Imagining Evil

IMAGINING *EVIL*

WITCHCRAFT BELIEFS AND ACCUSATIONS IN CONTEMPORARY AFRICA

Edited by
Gerrie ter Haar

Africa World Press, Inc.

P.O. Box 1892
Trenton, NJ 08607

P.O. Box 48
Asmara, ERITREA

Africa World Press, Inc.

P.O. Box 1892
Trenton, NJ 08607

P.O. Box 48
Asmara, ERITREA

Book design: Saverance Publishing Services (SPS)
Cover design: Ashraful Haque and SPS

Library of Congress Cataloging-in-Publication Data

Imagining evil : witchcraft beliefs and accusations in contemporary Africa /
edited by Gerrie ter Haar.
    p. cm. -- (Religion in contemporary Africa series)
  Includes bibliographical references and index.
  ISBN 1-59221-484-3 (hard cover) -- ISBN 1-59221-485-1 (pbk.)
  1. Witchcraft--Africa. I. Haar, Gerrie ter. II. Series.

BF1584.A53I43 2006
133.4'3096090511--dc22

                    2006012857

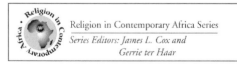

Religion in Contemporary Africa Series
Series Editors: James L. Cox and
Gerrie ter Haar

Table of Contents

1

INTRODUCTION: THE EVIL CALLED WITCHCRAFT

Gerrie ter Haar

INTRODUCTION

The belief in witchcraft is as strong as it is widespread in Africa, to the point that academic writers on the subject and other commentators have suggested a significant increase in witchcraft accusations in recent years.[1] Reports relating to belief in witchcraft or to witchcraft accusations are indeed very common in Africa and a popular topic for discussion in African mass media. An alarming element of such reports is the lynching or killing of alleged witches that often follows witchcraft accusations. It is striking that in most places women are the vast majority of those accused, although this is not exclusively so. Even more alarming is that children, too, are increasingly falling victim to witchcraft accusations—traditionally hardly ever aimed at children. In recent years disturbing reports have been recorded notably from the Democratic Republic of Congo,[2] a country riven by war, but also from other parts of the continent, such as Nigeria.[3] In 2005, reports in the British press of a case heard by a British court have brought to light the sad plight of some African children living in the United Kingdom who have received cruel treatment at the hands of their own families as a result of allegations of witchcraft.[4]

The obvious question to ask is why this is happening now. Some authors have sought the answer in the circumstances of the many African countries that are ravaged by war, poverty, or other forms of misery that affect daily life, causing many Africans in recent years to emigrate to other parts of the world. The spread of HIV/AIDS in Africa has introduced another powerful factor into the witchcraft debate, as a link with witchcraft is frequently made.[5] Other commentators have sought an explanation beyond material conditions, arguing that the crisis that is characteristic of so many African societies today has left metaphysical traces, resulting in a spiritual confusion that reflects the social and political chaos of the material world.[6] Hence, a crisis of governance in the material world may be reflected by types of interaction with the spirit world equally escaping the control of recognised authorities, becoming, in effect, 'privatised'. In such cases, a great number of competing spiritual techniques are on offer, causing confusion regarding both the nature of the spirit world and the authority of those considered competent to interpret it. An example of this is Liberia, an extreme case of a so-called failed state.[7] Some observers have particularly noted an aspect of 'spiritual insecurity' that is implicit in witchcraft fears.[8] However, spiritual confusion and spiritual insecurity, although connected, are different conditions. While spiritual insecurity may in theory be remedied by the creation of a stable environment, the notion of spiritual confusion refers to a deeper dimension, suggesting that not just the human world but the spirit world *itself* has gone out of control. This is not a recent development, but, rather, an escalation of a trend already perceptible during the time of colonisation and early missionary activities. Whereas in the past people had traditional means at their disposal to pacify angered spirits and to persuade them to resume their neutral stance to the human world, today the spirit world is often perceived to have assumed an inherently evil character in the face of which humans are rather powerless.[9] In many parts of contemporary Africa, 'witches' are believed to represent such type of inherent evil.

While both the material and the spiritual aspects of this situation have to be taken into account, it is undoubtedly the case that the spiritual dimension of the problem receives rather little attention in the best-known contemporary studies of witchcraft, which tend to take little notice of what African theologians, for example, have to say on the matter.[10] Hence, the religious nature of witchcraft beliefs and their religious implications are little explored in historical and anthropological studies of witchcraft in Africa.[11] Many works are written by Western anthropologists, who, by reason of their training, are little inclined to give attention to the religious aspect of the witchcraft phenomenon.

This is precisely the gap that the present volume aims to fill, thus enriching the literature on witchcraft beliefs and accusations in contemporary Africa by adding a religious studies perspective. Most of the contributors to this volume have a scholarly interest in religion, while some may also have an additional interest as practising Christians.

As a comment on witchcraft beliefs and accusations in contemporary Africa, the present volume may be distinguished from work in the same field in two major ways. First, most of the contributors are scholars living and working in Africa, which brings to their views an acuteness of observation—often based on lived experience rather than academic observation alone—that may otherwise be lacking. Most of the academic literature on witchcraft on Africa is actually produced by scholars working outside the continent, in most cases non-Africans. Second, the interest in the subject of authors in this volume is defined not only by scholarly insights, but also—even primarily—by the painful knowledge of the human suffering caused by witchcraft accusations. The personal tragedies that afflict the lives of those who fall victim to witchcraft accusations is almost never discussed in the academic literature on witchcraft, which is in danger of taking an excessively sociological approach at the expense of the moral and ethical dimensions involved.

Most of the contributors to the present volume are thus able to provide an unusual angle of approach to the question of witchcraft in Africa, acknowledging the spiritual nature of the issue without losing sight of its material aspects. Both are significant, but it appears that no lasting solution to the problems posed by witchcraft beliefs and accusations will be found unless full account is taken of the spiritual dimension of the matter.

THE ORIGIN AND STRUCTURE OF THIS BOOK

The original idea for this book grew from a collaborative research project concerning witchcraft problems in South Africa, conducted in the years 1999-2001 by two universities, the University of the North (now University of Limpopo) in South Africa and Utrecht University in the Netherlands. The project was financed by the Dutch government's South Africa-

Netherlands Research Programme on Alternatives in Development (SANPAD) with a view to helping reduce the number of 'witchcraft killings' in South Africa, notably in Limpopo Province (formerly called the Northern Province), where witchcraft-related incidents are most frequent. (The reason for referring to 'witchcraft killings' in quotation marks should become clear in due course). Three of the contributors to this volume participated in that project, representing different academic disciplines.[12] The project was based at the Theological Faculty of the University of the North. Although implemented with the help of staff and students from other departments, the project gained its main thrust from the perspectives provided by theological experts, with anthropologists, scholars of religion, law experts and others with a professional interest in the matter playing a complementary role.[13]

In the early 1990s, South Africa was experiencing its transition from the era of apartheid, with the first nationwide democratic elections held in 1994. The country also witnessed an upsurge of witchcraft accusations, which many observers suggested was related to the transitional process. During the preceding political struggles, South African youth, known as 'comrades', had come to prominence in many areas of the country and often took the lead in the persecution of alleged witches, resulting in the death of the accused often through the gruesome method known as necklacing.[14] The available statistics show the seriousness of the problem in those days. Between 1996 and 2001, more than 600 people lost their lives as a result of such lynchings of alleged witches in Limpopo Province alone,[15] while in 1998—in just one year—about 500 cases of witchcraft accusations were reported to the police in the same province.[16] The scope of the problem and the lethal consequences of witchcraft accusations were of serious concern to the post-apartheid government, which explored ways and means of tackling the problem. One of the best-known initiatives was the appointment by the government of the Ralushai Commission, named after its chairman, which held nationwide consultations on the subject and published its final report in 1996.[17] Another influential report was that published by the Commission on Gender Equality, which was particularly concerned about the gender bias in witchcraft accusations.[18] As will be seen below, this appears to be a major feature of witchcraft accusations in Africa generally.

It is notable that the new South African government considered both the material *and* the spiritual aspects of the witchcraft problem to be important perspectives, indicating that members of the government shared (or at least were aware of) a worldview of the public at large. Hence, it was entirely logical that the Theological Faculty of the University of the North, a training ground for professional expertise in spiritual matters, should respond positively to the government's call for help in finding solutions to the effects of witchcraft accusations, especially in the country's northernmost province. As can be gleaned from the present volume, it is not unusual in Africa for government policymakers to engage with people studying or working in the field of religion, and religious experts are often requested by governments to help find solutions to society's problems. This is also the case in regard to witchcraft accusations, which can be considered as both a symptom and an expression of social conflict. Hence, the SANPAD project adopted a strong policy orientation. Its research findings were discussed on several occasions in public meetings with representatives from various target sectors, resulting in a number of specific policy recommendations that were published in the final report emanating from the project.[19]

Students and staff who had taken part in the research project presented their findings also at the XVIIIth World Congress of the International Association for the History of Religions (IAHR), an international event attended by hundreds of scholars that was held in Durban in September 2000. Participants discussed the issue of witchcraft beliefs and practices in a wide context, both geographically and conceptually. Scholars from other African universities presented their views on the matter, based largely on the situation in their countries of origin. An exciting exchange of views ensued: this was eventually to lead to the production of the present volume.

Clearly, the belief in witchcraft is neither new nor unique to South Africa, or to Africa in general; the same can be said of the types of social conflict that result from witchcraft accusations.[20] It does seem, however, that the harmful effects of witchcraft beliefs in the form of witchcraft accusations, or through the 'pointing of witches', are at present more common in Africa than in any other part of the world. Documentary evidence exists from a large number of African countries indicating that witchcraft accusations are rampant and, in recent years, have led to the unlawful killing, exiling or imprisonment of many people. Such evidence comes from other countries in southern Africa, such as Namibia, Botswana, and Zambia, but also in West Africa, including, for example, Cameroon, Nigeria, and Ghana, as well as East Africa, such as in Tanzania, all of which receive attention in this book. The studies gathered in this volume amount to a set of case studies emanating from original research undertaken by African scholars in the countries concerned.

Thus, this volume discusses witchcraft beliefs and accusations in various parts of sub-Saharan Africa where these phenomena pose a serious problem today, cutting across divisions of class, age and gender. The book does not in any way attempt to provide an exhaustive overview of the state of affairs concerning witchcraft beliefs and accusations in African countries, but limits itself to some telling examples recorded from the above-mentioned countries and presented by scholars from those same countries. They demonstrate the tenacity of witchcraft beliefs and practices in Africa, but also the type of change these have undergone in recent years. Although the basic nature of belief has altered little, its concrete expressions, as this volume demonstrates, show a great ability to adapt to the ever-changing conditions of social and political life. Since the horizons of life for Africans can no longer be considered to stop at continental borders, this book also includes a perspective from Europe, where many Africans now live. When Africans migrate to other parts of the world, witchcraft beliefs and practices may accompany them and witchcraft accusations may continue to affect them.[21] But witchcraft accusations have also become transnational in a different way, such as in Zambia, where they have become linked to international networks of crime.[22]

The organisation of the chapters reveals the specific approach underlying the present volume. To place the theme of the book in a wider perspective, the first and last chapters provide a general framework for the case studies that form the bulk of this collection. Following the present introduction, the next chapter provides a historical perspective on the issue of witchcraft by testing the validity of the often-made comparison between witch-hunts in Africa and witchcraft persecutions in the history of Europe. Historical research shows that the comparison of Africa with Europe is problematic in many ways, to the point that it may actually prevent a deeper understanding of the phenomenon of witchcraft as it appears in Africa. The final chapter makes another type of comparison, namely of African societies in various parts of the continent that appear to have developed quite different responses to the social unrest that witchcraft beliefs can cause.

These opening and closing chapters frame the individual country studies, which range from West Africa to East and southern Africa. The first of these country studies is a phenomenological examination of witchcraft as it is traditionally seen in Ghana. This is followed by two further chapters on Ghana, one containing a discussion of witchcraft in contemporary conditions, the other an exposition on the subject from the perspective of a Ghanaian pastor in charge of an African congregation in the Netherlands. The following chapter then extends the pastoral dimension by means of a discussion of witchcraft in ethical terms, with specific reference to Cameroon. Further chapters on Nigeria, Namibia and Botswana provide a detailed insight into the complexities and subtleties of local witchcraft discourses, while illustrating some of the underlying social problems with examples taken from real life. The importance of social relationships, which in Africa typically extend into the invisible world, is evident in every case. The significance of this aspect of social relations in Africa is one of the main reasons why witchcraft-related problems there cannot be solved by an improvement of material conditions alone. Yet, as the chapters on Zambia, Tanzania and South Africa show, improvement of the material conditions in which people live may nevertheless go a long way towards reducing the level of witchcraft fears and consequent violence.

Considered collectively, the various chapters provide insights from a variety of perspectives, including history, anthropology, and theology, but also take into account economic aspects and including policy observations. Living and working in Africa as most of the contributors to this volume do, they, like many other scholars in Africa, are particularly inclined to consider the implications of their observations in the field of policy. For this reason the question of how to respond to witchcraft-related problems is addressed in every chapter, either explicitly or implicitly.

COMBATTING EVIL

In the original project that gave rise to this book, as described above, the participants adopted a working definition of witchcraft which stipulated that: 'Witchcraft is a manifestation of evil believed to come from a human source'.[23] This is a definition that simultaneously reflects a prominent way in which many Africans imagine and experience evil, while at the same time leaving open the question of whether witchcraft beliefs are founded or not. Determining the true or false character of witchcraft belief is of little relevance to those seeking solutions for its often lethal consequences; moreover, mystical powers and processes are not observable facts that can be verified or falsified by scientific means. A fact that is observable, however, is that many Africans profess to believe in the reality of witchcraft, considering it a most dangerous form of evil, and that they may act accordingly. Even though there may be a certain ambiguity in local perceptions of witchcraft in Africa as a potential power for both good and evil, the overriding association of witchcraft is with evil. In fact, witchcraft appears to constitute a major mode for imagining evil in Africa, giving rise to a great variety of concrete expressions, as can be seen from the various contributions to the present volume. For all their differences, what seems to bind these various expressions is a concern for the supposed effects of this form of evil, rather than its believed origin.[24]

These observations are important, since for a proper understanding of the issue is helpful to make a distinction between what people *believe*, on the one hand, and what they *do*—or how they act—on the basis of their beliefs, on the other. In legal terms, people almost everywhere are free to believe whatever they wish, even in cases where the majority of the population may find certain beliefs harmful or despicable. But people are certainly not free to act on the basis of their belief in whatever way they choose. Their freedom of practising their belief is restricted the world over, first, by national legislation and, ultimately, by international agreement on what is right or wrong, notably as decided upon by the United Nations. One of the most important instruments in this respect is the Universal Declaration of Human Rights which, among others, stipulates the right to life of every person.[25] The killing of alleged witches violates this most basic right of every human being in the most obvious manner. It is not belief that kills them, but the actions taken in consequence of belief. Therefore, it was the issue of witchcraft *accusations*, rather than witchcraft belief, that concerned the participants in the original project. In any event, it is notoriously difficult to change people's beliefs, particularly when these are as deeply entrenched culturally as is the case with witchcraft beliefs in Africa. The belief in witchcraft as a form of evil that humans may manipulate purposefully and unscrupulously to further their own interests is deeply rooted in the worldview of many Africans even today, as the present volume shows. From this arises the need to find an effective remedy against witchcraft in the defined sense, now as much as ever.

Witchcraft beliefs amount to a moral theory that can neither be legislated away, nor eliminated through formal education. As the present volume shows, the anti-witchcraft legislation introduced in African countries under colonial rule has brought no real solution to witchcraft-related problems. At the heart of this failure lies the fact that the law is unable to address the moral-spiritual dimension of the matter, which accompanies the moral-legal dimension upheld by the law. One result of this imbalance is a frequent lack of commitment in upholding the law on the part of law enforcement officers in Africa, either because they themselves believe that an accused person is a witch or because they are afraid of themselves being accused of witchcraft if they are seen to protect a witch, someone considered an enemy of society.[26]

Another often-touted solution, formal education, suffers from the same shortcoming, since this type of education is often not based on the worldviews of the people concerned. This was one of the main reasons why missionary attempts to change people's perceptions concerning the role of evil in African societies have largely failed. European missionaries, but colonial officers as well, often believed that, since at some stage in history witchcraft persecutions had ceased in Europe, they were likely to stop at a certain stage in Africa too. The argument can still be heard today. Witchcraft belief and witch-hunting in Europe—so the argument goes—were the products of ignorance and eventually terminated due to human progress in the form of a more enlightened approach to religion, the advance of science, and the correct use of reason.[27] But these assumptions have proved wrong, as political and economic changes in Africa have produced no perceptible diminution of witchcraft belief. Moreover, there are many educated Africans who are well-versed in Western culture and science but may nevertheless believe in the existence of witchcraft powers.

Concepts of evil are central to the religious beliefs of many Africans, in past and present times. In fact, the persistence of belief in the presence of evil has become a contentious issue in relations between former mission churches in Africa and home-grown African-initiated churches, creating a major line of division between them.[28] Combatting evil in whatever form it may appear is a constant theme in the life of African church communities, both in and outside the continent. It is also a prominent point that connects such communities, in spite of individual differences. In this respect, there is a historical continuity between the earliest African independent churches and the latest generation of charismatic churches in Africa. The common thread is a consciousness of the presence of evil, and the need to counter it.

On occasion, ideological differences in such matters have led to a crisis within the mainline churches. A well-known example concerns the Zambian Catholic Church in the 1980s.[29] At that time, the primate of the church, the archbishop of Lusaka, Emmanuel Milingo, was removed from his see as a result of a controversy concerning his healing ministry. The ground of this dispute was that Milingo had come to believe on the basis of his pastoral experiences that his Church should play a leading role in liberating Zambians from the evil spirits that they believed to be afflicting their lives. Milingo shared with many fellow-Zambians both a belief in the presence and power of evil, and a perception of how to rid people of it by spiritual means. Many non-African church officials, however, considered this to be unacceptable and incompatible with modern times. When Milingo started to exorcise evil spirits through the power of the Holy Spirit, he came into sharp conflict with the Vatican, which forbade his activities. Eventually, he was removed from his see. Milingo was correct, however, in his cultural understanding of the Zambian people, whose worldview he understood and whose symbolic language he articulated. He was able to provide them with the type of help- spiritual help—they needed, even if his methods seemed too unorthodox to his superiors in Rome. His approach was essentially a pastoral one, based on the biblical injunction to preach the gospel, heal the sick, and exorcise demons.

Although witchcraft and evil spirits are both perceived as manifestations of evil, with the result that those suffering from it may feel in need of liberation, they are not one and the same thing, as various authors in this book remind us. While evil spirits are believed to be an external force that enters a person involuntarily and takes up temporary residence, witchcraft powers represent a type of evil that is considered to be inherent, voluntary and permanent. This difference in character makes it far more difficult for a religious specialist, whether traditional or Christian, to free people from witchcraft powers than to liberate them from evil spirits.

In the present volume, the relevance of a pastoral approach to witchcraft problems is notably highlighted by Elias Bongmba and Hugo Hinfelaar. Both emphasise the need to address witchcraft fears, which are as real for the people concerned as the effects of it are for those who are made to suffer the consequences. But there is also a further pastoral dimension, as appears from the chapter by the present author recording a view from the Netherlands. Pastoral care is needed not only for those suffering the consequences of witchcraft accusations, but also for those who believe themselves to possess witchcraft powers. Daniel Himmans-Arday, founder and pastor of the oldest African-initiated church in the Netherlands, is one of many Africans who believe that witchcraft does indeed exist. However, his views on how to deal with it are inspired by Christian beliefs, and his ideas about evil are associated with a theology of spiritual healing and liberation.[30] It is significant in this context, that the leading paradigm of Christian belief in Africa is that of Jesus as the *Nganga* or the Great Healer.[31] Religious or spiritual healing, we may recall, is a major characteristic of African belief that transcends religious allegiances. The religious need for healing in Africa concerns all aspects of human life, including the need for healing human relations. This has an important bearing on the issue of witchcraft.

In this regard, Elias Bongmba argues that the Christian Church should not simply dismiss the issue of witchcraft powers and their negative use, but instead should reflect on the ethics of witchcraft beliefs in such a way as to address the reality of such powers in the African context, for which he suggests several approaches. Reflection along these lines may imply, as he shows, the need to 'de-witch' individuals believed to have used witchcraft power, most likely in cases where such people themselves believe that they have this power at their disposal.[32] Unlike most African independent churches, mainline churches in Africa do not offer this type of pastoral care, due to their historical allegiance with former missionary churches in Europe. One result of the neglect by mainline churches in Africa, as Bongmba points out, is the failure to prepare their leaders to deal with the problems associated with the belief in witchcraft.

Yet, the belief in the reality and presence of evil, including in the form of witchcraft, is not peculiar to Africa but is a feature of human societies worldwide. All societies have their own ways, shaped by their own cultures and specific histories, of expressing ideas about the existence of evil. All societies have developed their own mechanisms to eliminate evil and those believed to purvey it. This observation applies also to Europe, which, at a certain point in history, expressed such ideas in the form of a witchcraft discourse. In fact, as Stephen Ellis states in his contribution, the memory, or perhaps the morality-tale, of the great witch-hunts of the fifteenth to the eighteenth centuries is one of the most potent stories from Europe's past. In European history, the witch was portrayed as a person in active relation with Satan, the prince of darkness. This is an image that has not entirely lost its hold over the popular imagination. In some European countries at least, there still exists a notion of the existence of secret conclaves of utterly destructive people who, in league with the devil, aim to wreak havoc in society. Witch-stories are still transmitted in contemporary Europe through popular news and entertainment media, including fiction and children's stories.[33]

Europe, then, has its own history of witchcraft accusations. It has been an extremely painful one, having led to the death of thousands of people accused of practising witchcraft. But today, the traces of witchcraft belief that survive in Europe do not, in general, any longer lead to witchcraft killings. This is not the result of an inevitable historical process, as is often suggested by commentators who expect Africa to follow this purported line of historical development. Rather, it is the result of a profound change in political conditions in Europe in the first instance. Modern historical research shows that witch-hunts and witchcraft killings in Europe halted primarily because the balance of power between Church and State had fundamentally altered, from the time of the Reformation and the wars of religion onwards. One result of this redefinition of power was that the governing elites of the day came to see that there was no longer any political merit in persecuting witches, just as they gradually ceased to see merit in persecuting Jews or members of minority churches.[34] Interestingly, and vitally important to the argument, is the fact that while witch-*hunting* declined dramatically over a relative short period in European history, the *belief* in witchcraft continued to exist among the general population and even among intellectuals for some time to come. This is an extremely important observation, not least in its implications for present debates in and concerning Africa, as it shows that individuals and communities may adhere to a belief in witchcraft, even strongly, without necessarily resorting to the extreme course of killing or otherwise violating the basic rights of those whom they accuse of practising witchcraft.

Hence comes the importance of our analytical distinction between witchcraft beliefs on the one hand and witchcraft accusations on the other. This nuance is important for reasons of analysis and does not in any way deny the close connection that normally exists between the two. While a belief in witchcraft may continue to exist, it is witchcraft accusations that may ultimately lead to the killing of people, and these latter should be the focus of our attention. It appears that there is neither a necessary nor an inevitable connection between the belief in witchcraft and the unlawful killing of alleged witches. This, in fact, was one of the most important outcomes of the South African research project that formed the basis of the present book. On the basis of field research carried out by South African students in their local communities, Walter van Beek developed a 'witchcraft escalation model', in which he compares the handling of witchcraft accusations in different African countries, represented in the form of a step-ladder.[35] The significance of this model lies in the demonstrations that policy interventions are possible at specific steps on the ladder, with a view to reducing social tension and preventing the killing of alleged witches. For communities to proceed from witchcraft belief to the killing of witches, six key variables can be identified, forming a logical series of rungs on the escalation ladder, each leading towards increased danger for the accused. The ladder shows how in societies where witchcraft belief exists, people may act rather differently on the basis of their belief: they can ignore the problems believed to emerge from it; they may recognise the problems but desist from taking action; they may express suspicions, or pursue them; they may accuse specific people of using witchcraft; they may actually formulate witchcraft accusations; and, finally, they may kill alleged witches. But at each step on the ladder those who fear that witchcraft may be involved have the option of halting the escalation. It is at these points that policymakers seeking to halt witchcraft-related violence may intervene and influence the process. Since the contributors to the present volume all share an interest in exploring these possibilities, they have also made recommendations to minimise the threat of witchcraft accusations in each country under study.

It is appropriate at this point to draw attention to another relevant factor. In popular speech, in and outside Africa, the term 'witchcraft' has become an umbrella concept, used to refer to a great variety of ideas and practices related to the manipulation of mystical powers. References to 'witches' are made in common parlance, but also frequently in academic language. If these terms are uncritically adopted in academic discourse, this not only tends to perpetuate popular ideas and attitudes concerning the matter, but it may even inadvertently contribute to witchcraft-related violence. Through their uncritical usage of terms, academics may unwittingly help in the construction of witchcraft in Africa as a social fact, strengthening local beliefs that witches 'really' exist. As has been argued elsewhere,[36] the current revival of witchcraft studies is helpful inasmuch as it focusses attention on an important expression of deep moral concern in many African societies. But it is precisely because they often devote insufficient attention to the moral aspects of witchcraft that academic studies may risk contributing to the stigmatisation of people who are accused of being witches, with at times fatal consequences. This calls for a careful use of language in studies of witchcraft.

It is not insignificant, in this context, to refer to the observation that the term 'witchcraft' was popularised in regard to Africa only in the later nineteenth century by Europeans who were applying to Africa ideas derived from their own historical memory of witchcraft in Europe. Before the mid- or late-nineteenth century, some aspects of African religious or spiritual belief that were subsequently labelled as 'witchcraft' did not go under that name.[37] The same is broadly true regarding the current popular use of the term by Africans themselves. As various authors show this book, local communities originally had a far more subtle language to describe the different meanings and conceptions of what today is often simply termed 'witchcraft'. People may mean different things by the word at different times.[38] In all cases, the concept of witchcraft has to be considered in the wider context of the spiritual universe that most Africans believe to exist, and that traditionally is of an enormous complexity. This matter is further complicated by the fact that as a result of historical change original indigenous concepts have often undergone changes of meaning.

Yet, the task remains to find a common language that can adequately describe and analyse the different forms and manifestations of 'witchcraft'. As long as this is lacking it remains important to use a working definition of witchcraft, as an analytical tool selected for its ability to help understand the specific phenomenon under discussion. This is precisely what the different authors in this volume have attempted to do, indicating a variety of meanings associated with the concept of witchcraft in different contexts and in different circumstances. These, it appears, are related to specific traditional ontologies. The complexities of traditional ideas are investigated by Umar Danfulani in his analysis of mystical powers and their use among the Mupun in Nigeria. He shows, for example, how their concept of witchcraft is closely related to the notion of anger, the deep anger that consumes the person at whom it is targetted, diminishing the life-force of the victim in the same way that witchcraft is believed to do. Samuel Mbambo makes a comparable point in discussing one particular type of witchcraft among the Vagciriku in Namibia. This is known as *shitera*, the witchcraft of revenge. Using anger as a metaphor of witchcraft reveals a crucial insight into what is believed to be the essential nature of witchcraft, namely a deadly force in interpersonal relationships. In her discussion of witchcraft among the Batswana, Seratwa Ntloedibe points to the fundamental paradox in witchcraft beliefs, namely that the people closest to one, with whom one is expected to maintain good relations, are the very people accused of witchcraft, thus undermining traditional ideas of community. Or, as Thias Kgatla puts it, most witchcraft accusations emanate from the home. Both of them show how jealousy and aggression often reign where solidarity and trust should exist.

Witchcraft discourse, it appears, is a self-perpetuating discourse, where a minor indication leads to a chain of accusations. It is also a 'foolproof' discourse, that cannot be negated as it does not allow for any counter-evidence. Whatever argument an accused person may bring to the fore will be interpreted within the same discourse.[39] This is confirmed by an investigation of views on the subject of witchcraft among educated youth conducted in Botswana.[40] It was found that all social categories are liable to witchcraft accusations, even contrasting ones, including both rich and poor, those who are successful at school and those who fail, etc. In a similar vein, it appears that Christian community leaders hardly dare refuse to participate in traditional rituals intended to cleanse their area of witches lest they be accused of themselves practising witchcraft, with unpleasant consequences.[41] In this way witchcraft beliefs and accusations become an effective instrument, or even a weapon, to force individual members of a community into a state of submissiveness. This has important consequences in the fields of development and human rights.

WITCHCRAFT, DEVELOPMENT AND THE LAW

The belief in witchcraft in the sense we have defined, with its harmful consequences, caused colonial governments to promulgate anti-witchcraft laws. In general, such laws forbade both accusations to be made against others and the practice of techniques likely to be considered as witchcraft-related activities. Colonial governments did not take any position on the reality of witchcraft, trying only to suppress witchcraft accusations in an attempt to make African societies conform to European ideas of right and wrong. In practice, this meant that colonial magistrates often ended up condemning the accusers rather than the perceived manipulators of evil, or 'witches', in any specific incident. As a result, African communities felt abandoned to the capricious powers of witches, against whom they had no legal defence. Whatever defensive measures were taken by them would be implemented outside the formal jurisdiction of the colonial law.[42]

Most, if not all, African countries retained the corpus of colonial laws intact after independence, including the colonial Witchcraft Suppression Acts. At the same time, however, witchcraft-related problems continued to emerge and frequently continued to be resolved by people taking the law into their own hands, up to the present day. In South Africa, individuals accused of being witches are regularly chased out of the community, beaten up or even killed. Those who survive may end up in so-called 'witch villages', where they may enjoy a certain degree of protection while living generally in miserable conditions.[43] In Ghana too, there are special places popularly known as 'witch camps', where individuals accused of witchcraft—almost exclusively women—have sought refuge and escaped from certain death.[44] In South Africa, such places of refuge are notably found in Limpopo Province, while in Ghana they are mostly in the north of the country. Both regions are among the poorest in their respective countries, suggesting the possibility of a causal connection between witchcraft accusations and the state of the economy.

The 'witchcraft mentality', as it is often referred to in Africa, is frequently seen by outsiders as just another stumbling-block on the road to development. But Africans, irrespective of whether they share a general belief in witchcraft, are deeply concerned about its effects in many areas of life, of which socio-economic development is one. Witchcraft, as an ideology and as a practice, is a development issue in the sense that it hampers economic progress as people, afraid of being accused of practising witchcraft, refrain from any activity that may make them appear more successful in life than others. This aspect of witchcraft accusations receives particular attention in some of the chapters in this volume. Fear of witchcraft often inhibits people from undertaking any productive activity in areas where this is often most needed. As a result, ambitious young people will move away and start businesses elsewhere, while outsiders, who traditionally cannot be affected by witchcraft, will take their place and profit from this situation. This is the case, for example, in Tanzania.[45] Equally, in South Africa witchcraft accusations are often made against those who initiate development projects or otherwise try to improve their conditions of life.[46] In other words, the witchcraft mentality thrives on fear, as Abraham Akrong argues with regard to Ghana. It encourages a culture of passivity that leads to the development of a mentality of dependency, with lack of creativity and initiative as its by-products.[47] Elom Dovlo provides evidence of this in his discussion of the economic consequences of some of the punishments meted out in Ghana, especially to women who have been accused as witches. Since their economic achievements are often attributed to the use of witchcraft powers, such accusations effectively block women's initiatives in economic productivity, with a negative effect on the country's development.[48]

All over Africa, in fact, it is mostly women who bear the brunt of witchcraft accusations, as the chapters in this book testify. To be labelled a witch in many cases is tantamount to being declared liable to be killed with impunity. Those accused of witchcraft are likely to be deprived of their human rights, and are deemed to have brought their fate upon themselves. Ghana is only one example where witchcraft accusations frequently lead to the abuse of the human rights of women.[49] There are even women in Ghana today past child-bearing age who opt for voluntary exile at one of the 'witch camps' to avoid being branded witches and sent there later by force.[50] In any event, it saves them from the risk of being lynched. Typically, it is women whose association with mystical powers is usually considered negative, in contrast to the positive associations made when it concerns men.[51] In other African countries too, the worst types of witchcraft are associated with women. A gender bias can also be observed in the belief that women are generally held responsible for passing on witchcraft powers from one generation to another, while men are more likely to be seen as acquiring witchcraft powers by purchasing them, for example from traditional healers.[52]

The cruel treatment meted out to those accused of witchcraft throws light on a much neglected dimension of witchcraft accusations, namely their relation to human rights. For Western academics the subject of witchcraft is more likely to be regarded as an absorbing field of study than as the matter-of-life-and-death reality it is for many Africans. International human rights organisations such as Amnesty International have so far not pronounced witchcraft accusations to be a specific category of offence against human rights, probably because they have never thought about the matter in those terms in the first place. Neither have human rights lawyers or others with a professional interest in human rights. The matter of witchcraft accusations seems simply to escape their attention, and recent witchcraft studies have done little to remedy this oversight, as they normally fail to include a human rights perspective. International human rights discourse, I have argued elsewhere, has tended to develop an exclusively moral-legal approach due to its single-minded emphasis on only one dimension in the concept of human rights. It has failed to pay equal attention to the first element of the composite term—the human dimension—which in many parts of the world suggests the utility of a moral-spiritual approach.[53] This is illustrated in a particular manner by Hugo Hinfelaar in his explanation of differences between the Bantu concepts of *muntu* and *musungu*, and the cosmological shift of position this entails regarding witchcraft accusations.[54]

Abraham Akrong rightly argues that it is not just a mob of villagers that can be held responsible for witchcraft accusations and the persecution of alleged witches: society as a whole is to blame in its role as a tacit accomplice. This argument may even extend to parts of the international community, as becomes clear from Hugo Hinfelaar's account from Zambia, where unrestrained market forces and a philosophy of *laissez-faire* have created a situation whereby witchcraft accusations are used as a means of dispossessing local people of their ancestral lands in order to make way for international investors in tourism and game-ranching. Here as elsewhere, inhumane treatment is the fate of all alleged witches. The dehumanisation of people accused of practising witchcraft which normally precedes their maltreatment or death, has proved a typical prelude to mass killings, and is possibly even a necessary condition for such atrocities.[55] Human rights are applied only to 'real' human beings, and not to those who are seen by a community to have placed themselves outside the category of normal humanity.

The problems posed by witchcraft accusations are, then, also a human rights issue. The constitution in most countries forbids any action of the sort often meted out to those accused of witchcraft. Such action is also contrary to the basic principles of the Universal Declaration of Human Rights, as well as the letter and spirit of the African Charter of Human and Peoples' Rights. Nevertheless, in many African countries current legislation appears insufficient to deal with the problem of witchcraft. South Africa is only one of several African countries where a discussion is taking place as to how to the law may be adapted to deal with this lacuna. The Witchcraft Suppression Act that is still in force in South Africa appears to have done nothing to reduce the widespread fear of witchcraft. According to Thias Kgatla, this is primarily because the law has never had the benefit of public consent. But, he argues, it would be irresponsible to repeal the law on that ground, because, imperfect as it may be, the law still protects innocent people from being branded as a witch by witch-hunters. Those who accuse others still have to face the force of the law.

Today, there are other views on the matter. The solution advocated by some politicians and other proponents is to abolish the anti-witchcraft legislation that is currently on the statute books in South Africa on the grounds that it is a remnant of colonialism and apartheid, and replace it with a law that makes 'witchcraft' a criminal act punishable by the state. If this were to happen, it would mean that, in effect, anybody accused of practising witchcraft would run the risk of being prosecuted in court, convicted, and subjected to a heavy penalty. This is a matter of concern for a number of reasons, but particularly because such a course would seriously undermine the integrity of the law. Whereas the law properly operates on the basis of written rules and strict procedures that follow international standards, the witchcraft discourse that leads to the accusation of certain individuals is generally based on gossip and hearsay that lacks actual proof since it is based on belief, and not on evidence of a type normally required in court. Whereas law enforcement is fully institutionalised, witchcraft accusations operate beyond any institutional control. Witchcraft accusations imply that the accused is guilty, and denial of the charges makes things worse for the accused. The position in a court of law, however, is based on the principle that the accused is innocent until proven guilty.[56]

These are only some of the characteristic differences between the use of witchcraft discourse on the one hand and the application of the law on the other: each is the structural opposite of the other. There is also a clear political aspect to the matter, which makes allowing witchcraft discourse into the rule of law very hazardous. It opens the way to accusing political or personal opponents of practising witchcraft, thus providing an excellent— legal—opportunity to eliminate them. We know from experiences in Cameroon, for example, that witchcraft accusations may become a convenient tool to get rid of political dissidents.[57] In Ghana, too, the witchcraft mentality has been transferred to the political arena, notably in the way in which political opponents are dealt with. A political opponent shares the same epistemological status as a witch. Both are seen as enemies of society.[58]

The comparison with Europe may once again shed light on developments in Africa. Generally speaking, as indicated above, Europeans stopped persecuting witches not because they had ceased to believe in witchcraft, but because they ceased to believe that issuing an indictment through a formal judicial organ was the best means of dealing with it. Public officials ceased to consider witchcraft as a political problem. They might see it as a social or a religious problem, but in any event a problem outside the political realm.[59] It seems that there may be an important historical lesson to draw from that experience.

These considerations concerning development and human rights make it particularly urgent to find practical measures to cope with the problems posed by witchcraft. All the evidence suggests that, for an effective approach, solutions should not be sought exclusively in the moral-legal sphere, but also in the moral-spiritual domain. In his final observations, Umar Danfulani provides several arguments as to why the current legal system in Africa cannot deal effectively with the problem of witchcraft, and may even have unwittingly increased it. Reducing the level of violence associated with witchcraft accusations will require a combined effort by political and religious authorities, as the following paragraphs will show.

THE WAY FORWARD

The violation of human rights that is inherent in witchcraft accusations, whether it is by way of banning, killing, or otherwise suspending the full human rights of the accused, occurs in many countries in Africa. Government bodies and public servants, churches and other religious organisations, teachers, educationalists and human rights activists, have gathered on many occasions to address the issue or, as they often put it, to consider 'the way forward'. In a public address at a roundtable conference on the matter, Ghana's Human Rights Commissioner stated the problem as follows:[60]

> as a nation we face daunting challenges in effectively grappling with these issues, and in preventing the violation of the rights of persons accused of witchcraft. We recognize that input from each and every

segment of society is crucial to attainment of a lasting solution to these problems.

In South Africa, people from all walks of life gathered in 2001 for a Summit on Social Conflict at the University of the North, where they discussed ways to reduce the social damage caused by witchcraft accusations. To them, the 'way forward' fell into two categories. The first one consisted of outlining the various problems associated with witchcraft accusations. The second was the formulation of a number of suggestions for long- and short-term solutions, with specific recommendations for different target groups, including the general public, the academic community and policymakers.[61]

All the contributors to the present volume have reflected on the question of how to solve the different problems that arise from the belief in witchcraft as a lethal form of evil. Several of them emphasise that a significant improvement of people's material life will reduce the need, if not for witchcraft beliefs, then in any case for witchcraft accusations. Kgatla considers poverty as the dominant factor in the escalation of witchcraft accusations in South Africa. Hinfelaar argues that, in the case of Zambia, the provision of title deeds for rural people with smallholdings would provide some security against the type of land-grabbing that now induces many witchcraft accusations. Stephen Nyaga argues in favour of sensitisation and awareness programmes at a local level, and the provision of opportunities for community leaders to be exposed to other views and circumstances. Simple scientific explanations that can account for certain problems, such as in the area of health, are often lacking, as are scientific explanations of natural phenomena such as lightning, which in the Limpopo Province of South Africa, for example, is usually ascribed to the evil machinations of witches.

It is clear that the search for effective solutions will be a long-term process that requires the active engagement of civic organisations, notably at the local level, where witchcraft accusations are most rampant. According to Umar Danfulani, the lack of a strong civil society that devotes attention to the development of the human person is the main reason for the persistence and increase of witchcraft beliefs. He is supported in his views by Thias Kgatla who, on the basis of his own experiences, is convinced that where civil society works effectively, witchcraft accusations can be curtailed. He identifies churches and non-governmental organisations (NGOs) as two types of entity that have played a significant role in the transformation of South African society, and which could also spearhead other changes.

These considerations raise some pertinent questions about what 'development' actually is. For most international NGO's, its meaning is limited to the field of socio-economic development. Religious believers, however, generally extend the meaning of the term to include the element of spiritual progress. In such a case, the emphasis is not exclusively on the material result of a development project: at least equal importance is attached to the means by which it is realised. This is summarised in the slogan 'We build the road and the road builds us.'[62] From such a perspective, it makes a good deal of sense to insist, as Kgatla does, on the development of individual character as a first step in what he refers to as 'transformational' education.[63] He proposes an educational model that is informed by principles that may lie beyond the normal scope of a school curriculum, one that emphasises the fostering of healthy interpersonal relationships. Working on human development in such a way, he suggests, would encourage the socio-economic development of local communities.

The important point that various writers make in this volume is the need to address the spiritual dimension of the problem of witchcraft alongside other measures. The challenge, they suggest, is not to seek solutions exclusively in a Western tradition of logic while ignoring African experience, but to address the issue while considering both. This is also important from a development perspective. Hugo Hinfelaar once made the point that if local communities in Zambia were to be asked about their development priorities, the liberation from witchcraft would rank first on their list, taking priority over the establishment of schools and health facilities.[64]

Changing witchcraft beliefs in Africa, then, can only be the result of a long-term process. What is needed, according to Abraham Akrong, is to cultivate alternative modes of interpretation of life-events in order eventually to undermine the witchcraft mentality. But any type of education in this regard, as Dovlo argues, must be culturally based in order to be effective. He identifies a number of areas where this could be done. One area is human rights, where the use of traditional proverbs and sayings will have a greater effect in raising human rights awareness among ordinary people than teaching them relevant articles from the Universal Declaration of Human Rights.[65] The use of appropriate media is another important area for attention, particularly given the popularity of local films and videos in many African countries. The use of videos on national television is one of the means by which the Catholic Church in Zambia, for example, tries to 'objectify' and demystify witchcraft, exposing some of the methods employed by rural witch-finders to identify witches.[66]

During an international workshop on religion and human rights held in Ghana in 2002, participants considered among other things the human rights problems arising from witchcraft accusations.[67] In their view, religious functionaries and traditional leaders in particular can play a crucial role in influencing people's perceptions. This makes it essential to involve them actively in any attempt to change popular attitudes to problems ascribed to witchcraft. In the case of religious leaders of all religious persuasions, it was suggested that one of the most urgent tasks would be to develop new theologies that address the issues emerging from people's lived experiences.[68] Generally speaking, there is a great lack of original, grassroot theologies in Africa that take the situations in which people daily live and work as their point of departure. Often this is a context of close-knit communities and extended kinship networks in which witchcraft accusations easily flourish.

Addressing the problem of evil as this is experienced by African communities, then, is among the most urgent tasks. This also applies to religious communities that have generally avoided addressing the issue, such as the mainline churches. As Bongmba shows in his exploration of ethical solutions from within the Christian tradition in Africa, the neglect of the issue of witchcraft by the Christian Church has contributed to a simplistic identification of witchcraft with the devil, instead of encouraging relevant theologies based on key biblical concepts such as hospitality, love, freedom and reconciliation. The Christian worldview, he and other authors suggest in this book, offers ways of empowering people to deal with witchcraft-related problems that are based on a critical, contextual reading of the Bible.

The need for new theologies is all the more pressing in the light of the popularity of charismatic churches in Africa. Many academic observers have commented on the important role of combatting evil in those churches, which appears one of their most attractive features from the point of view of their religious clientele. The new Christian demonology that has become so popular in Africa today provokes disconcerting comparisons with the history of witchcraft in Europe. The emergence in early modern Europe of a new type of demonology was a factor in the enormous upsurge of formal witchcraft accusations, resulting in the violent death of many in early modern times. People accused of witchcraft were increasingly depicted as agents of the devil and therefore as a threat to both Church and society. In view of this historical comparison with Europe, there seems to be a valid reason for concern regarding the extreme interest of charismatic churches in Africa in the development of full-fledged demonologies.

Some churches even run a great risk of encouraging and legitimising the killing of alleged witches. In press reports of witchcraft accusations against children among African communities in Britain, quoted at the beginning of this chapter, reference was made to the involvement of some African church leaders in this sad episode which, it appeared, was not a unique case. 'Some churches', one spokeswoman was reported saying, 'believe that their role is to beat the devil out of a child'.[69] She explained how such churches believe they need to inflict physical pain to make the body uncomfortable for the devil. This not only causes harm to individuals, but is likely to strengthen fears of witchcraft rather than helping to reduce them. This is an issue that is also commented on by the Ghanaian pastor in the Netherlands quoted in this book, when he describes the misguided views of some of his colleagues. The 'spiritual confusion' that Stephen Ellis identified in his work on war-torn Liberia[70] seems to also have affected some of Africa's religious and spiritual leaders inasmuch as they resort to extreme and inhumane measures to rid society of its perceived evil. Addressing confusion of this type is yet another challenge.

Notes

1. There is a growing literature on witchcraft in Africa today, some of which is reflected in the bibliography at the end of this volume. For an overview of the recent literature, see the introduction in Henrietta Moore and Todd Sanders (eds), *Magical Interpretations, Material Realities: Modernity, witchcraft and the occult in post-colonial Africa*. London: Routledge, 2001.

2. Filip de Boeck and Marie-Françoise Plissart, *Kinshasa: Tales of the Invisible City*, Gent: Ludion, 2004.

3. Umar Danfulani, Simon Mwadkwon and Vincent Parlong, 'Children at the centre of witchcraft accusations: The rise of modern witchery; secret societies and anti-witchcraft Christian prayer houses in Nigeria', paper presented at the International Workshop on Religion and Human Rights, 4-8 November, 2002, Dodowa, Ghana.

4. Vikram Dodd, 'More children "victims of cruel exorcisms"', *The Guardian*, 4 June 2005, p. 10.

5. Cf. Elias Bongmba (p. 123), Seratwa Ntloedibe (p. 221) and Hugo Hinfelaar (p. 234) in this volume. See also Christine Brandsma, 'HIV/AIDS and witchcraft: an exploration of a possible relationship on the discourse of HIV/AIDS and witchcraft in South Africa', M.A. diss., Utrecht University, 2004.

6. Stephen Ellis and Gerrie ter Haar, *Worlds of Power: Religious thought and political practice in Africa*, London: Hurst & Co./New York: OUP, 2004.

7. Stephen Ellis, *The Mask of Anarchy: The destruction of Liberia and the religious dimension of an African civil war*, London: Hurst & Co., 1999.

8. Adam Ashforth, *Witchcraft, Violence and Democracy in South Africa*, University of Chicago Press, 2005, notably pp. xiii-xv, 3-4, 17-18.

9. Cf. Gerrie ter Haar, *Spirit of Africa: The healing ministry of Archbishop Milingo of Zambia*, London: Hurst & Co./Trenton, NJ: Africa World Press, 1992.

10. A helpful overview is provided by Leny Lagerwerf, *Witchcraft, sorcery, and spirit possession: Pastoral responses in Africa*, Gweru:

Mambo Press, 1987. A recent exception is Ashforth, *Witchcraft, Violence and Democracy*.

11. Religion is defined here as 'a belief in the existence of an invisible world, distinct but not separate from the visible one, that is home to spiritual beings with effective powers over the material world'. Cf. Ellis and Ter Haar, *Worlds of Power*, p. 14.

12. Thias Kgatla, Gerrie ter Haar and Walter van Beek.

13. See S.T. Kgatla and G. ter Haar, 'Crossing witchcraft barriers in South Africa: Power, politics, healing, beliefs and social empowerment. Preliminary Report', notably pp. 5-6.

14. Ineke van Kessel, *'Beyond Our Wildest Dreams': The United Democratic Front and the transformation of South Africa*, Charlottesville: University Press of Virginia, 2000, pp. 125-36.

15. See Thias Kgatla in this volume, p. 269.

16. Kgatla and Ter Haar, 'Preliminary Report', p. 2.

17. Ralushai, N.V. et al., 'Report of the Commission of Inquiry into Witchcraft Violence and Ritual Murders in the Northern Province of the Republic of South Africa', Pietersburg, 1996.

18. The Thoyandu Declaration on Ending Witchcraft Violence, Johannesburg, 1998.

19. See S.T Kgatla, G. ter Haar, W.E.A. van Beek and J.J. de Wolf, *Crossing Witchcraft Barriers in South Africa. Exploring witchcraft accusations: causes and solutions.* Utrecht: Utrecht University, 2003, pp. 33-5.

20. Examples have been recorded from a variety of countries in different continents. See e.g. Pamela J. Stewart and Andrew Strathern, *Witchcraft, Sorcery, Rumors and Gossip*, Cambridge University Press, 2004. See also data presented by Wolfgang Behringer in *Witches and Witch-Hunts: A global history*, Cambridge: Polity Press, 2004.

21. See the chapter by Gerrie ter Haar in the present volume (ch. 4).

22. Hugo Hinfelaar in the present volume. Unless otherwise stated, all future references to work by contributors to the present volume refer to the individual chapters in this volume.

23. Kgatla et al., *Crossing Witchcraft Barriers*, p. 5.

24. As discussed at some length by Abraham Akrong in this volume.

25. Article 3 of the United Nations Universal Declaration of Human Rights.

26. Cf. Riekje Pelgrim, *Witchcraft and Policing: South African Police Service attitudes towards witchcraft and witchcraft-related crime in the Northern Province*, Leiden: African Studies Centre, 2003.

27. Cf. Stephen Ellis in this volume.

28. Cf. Richard Gray, *Black Christians and White Missionaries*, New Haven: Yale University Press, 1990, notably chapter 5: 'Christianity and concepts of evil in sub-Saharan Africa'.

29. Ter Haar, *Spirit of Africa*.

30. Gerrie ter Haar, ch. 4.

31. As pointed out by Mathew Schoffeleers, 'Christ as the medicine-man and the medicine-man as Christ: a tentative history of African christological thought', *Man and Life*, vol. 8, nr. 1/2, 1982, pp. 11-28. See also Aylward Shorter, *Jesus and the Witchdoctor: An approach to healing and wholeness*. Maryknoll, NY: Orbis Books, 1985.

32. Cf. Gerrie ter Haar, ch. 4, p. 99.

33. Stephen Ellis, p. 31.

34. Cf. Ibid., p. 42.

35. Walter van Beek, p. 308. See also Kgatla et al., *Crossing Witchcraft Barriers*, p. 23.

36. Ellis and Ter Haar, *Worlds of Power*, pp. 149-50.

37. See Stephen Ellis, p. 33.

38. As pointed out by various contributors, notably by Umar Danfulani, Samuel Mbambo, and Stephen Nyaga.

39. Walter van Beek, p. 301.

40. Investigation by Seratwa Ntloedibe, see pp. 215-16.

41. See Hugo Hinfelaar, p. 234-5.

42. See e.g. the special issue of *African Legal Studies*, a journal published by the Faculty of Law in the University of the North in South Africa, which was in 2001 devoted to the problem of witchcraft violence and the law in South Africa.

43. The SANPAD report *Crossing Witchcraft Barri*ers contains some relevant pictures.

44. See the chapter by Elom Dovlo.

45. See Stephen Nyaga, notably pp. 264-5. Also Dovlo, pp. 82-3.

46. Thias Kgatla, p. 270. See also Frederick Golooba-Mutebi, 'Witchcraft, social cohesion and participation in a South African village', *Development and Change*, vol. 36, nr. 5, 2005, pp. 937-58, who discusses the long-term consequences of witchcraft-related conflicts

for intra-community relations and their implications for development policy and practice.

47. Akrong, pp. 59-61.

48. Dovlo, pp. 82-3.

49. Cf. Akrong, pp. 61-5.

50. Dovlo, p. 77.

51. Cf. also Ter Haar, p. 106.

52. Ibid, p. 106-7.

53. Gerrie ter Haar, *Rats, Cockroaches and People Like Us: Views of humanity and human rights*, The Hague: Institute of Social Studies, 2000.

54. Hinfelaar, p. 243.

55. Gerrie ter Haar, *Rats, Cockroaches and People Like Us*. Revised and shortened version published in Joseph Runzo, Nancy M. Martin and Arvind Sharma (eds), *Human Rights and Responsibilities in the World Religions*, Oxford: Oneworld, pp. 79-95.

56. Kgatla et al., *Crossing Witchcraft Barriers*, p. 28.

57. See Cyprian Fisiy and Peter Geschiere, 'Judges and witches, or how is the State to deal with witchcraft? Examples from southeast Cameroon', *Cahiers d'études africaines*, vol. 30, cah. 118, 1990, pp. 135-56.

58. Akrong, p. 61.

59. Ellis, 'Witching-times'.

60. Report on the Round Table Conference on the Treatment of Suspected Witches in Northern Ghana, Picorner Hotel, Tamale, 17th December 1998, p. 17.

61. Kgatla et al., *Crossing Witchcraft Barriers*, pp. 31-5.

62. This is the slogan of the Sarvodaya Shramadana Movement, a Buddhist development organisation founded in Sri Lanka in 1958.

63. Kgatla, pp. 275-82.

64. Personal communication.

65. International Workshop on Religion and Human Rights, 4-8 November, Dodowa, Ghana, 2002.

66. Hugo Hinfelaar, pp. 239, 242.

67. Interim Report International Workshop on Religion and Human Rights, 4-8 November, Dodowa, Ghana.

68. Ibid., pp. 10-11.

69. See note 4.

70. Ellis, *The Mask of Anarchy*.

2

WITCHING-TIMES: A THEME IN THE HISTORIES OF AFRICA AND EUROPE

Stephen Ellis

INTRODUCTION

The memory, or perhaps the morality tale, of the great witch-hunts of the fifteenth to eighteenth centuries is one of the most potent stories from Europe's past. The image of the witch propagated by early modern demonologists – that is, a purveyor of death and destruction in active relation with Satan, the prince of darkness – has not entirely lost its hold over the popular imagination. In some European countries at least, the notion occasionally resurfaces that there exist secret conclaves of utterly cruel and destructive people who, in league with the devil, wreak havoc in society.[1] Witch-stories are still transmitted in Europe through popular news and entertainment media, including fiction and children's stories.

Historians professional and amateur have been producing accounts of European witchcraft and European witch-hunting since the late nineteenth century.[2] For much of this time, the view most commonly held among European and North American writers on the subject was that witch-beliefs and witch-hunting arose from the ignorance of an earlier age, and that they eventually succumbed to the onward march of progress in the form of a more enlightened approach to religion, the advance of science, and the correct use of reason.[3] The general public in Europe and North America today probably still holds a similar view of why their ancestors ceased to believe in witchcraft and why they stopped persecuting alleged witches.

Extensive historical research in the last few decades, however, making systematic use of archives and of the original works of writers living at the time of the great witch-hunts, has effectively demolished older theories that the fall of European witch-hunting was a consequence of a general decline in the belief in witchcraft. Moreover, it is now clear that the persecution of alleged witches in early modern times was not a medieval practice that survived until it eventually became obsolete due to more enlightened thinking. On the contrary, while there were comparable campaigns against various minorities during the Middle Ages, such as lepers, Jews, heretics and Muslims,[4] there was little persecution of alleged witches in that period. The great witchcraft persecutions were essentially an innovation of the period of the Reformation and the Renaissance, reaching their peak in the sixteenth and early seventeenth centuries. Moreover, although the witch-persecutions did indeed cease during the period of the Enlightenment, this was not because of an overall loss of belief in the existence of witchcraft,[5] for many Europeans, including some famous names in the history of science, continued to believe in the existence of witchcraft even after people had ceased to be executed as alleged witches.

It has therefore become necessary to find other explanations for the rise and fall of European witch-hunting. It is also necessary to explain why the persecutions eventually stopped, in spite of the fact that many people continued to believe in the existence of witchcraft. It has become increasingly evident that belief in witchcraft does not inevitably result in murderous bouts of persecution and, vice versa, that bouts of murderous persecution of people considered to be inherently evil and threatening to society have occurred in some twentieth-century societies that formally disclaim any belief in religion or related metaphysical ideas. According to historians, the purges in Stalin's Soviet Union, for example, show 'many similarities'[6] to the witch-hunts of past centuries. Such insights suggest that it might be possible to investigate a comparative sociology of scapegoating in a broad variety of societies, not all of which profess a general belief in witchcraft or religion.[7] However, it would also be necessary to consider how the action of hunting down perceived subversives relates to the wide variety of ideas associated with 'those who commit acts perceived as transgressing the fundamental moral axioms on which human nature, and hence social life, is based'.[8] Pedophiles, Trotskyists, Jews, communists, asylum-seekers and many other groups have been placed in such a category in twentieth-century Europe and North America, without people labelling them as 'witches'. In short, we also need to consider under what circumstances a belief in the existence of transcendental evil, channelled through a person, can properly be described as witchcraft.

HOW EUROPEANS FOUND WITCHCRAFT IN AFRICA

For present purposes, in addition to considering the historical record of witchcraft belief and witch-hunting in Europe, it is also useful to consider how European beliefs in the existence of such an absolutely evil, mystical power, able to be manipulated by at least some human beings, became connected to Africa. To be sure, Europeans who left accounts of their travels in Africa during the centuries when the witch-hunts were at their height in Europe often lamented what they considered to be the superstition and false religion of its inhabitants. Nevertheless, early European travellers and missionaries did not generally detect 'witchcraft' in those African religious practices that they were able to witness or document, but more commonly considered them to be other forms of 'wrong' religion, which they sometimes labelled as 'superstition', 'fetishism' or 'idolatry'. The first wave of European missionary endeavour in Africa, in the seventeenth century, was aimed at converting Africans in order to outflank Islam much more than it was motivated by any perception that Africans were engaged in witchcraft.[9] The identification of African religion with witchcraft came only later, perhaps not until the later nineteenth century, via the popular missionary and travel writings of David Livingstone (1813-73) and others. However, according to the anthropologist Peter Pels, it was the English popular literature of the late Victorian period, especially H. Rider Haggard's best-selling novel *She* (1887), that was instrumental in fixing a view of Africa in the English-speaking world as 'the heartland of witchcraft and magic', as opposed to other forms of supposed religious error.[10] A roughly similar pattern could probably be found in the literature of France and other Western European countries, whereby the historical memory of European witchcraft and the associated persecutions was applied to Africa during the course of the nineteenth century.

The creation of a popular literature depicting Africa as the Dark Continent, as backward in religion as it was said to be in most other manifestations of human culture, was consistent with nineteenth-century developments in science. Early practitioners of the new science of anthropology specialised in gathering data on people previously unknown to the West. Among the examples of behaviour, thought and social organisation that ethnographers identified as forming distinctive patterns and systems were some that European intellectuals considered reminiscent of bygone periods of Europe's own history. It became common throughout Western Europe and North America in the late nineteenth century to conceive of history as a story of evolution in which different peoples (and different 'races', in those days regarded as a sound scientific category) had progressed at different speeds. European scholars came to think of the world's people as divided into distinct societies, of which Europeans were the most advanced. Africa came to be widely seen by Europeans both educated and uneducated as a reservoir of institutions and types of behaviour that had become obsolete in more advanced countries. By this token, anthropological data on Africa were considered not only as an addition to the world's stock of general knowledge but also as a source of comparative information on the origins of those institutions of government, society and religion that Europeans conventionally thought had reached unprecedented heights of development in their own countries.[11]

Hence, for Europeans and North Americans in the nineteenth century – and for a good part of the twentieth as well—it was reasonable to consider the religious ideas and activities that were being discovered by explorers and recorded by ethnographers as evidence of archaic forms of belief and ritual that had been abandoned in Europe but still existed elsewhere.[12] They saw little difficulty in comparing Africa's present with Europe's past, since it was assumed that such a comparison had a firm scientific grounding in theories of evolution. Any activity in Africa that could be identified as witchcraft was considered to be rooted in ignorance and irrationality, just as it was thought to have been in the history of Europe itself. This scheme was equally attractive from both an agnostic and a Christian point of view. By the same token, any religious activity by Africans that did not have some clear equivalent in the practice of contemporary European Christians risked being vaguely consigned to the category of 'witchcraft', and campaigns of ritual purification labelled as 'witch-hunting', [13] while indigenous healers and specialists were described as 'witch-doctors'. There can be no doubt that many African practices of divination, healing and initiation were subsumed into the category of 'witchcraft' in this way without any deep consideration of the moral value attached to such practices within the societies where they were extant. In this way, some of the evil character inherent in the idea of witchcraft emanating from Europe's own history became attached to African practices that originally had other, less uniformly negative, associations. [14]

A nineteenth-century European and North American view of Africa as a continent of primitive and often sinister religion has never been entirely dispelled. Contemporary African 'witchcraft' is, then, like many other aspects of life there, neither authentically African nor a pure imposition. It is an unfortunate amalgam created in part by comparing religious ideas and practices from different places without sufficient precaution.

This last remark does not mean that comparisons should not be made. On the contrary, comparison is necessary if contemporary African 'witchcraft' is not to be considered a problem peculiar to Africa in the modern world. Comparison, however, needs to be on the basis of the best possible data and to take what one thoughtful anthropologist called 'those cautions we observe in the translation of culture in connection with other problems'. [15] Accordingly, the following paragraphs will first examine some new insights into the nature of witchcraft and witch-hunting in early modern Europe that have emerged from what is now a large and sophisticated corpus of historical research. Only then are we in a position to discuss what, if anything, could be a proper basis for a possible comparison between this phenomenon in European history and certain phenomena recorded as occurring in modern Africa or elsewhere that are often labelled as 'witchcraft' or 'sorcery' [16] by scholars writing in English. The classic definitions of these terms are offered by Evans-Pritchard, the founder of modern anthropological studies of the subject. He describes sorcery as 'magic that is illicit or is considered immoral', a mystical power considered in some societies to exist in nature, whose use is normally forbidden. In this respect sorcery is rather like a firearm: anyone is capable of using it, but because it can be lethal, in practice its use has to be restricted. 'Witchcraft', on the other hand, Evans-Pritchard sees as a type of destructive power inherent in only some people.[17]

THE NEW HISTORIOGRAPHY OF EUROPEAN WITCH-CRAFT

The idea of comparing witchcraft beliefs between societies, as well as associated practices including accusations and confessions of witchcraft, was assumed by many scholars to be straightforward until perhaps forty or fifty years ago. Leading social scientists produced general studies of witchcraft in which evidence drawn from Europe and Africa was used without much distinction.[18] Edited volumes contained papers on witchcraft in early modern Europe alongside analyses of Africa and other parts of what was then called the third world.[19] Many scholars reasoned that an accusation of witchcraft could best be analysed by reference to the function it fulfilled in any society where belief in witchcraft was widespread. They saw such accusations primarily as a technique used in overwhelmingly pre-industrial communities for redressing tensions in society that typically had an economic or social cause.[20] Some of the most influential anthropologists of the time, including some distinguished Africanists, tended to see individual societies as integrated units, in which every process has a function and provokes a corresponding readjustment in the society in such a way as to maintain order and equilibrium. According to this point of view, the root of a perceived case of witchcraft might actually be a dispute between relatives or neighbours, fear of an individual thought to be amassing excessive wealth or power, or some similar problem likely to occur in any small community where people know each other well and cannot easily escape from the petty jealousies and disputes of everyday life. Many academic analysts considered that an accusation of witchcraft served as what we would now call a conflict-resolution mechanism, a means of relieving economic or social tensions by channelling them into a ritualised form that could then be dealt with by appropriate specialists. By this reasoning, the occurrence of large-scale, lethal witch-hunts indicated a fundamental breakdown in the normal means of regulation.

One of the implications of such an analysis was that the great European witch-hunts of the sixteenth and seventeenth centuries must have resulted from a breakdown in habitual modes of regulating social problems so massive as to imply a crisis of the utmost gravity.[21] In the 1960s, a leading historian, Keith Thomas, and a historian/anthropologist, Alan Macfarlane, both working on separate books, set out to apply to English history methods of functional-structural anthropology previously used in regard to African societies.[22] They found evidence to support the notion that witchcraft accusations in English villages three or four centuries earlier often arose from conflicts based on changing notions of proper behaviour in tightly-knit communities, such as a refusal to give customary alms or charity. A person who refused to help out a neighbour who had fallen on hard times might be accused of being a witch. Others particularly liable to be accused of witchcraft in this period were 'cunning men' and 'cunning women', as they were called in Shakespeare's day, in other words people practicing forms of healing and divination derived from folk knowledge.[23] For the many Europeans who lived from the land, fertility and the protection of crops was of the utmost importance, and indeed this was 'the main purpose of most communal Christian rites'.[24] People at all levels of society believed in a wide variety of forms of mystical power, including in regard to such mysterious processes as the transubstantiation of the host in the Catholic mass, miracles, and the reality of the resurrection of the dead. Some mystical powers were held to be destructive in nature and related to witches. Witch stories 'invoked a mythical world, in which the tensions of personal and communal life were personified in the devil and his agents'.[25] The fact that the persecution of alleged witches declined sharply in the later seventeenth century in most of Western Europe seemed to be commensurate with the overall view that witch beliefs were an essentially medieval idea that, like other aspects of the medieval world, was fated to disappear in proportion as ideas which we would now regard as typically modern became more current.

Historians using methods derived from mid-twentieth century anthropology, intent on identifying the factors underlying changes in belief, considered that the rise of the great witch-persecutions arose from a clash between the traditional structures and values of medieval life, in retreat before modern values associated with the spread of learning, systematic Christian theology, centralised government and individualism, all of them processes at work in sixteenth- and seventeenth-century England. It has been established beyond doubt that changing views of the types of activity that were believed to constitute witchcraft were influenced in much of Europe, although generally less in England than on the continent, by the spread of advanced, dogmatic opinions of Christian orthodoxy that circulated through texts printed during the great religious and political upheavals of the Reformation.[26] Clergymen, both Protestant and Catholic, were concerned to spread piety among the lay populations of Europe, to redefine correct religion, and to root out forms of belief and ritual which they considered to lie outside the scope of their definitions.[27] A new type of demonology emerged that was based not on folk belief but on the work of scholars, who tended to represent any mystical powers not approved by the Church as being necessarily satanic. Such ideas, which in Catholic areas particularly were replete with the theory of the witches' sabbath and all its accoutrements, spread from theologians and lawyers to more lowly magistrates and the population at large.

A historian looking for patterns in series of data could identify a clear tendency over the course of time for an accusation that a person was a witch to become considered as tantamount to the charge that they had had some form of liaison with Satan, the prince of evil. In an age when rival Christian creeds were striving to evangelise a European population only superficially Christian in many respects, and to persuade people of the necessity of highly disciplined forms of belief, and at a time when satanic attacks were generally expected, this was the essence of the matter. An accusation of witchcraft became a most serious charge, since the presumed presence of human agents of Satan threatened states and societies alike. Anyone thus accused was at risk of being judicially investigated, sometimes by means of torture, with a view to establishing whether they had had dealings with the devil such as in the form of sexual congress or through attendance at the witches' sabbath or through an animal familiar.

The search for a deeper explanation, located not just in the records of people's shifting ideas but in the structures underpinning society, led historians, as it had done anthropologists, to examine the social and institutional patterns of witch-hunting, rather than studying witchcraft beliefs in and of themselves.[28] Historians noted that one innovation of the sixteenth century was the use of civil courts to try people accused of witchcraft, an offence which had earlier been dealt with less stringently by ecclesiastical courts. This produced evidence suggestive of a political aspect to the great witch-hunts, all the more persuasive because many of the archives most useful for the historical study of witchcraft beliefs were the records of judicial proceedings taken against people accused of witchcraft. The great age of witch-trials broadly coincided with the rise and fall of the great absolutist monarchies of early modern Europe. These developed powerful bureaucracies able to standardise procedures and legal texts, having the means to penetrate directly to the heart of the societies they aspired to govern. The witchcraft persecutions were evidence of the power of growingly authoritarian states to impose themselves on society inasmuch as the prosecution of legal charges against people accused of witchcraft required a judicial apparatus capable of handling such cases. As a historian of Scotland summarises it, 'The rise of nation states was marked by new regimes establishing more centralized, more secular governments, which demonstrated their independence of the papacy either through direct adoption of the Reformation or through the nationalization (secularization) of areas of ecclesiastical law, including sexual offences and witchcraft'. She continues, 'At the same time it was necessary for these regimes to demonstrate their legitimacy to their peoples, their allies, and their enemies, by appropriating the religious authority previously attributed to the Roman church'.[29] Nevertheless, it has been demonstrated that there is no precise correlation between the incidence of witchcraft prosecutions and the areas most strongly exposed to central government.[30]

The growth of an enhanced fear of witchcraft can be detected from the mid-fifteenth century, beginning in the area on the northern side of the Alps and gradually spreading throughout Europe. There were probably some 100,000 witchcraft trials in Europe between 1450 and 1750, resulting in perhaps 40-50,000 executions. Seventy-five to 80% of victims were women,[31] typically a woman past child-bearing age, although many other people were accused as well. Women were considered the weaker sex, and therefore more open to temptation by the devil. Female or male, victims could be rich or poor. There is no completely consistent sociological pattern of accusations; all sorts and conditions of people believed in the reality of witchcraft in the sense that they believed it was possible for people to harm others, or create superhuman effects, by the use of mystical powers.

By no means everyone at the time believed that it was necessary to hunt down and punish alleged witches. 'After all,' wrote the great humanist Michel de Montaigne (1533-95), 'it is putting a very high price on one's conjectures to have a man roasted alive because of them.'[32] Nevertheless, witch-hunts increased in scale and frequency, becoming particularly acute in parts of France and the Rhineland and occurring among both Catholic and Protestant populations. Recent studies of Scandinavia, eastern Europe and other areas previously ignored by historians writing in English have given us a sharper appreciation of the considerable differences between different parts of Europe and of the spread of witch-hunting from one region to another.[33] England, in fact, suffered relatively few severe bouts of witch-hunting. The Netherlands witnessed very few cases at all. Witch-hunting declined sharply in Scotland, England and France in the late seventeenth century, but continued in other areas until after 1750. The last known European witchcraft trials that led to executions took place in Poland in the late eighteenth century.

THINKING WITH EARLY MODERN DEMONS

The work of Thomas and Macfarlane in the 1960s and 1970s in many ways was the pioneer of a major interest in the history of European witchcraft beliefs, now amounting to a vast literature. In recent decades, historical research has tended to turn away from an attempt to detect patterns or structures in records of persecutions and rather more towards the study of witchcraft beliefs in their own terms. There are several reasons for this change in emphasis. They include a concern with reconstructing the mentalities of earlier periods in all their diversity and an interest in investigating the ideas connected with the work of Michel Foucault concerning the way power expresses itself not only through repression, but through investing in social relations and imposing particular forms of knowledge on societies. One of the perhaps surprising discoveries that have been made as a result of studying witchcraft beliefs as ideas, situating them in the mentalities of their time, is that such beliefs were quite compatible with a range of rational opinions on natural science.[34] Some of the most famous intellectuals of the period believed strongly in witchcraft, such as Robert Boyle, one of the founders of modern chemistry and physics. (Isaac Newton, we may note in passing, was a keen alchemist, who also believed in witchcraft). Many advanced intellectuals of the seventeenth century understood witchcraft as a natural force that would therefore work according to certain regular 'rules' that could be identified, like the laws of gravity or planetary motion. Thus, the hypothesis that witchcraft is an archaic belief that was forced to recede in Europe due to the introduction of modern government and rational thinking about science has to be reviewed. This finding is of particular relevance for Africa, where there appears to be a widespread supposition that witchcraft beliefs and witchcraft accusations will disappear of their own accord as countries develop economically and with the spread of Western-style systems of formal education.

Perhaps the most significant light to have emerged from the new research on European witchcraft, then, concerns the distinction that needs to be made between changing beliefs concerning the invisible world and the chronology of the great witch-hunts. The great witch-hunts were not caused solely by belief in witchcraft, since such a belief was prevalent both before and after the period of the most intense persecutions. Therefore, the question of why Europeans ceased to believe in the reality of witchcraft and why the witch-persecutions stopped are best regarded as two separate (although of course related) questions, rather than as cause and effect. The great witch-hunts occurred in a phase of European history that witnessed profound changes in government, in views of society, and in the mechanisms by which the strong could exercise power over the weak, the period of the Reformation, the spread of printing, wars of religion in France, England and Germany, and the birth of bureaucratic states that had the means to formulate and implement policies in regard to a range of social matters. The fear of witches was connected to 'an eschatological reading of current affairs,'[35] an analysis of events and trends interpreted in the light of an intensive reading of the Bible. Amid a widespread perception that the End-Time predicted in the Bible was at hand, patterns of behaviour among the general population that might have excited rather little attention in earlier times were now subject to critical examination by authorities that were more disposed than previously to see the hand of Satan in events on earth. A rigorous new academic discipline of demonology developed as a way of trying to understand these diabolic activities in a systematic form. In an age when religious identity was also considered a civil identity, the witch's nature as 'a social *and* religious criminal' was significant,[36] for a witch was not just a bad person, but also the bad subject of a prince or king.

If some monarchs concluded that the solution to the problem of religious dissidence was to require all their subjects to show allegiance to the same church, others reasoned that a better solution was to distance the state itself from factional disputes of a religious nature that risked bringing it into discredit. In England, a consensus emerged in political circles after the excesses of the civil war of the 1640s, which had coincided with some of the bloodiest witch-hunts, that witchcraft accusations had been abused by fanatics in a manner that, on balance, was detrimental to public order. The restored monarchy of 1660 wished to retain the sacral nature of the state, which implied standing above such controversies. [37] A reluctance for the state to involve itself in accusations of witchcraft, particularly when it became clear that these risked miscarriages of justice through confessions extracted by torture, was part of a wider tendency among European states to distance themselves from religious quarrels of various sorts. In France, such episodes as the notorious burning of Urbain Grandier, a parish priest convicted of causing the devil to possess a convent of nuns, came to be seen as excesses of such a type. It was so obvious that Grandier's prosecution was manipulated by powerful people for the most worldly of reasons, and the official account of his alleged crime was so full of contradictions, as to cause widespread doubts about explanations of his case advanced by theologians and jurists.[38] Confessions extracted under torture were often the main basis for judicial conviction. Scepticism about officially proclaimed cases of witchcraft was politically damaging, as it could undermine the authority of kings whose power was still closely associated with that of the Church. The contradictions inherent in many accounts of supposed diabolic possession were later to be mocked by Voltaire, for example, in such a way as to cast doubt on closely related doctrines concerning Christian miracles and resurrection.[39]

Hence, generally speaking, Europeans stopped persecuting witches not because they had ceased to believe in witchcraft, but because they ceased to believe that issuing an indictment through a formal judicial organ was the best means of dealing with it. Public officials ceased to consider witchcraft as a political problem, but perhaps as a social one or a religious one only, but in any event a problem outside the political realm. In France, Austria and Prussia, the prosecution of people accused of witchcraft was halted as a result of central government decree, even though those who promulgated such measures themselves generally continued to believe in the existence of witchcraft.[40] Over time, the number of people grew who, while still regarding witchcraft as a reality, came to regard it as a problem that should not be pursued through the civil courts. This may helpfully be seen in the context of evolving theological ideas concerning relations between the visible and invisible worlds or between nature and supernature. To scholars, an orderly creation implied that God did not ordinarily intervene in the affairs of a world that he had set in motion, and that God no longer took human form. If the frontier of the visible and invisible worlds was less permeable than had previously been thought, then the likelihood of the devil recruiting human agents was much diminished. 'Scholars are now more aware that religious toleration was a political means to the formation of strong state power 'that emerged from the sectarian wars of the sixteenth and seventeenth centuries rather than the gift of a benign intention to defend pluralism', Talal Asad notes.[41] He adds the telling remark by a French jurist of the period that 'heresy no longer exists in religion today, it exists in the state'.[42] If heretics and other people perceived to profess a 'wrong' brand of religion could now be tolerated, so could alleged witches.

THE ANTHROPOLOGY OF WITCHCRAFT IN AFRICA

Recent years have also seen a marked revival of anthropological interest in witchcraft in Africa.[43] In brief, leading anthropologists in this field have sought to overturn an old-fashioned view that witchcraft in Africa is part of a traditional mode of thought that is fated to disappear in the face of modern life.[44] They observe that mystical conceptions of malice are used in a wide variety of situations in Africa today, including some that may be considered as belonging in the most modern sectors of life. As summarised by the anthropologist Blair Rutherford, witchcraft is represented in the new anthropology of Africa as a set of 'shifting and versatile practices and idioms deployed within local communities in response to wider social forces', and most particularly as a way of contesting or appropriating modernity.[45] This point of view broadly corresponds to the findings of historians that people in early modern times – even major scientists and philosophers—found no inconsistency in believing in witchcraft at the same time as they believed in the existence of a cosmos governed by orderly rules. In other words, both historians and social scientists have come to suppose that there is in principle no reason to doubt that people may believe in the reality of witchcraft at the same time as they live in the modern world.

Historians and social scientists fifty years ago were able to assume with little apparent difficulty that 'witchcraft' was the same thing in a wide variety of times and places largely because they saw it as a mechanism of predominantly agrarian societies. The corollary of this supposition was that 'witchcraft' would disappear with modernisation. If, then, as has become increasingly apparent, similar beliefs may transfer themselves to urban settings and modern sectors of life, then 'witchcraft' cannot be assumed to be something that is fated to disappear with eco-nomic or scientific development. Moreover, social analysts have come to appreciate that the mystical power which some people refer to as 'witchcraft' can be seen to have similarities to many other forms of power, based on relations between people, that can be considered real despite being invisible. 'It is an old empiri-cist prejudice,' Talal Asad remarks, 'to suppose that things are real only when confirmed by sensory data, and that therefore people are real but structures and systems aren't.'[46] Seen from this point of view, positing the existence of a mystical power that can be used for harmful purposes is no more inherently anti-modern than supposing the existence of life expectancies, voting patterns, rates of productivity, race, or the self.[47]

Since it may be demonstrated that people may believe in artefacts such as these in a great variety of societies, and that such a belief does not always have the same function in each one, it becomes a problem to know what precisely is meant by the term 'witchcraft'. However, none of the leading authors writing on the subject with regard to Africa today seems to have addressed this question in any depth. In part, their reluctance probably arises from a theoretical distrust of definitions, which can become unac-ceptable impositions of meaning on masses of data. Many anthro-pologists prefer to work with a 'thick' description of particular contexts. Since there is no doubt that, in many parts of Africa, people routinely refer to 'witchcraft', when they are speaking in English, in a wide variety of circumstances, anthropologists some-times justify their use of the term (or the French equivalent *sorcel-lerie*) on the grounds that it is one that their African informants use. This, however, is not sufficient reason for scholars to adopt the term without further inquiry. (Africans, after all, commonly talk of 'tribes', 'juju' and so on, without social scientists finding it permissible to take over these expressions.) Social scientists make use of categories and vocabularies that they believe to be stable and to have explanatory power, and do not in all circumstances repro-duce uncritically the language of the people they write about.

This is more than merely playing with words. As we have seen, the word 'witchcraft' carries with it a heavy historical baggage, inherited not only from the gruesome history of European witch-hunting, but also from the application of the term 'witchcraft' to Africa in colonial times. It is just one key item of religious vocabulary applied to, or used in, Africa today that reflects the habit of European missionaries, secular intellectuals and government officials in the quite recent past of regarding all forms of indigenous religion as suspect, and possibly even satanic, causing them to label whole areas of thought and practice as 'witchcraft'. Such a categorisation was often made with little consideration of the moral nature of the practices thus designated, which seems to be a crucial point. The philosophers Hallen and Sodipo have cited as an example the intricate theologies of the Yoruba of Nigeria concerning the soul, destiny and the moral self that have sometimes been labelled as 'witchcraft' by authors writing in English.[48] Since the beginning of the colonial period, much of this vocabulary has been taken over by Africans and is used by them when they speak English.

The continuing use in postcolonial times of what was originally a colonial language, particularly when accompanied by a vast range of other transformations initiated in the colonial encounter,[49] has encouraged the development of new moral connotations for a wide range of traditional practices and ideas. Whereas the orthodox Christianity that emerged from the Reformation considered the metaphysical world to be divided into principles of absolute good and evil, much African religious thought has regarded the metaphysical world as being a-moral. Spiritual forces, traditionally, were seen as intrinsically neither good nor bad, although their power could be channelled for moral or immoral purposes. Hence, some recent studies of witch persecutions in Africa point out how the performance of actions or rituals that were once respectable, or at least permissible, may, under the influence of a dualistic Christian theology, become perceived by people as witchcraft, considered to be a form of lethal, radical evil inspired by Satan.[50] In other words, traditional practices, in becoming sublimated in the category 'witchcraft', have also gained a new moral character—an evil one. Just as European witchcraft has a history, so does the jumble of ideas and practices that may be designated by that term in Africa.

In these circumstances, it is unsafe to assume that beliefs extant outside Europe, which bear a superficial resemblance to witchcraft as it was perceived in Europe's own history, are necessarily the same as the historical European version. The apparent similarities between European and non-European variants may be due to a mixture of poor labelling by colonial officials and missionaries combined with the way Western scholars have thought about certain types of religious belief in Africa. As the anthropologist Malcolm Crick wrote over 25 years ago in regard to the literature on Africa, 'It is most likely that witchcraft may have become a separate topic for anthropology because of its appearance in the history of our own [i.e. British] society.'[51] Social scientists working in Africa may simply have taken the memory of European witchcraft belief, with many of its associations, as a ready-made term, without thinking deeply about its suitability. This is all the more serious in that historians of Europe have themselves borrowed much of their terminology from early modern demonologists inspired by the notorious witch-hunter's manual, the *Malleus Maleficarum*.[52] One could extend this argument further than just to the identification of 'witchcraft' in Africa, by agreeing with the historian Steven Feierman that it has become apparent from the study of African history over the last fifty years that specific events that occur in Africa can never automatically be assimilated into 'categories of analysis...drawn from Europe,' such as building European-style states or the growth of capitalism,[53] or, indeed, the rise and fall of witch-hunting. 'Witchcraft' cannot be used straightforwardly as a technical term that, like other standard items in the lexicon of social science, aspires to describe something of universal application.

In addition to a need to ascertain the nature of mystical beliefs and practices glossed by anthropologists as 'witchcraft', there are also further questions that could usefully be elaborated concerning their interpretation. The new anthropology on witchcraft in Africa generally argues that witchcraft accusations and witchcraft belief—the two being not always distinguished—are, at bottom, a means of apprehending forces or factors such as globalisation or modernity that are considered the common currency of social science. This implies that the real cause of certain forms of social disruption is not witchcraft itself but modernity, which then becomes expressed in the language of witchcraft. The implication in such an analysis is that those Africans who speak of witchcraft are not able to identify the forces of globalisation or modernity that are really shaping their lives or, if they are able to do so, they still prefer to express them as 'witchcraft'. 'Such a social science translation adds nothing to what is self-evident to victims and can trivialize the events of sorcery as they are experienced', notes an anthropologist who has studied comparable perceptions in Sri Lanka,[54] here referring to mystical forms of assault not as witchcraft but as sorcery. In fact, interpreting witchcraft in the first instance as a translation of a secular force, social or economic, seems little different from the functional analysis that was in vogue among anthropologists fifty years ago, in which a mystical belief is interpreted as a function of an economic or social force.

CONCLUSION

This, it should be emphasised, is not a plea to scholars to ignore the phenomena which Africans themselves often call 'witchcraft'. On the contrary, there are reasons to suppose that these are in urgent need of study. It is a plea to examine such phenomena with appropriate sensitivity to the nuances of meaning attached to such ideas,[55] both in the communities where they can have such powerful consequences and in the industrialised world that made use of the notion of Africa's barbarism to justify taking possession of the continent. It is no longer acceptable to assume, as was common in the mid-twentieth century, that practices or beliefs labelled as 'witchcraft' in different times and places are necessarily one and the same, nor that unorthodox forms of religious belief and observance can acceptably be categorised in this way. Such a realisation, however, need not hamper careful comparative study.[56] A helpful comparison should perhaps begin with a reflection on method, concerning how mystical beliefs may be analysed in general. While historians have made considerable advances by considering ideas in their own terms, it is also clear that, in the last instance, what people think cannot be separated from what they do: if Europeans four centuries ago became convinced of the reality of the witches sabbath and of couplings with Satan,[57] it was in part because they knew of people who had confessed to such things in trials. Specialists of different times and places may learn much from each other about how to frame the object of their inquiry, and this in time might lead to a higher level of comparison than has previously been possible.[58] No interpretation is possible without a clear identification of the nature of 'witchcraft' in different societies.

This is not an original thought: the same was said more colourfully by the seventeenth-century thinker John Selden. He put it thus:[59]

> The reason of a thing is not to be enquired after, till you are sure the thing itself be so. We commonly are at *what's the reason of it?* before we are sure of the thing.

Notes

1. Jean La Fontaine, *Speak of the Devil: Tales of satanic abuse in contemporary England,* Cambridge University Press, 1998, esp. pp.180-8.

2. Alan C. Kors and Edward Peters (eds), *Witchcraft in Europe, 1100-1700: A documentary history* (Pittsburgh: University of Pennsylvania Press, 1972) includes useful extracts from early sources. On the historiography of witchcraft in Europe, see e.g. Jonathan Barry, Marianne Hester and Gareth Roberts (eds), *Witchcraft in Early Modern Europe: Studies in culture and belief,* Cambridge University Press, 1996, pp. 1-45, and the preface to Stuart Clark, *Thinking with Demons: The idea of witchcraft in early modern Europe,* Oxford: Clarendon Press, 1997. An excellent summary of modern scholarship is Robin Briggs, *Witches and Neighbours: The social and cultural context of European witchcraft,* London: Fontana, 1997.

3. For an expression of this, see Kors and Peters, *Witchcraft in Europe,* pp.3-21.

4. Carlo Ginzburg, *Ecstasies: Deciphering the witches' sabbath*, Harmondsworth: Penguin, 1992, pp.33-86.

5. Cf. Ian Bostridge, *Witchcraft and Its Transformations, c.1650-1750,* Oxford University Press, 1997, pp.4-5.

6. The phrase is from J. Arch Getty and Oleg V. Naumov, *The Road to Terror: Stalin and the self-destruction of the Bolsheviks, 1932-1939,* New Haven: Yale University Press, p. 7.

7. Cf. Stephen Ellis, 'Witch-hunting in central Madagascar, 1828-1861', *Past and Present,* nr. 175, 2002, pp. 90-123.

8. La Fontaine, *Speak of the Devil*, p.14.

9. Cf. the essays by Jacques Razafimbelo-Harisoa and by Bruno Hübsch in *Madagascar et le christianisme,* ACCT, Karthala and Ambozontany, Paris and Antananarivo, 1993.

10. Peter Pels, 'The magic of Africa: reflections on a Western commonplace', *African Studies Review,* vol. 41, nr. 3, 1998, p.195.

11. Sally Falk Moore, *Anthropology and Africa: Changing perspectives on a changing scene,* Charlottesville: University Press of Virginia, 1994, pp.8-14.

12. Perhaps the supreme literary product of this line of thought is Sir J.G. Frazer, *The Golden Bough* (1890). The London *Times* thought it 'a great book', which described 'the greater part of the magical beliefs and practices of the lower races and peasant peoples of the world, with a scientific precision and completeness superior to those of the encyclopaedic biologist', while also narrating 'the tragi-comedy of human superstition': quoted in the endpapers of the abridged version (London: Macmillan, 1933).

13. Cf. Willy de Craemer, Jan Vansina and Renée Fox, 'Religious movements in central Africa: a theoretical study,' *Comparative Studies in Society and History*, vol. 18, nr. 4, 1976, pp. 458-75.

14. For some examples drawn from the history of Liberia, see Stephen Ellis, 'Mystical weapons: some evidence from the Liberian war', *Journal of Religion in Africa*, vol. 31, nr. 2 , 2001, pp.222-36.

15. Malcolm Crick, *Explorations in Language and Meaning: Towards a semantic anthropology,* London: Malaby Press, 1976, p.112. This forms part of a discussion of 'witchcraft' on pages 109-27.

16. Evans-Pritchard makes a distinction between these two terms. Some other authors, however, do not. See Max Marwick (ed), *Witchcraft and Sorcery: Selected readings*, Harmondsworth: Penguin, 1970, pp. 11-14. An important recent study of Sri Lanka uses 'sorcery' where Africanists would be more likely to speak of 'witchcraft': Bruce Kapferer, *The Feast of the Sorcerer: Practices of consciousness and power,* University of Chicago Press, 1997, p.8.

17. E.E. Evans-Pritchard, *Witchcraft, Oracles and Magic among the Azande*, Oxford: Clarendon Press, 1937, pp.9-10.

18. E.g. Geoffrey Parrinder, *Witchcraft: European and African*, London: Faber and Faber, 1963, especially the comments on pages 128-9.

19. E.g. Marwick, *Witchcraft and Sorcery*.

20. See Mary Douglas (ed), *Witchcraft Confessions and Accusations*, London: Tavistock, 1970, although Douglas in her introduction (page xx) expressed distrust of 'the superbly untestable' assumption that witchcraft accusations were 'a symptom of disorder and moral collapse'.

21. Marwick, *Witchcraft and Sorcery,* pp.11-18.

22. Keith Thomas, *Religion and the Decline of Magic: Studies in popular beliefs in sixteenth- and seventeenth-century England*, London: Penguin, 1973; and Alan Macfarlane, *Witchcraft in Tudor and Stuart England*, London: Routledge and Kegan Paul, 1970. These works inspired some useful exchanges: see e.g. Mary Douglas's introduction to *Witchcraft Confessions*

and Accusations, and Hildred Geertz, 'An anthropology of religion and magic', *Journal of Interdisciplinary History*, vol. 6, nr. 1, 1975, pp.71-89.

23. Thomas, *Religion and the Decline of Magic*, pp.252-64, 518.

24. Briggs, *Witches and Neighbours*, p.40.

25. Ibid., p.31.

26. Thomas, *Religion and the Decline of Magic*, pp.517-98; Clark, *Thinking with Demons*, pp. 437-545.

27. Clark, *Thinking with Demons*, pp. 437-545.

28. Ibid, pp.vii-x.

29. Christina Larner, *Witchcraft and Religion: The politics of popular belief*, Oxford: Blackwell, 1984, p.89.

30. Wolfgang Behringer, 'Witchcraft studies in Austria, Germany and Switzerland', in J. Barry et al., *Witchcraft in Early Modern Europe*, pp.88-94.

31. Briggs, *Witches and Neighbours*, p.8; Brian P. Levack, *The Witch-Hunt in Early Modern Europe*, London: Longman, 1995, pp. 21-6, gives a slightly higher estimate of numbers executed.

32. *The Complete Essays of Montaigne*, excerpted in Kors and Peters, *Witchcraft in Europe*, p.337.

33. Bengt Ankarloo and Gustav Henningsen (eds), *Early Modern European Witchcraft: Centres and peripheries*, Oxford: Clarendon Press, 1990; Gábor Klaniczay, *The Uses of Supernatural Power: The transformation of popular religion in medieval and early-modern Europe*, Cambridge: Polity Press, 1990.

34. Clark, *Thinking with Demons*, p.152.

35. Ibid., p.316.

36. Bostridge, *Witchcraft and Its Transformations,*, p.109.

37. Ibid., p.54.

38. Michel de Certeau, *La possession de Loudun*, Paris: Julliard, 1970.

39. Klaniczay, *The Uses of Supernatural Power*, pp.185-6.

40. Ibid., pp.170-2.

41. Talal Asad, *Genealogies of Religion: Discipline and reasons of power in Christianity and Islam*, Baltimore: John Hopkins University Press, p. 206.

42. Ibid. My translation.

43. See especially Jean and John Comaroff (eds), *Modernity and its Malcontents: Ritual and power in postcolonial Africa*, University of Chicago Press, 1993, and Peter Geschiere, *The Modernity of Witchcraft: Politics and the occult in postcolonial Africa*, Charlottesville: University Press of Viriginia, 1997; the French version was published by Editions Karthala, Paris, in 1995 under the title *La sorcellerie en Afrique: la viande des autres*. A summary of the recent anthropological writing on witchcraft in Africa

is Henrietta L. Moore and Todd Sanders, 'Magical interpretations and material realities: an introduction', in Ibid. (eds), *Magical Interpretations, Material Realities: Modernity, witchcraft and the occult in post-colonial Africa*, London: Routledge, 2001, pp.1-27.

44. Comaroff, *Modernity and its Malcontents,* introduction and esp. pp.xviii, xxv-xxx.

45. Blair Rutherford, 'To find an African witch: anthropology, modernity and witch-finding in north-west Zimbabwe', *Critique of Anthropology*, nr. 19, 1999, p. 91.

46. Asad, *Genealogies of Religion*, p.6.

47. Cf. Karen E. Fields, 'Political contingencies of witchcraft in colonial central Africa: culture and the state in Marxist theory', *Canadian Journal of African Studies*, vol. 16, nr. 3, 1982, p.586.

48. Barry Hallen and J.O. Sodipo, *Knowledge, Belief and Witchcraft: Analytic experiments in African philosophy*, London: Ethnographica, 1986, pp. 86-118.

49. Cf. Stephen Ellis and Gerrie ter Haar, *Worlds of Power: Religious thought and political practice in Africa,* London: Hurst & Co., 2004, chapter five.

50. Mary Douglas, 'Sorcery accusations unleashed: the Lele revisited, 1987', *Africa*, vol. 69, nr. 2, 1999, pp.177-93; Isak Niehaus et al., *Witchcraft, Power and Politics: Exploring the occult in the South African lowveld*, London: Pluto Press, 2001, pp.31-6.

51. Crick, *Explorations in Language and Meaning*, p.112.

52. Wolfgang Behringer, *Witchcraft Persecutions in Bavaria: Popular magic, religious zealotry and reason of state in early modern Europe*, Cambridge University Press, 1997, p.13.

53. Steven Feierman, 'African histories and the dissolution of world history', in R.H. Bates, V.Y. Mudimbe and Jean O'Barr (eds), *Africa and the Disciplines: The contributions of research in Africa to the social sciences and humanities*, University of Chicago Press, 1993, 178-9.

54. Kapferer, *The Feast of the Sorcerer,* p.43.

55. Cf. Comi Toulabor, 'Sacrifices humains et politique: quelques exemples contemporains en Afrique', in G. Hesseling, P. Konings and W. van Binsbergen (eds), *Trajectoires de libération en Afrique*, Paris: Karthala, 2000, p.207.

56. See e.g. a new attempt at a global history by Wolfgang Behringer, *Witches and Witch-hunts: A global history*, Cambridge: Polity Press, 2004.

57. Cf. Walter Stephens, *Demon Lovers: Witchcraft, sex, and the crisis of belief*, University of Chicago Press, 2002.

58. Cf. Marcel Detienne, 'L'art de construire des comparables: entre historiens et anthropologues', *Critique internationale*, nr. 14, 2002, pp.68-78.

59. John Selden, *Table Talk* (1689), quoted in Thomas, *Religion and the Decline of Magic*, p.517.

3

A PHENOMENOLOGY OF WITCHCRAFT IN GHANA

Abraham Akrong

GHANAIAN PERSPECTIVES ON WITCHCRAFT

For many Ghanaians witchcraft is a phenomenon they take for granted at the pre-suppositional, as a reality without any doubt. There are people for whom witchcraft is a tantalising and overwhelming phenomenon that puts limitations on their lives. For others, witchcraft is essentially a disruptive force that disturbs their life project. And still for others, witchcraft provides a supernatural power or ability that allows one to excel, or move beyond, normal human capabilities. The different and often contradictory perspectives on witchcraft pose a problem for the categorisation of witchcraft. The problem with the concept of witchcraft is that in popular usage, witchcraft could be either good or evil. And indeed, in everyday parlance, witchcraft is used either as an explanation for extra-ordinary human feat or the concrete manifestation of evil. This creates a problem of conceptual clarity for the discourse of witchcraft.

This imprecision and ambiguity about the nature of witchcraft makes research and analysis of the phenomenon difficult, because one can interpret it from different perspectives.[1] The question is: what is witchcraft? On this subject, it seems that in Ghanaian society generally, witchcraft is often associated with supernatural activities that are believed to bring about negative or evil consequences for individuals and families. There is an equally strong view about witchcraft that defines it in terms of a benign supernatural power that can enhance one's ability to perform extraordinary feats. This perspective leads to the view in some circles, especially in popular music, that it equates the scientific achievement of the West to what they term the 'white man's witchcraft'.

These varying perspectives on witchcraft give the impression that the witchcraft spirit, which people believe to exist, is neutral and takes its character from how it is used. If one uses witchcraft for evil, it will become an evil destructive force; on the other hand, if one uses it for good, it will be a positive force that can be used for one's personal improvement or social advancement. From these different perspectives on witchcraft, there is a common thread that justifies people to describe witchcraft as a spiritual power that individuals can manipulate for good or evil. This then puts the genre of witchcraft broadly within the domain of 'magic', in the sense that witchcraft is associated with the manipulation of spiritual power, driven by the will of a person either for good or for evil.

Generally, witches in Ghana are believed to operate in groups or guilds of about ten to twenty under a leader.[2] They are supposed to hold nocturnal meetings in inaccessible places to which they travel by familiars, such as snakes, owls, leopard, and others. It is believed that the spirit of witchcraft is kept in earthenware containing blood. The witchcraft spirit is believed to leave the body while the witch is asleep: the operation of the witch is believed to be done in the spiritual realm through the soul of the witch.

According to traditional witchcraft lore in Ghana, a witchcraft spirit can be acquired in several ways. It can be transmitted to a child at birth, or from a mother who is a witch. However, even a mother who is not a witch can still transfer witchcraft to a child if she is contaminated unwittingly by the witchcraft substance that is left behind after witches have bathed in a river. The witchcraft spirit can also be acquired through gifts, or may be purchased from a wizard.[3]

The spiritual nature of witchcraft, and the way in which it is believed to operate, has given rise to many strange and often mysterious accounts of the nature and function of witches. It is believed, for example, that witches operate in the spiritual realm but that this spiritual operation is expressed in actual events and occurrences that effect human life. This assumed correlation between the spiritual activities of witches and real life is what accounts for their supposed ability to engage in various bizarre spiritual activities that are not subjected to the laws of nature, but can nevertheless have an effect on life. This view of witchcraft is premised on Ghanaian traditional ontology and principles of the human person.

In traditional metaphysics there is an assumed necessary connection between the world of nature, or the material world, and the spiritual dimension that is deemed to be the real essence of the material world and its ultimate cause.[4] This view of the nature of reality supports the idea that there are spiritual reasons for ordinary everyday occurrences. The metaphysical framework of traditional thought, in other words, provides the social lexicon, vocabulary and concepts by which the witchcraft phenomenon is described and articulated; hence it is often a mysterious and bizarre characterisation.

The principles of personality in Akan thought postulate what might be described as a multiple personality, made up of different component selves.[5] The blood (*mogya*), which is believed to be the source of one's personality, can be described as the social self. It determines and defines the social rights and status of the individual. The blood expresses a person's social identity, because it is the blood—either through the father (patrilineal) or the mother (matrilineal)—that links the individual to the family, where the family ancestors are believed to protect one from witches. There is also in Akan thought what might be described as the moral self (*ntoro*), which is normally received from the father. This moral self is believed to determine the moral character of the individual. The moral self links individuals to the protective spirits of their father's family that protects the person from witches. This means that one's family, both from the fathers and the mother's side, can provide spiritual protection against the attack of witches.

There is also what might be called the ego self or human spirit (*sunsum* or *sunsuma*). This is what distinguishes one individual from another, and could be described as the principle of individualism: that which gives human beings their unique identity as an individual. It is believed that if one has a strong *sunsum* or ego, a witch cannot capture one's *kra* or soul. The Ga people of Ghana believe that the *kra* is the carrier of the destiny that God gives to every individual at birth. The *kra* is supposed to direct the life of individuals according to what is contained in their destiny. The concept of *kra* is very imprecise in its usage and has been the subject of much controversy. Usually it is described as the soul, but other ways of designating it, especially in a ritual context, suggest that the *kra* is at times treated more as a double, or as a shadow or ethereal form of the physical body, and that anything that happens to it affects the body. The concept of the *kra* as the double or shadow of the body is what features prominently in witchcraft lore. It is believed that when the witches attack the *kra*—understood as the soul or the double—then whatever happens it automatically happens to the person. It is this understanding of the relationship between the body and the *kra* that provides the medium through which the effects of witchcraft on human life is articulated. For example, witches are believed to cause barrenness in a woman by removing the womb of the *kra*. Or, people may interpret alcoholism as a disease caused by witches who have placed a 'big bowl' in the stomach of the *kra*, in which drinks are stored. It is believed that when a person drinks, the drink is passed on into the bowl in the stomach of the *kra*. In this way, he can continue to consume alcohol without feeling that he is drinking. Or, people may can interpret dullness in school as the result of the witches having removed the brains of one's *kra* and added these to someone else's brain. This then can account for the fact that the person may be learning but lacks the brains to absorb the knowledge. For this reason some people explain chronic headache in terms of witches playing football with the head of one's *kra*. We can multiply the examples of how the assumed correlation between the *kra* and the body provides the language that allows somebody to believe that whatever damage a witch may cause to one's *kra* will have a corresponding effect on the body.

The most problematic of witchcraft lore is the belief that witches feed on human bodies and their blood in order to survive. They are believed to gather for ritual meals at night, where they feed on parts of the bodies of their victims. This is done by capturing the *kra* of the victims and whatever part of it is eaten, this will be damaged in the physical body of the victim. This means that once witches are able to capture someone's *kra*, then in principle they have got hold of the body of the victim. The issue is, in this context, whether witches need to feed on human body parts for their survival, or that they do so in order to harm the *kra* of those they do not like. There are indeed stories about witches who have partaken in feasting on other people's children and relatives as nourishment, but have refused to bring their own children and relatives for a witches' feast. The idea of an exchange of relatives and children in witches' operations, which is common in witchcraft lore in Ghana, is based on the belief that the witchcraft spirit can only operate among blood relations. It is for this reason that witchcraft accusations are very common within families.

In recent times, witchcraft accusations have increased within families due to the pressures of social change and new challenges from modern culture. These entail moving from traditional social structures into a modern world with conflicting demands and new challenges. The fundamental challenge facing individuals in families is how, on the one hand, to continue kinship obligations that sustain the extended family and define its identity with the ethics of modern society and its emphasis on individual success and personal well-being on the other. The question is how to be loyal member of an extended family and also fit into the emerging modern society. This brings into sharp conflict the sense of community based on kinship solidarity supported by a communal ownership of property, and the modern idea of individual capital accumulation and success. Usually, individual success or wealth accumulated outside the family, which cannot be shared by it, arouse suspicions of witchcraft. In such cases, witchcraft accusations are used as a levelling mechanism that does not allow for the success of the individual to undermine the kinship structure and its associated values.[6] During the post-second world war cocoa boom in Ghana, for example, witchcraft accusations became rife among families of cocoa farmers. Its ensuing prosperity made a local protective witchcraft cult, known as Tigare, very popular as many people sought its protection against witchcraft.

WITCHCRAFT AND THE METAPHYSICS OF EVIL

The perspectives that emerge for a description of the witchcraft phenomenon in Ghanaian folklore provide us with a context from which some analytic comments can be made about it. For most people in Ghana witchcraft is a social reality. Reducing it to psychological or social phenomena does not alter the reality of witchcraft and its implications for the life of individuals. For this reason, the tendency on the part of anthropologists to reduce witchcraft to certain social and psychological epiphenomena denatures the belief in witchcraft and its place in Ghanaian society. Witchcraft beliefs exercise great influence, especially on family relationships and other networks of social relations. Precisely because of the psychosocial and social dimensons of witchcraft, there is always the temptation to define it in terms of its social and psychological effects, ignoring the fact that such beliefs continue to shape the life and relations of individuals and families. However, an analysis of Ghanaian witchcraft folklore shows that it is difficult to ascertain spiritual claims about witchcraft. This creates an epistemological problem about the way in which to handle witchcraft discourse. The real issue does not concern the alleged existence of witches, or even the claims that are made about witchcraft. It is rather about how to investigate and verify such claims. Our procedure is therefore to bracket all issues concerned with the existence or non-existence of alleged witches and focus on what people believe about witchcraft and the implications of these beliefs for their social interaction, as well as the way in which they deal with misfortune and how victims of witchcraft accusations are treated.

Certain concepts, such as evil, are boundary concepts that deal with the negation of life. The concept of evil is usually employed to explain those experiences that are believed to be inimical to people's well-being. Generally speaking, the problem lies with the origin of evil, or, in other words, with he question: where does evil come from? In many religious traditions, theories have been advanced to answer this question. In Ghana, the issue of evil is not so much about its origin but rather about its supposed effects on human life. This pragmatic approach to the problem of evil is concerned with the threat it poses to life, or with evil as a disruptive force that robs human life of its meaning. The absence of any doctrine concerning metaphysical evil leads many Ghanaians to a more concrete view of evil as that which disrupts or destroys human life. This view of evil can be said to be more concrete, direct, and related to specific acts or events that disrupt or disturb the life process or the life of a community, a family or an individual. In this sense, evil is more an obstruction, a disturbance or diminishing of being. This means that in Ghanaian thought the subject of evil is not so much about its nature as about its consequences for human life and its fulfilment.

Witchcraft, to the Ghanaian mind, is what can be described as a concrete manifestation of evil that disrupts the life process. Witchcraft in this sense is any type of evil that diminishes a person's being and threatens life's fulfilment. There is in Ghana a popular belief that witches can tamper with one's destiny, given at birth by God. This can bring about confusion in the life of an individual, usually expressed in acute immoral acts and social disorientation. For this reason one way of treating what might be called social deviance, is to enquire from an oracle whether a person's behaviour should be attributed the activities of a witch.

WITCHCRAFT MENTALITY

The evil of witchcraft as a concrete manifestation of evil can make evil so pervasive and so palpably real that almost everything experienced as inimical may be attributed to witchcraft. Such views create the condition for the development of what may be called a 'witchcraft mentality'. The witchcraft mentality is a constructed interpretative scheme that attempts to account for misfortune, or anything inimical to a person's well-being, as traceable to the activities of witches.[7] In this scheme of interpretation all causality is deemed to have originated primarily from the spiritual realm; the material causes are considered secondary, or seen as the medium through which the primary spiritual causality finds its expressions. Such an interpretation tends to discount a material causal explanation of events, focusing attention on external agents, usually witches. This then creates a mindset that attempts to account for misfortunes not in the actions, behaviour or attitude of the victim, but rather in the activities of an enemy or malefactor. It is not uncommon to hear people exclaim in dismay in the face of problems: 'Who is doing these things to me?', instead of 'What is causing these things?' In the context of this mindset, which is becoming more popular with the advent of neo-pentecostal and charismatic theology, there is a certain personalisation of events and occurrences in everyday life. The witchcraft mentality is premised on the assumption that every cause must have a personal agent as its originator, usually a spiritual force.

The attitude of personalising events that people experience as negative, is deeply rooted in the way in which personal identity is defined. The personalisation of events introduces the principle of what might be termed 'agentive causality' into the discourse of interpretation of events.[8] The communalistic ethos of Ghanaian society leads to a socio-centric construction of individual identity. This idea is captured succinctly in John Mbiti's celebrated dictum: 'I am because we are, and since we are therefore I am.'[9] The other, who is included in the definition of my identity, is not a neutral 'other'. This 'other' could be my enemy or my benefactor. This idea is expressed beautifully in a saying of the Ga of Ghana: 'once you are born, both your enemy and your benefactor are born with you'. This socio-centric definition of identity, which makes the 'other' a necessary part of the world of the individual, may be responsible for the fortune or misfortune of the individual. The 'other' can be represented both as human and non-human, or as a spiritual agent that is for or against the individual.[10] Thus, irrespective of whether the 'other' who co-inhabits people's social world is either benevolent or malevolent, there is always an agent who can be held accountable for whatever may happen to them.

From the perspective of those with a 'witchcraft mentality', witches are the source of all evil. Instead of looking for reasons and explanations for particular events, they look for a witch as the cause of their problems. The consequence of such a mentality is that it absolves people from taking responsibilities for their own actions. The usual explanation is that the victim has done the right thing, but that a witch has intervened to turn a well-calculated and well-intended act into something dangerous, negative and harmful. Today, this idea has also been incorporated into much of charismatic theology, which teaches that it is the right of a born-again person to have success and prosperity and, therefore, failure and lack of success must be the work of demons or witches. In the final analysis, the witchcraft mentality appears to provide a very simplistic scheme for the interpretation of life, where the good things that happen to someone are deemed to have escaped the attention of witches, while the bad things can be traced to their activities. Such simple explanations of evil are at the expense of individual freedom, creativity and industry. Those who descry the presence of witches everywhere tend to limit their own freedom to operate. They allow the idea of witchcraft to occupy almost every available space in their life, leaving very little scope to themselves to live their life in fullness. Witchcraft in this sense, although it provides an easy and responsible-free attitude to ownership of the consequences of individual actions, eventually limits the scope for the creative expression of human life. Lastly, the witchcraft mentality brings a lot of fear into people's lives, thereby equally limiting their creativity.

One cannot help noticing, if even remotely, the transfer of the witchcraft mentality into the political arena, especially in the the way people deal with political opponents. The construction of the 'other', who in this case is a political opponent, resembles the way in which witches are viewed, namely as an enemy seeking our downfall. In fact, it appears that political opponents are seen through the prism of witchcraft as malefactors and enemies. This point cannot be stretched too far, but I believe that the construction of the other who is a political opponent, shares the same epistemological status with the witch, who is seen as the enemy of society.

WITCHCRAFT AND THE ABUSE OF WOMEN'S HUMAN RIGHTS

For some strange reason, women, especially older women, are in Ghana associated with witchcraft. In the northern part of Ghana, there are actually so-called 'witch villages', where banished 'witches', usually older women, live separate from the rest of society. This indicates that in popular Ghanaian folklore, the face of witchcraft is feminine. The reason for this is difficult to understand. One can conjecture that there are structures in traditional thought that predispose Ghanaians to identify witchcraft with women, or use the concept of witchcraft to explain women's behaviour. Identifying witchcraft with women can lead—consciously or unconsciously—to their marginalisation in society, preventing women from active participation in leadership roles and other prominent social positions. The marginalisation of women has its roots in the way traditional society constructs gender relations.

Invariably, women's gender roles in traditional society are based on concepts of femininity associated with the biology of women. Traditional society defines the role of women in terms of their biological functions of giving birth, caring for the children and the related function of caring for the home, regardless of the individual gifts and qualities of women. It is important to note that the gender roles in traditional Ghanaian society are often very rigid, and society frowns on crossing the boundaries between them.

Witchcraft is often used as one of the ways of enforcing these rigid gender roles, especially for women in order to keep them from 'gate-crushing' into roles traditionally reserved for men alone. The association of witchcraft with evil makes it a very dangerous tag to put on anybody, because once a person is identified as a witch, she becomes a social outcast, who loses all her human rights. This is the main reason why in certain parts of northern Ghana women accused of witchcraft stay in 'witch villages'. People believe that during their operations witches feed on human beings, and mischievously disrupt and disturb people's social mobility and well-being. In the view of many Ghanaians this renders them enemies of society, who act against the ideals concerning human well-being. Indeed, witchcraft is perceived as the total negation of those fundamental human values that are believed to give meaning and shape to human existence. Therefore, witches must be destroyed in order to rid society of evil.

To be labelled a 'witch' carries grave social consequences. In traditional logic, witchcraft is an anti-social act that attracts to itself the greatest social sanction: public humiliation and the loss of one's rights. This frightful sanction on perceived acts of witchcraft has been used to marginalise women in society. The reason, as we noted above, lies in the perception that women who attempt to move beyond their traditional roles in society and aspire to roles normally reserved for men, must be witches. It is not uncommon even today to hear men describing enterprising and brilliant women as 'witches', simply because they are seen as renouncing their traditional roles and venturing into roles that are reserved for men, thus crossing the gender boundaries. As a result, many women do not want to go beyond their respective roles, for fear of becoming the object of witchcraft accusations, including by other women who may be jealous of their success.

In this way witchcraft accusations are used as a marginalising mechanism that keeps women within the confines of the biological roles assigned to them by society. It is in the violation of these assigned roles that women who are suspected of witchcraft are abused, beaten, or even lynched. In witchcraft situations, there are normally three parties involved: the person accused of witchcraft, the one who claims to be the victim of the witch, and the public. The witch is feared, and until she is accused, no one dares to cross her. But once an acclaimed witch is accused of having practised witchcraft, then she loses all rights to self-defence and security. Every human rights abuse may be perpetrated by her accusers to make her confess, and they will continue to torture and beat her up until she does so. Once she confesses, she will be taken to a medicine-man or 'witch doctor' to have the witchcraft spirit exorcised.

Once accusers start torturing the alleged witch, her only salvation is to confess she is one. Another extreme form of human rights abuse that may lead to the torture and sometimes death of the accused by mob-lynching, is when an oracle traces certain problems to the activities of a witch. This has often resulted in instant cold-blood murder of the accused, usually women. Stories about witchcrafts in our newspapers abound in such types of cold-blooded murder of women accused of witchcraft. Once a witch has been identified, there is a demand for confessions. People beat and torture the accused, which sometimes results in the death of the suspected witch, with the complicity of the bystanders. The critical point is that, since Ghanaian society in general holds a strong belief in witchcraft and its horrible consequences, those accused of witchcraft are seen as legitimately being deprived of their human rights and dignity and therefore easily become the object of torture and even death. Witches have no sympathisers. The dominant logic that rules Ghanaian social conscience with regard to witches is that those accused of witchcraft have brought a curse on themselves and deserve their fate. In this way, Ghanaian society is tacitly complicit in the abuse of the human rights of people accused of witchcraft. In passing, we may note, it might not be too far-fetched to suggest that the construction of the concept of 'enemies of the state' during the so-called revolutions in Ghana, aroused sentiments similar to those connected with alleged witches.

It is important to note in this context that the same witchcraft discourse that leads to the human rights abuse of women, has also found its way into the widowhood rites that are imposed on women who have lost their husbands. Widowhood rites in Ghana have traditionally served a number of goals. First, they have in-built mechanisms to help the widow cope with the loss of her husband. Second, through these rites, especially those elements that involve rituals of separation, the widow is helped to come to terms with the separation from her husband. And third, widowhood rites confer on the woman concerned the right to enjoy the benefits of a woman who has lost a husband. These are in itself noble objectives, intended to deal with the pain of a loved one. However, on many occasions these rites are manipulated to punish the widow, who is often suspected of being responsible for the death of her husband through witchcraft.

It is a commonly held belief that, since women are likely to be witches, they must be somehow responsible for the death of their spouses. The witchcraft premise leads to a harsh treatment of the widow, as if she actually killed the husband through witchcraft. Usually the in-laws of the woman convince themselves that the wife of their relative is the one who caused his death. Hence, they use certain aspects of the widowhood rites as a means to revenge the death of their relative. Part of the widowhood rites demand the widow to go through some hardship, such as sleeping on the bare floor or enduring the pain of hot pepper being put into her eyes to show her sorrow for the death of the husband. In-laws who do not like the widow often exaggerate or intensify these traditional rites in order to punish the widow for killing their relative through witchcraft.

CONCLUSION

Witchcraft, we may say, constitutes a social reality in Ghana. It relates to a belief system that Ghanaians may use as explanation for those aspects of life that are perceived as inimical to their well-being. Witchcraft belief is also associated with a mindset that supports the marginalisation of women whom, as we noted, are frequent victims of witchcraft accusations. 'Witchcraft' is used as a category to explain the nature of evil, experienced as the disruption of life that affects the fulfilment of human life. As a concrete expression of evil witchcraft evokes in people the greatest fear for their survival which, in turn, leads them to treat those associated with it with the greatest form of cruelty, regardless of their human rights and dignity. This may lead to the torture and even death of those accused of practising witchcraft. In this frenzied state, when everyone is seized by fear of witches and their perceived potential for evil, the mood is the destruction of the witch.

Ghanaian society as a whole stands accused by the way it treats alleged witches, as it allows the torture, and even death, of innocent people who are so unfortunate to be accused of witchcraft in a situation where they have no defence except accepting the charge of witchcraft, if only to escape further suffering. What needs to be done is to cultivate an alternative mode of interpreting events in people's lives. These alternative interpretations of events in life can gradually help people to realise that it is possible to look at things in a different way, outside the mindset fashioned by the witchcraft mentality. Such alternative views can gradually undermine the structures of a witchcraft mentality, and therefore instead of pointing accusing fingers at alleged witches, people may then begin to reflect on their own responsibilities for their lives. Rather than searching for witches who can be made responsible for their problems, they will then look for the real causes of and reasons for their problems within the context of normal material causality, which include their own attitudes, actions and behaviour.

Notes

1. See Abraham Akrong, 'Researching the phenomenon of witchcraft', *Journal of African Christian Thought*, vol. 2, nr. 2, 1999, pp. 44-6.

2. Margaret Field, *Search for Security: An ethno-psychiatric study of rural Ghana*, London: Faber & Faber, 1960, p. 35.

3. Kofi Asare Opoku, *West African Traditional Religion*, Accra: FEP International Private Ltd., 1978, p. 143.

4. Dominique Zahan, *The Religion, Spirituality and Thought of Traditional Africa,* University of Chicago Press, 1979, p. 10.

5. Abraham Akrong, 'An African philosophy of religion' [unpublished manuscript, 1993, p. 50].

6. Abraham Akrong, 'Neo-witchcraft mentality in popular Christianity', *Research Review,* n.s., vol. 16, nr. 1, 2000, notably pp. 3-4.

7. Akrong, 'Neo-witchcraft mentality'.

8. Ibid.

9. Cf. John S. Mbiti, *African Religions and Philosophy*, London: Heinemann, 1969.

10. Glen Adams et al., 'The collective construction of friendship and enemyship in Ghana and the US: interview evidence and implications for development [note 1]'. Paper presented at the Tamale Institute of Cross-Cultural Studies (TICCS) seminar on 'ATRs and Development', 1-2 November, 1999.

4

WITCHCRAFT IN CONTEMPORARY GHANA

Elom Dovlo

WITCHCRAFT AS BELIEF

Witchcraft beliefs in contemporary Ghana are prominent. At times they are a frighteningly real aspect of everyday life for many people. Although the belief in witchcraft is part of traditional religious belief, Islam and Christianity in their development in Ghana have accepted the worldview that supports the belief system by providing preventive and curative measures against witchcraft attacks and by neutralising supposed witches.

The Ghanaian sociologist Max Assimeng notes[1]:

> Some writers have made an attempt to elicit direct responses whether or not people in Ghana believe in witchcraft. But such an approach seems inadequate (...) A better approach in any such inquiry should, therefore, stress, not belief or disbelief as such, but rather the attitudinal and behavioural pattern that man would adopt in certain types of problem solving situations.

In conducting such an analysis we find that many such witchcraft beliefs emerge both in crises situations and in conditions of well-being in Ghanaian society. Witchcraft belief cuts across religious, educational and social boundaries in Ghana. The tenacity of these beliefs reveals their true nature as a deeply entrenched part of the West African worldview.

Asare Opoku has defined witchcraft as 'the exercise or employment of esoteric power for a definite purpose, good or evil.'[2] Similarly, Assimeng states that the core of witchcraft beliefs is the search for an extraordinary power that enables a person to regenerate a phenomenon from evil intentions for destruction.[3]

These two definitions point to certain components deemed essential to witchcraft. First, it is considered a power inherent in an individual, that requires no incantations or manipulation of objects for its effects to take place. This is quite distinct from what is known as sorcery or divination, where manipulatory rituals are performed. Furthermore, witchcraft is believed to be a power with a potential for both good and evil, but it seems generally to be more associated with evil intentions than with good ones. Traditionally, when witchcraft is seen as good, it is associated with men, while the evil use of witchcraft power is normally associated with women.

Powers attributed to 'witches' include the ability to inflict material loss through fire, theft, crop failure, or poor spending. Witches are also believed to cause sterility, impotence or diseases such as leprosy. They are held resonsible for addictions such as drunkenness, for poor performance by school children, or for insanity, death, and other misfortune. Witches are most commonly identified through a combination of physical attributes and personality traits. They include those who live alone, or who reach very old age; people who live with animals, act as loners or misers, or maintain an unpleasant disposition; persons who have red eyes, who are fair in complexion, or who suffer from blindness, lameness or other physical defects, as well as those who have attained great wealth. The great variety in marks of identification means that people intent on accusing others of witchcraft can always do so.

The general trend that seems to underlie all particulars of witchcraft accusations, is a tendency to consider witchcraft activities, though seen as spiritual, as anti-social, which could potentially destroy the ever-important concept of community in African life. Thus the definition of witchcraft, according to Asare Opoku,[4]

> ...may also be considered a moral theory. The witch is essentially a bad person – she is anti-social, full of envy, spite and malice (...) The idea of witchcraft, therefore, draws a moral distinction between the

good and bad people. This distinction helps to influence the conduct of people in society by spurring them on to show their virtues, which receive social approbation, and to try to suppress their anti-social tendencies.

Witchcraft belief has a long-standing role within traditional religion in West Africa. Yet, many scholars attribute its recurring manifestations to various factors. What is disturbing about these factors, is that the incidence of witchcraft accusation increases both in cases of economic well-being and disaster. Thus, some scholars have suggested, for instance, that a rise in witchcraft accusations in West Africa during the first half of the twentieth century may be attributed to a boom in the cocoa industry.[5] They argue that westernisation, coupled with new economic trends that led to the development of individualism, created a new social ladder with those newly at the top being afraid of relatives at the bottom of the ladder, who might envy them.

The connection between witchcraft beliefs and social change allows us to consider the role of witchcraft as a means by which social tensions are made public. It is essential to note, therefore, that witchcraft beliefs cannot simply be seen as a random grouping of vague superstitions. Rather, as Assimeng notes, 'they constitute a coherent interrelated set of ideas.'[6] Witchcraft beliefs are in fact a group of ideas dominated by an internal logic based on the cultural and experiential surrounding from which they emerged. Without acknowledging this fact, the complex set of social implications around witchcraft becomes reduced to a form of paranoid, neurotic superstition. Such a reduction is quite incorrect, however, for reasons which will become apparent.

Evans-Pritchard, probably the most acknowledged theorist on the subject of witchcraft, finds in his study of the Azande (Sudan) that witchcraft can be considered best through the act of accusation.[7] Generally, accusations of witchcraft occur within a family, or among those close to the accuser. Evans-Pritchard found that they arise due to the competing relations between the alleged witch and her or his accuser. For example, a wife may be likely to accuse her mother-in-law, as they both compete for the attention of the same man. In a traditional polygamous context, accusations are also rife among co-wives. Nukunya confirms the belief that witchcraft operates among close relations in West Africa, noting that 'the most frequent accusations are among kinsfolk, affines and others among whom there is frequent inter-action.'[8]

While Evans-Pritchard seems to have discovered a fact highly relevant to the belief in witches, this belief must be distinguished from that in witchcraft, and different functions apply. The act of accusation, and the social tensions this reveals, seems in many ways of secondary importance to the effects that a communal fear of witchcraft has on a given community. This fear brings numerous people together in dramatic settings to repulse and react against what they perceive to be an inherently evil force which plagues them all. The preponderance of anti-witchcraft cults such as Tigare in the 1950s and 1960s in Ghana is a perfect example of this type of corporate action against perceived evil. Tigare is an anti-witchcraft cult that originated in northern Ghana and spread through the rest of Ghana and some other West African countries in the early 1940s. It claimed to detect witches, offer protection against witchcraft and evil in general, and to enable progress and prosperities for its members. Tigare shrines were home to titular spirits that identified and exorcised witches of their evil power. After exorcism, the accused were accepted back into the community, but they carried a stigma forever.

Tigare drew not only traditional believers but also attracted many Christians.[9] Several modern Christian prophets equally affirm belief in witchcraft and lead followers in rituals of detection and exorcism. These rituals validate cultural beliefs and sustain a reaction against, and attempts to control, a widespread fear of evil. It may be argued that such rituals and the beliefs they depict can be linked with economic life and form a vital outlet for many people leading a difficult live in an impoverished land.[10] This would seem possible, especially considering the supposed outbreak of witchcraft practice after colonialism and the emergence of anti-witchcraft shrines noted by so many scholars, and given that the cocoa industry created a number of rich people, thus highlighting the misfortune of so many others. It would also help to explain the frequent accusations of witchcraft against those who have managed to succeed.

According to some scholars witchcraft beliefs constitute a form of social control, which they see as another central function of such beliefs.[11] Since witches can be identified through certain traits, these traits must be avoided. Showing misery or anti-social behaviour thus become dangerous actions, illustrating the importance of reciprocity in a community-oriented African society. Arrogance or flashy displays by wealthy persons also draw accusations, forcing the rich into a more humble existence.

There is also a widely held belief that women, especially old women, are potential witches. Being often one of the most marginalised groups in post-colonial African, dependent on their children and probably less educated than even younger women, could witchcraft accusations be a means of expressing frustration over their inevitable position in society? Some of the negative stereotypes often ascribed to women, such as maliciousness, jealousy, anger, animosity and spite for others, and anti-social behaviour, are also the characteristics that reveal witchcraft powers. In this vein it can be argued that witchcraft accusations constitute a social control mechanism that regulates the behaviour of women.

Though often dismissed as 'superstition', the reality of the situation is that witchcraft beliefs continue today in West Africa. Below I will discuss some contemporary expressions of such belief in Ghana and their effects, and discuss current attempts at solution. I will conclude with my own suggestions for possible interventions.

EXILE

In the past few years the incidence of witchcraft accusations and the treatment of supposed witches has been a popular topic, making headlines in the Ghanaian media. This has aroused the concern of the government, but also of non-governmental organisations and churches. It has also led to a number of seminars and workshops on the issue and its effects on Ghanaian society.

Stories in the media regularly report about individuals attacking, and at times killing, people they suspect to be responsible for their misfortunes. For example, in 1996 *The Mirror* reported under the caption 'DRIVER BUTCHERS MUM FOR BEING A WITCH' that Kwesi Prah, a Ghanaian employee at the Zimbabwe Embassy in Berlin came home to have his stomach ache and leg pains cured. A prophet told him that the mother was the cause of his ailment. He lured his mother into a bush where he butchered her to death.[12] In January 2000 the *Ghanaian Times* reported with the headline 'WOMAN BURNED TO DEATH AT GAMBAGA' that in northern Ghana a 54-year old woman was burnt to death a few days after she had been accused of being a witch.[13] Many tabloids in Ghana, however, do not simply report such incidents. They actually foster the belief in witchcraft by carrying stories of witchcraft confessions and particularly of pastors exorcising people of witchcraft (often with pictures). This is also a popular theme of video films, mostly produced in Nigeria, that sell in Ghana and are shown to the public in video theatres but also on Ghana television.[14]

In Ghana the traditional treatment of people accused of witchcraft is to exile them from their communities, if they survive being lynched. However, in recent years a practice in northern Ghana became a matter of national interest. Special communities, known as 'witches homes' have been established in this part of the country that provide a refuge for alleged witches, who have been driven away from their communities. The majority of them are women. A report of the Commission for Human Rights and Administrative Justice (CHRAJ) noted in 1998 that 'out of a total of 815 people found in witches homes in the four districts of the Northern Region of Ghana only 13 were males'.[15] This confirms that women are the main victims of witchcraft accusations and subject to maltreatment associated with these. The age of those committed to the homes, popularly designated as 'witch camps', generally ranges from around forty to ninety years. These places of refuge will form the focus of our discussion as their geographical location, as well as their links with specific communities and traditional authorities have caused a debate about government action, but also about the activities by NGOs, churches and other interested bodies.

Some of these witches' homes, which have been identified mostly in northern Ghana, are located at Ngani, Gambaga, Kukuo, Kpatinga, and Nalerigu. One such camp has also been found in Duabone near Atebubu in the Brong Ahafo region of Ghana. These 'homes' were originally created as refuges for people who had been exiled or faced the threat of being lynched. The Gambaga home was the first to be established, around 1870. Gambaga, which served as the administrative capital of the northern territories under colonial rule, is currently the capital of the East Mamprusi District. Recounting the tradition regarding the home, Hajia Amina Adam writes:[16]

> History has it that the Gambaga witchcraft camp dates as far back as 1870 (...) In the mid-17th century the then paramount chief of the Mamprugu by the name of Naa-Bariga had to judge a case in his palace whereby a woman accused of witchcraft was almost lynched to death by her relatives.
>
> The then Imam of Mamprug called Imam Baba was touched by the torture meted to this old woman. Out of sympathy he pleaded with Naa-Bariga to rescue her from being killed, by allowing him to take her away from Nalerigu to Gambaga, where he lived as the Muslim religious leader.
>
> Naa-Bariga agreed for Imam Baba to take the woman to Gambaga, where she lived as a refugee. Consequently, any similar case was referred to Imam Baba in Gambaga and the numbers of such outcasts kept increasing as the years passed by with the succeeding paramount chiefs and Imams until in the early 18th century when the then Imam Abudu declared he could no more handle both religious and traditional duties together. He therefore handed over the traditional duty of keeping the outcasts as refugees to Nayina and Nachinaba, who were both elders of Gambaga.

These elders explained to Imam Abudu that they would confer with the Gambaraan Bawumia, who was then the chief of Gambaga. After consultations, it was agreed that since Gambaraan Bawumiah is the traditional ruler and he performs sacrifices to the gods of the land, it would be appropriate for him to take custody of the outcasts. Gambarana Bawumiah then took over as the custodian of these outcasts and established a settlement which I would comfortably call a sanctuary for these unfortunate old ladies.

The writer's use of two terms, 'camp' and 'sanctuary', reflects the debate in Ghana, revealing the modern and traditional perceptions of these places. When these places became nation-wide known through the media in the late 1980s and more prominently in the 1990s, the word 'camp' was used by the media to describe them. Media language connoted a place where the women were being held prisoners against their will. They portrayed a restricted area, bounded, probably even surrounded with barb wire, and traditionally policed. The use of the word 'sanctuary' actually reflects the history narrated above, in which the origin of the practice suggests that Gambaga was supposed to serve as a town of refuge for those accused of witchcraft, preventing them from being molested and killed. As Hajia Amina Adam further noted, 'It must be emphasized that the Gambaraan is only a custodian of these unfortunate women. The camp serves as a haven or sanctuary. The Gambaraan does not keep them in bondage. It is the society which they come from which has stigmatised them and treated them with total reject and contempt.'[17] Indeed, the current Gambaraan sees himself as offering a sanctuary to persecuted women who would otherwise have been killed in their own communities.[18]

The 'home' at Gambaga is actually a ward of the town and can hardly be differentiated from the rest of it by a stranger. Generally, the women are engaged to farm at a certain fee, and gather firewood on their own initiative for sale to the community. They are allowed visits from their families and some even have children and grand-children living with them. But from the 1960s the number of alleged witches in the so-called witch homes became so large that accommodation, feeding, medical care and clothing became a problem. It appears that in the course of time, what had originally started as a relief effort became increasingly institutionalised, and rather than a haven these places of refuge have now become places in which inmates face various hardships. In an interview in 2001, however, the current chief of Gambaga, Gambaraan Wuni Yahaya, claimed still to provide for the women by allocating a third of his harvest to them.[19]

However, it is not clear whether it was after the Gambaraan took over the custody of the women that a new practice developed. For whereas the impression is gathered that Imam Baba simply offered refuge to women accused of witchcraft, the Gambaraan performs rituals to determine whether they are indeed witches or not. He is believed to have the power to detect whether the accused are really witches or not, and to neutralise the power of witchcraft in the women who are allegedly found to be witches. The first type of ritual is normally a type of trial by ordeal popular in Ghana. It involves the slaughter of a fowl, which is released to die. As it flutters around it finally dies, and the position in which it eventually falls and dies—with the breast down or up—is held to prove either the guilt or innocence of the accused.

Even where she is found innocent, this does not mean that women already stigmatised in their own communities can return home safely. They are not normally welcomed back. When a person supposedly found to be a witch denies the accusation, she is threatened with a second ritual. She is made to understand that she will be given a concoction by the Gambaraan to drink; if she knows that she is guilty but drinks it, she will die. This threat makes many women accept and 'confess' that they are witches.

Whenever the accused accepts the outcome of the trial by ordeal and 'confesses' to be a witch, she is made to go through a 'de-witching' ritual. Upon the payment of a fee, a herbal preparation is given to the accused to drink and bathe. This latter treatment is believed to exorcise supposed witches of their evil potency, rendering them powerless forever. Rendered powerless, the women can then in theory return home since they no longer pose their alleged threats to the society. When the cleansing rituals have been performed, relatives of the accused are expected to pay some minimal amount in money, cola nuts or other items, such as sheep, and may then take the woman away. Relatives however, hardly fulfil this obligation to take the women home. Subsequently, the number of women has been increasing year after year. For example, in 1991 there were about 123 women at the Gambaga 'home', but by 1997 the number had increased to about 200.

It seems that other camps developed along the lines of Gambaga. The largest home is at Kukuo, near Bimbilla, whose inmates often outnumber those of Gambaga. In 1995, for instance, 450 suspected witches were expelled from their homes to Kukuo. Another witches' home, eight kilometres from Yendi, capital of the kingdom of Dagbon, is Gnani. During inter-ethnic conflicts in the northern region of Ghana in 1994 this village of unprotected alleged witches, mostly women, was virtually wiped out. Women accused as witches who have been sent to these camps have to undergo trial by ordeal such as described above, administered by the local earth priests to find out whether they are guilty or innocent. But either way they hardly go back home. For the divination to ascertain by ordeal whether a person is a witch or not does not even take place in the location of the accused. The person is virtually exiled before the test is performed!

The incidents of witchcraft accusations leading to exile are the same as those listed earlier. Vincent Azumah provides various accounts of such accusations. Examples include the following:[1]

- On September 20, 1999 Memuna Idana was accused of killing the brother's son through witchcraft. All her pleas of not being responsible for the death of the 14-year old boy who apparently died of malaria went unheeded. Within 48 hours she was on her way away from her family amidst stone-throwing and jeers and boos, and with only a polythene bag to convey a few of her clothing to Gnani Tindana, a village southeast of Yendi. Memuna's son brought her to the village and left a two thousand cedi note with her. He was not seen again.

- Madam Berkpema was in a polygamous marriage. Her children were doing well academically, but her rivals' children were performing poorly. She was accused of 'eating out the brains' of the children of her two rivals after 'two of their children claimed they saw me in a dream'.

- Another dream case is that of Asumi Azuma at Gnani, who was sent there because someone in her family had dreamt that she turned into a lion and was about to devour her.

Albin Koram offers the following example of a false accusation that led to the exile of a woman:[21]

- In the village of Samwusi, one man borrowed one bag of millet from an old lady. When the woman later insisted on the man replacing that bag of millet, the man accused her of being a witch. The unfortunate woman was condemned to live for the rest of her life in the witches' camp at Gambaga (...) Later, the man became ashamed what he had done, but no one was able to help the unfortunate woman anymore.

It appears that some women who are past child-bearing age do not even wait to suffer the humiliation of witchcraft accusation, but relocate themselves to one of the witch villages. Akwele Adjavon cites the example of sixty years' old Zenabu Seidu, who lives in voluntary exile at Kukuo:

> ... According to her, she was suspected of causing all the diseases that afflicted people in her village. 'I wasn't openly accused. But to avert any hostility, I left the village on my own. Besides, I had ten children but only four survived. And in my village, when you lose a lot of children, people begin to call you names'[22]

Another case is that of Puone Andani, a widow of over 80 years, who had ten daughters who all got married, and therefore she had to fend for herself. She did not wish to live with any of her daughters and rather than run the risk of remaining on her own in town, she opted to relocate to Kukuo.[23] The examples show that some women who are likely to become unpopular because they might fit into the witchcraft belief profile of the people, volunteer to go to Kukuo, for fear that if they did not, they may later be branded witches and sent their anyway.

Witchcraft accusations became intensified after 1995, and a lot of women were exiled to the various homes. When the present author investigated the matter, he was informed that one of the main causes of the rise of witchcraft accusations that occurred in the aftermath of the northern ethnic wars of 1994, especially in Dagbon, was the acquisition of new gods. It is recounted that during the war the quest for spiritual support against the enemy led to the introduction of a new god from northern Togo, called Tsamkpana. It is alleged that part of the potency of this god is the ability to detect witches. This led to an increase in the incidence of witchcraft accusations after 1995. Indeed, at Kukuo the fetish for de-witching was acquired in Yaounde, in Cameroon. This reveals that though the belief system may be local, it is open to 'foreign', transethnic and transnational techniques of dealing with witchcraft accusations.

From the various incidents of witchcraft accusations narrated above, it is clear that existential problems form a reason for witchcraft beliefs and accusations. These include unexplained deaths, even the death of one's own children, ill health, and the lack of prosperity or of the success of people within one's own kin group or marriage structures. Traditionally dreams constitute legitimate grounds for such accusations, revealing how difficult it is to deal rationally with witchcraft accusations. Indeed, the belief system has clearly profiled such accusations, so that some people even opt to go and live in the witches' homes voluntarily to avoid the brutalities associated with forced exile.

However, witchcraft accusations can be explained. People who have researched the incidence of witchcraft accusations have noted an increase in accusations linked with two disease-prone seasons in the northern part of Ghana. The dry season that runs from September to January is typically a period in which cases of Cerebral Spinal Meningitis (CSM) frequently occur, leading to many deaths. People also easily contract guinea worm and food poisoning. The deaths resulting from such diseases are normally ascribed to witchcraft and lead to frequent witchcraft accusations. Moses Nabla, a minister in the Presbyterian Church, also notes that the number of witchcraft accusations is particularly high during the dry season when there is less work to do, and relatively low in the rainy season when people are busy on their farms.[24] This suggests that one of the causes of witchcraft accusations could be idleness. But in spite of Nabla's assertion, other sources note that the rainy season is equally marked by witchcraft accusations. During the rainy season the high incidence of malaria is often attributed to witchcraft. Without disputing people's traditional belief, the evidence suggests that health problems, which are not addressed scientifically, can aggravate the problem of witchcraft accusations. Comfort Ntiamoah-Mensah, who works on the Presbyterian Church's programmes for the homes, confirms that poverty, ill health and illiteracy are prevalent in these areas.[25]

In summary, two main issues emerge from witchcraft cases in Ghana, especially in connection with the 'homes' for supposed witches in northern Ghana. The first one relates to the facilities and conditions at the homes. Though seen as havens, the procedure involved in the identification of alleged witches and the conditions they are subjected to have recently been the subject matter of public discussions in Ghana in relation to human rights. The second issue relates to how witchcraft belief and practices undermine various facets of socio-economic development in Ghana.

AT STAKE

The issues at stake are many. For present purposes I wish to touch on four of them, namely issues of human rights, of religion, and of social and economic life.

Human rights

Globalisation and modernity have queried many traditional practices in Ghana, especially those that are seen as violating human rights. This includes the treatment of alleged or suspected witches, which raises a number of issues. Traditionally, such persons are deprived of any rights as they are assaulted, harassed, and may even be lynched. Often the accused women have to undergo trial by ordeal to ascertain their guilt. Moreover, the fact that there might be purely medical causes of death questions the suspicion of witchcraft associated with them. It should also be noted that the original traditional practice in northern Ghana recognised a chief as the only person with the authority to proclaim a person a witch. In recent times however, anybody can declare somebody else to be a witch.

Further, even though the inmates of the camp are not subjected to any maltreatment, they suffer various hardships. The women at the camps are sickly, worn out, anaemic, malnourished and dirty. Some are crippled, dumb, and blind. Mr. Emil Short, the Commissioner for Human Rights and Administrative Justice in Ghana, therefore, declared that a major concern of the Commission is that '...plight of the fairly old women, who are forced by circumstances of poverty or destitution and family and community rejection to till the land as a means of livelihood in these places.'[26] The effect of a long stay at these camps is that the victims have a low self-esteem, affecting not only their productivity but also entire life.

Religion

Though originally linked with traditional religious belief in Ghana, witchcraft belief more generally is an international phenomenon. It is therefore not surprising that Islam and Christianity in Africa also uphold this belief. In northern Ghana, where Islam has operated for a long time, many *mallams* or *afa* (Muslim clerics and healers) help in diagnosing witchcraft when patients are brought to them. But it is worth to recall that it was a chief Imam (that is, a leader of the Muslim community) who took the initial step to ameliorate the plight of alleged witches by establishing the refuge home at Gambaga. With Christianity arriving on the scene, the missionary churches often treated witchcraft as a form of superstition. This has not prevented their members to seek other avenues to address this traditional belief. Both African independent churches (AIC's) and, more recently, charismatic churches uphold the traditional worldview and offer remedies to witchcraft. In fact, these newer Christian churches have made evil and its removal fundamental to their message and activities. At the same time this has bereft them of much of the positive thrust of religion as an agent of progress and development, as it is assumed that the removal of evil frees a person to attain the good.

Indeed, the position taken by contemporary Christianity in Ghana on witchcraft has led to counter-arguments by neo-traditional movements such as Afrikania Mission. In a radio broadcast, Afrikania Mission acknowledged the existence of witchcraft but insisted that its power can be used for good purposes and channelled into that direction. It should therefore not be condemned totally.[27]

In general, the diagnosis of witchcraft offered by various religious bodies has had negative consequences and led to social conflicts. For more often than not, witchcraft accusations focus on close relations and often end up with physical attacks on the accused, who are subsequently ostracised.

Social life

One of the paradoxes of witchcraft accusations is that although sociologists theorise that they constitute a form of social control, witchcraft accusations are actually socially disruptive. Since they mainly occur within kinship relations and between neighbours, they often lead to strife. As indicated above, physical violence, including murder, may be meted out to those accused by their own kith and kin.

It must also be borne in mind that the corporate nature of social life in Ghana causes such accusations to go beyond the individual person identified as a witch to include his immediate family. Hence, the stigma associated with witchcraft belief affects other members of the family, even after the punishment has been meted out to the supposed witch. Witchcraft accusations naturally also affect marriage stability and lead to divorce. For when a woman is exiled from the village, the husband is bound to divorce her and take a new wife. Some of the children of the accused may also be seen as potential witches and become socially stigmatised.

Where the accused is driven away from the community at the age of about 30 to 40 years, that person's role as parent is abrogated and the socialisation and parenting of her children become a problem. This is particularly relevant when we consider the fundamental role of women in parenting. The punishment associated with witchcraft contributes thus to the disintegration of the family. Even when the accused person is of old age, a social problem is created when people who have contributed to the good of society are cast out at a time they need its help most. It means that those who approach old age must always dread the prospect of witchcraft accusations.

It is also sad to note that suspected witches face assault, harassment and lynching in their communities. Mostly it is children who are used to perpetrate such 'punitive' practices as stoning the accused. This amounts to a process of socialisation that ingrains lawlessness in children in their dealings with people declared as deviants in society. It also affects their respect for adults, particularly women, as male suspects are never lynched. This has the potential of making such children grow up without much respect for women. In addition, the involvement of children in the societal response to witchcraft contributes in their growing up with a strong belief in witchcraft accusations, making it difficult to erase such beliefs in Ghanaian society.

Economic life

Witchcraft accusations naturally affect the economic life of Ghanaian communities. Where able-bodied people are exiled or sent to camps in an agrarian community, which is labour intensive, human resources are lost and this affects productivity. Even with people of age who are exiled, the problem remains the same. For in Ghanaian traditional societies, they are the ones who babysit free of charge in the family, thus allowing the younger people to engage in economic activity.

At times witchcraft accusations also lead to ecological destruction and subsequently the destruction of economic resources. For example, in the village of Sakogu in Ghana in 1997, a diviner claimed that the witch-power of a woman was hidden under a paw-paw tree, leading to the destruction of all such trees in the village.[28]

But the greatest effect of witchcraft in economic terms concerns the contribution of women in the field of development. In Ghana, the hard-earned achievement of women is often attributed to witchcraft. Elisabeth Amoah has pointed out that there exists a traditional practice of accusing successful women of witchcraft.[29] This is confirmed by Nabla, who notes that in northern Ghana women who become rich through trade are accused of using witchcraft power to convert human souls into items sellable at the market, such as animals, groundnuts and shea butter.[30] Naturally, such accusations pose great obstacles to women's initiative in productivity and affect the country's development. The attitude that achievement by women cannot be accounted for rationally and can only be based on occult powers, fails to give credit when it is due and to inspire. The paradox is that women are accused of witchcraft, whether in adversity or prosperity. This reveals an attitude that a woman's life is supposed to be established along mediocre lines. She must not fall below expectation, neither should she rise above it.

Apart from women as the main targets of witchcraft accusations, the belief in witchcraft affects the economy and general development of the country. For instance, it has been noted in northern Ghana that witchcraft belief creates fear in the youth. As a result, they will not face challenging tasks for fear that their success will lead to witchcraft attacks. Nabla notes that young people are afraid of putting up good buildings for fear that this may be regarded as a show-off of wealth and lead 'witches' to harm them.[31] It has also been asserted that people in northern Ghana are afraid to inherit property for fear of becoming bewitched. Hence, property bequeathed by a deceased is not utilised effectively in productivity and development. This is particularly sad as the northern region is one of the most economically deprived areas of Ghana.

SOLUTIONS

Like most other countries in Africa, Ghana recognises that the problems embedded in witchcraft beliefs need to be addressed in order to enhance the development of our nations. As a people we are faced with two challenges: how to address the inhuman treatment meted out to alleged witches, and how to put a halt to this type of belief, some of the effects of which have been enumerated above.

The frequent incidence of witchcraft accusations raises the problem of how to handle religio-cultural issues in a modern state. Even though the 1992 Constitution of the Republic of Ghana contains provisions which are against customs, practices and traditions that demean the quality of human life and undermine the sense of dignity particularly of vulnerable groups, experience shows that cultural and metaphysical beliefs such as witchcraft cannot be legislated away. Neither can they be dealt with in courts of law where, because of their metaphysical nature, concrete evidence is lacking. Indeed, Justice Apaloo, one time Chief Justice of Ghana and later Kenya, is reputed to have declared that the arms of the law are too short to reach to the realm in which witchcraft operates![32]

Nevertheless, the national government, prompted by the media and women's organisations, has tried to address the issue of witchcraft especially in connection with the 'camps' in northern Ghana. The government acknowledges that the witches' home concept is a deep-seated cultural norm that involves close relations and family members, and considers this in its policy. Recently, the Deputy Minister of Social Welfare, Mrs. Ama Benyiwa-Doe, and the Commissioner of Human Rights and Administrative Justice, Mr. Emile Short, have initiated action by requesting that a thorough investigation be carried out to enable a well-planned resolution of the issues at stake and to facilitate a possible reintegration of the women at the camps into their communities. Another government official, Chairman of the Council of State Alhaji Mumuni Bawumia, who is himself from northern Ghana, has presented a report to the President of Ghana. In August 1999 the women caucus in Parliament visited the Gambaga camp. So far, what has happened is to register a political awareness of the problem, and leave it at the door of the Commission for Human Rights and Administrative Justice as a human rights issue.

Long before issues related to the 'witch camps' were brought to the attention of the nation through the media, various church organisations and non-governmental organisations have tried to help victims of witchcraft accusations. We noted already that the establishment of the camps was due to the initial effort by a Muslim cleric to offer a place of refuge to those accused. In contemporary times other religious bodies, such as the Presbyterian Church of Ghana (PCG) which operates at Gambaga and Kukuo, have been very active in handling the incidence of 'witch camps'.

The Presbyterian Church started its work at the Gambaga camp in the early 1960s. It regarded the accused women as outcasts and therefore preferred to use the name 'outcast homes'. The church mainly offered clothing and food to the women. It also tried to rehabilitate the women with income-generating projects that would enable them to earn money to improve their living conditions. The church was assisted by other organisations, such as the Catholic Relief Services and other churches, such as the Assemblies of God.

In 1994 the Presbyterian Church of Ghana instituted a new and ambitious project, called the 'Go Home Project of the Outcast Home', aimed at returning victims to their families and communities. As noted by Dahamani, 'the main aim of the project was to bring about the reintegration of the women back into their original communities where they could live with their families and enjoy life meaningfully as active members.'[33] Comfort Ntiamoah-Mensah further outlines the objectives of the project as follows:[34]

- to educate the communities to desist from sending women to Gambaga as witches and accept those already in the home back and to be reintegrated;
- to assist returnees to be rehabilitated and integrated in their families through the necessary support;
- to assist the women in Gambaga to farm and engage in income-generating projects to fend for themselves;
- to provide essential medical support to the women, in collaboration with the Baptist Medical Center and other existing support systems;
- to provide food and other basic support when crops fail;

- to educate the girl-child or grand-child of the women in the home and returnees, since there is a basic belief that witch-craft is passed on to them.

The church organises outreach and counselling in villages from which the women come for the community leaders, family members and women groups to make them open to receiving the women back into the community. Women chosen to return home are encouraged to visit home six months before their final return with a field worker, to have a feeling of reassurance. When a woman finally returns she is assisted to have her room in the family compound and is given farming inputs to start a farm.

The women who return are joined with other women into cooperative groups for economic purposes and given small grants for their operations. Health care programmes are also put in place to educate the people on the causes of diseases such as CSM, high fever and others which are often wrongly attributed to witchcraft.

Though about ten women are currently said to return home annually, two factors have adversely affected this programme. First of all, even though some victims went back home this did not stop new ones from being sent to the camp as intended in the programme. Thus while between 1994 and 1998 137 victims went back home, 126 others were admitted into the Gambaga camp.[35] Indeed, it has been reported that some women who returned to their communities were found dead in mysterious circumstances. The *Daily Graphic* reported: 'It has been alleged that some supposed witches from the Gambaga Witches Home who are reintegrated into their communities through the inter-vention of the Presbyterian Outcasts Home project are some-times maltreated or killed and their murders hushed up.'[36]

Other NGO's are also active in trying to reduce the burden of the women in the witches' homes. At another such home, in Gnani, one NGO, Management AID (MAID), has designed a credit scheme for the women there and assists them in starting some small agricultural-based businesses. MAID also counsels to these women, who have to overcome their traumatic experiences. Efforts by other NGO's are geared towards the provision of potable water and a balanced diet for the women in the camps. One local NGO, Timari-Tama, also assists these women by initiating income-generating ventures to alleviate poverty, since it holds that poverty is the root cause of witchcraft accusations, as it leads to disease and frustration.

CONCLUSION

Witchcraft beliefs and accusations in Ghana are very common. The key variables in witchcraft accusations fit up to the fifth level of the logical chain constructed in the SANPAD Research Report about witchcraft accusations in South Africa.[37] These variables include people's notion of evil, definition of relationship, notions of agency, divination practices and intergroup relations as discussed in the report.[38]

So far, all attempts in Ghana to address witchcraft beliefs have focused on the alleged witches, some of whom are said to have confessed to being witches. The witchcraft problem, however, lies not with those who confess it, but with those who believe in it and live in fear of its alleged powers. A confession by a 'witch' does not confirm that she is one, as she might be pressured into such a confession. But it is the belief in, and subsequent accusation of, witchcraft that get the accused woman punished. Those who believe in witchcraft will magnify its alleged effects and enforce its validity. The task in finding a solution, therefore, is to address the belief system holistically so as to nip its consequences in the bud.

As noted earlier, witchcraft belief is a religio-cultural phenomenon that cannot be legislated and banished into oblivion. The state does not have the law enforcement apparatus to completely enable this. This has been the experience with a law banning another socio-cultural practice in Ghana, known as *trokosi*, in which young girls are made to serve at traditional shrines for years, in reparation for the misdeeds of family members. Since the the Criminal Code Amendment Act (Section 314) was passed in 1998 against this practice, no case has been brought to court, and yet the practice continues. This is mainly because the people who must report such cases, close relations of the girls, are the very people who send the girls to the shrines. Similarly, it is close relations who send women accused of witchcraft to the witch 'homes' in northern Ghana.

Generally, in situations such as witchcraft accusations, the law can address individual cases of maltreatment of alleged witches, such as when an individual kills his mother. However, cases that affect the community are more difficult to address. They require education on human rights, as well as on the effects of community actions against alleged witches on society as whole, even when traditionally such actions may be conceived of as cleansing the community of evil.

Such education on human rights must be culturally based to be effective. In my personal experience of dealing with human rights abuses during interventions concerning the *trokosi* practice alluded to above, it was realised that using cultural idioms of human rights was more effective than citing the Universal Declaration of Human Rights and other international protocols that the people have not even heard of. Rather, the international tenets were woven into traditional proverbs, sayings, lyrics and practices that place value on the human being. These were used to question the practice, until it dawned on some of the practitioners that clearly there must be some contradiction between the value they place on human life and the abuse perpetuated through some cultural practices. Indeed, this method could serve as a useful tool in intervening at the point described in the SANPAD Research Report as 'notions of agency' in witchcraft discourse. These are defined as 'cultural notions of personhood, especially about human agency (...) The position of the individual versus the group, the amount of freedom allowed to an individual and the amount of peer control [which] all help shape witchcraft accusations.'[39]

Such a program of education must be multidimensional in sensitising different groups of people through a variety of methods. This is important because different groups in society can cause intervention at different levels of the witchcraft discourse. Thus law enforcement agencies, ritual specialists at local shrines, local political authorities who traditionally adjudicate witchcraft cases, and the general public must be sensitised in specialised ways. The law enforcement agencies such as the police force, need to be well sensitised to the human rights violations and other negative effects resulting from witchcraft accusations. It must be borne in mind that they themselves may hold such beliefs, which they must be helped to eradicate in other to help the government effectively stem witchcraft accusations. The ritual specialists at the shrines, in particular, would serve as an important point of intervention, because though suspected witches are maltreated prior to divination, their ritual normally seals their doom. The priests traditionally cannot practice without the permission of the chief or traditional rulers. Traditional rulers therefore need also to be sensitised to control this aspect of the work of the shrines, as to intervene in the public support for such accusations, which normally results in brutalising the accused. The general public needs to be educated with respect to notions of evil and notions of agency, and as to how witchcraft accusations and the ostracising of alleged witches adversely affect their communities.

In all education efforts, the appropriate media should be employed. For example, popular drama can be a helpful medium of educating a non-literate society. The performers should mainly consist of the youth, who at a tender age participate in the process of witchcraft accusation by maltreating supposed witches. This will contribute to bringing about a generational change in attitudes. Modern media, such as FM radio stations in the Northern and Upper Regions of Ghana, can be used to sensitise people against such human rights abuse. On the other hand it is also important that films shown on Ghana television that encourage witchcraft belief are controlled. The theme of witchcraft appears to be a popular one with Ghanaian producers of video films, and they may need to be sensitised to the damage their films cause to the national psyche and to national development by reinforcing witchcraft belief.

The promotion of formal education may also reduce the incidence of witchcraft accusations. Access to education will not resolve the problem itself, but reduce the maltreatment of alleged witches. There is also a need to resolve problems of disease and poverty, which often lead to accusations of witchcraft. As noted above, certain seasons are prone to certain types of disease, some of which are fatal. Preventive measures and education on the causes of ill health by health authorities may reduce the incidence of witchcraft accusations. Economic development programmes to alleviate poverty, such as irrigation facilities for dry season gardening as recommended by Nabla,[40] are also useful in bridging the social gap that at times leads to witchcraft accusations.

Such solutions demand advocacy by civil society, for left to the government alone there may be the political will but little action to solve the problem. The role of NGO's and other civic organisations is therefore crucial. They must not only help in achieving the above, but offer social and religious reprimand to those who perpetuate the belief system. Above all, since women are the majority of those accused of witchcraft, empowering women is important so as to stem the tide of such accusations.

Notes

1. Max Assimeng, *Religion and Social Change in West Africa: An introduction to the sociology of religion*, Accra: GUP, 1989, p.168.

2. Kofi Asare Opoku, *West African Traditional Religion*, Accra: FEP International Private Ltd, 1978, p.146.

3. Assimeng, *Religion and Social Change*, p.168.

4. Opoku, *West African Traditional Religion*, p.146.

5. Margaret Field, *Search for Security: An ethno-psychiatric study of rural Ghana*, London: Faber & Faber, 1960; Hans Debrunner, *Witchcraft in Ghana: A study on the belief in destructive witches and its effects on the Akan tribes*, Accra: Presbyterian Book Depot, 1961; Andrew Apter, 'Atinga revisited: Yoruba witchcraft and the cocoa economy, 1950-51', in Jean Comaroff and John Comaroff, *Modernity and Its Malcontents*, University of Chicago Press, 1993, pp. 111-28.

6. Assimeng, *Religion and Social Change*, p. 167.

7. E.E. Evans-Pritchard, *Witchcraft, Oracles and Magic among the Azande,* Oxford: Clarendon Press, 1976.

8. G.K. Nukunya, *Tradition and Change in Ghana: An introduction to sociology*, Accra: GUP, 1992, p. 58.

9. The challenge this anti-witchcraft cult posed to Christianity led the Christian Council of the Gold Coast to come out in 1949 with a pamphlet entitled *Tigare or Christ.*

10. Birgit Meyer has written extensively on contemporary pentecostal discourse on witchcraft and demonisation in Ghana. See e.g. *Translating the Devil: Religion and modernity among the Ewe in Ghana,* Edinburgh University Press, 1999; 'Delivered from the powers of darkness: confessions of satanic riches in Christian Ghana', *Africa,* vol. 65, nr. 2, 1995, pp. 236-55; 'Commodities and the power of prayer: pentecostalist attitudes towards consumption in contemporary Ghana', *Development and Change,* vol. 29, nr. 4, 1998, pp. 751-76.

11. See Field, *Search for Security.*

12. *The Mirror,* 25 May 1996, p. 3.

13. *Ghanaian Times,* 8 January 2000, p. 1.

14. For a detailed discussion, see Birgit Meyer, 'Popular Ghanaian cinema and "African heritage"', *Africa Today,* vol. 46, nr. 2, 1999, pp. 93-114; Ibid., 'Ghanaian popular cinema and the magic of film', in Birgit Meyer and Peter Pels (eds), *Magic and Modernity: Interfaces of revelation and concealment,* Stanford University Press, 2003, pp. 200-22.

15. 'Report on the Round Table Conference on the Treatment of Suspected Witches in Northern Ghana, Picorner Hotel, Tamale, 17th December 1998', p. 16. The Commission for Human Rights and Administrative Justice (CHRAJ) is a statutory body of the Fourth Republican Constitution of Ghana (1992). It is responsible for investigating human rights abuses in Ghana and generally replaced the office of the ombudsman in previous constitutions.

16. Hajia Amina Adam, 'What goes on at Gambaga "witches' camp"?' *The Mirror,* 5 August 2000, p. 19.

17. Ibid.

18. Personal interview with Gambaraan Wuni Yahaya, Chief of Gambaga, at Gambaga on 3 February 2001.

19. Ibid.

20. Vincent Azumah, 'Is it a crime to be a woman?', unpublished research notes (undated), made available to the author in 2001. See also his article 'Witchcraft—is it for women only?', published in the Ghanaian daily *The Mirror,* 28 June, 1997.

21. Albin Koram, 'Witches' camp: cruelty against women', *Weekly Spectator,* 20 September, 1997.

22. Akwele Adjavon, 'Women in struggle: something to blame... when things go wrong', *Daily Graphic*, 18 March, 1988, p.3.

23. Ibid.

24. Moses Nabla, 'Rehabilitation of the witches in Gambaga: The role of the Presbyterian Church of Ghana', BA Hon. diss., University of Ghana, 1997.

25. Comfort Ntiamoah-Mensah, 'Gambaga outcast home: The experiences of the Presbyterian Church of Ghana', paper presented at the International Workshop on Religion and Human Rights, Dodowa, 4-8 November, 2002.

26. 'Report on the Round Table Conference'.

27. Broadcast at Afrikania Hour, GBC FM, 11th May, 2000.

28. Nabla, 'Rehabilitation of the witches in Gambaga', p. 3.

29. Elisabeth Amoah, 'Women, witches and social change in Ghana', in Diana Eck and Devaki Jain (eds), *Speaking of Faith: Cross-cultural perspectives on women, religion and social change*, Delhi: Kali for Women, 1986, pp. 77-87.

30. Nabla, 'Rehabilitation', p. 2.

31. Ibid.

32. Cf. Santuah Naga, 'Emile Short and the 200 witches', *Daily Graphic*, 1 October, 1997, p. 7.

33. 'Address by Edward Dahamani, Presbyterian Church of Ghana "Go Home Project"', in 'Report on the Round Table Conference on the Treatment of Suspected Witches in Northern Ghana', p. 20.

34. Ntiamoah-Mensah, 'Gambaga outcast home', p. 4.

35. See Dahamani in 'Report on the Round Table Conference', p. 24.

36. *Daily Graphic*, 24 August 1999, p.1.

37. See S.T. Kgatla, G. ter Haar, W.E. A. van Beek and J.J. de Wolf, *Crossing Witchcraft Barriers in South Africa. Exploring witchcraft accusations: Causes and solutions*, Utrecht University, 2003. See also the chapter by Walter van Beek in the present volume.

38. Kgatla et al., *Crossing Witchcraft Barriers*, pp. 23-5.

39. Ibid., p. 20.

40. Nabla, 'Rehabilitation of the witches in Gambaga', p. 80.

5

GHANAIAN WITCHCRAFT BELIEFS: A VIEW FROM THE NETHERLANDS

Gerrie ter Haar

INTRODUCTION

It is not only in Africa itself that witchcraft beliefs and accusations are a feature of life; they are also quite common among Africans who have migrated to other parts of the world.

Substantial numbers of Africans have settled in Western Europe in recent decades, including a high number of Ghanaians. In the case of the Netherlands, the largest Ghanaian community is in the Bijlmer district in the southeast of Amsterdam. According to official statistics, there are about 12,000 first-generation Ghanaian immigrants living in the Netherlands, about half of whom are resident in the Bijlmer.[1] Unofficial figures, however, suggest a much higher figure of Ghanaians in the Netherlands, due to the large number of undocumented migrants.

Not surprisingly, Ghanaian immigrants brought their religious and cultural beliefs and practices with them when they migrated to Europe. These include not only traditional African beliefs and practices, but also Christian ones, as many Ghanaian immigrants were raised as Christians in their home country. For many of them, their first encounter with the Netherlands came as a shock: they had not expected to land in a highly secularised country where increasingly fewer people attend church. Hence, one of the main problems which the first Ghanaian Christians in the Netherlands faced on arrival in the 1970s and 1980s was the lack of places of worship. As a result they started prayer groups and home congregations, which soon developed into fully-fledged church communities, even though they could find only temporary space in places that had not been designed for that purpose. Many places of worship emerged under the big multi-storey parking garages that formed part of the tower-blocks in the Bijlmer.[2] Today, African-initiated congregations can be found in many places in the Netherlands where Ghanaian and other African immigrants have settled.

Some ten years ago, I conducted extensive research regarding these new African congregations, in Amsterdam's Bijlmer district.[3] I particularly frequented the True Teachings of Christ's Temple, the oldest of the African-initiated churches in the Netherlands, founded in the 1980s by the Ghanaian pastor Daniel Himmans-Arday. Over the years I have had several interviews with him on particular aspects of his work, since he is known among his fellow-Africans as a prophet and healer. Fear of witchcraft is one among many reasons why Africans (but also some Dutch people) consult him for advice or for healing. Generally speaking, African Christians in the Netherlands believe as much in the presence and reality of witchcraft powers as they do in Africa itself. Hence, witchcraft is something that is discussed and that receives pastoral attention in the African congregations.

The aim of this chapter is to explore how witchcraft beliefs that are widespread in Ghana are perpetuated among Ghanaian Christians in the Netherlands. I examine how African congregations in the Netherlands respond to the problems posed by such beliefs, notably when they lead to witchcraft accusations, and I consider whether the circumstances of migration have altered some of these ways.

Below, I will discuss these matters as they emerge from an exchange of views with Reverend Himmans-Arday, whose spiritual insights I have found helpful for my own understanding of the matter. In the empirical tradition of the study of religion it is considered of vital importance to study the religious ideas of believers in their own words and in their own context in the first instance.[4] In this case, these are the ideas of an African Christian leader, who developed his thoughts originally in Ghana, later elaborating them in the Netherlands. From an emic perspective, it appears from the following that witchcraft beliefs and practices are related to ideas concerning the presence of evil. African Christians have incorporated such ideas into a Christian ideology of good and evil, and associate them with a theology of spiritual healing and liberation. This is particularly the case in those African congregations that do not trace their origin to the European missionary tradition.

In the following pages, I will first provide background information on the life and work of Daniel Himmans-Arday. I will then discuss the problem of witchcraft as part of his spiritual healing work. Finally, I will consider how, in his view, migration has affected witchcraft beliefs among African Christians in the Netherlands, and how their harmful effects may be reduced.[5]

A SPIRITUAL JOURNEY

In the late 1970s, Daniel Himmans-Arday left Ghana, his country of origin, to follow the vocation that had been revealed to him one night, when he was suffering from a serious illness. Only 25 years of age, he had a vision that he described as follows:[6]

> For that night I saw the heavens opened, and there appeared twelve men in a huge basket with each holding a Holy Bible with their names written on their chests. A voice in their midst shouted, 'Daniel, your salvation is at hand. I am here to heal you and then send you away to bring home all lost souls. As many as those whom you will be inspired to contact they will see salvation and here are your instructions: 'Abide by Matt. 10: 7-10 all your life and you as well as those touched to come to you will see wonders upon wonders in your lives.'

He interpreted his vision as an act of divine intervention that led to the restoration of his health. It was a profound experience that changed his life and eventually caused him to embark on a journey into the unknown, confident of divine guidance. He set forth on a mission that eventually took him to the Netherlands in order to do to others what he believed God had done to him: to bring healing. Almost forty years later, the event is still vivid in his mind. 'It is an experience that I will never, never forget', he says. 'It is like a photograph in my conscience. I cherish it a great deal, and I stand on this to tell all Christians that the gift of healing is still available'.

Daniel Himmans was born in 1943 in Agogo in the Ashanti region of Ghana, in a family of the Ga people in Ghana.[7] He was the second of three sons. One brother became famous in Ghana as the coach of the national football team, and Daniel Himmans was himself was a talented footballer in his younger days. Born into a Methodist family, he was raised as a Christian. His parents were, by his own account, 'extremely religious'. He remembers his earliest years as very happy, although due to his father's duties as a police officer the family was separated for some years, during which he was brought up by a foster-family. When he was four years old the family was briefly re-united. Two years later, when his mother died, the family was broken up again. At the age of six, when his mother died, he was afflicted for eight months with an illness that was never fully diagnosed but which was serious enough to necessitate a long spell in hospital.

This was followed by a time of hardship, during which Daniel Himmans experienced periods of extreme loneliness. He suffered from a series of unidentified illnesses, and had a range of spiritual experiences that in retrospect made him believe, in his own words, that God had a special plan for him. One time, for example, he almost drowned in a river but was saved by what he perceived as the experience of a 'strange hand' lifting him up from the bottom of the river and depositing him on a rock. Due to sickness and the regular transfers inherent in his father's job, Himmans's education was interrupted, but he nevertheless passed his exams successfully, and after finishing secondary school he began a career in the army as a compositor with the Armed Forces' Printing Press. He left the army after another serious illness. It was this last episode that led to his religious vocation, marking the beginning of his new career as a church minister.

Sickness is a recurrent factor in Daniel Himmans's life. This reflects a pattern well-known in African religious biographies, whereby a childhood illness turns out to be the start of a spiritual trail leading to a religious career. In the following years he continued to have experiences of a spiritual nature, accompanied by various forms of illness and at least one other near-death experience. This culminated in the last and crucial experience preceding his call, at the time he was working with the armed forces. While taking a shower, he experienced a sensation of paralysis and breathlessness, a sensation similar to that of his earlier near-drowning experience. Once again he felt himself on the boundary of life and death, as he began losing consciousness. At that moment he felt that 'someone' was pushing him away from under the shower. He was rushed to the emergency ward of the army barracks, and later transferred to a general hospital. The spiritual nature of this last experience caused him to be ill for the next three years, during which time he felt he had to struggle for his life. He was taken to various places in search of healing, but to no avail. Neither traditional nor Western medicine was successful. It was only after the profound spiritual experience described at the beginning of this section that preceded his vocation as a Christian healer that he found full recovery.

It took Himmans some more years to prepare for the mission which brought him to his final destination, the Netherlands. In 1976 he arrived in Amsterdam, where he lived in a hostel, making a living by manual work like many other African immigrants do. In the early days he simply went out into the streets of Amsterdam with his Bible, inviting people to pray and read the Bible with him. He gradually gathered a number of Africans, particularly from Ghana, who became the core of what later developed into a congregation with the name The True Teachings of Christ's Temple. In the following years Himmans-Arday became increasingly involved in the lives of the Ghanaians who settled in large numbers in the Bijlmer district of Amsterdam from about the mid-1980s. In the meantime he studied theology through a correspondence course with the London Bible College in Britain. The new congregation found its own space of worship under one of the multi-storey car-parks, with Daniel Himmans as its head pastor. His ministry focused on preaching the gospel, healing the sick and exorcising evil spirits in conformity with the injunction in Matthew 10 that forms the basis of his vocation.

WITCHCRAFT AND HEALING

Himmans-Arday's ideas about witchcraft have been greatly influenced by his own experiences of sickness and subsequent healing. Healing, in his view, refers to 'the method by which a person is restored', when one's integrity as a human being has been violated or affected in some respect. This includes those whose human integrity is believed to have been violated by the spirit of witchcraft, which he describes as 'the power that goes into a person to let him do monstrous things against his fellow men.' In his perception, witchcraft refers to 'someone with a supernatural power that is not meant to help but to hurt others.' A 'witch', then, in his understanding of the subject, is a person who deals with bad spirits or with the devil himself, and whose aim is to damage and destroy the life of a fellow human being. In other words, witches act under the influence of an evil power that they cannot resist on their own. In order to overcome the powers of evil, another and stronger force must be introduced, in this case the power of good. From an African Christian perspective, witchcraft is a form of evil that can be removed by the power of Christ through the Holy Spirit.

Witchcraft is only one of the reasons why Ghanaians in the Netherlands call on Himmans as a Christian healer. While Westerners may seek his help for psychological problems such as stress and depression or to be healed from a particular physical ailment, in the case of his African clients he addresses a much broader spectrum of problems, both physical and mental. The conditions of Africans' lives in Europe easily lead to marital instability and difficulties with the education of children, to financial problems or to anxieties about obtaining a residence permit. Physically, certain ailments commonly known to Africans are unfamiliar to European doctors. For most Africans, healing concerns human well-being in all its dimensions, treating the human person as a whole rather than as the sum of many parts. For them, spiritual healing is a normal aspect of the healing process, and African Christians find ample support in the Bible for this point of view.

Bible study and prayer are central to the experience of faith of African Christians, in and outside Africa. 'I live according to the Bible', Himmans says. 'Whenever I am given a [spiritual] message, I refer that message to the Scripture.' In the same way he always relates his healing activities to some passage from the Bible. This, he believes, is in fact the work of the Holy Spirit, who leads him to a particular quotation in order to show him what to do and how. There are different ways, he explains, by which he may be commanded to heal. One is what he refers to as 'direct intervention', which works through the laying-on of hands: 'the Lord can tell you that'. This may happen, for example, when somebody comes to him with a particular ailment or pain. By touching the painful spot, the pain may be taken away directly. Another way he describes as 'methodical healing', 'by which the Lord will tell you what exactly to use to heal the person.' He illustrates the point with examples from the Old Testament, such as the healing of King Hizkiah through the prophet Isaiah,[8] as well as the New Testament, for example when Jesus healed a man who had been blind all his life.[9] The use of oil and blessed water, which is common in many African-initiated churches, in and outside Africa, is a normal part of his methodical method of healing. The crucial issue with these forms of healing, he explains, is not to follow one's own intentions, but to open your mind to the instructions of the Holy Spirit. In order to be sure that it is indeed the spirit of God and not a different spirit that speaks, it is necessary to anchor the spiritual inspiration in the Bible.

Divine guidance also leads him to liberate people from the witchcraft powers they believe to possess, which in many cases they cannot control themselves. Himmans describes how he goes about healing such persons. First, he says, he asks for God's approval and guidance. Then, he continues, 'I place one hand on the forehead of the person and place the other hand at the back of the person and start prayerfully, sliding it [the witchcraft power] downwards. Believe me, when I start I get magnetised, I can feel the electrical chain, and the person can feel that something is moving. I tell the person: "if you are not feeling anything, say: 'I'm not feeling anything'". But the person says: "it is coming down, it is coming down, it is coming down!". So I get to the feet of the person and then I wash the person; I know that it is gone. Because it is meshed into the whole flesh'.[10]

This description is an example of the healing method referred to above as 'direct intervention', which depends on spiritual guidance from the Holy Spirit. When asked whether he is never afraid that the Holy Spirit might one day stop speaking to him, Himmans laughs. He has no doubts, he answers, because he calls on the infinite power of the almighty God. This is quite different, he explains, from somebody who derives his power from a different source and must fear that one day it will dry up.

According to Himmans, it is not easy to identify a person as in possession of witchcraft powers. It requires the spiritual gift of foresight. 'If you are spiritually endowed with foresight' he relates from his own experience, 'you can easily identify the person as possessing a spirit that does not belong to good.' This may emerge in different ways, he explains. 'Sometimes, through prayer the person confesses; sometimes, through experience with the person, you know that he possesses a power that suppresses others. In the presence of the person, he will say one word and then somebody will feel ill; in the gathering, he can look at somebody and that person gets a headache'. He knows how risky it can be to decide on the type of spirit that motivates people into certain actions and, by implication, to expose such a person as a witch. 'That has always been the problem', he says, 'because to be able to describe [witchcraft] would be easier, to be able to prove is something else. And always I depend upon the person whom I have exposed to prove that he or she possesses the witchcraft [powers]. That's why I do not go about just calling people witches. Before I can say: "this person possesses a bad spirit", the person will confirm it. That is the only way by which I can explain my observation. It is the only way that I can say: "this person is no good", or: "this person is good"'. All human beings have both good and bad in themselves, he maintains; hence a person behaving badly on one particular occasion does not therefore merit the label of witch. 'This is a very serious matter', he states, 'and that is why many of the churches are having problems, breaking down marriages and breaking down families by casting remarks on people who probably look very bad in the eyes of the public but possess no witchcraft powers at all.' It is only when a person is constantly behaving abnormally that the suspicion may arise that there are witchcraft powers at work. It is in such cases that Himmans takes up his task as a pastor: 'I start to go into the person's life spiritually by prayer. That is how I always observe those things'.

Himmans finds support in the Bible for his emphasis on the importance of discerning the spirit, a point of view he passionately defends. 'The Bible tells us that we must test all the spirits', he maintains, 'and we will know which one is who.' It is important to discern them because there are different types of spirits, some of which have good intentions, but there are also others that have evil intentions. For example, he explains, 'we have the Holy Spirit, that tells us only good things. The Holy Spirit will never tell you to harm anybody. It is not mischievous, it is not a danger to life. It sees to it that the progress that you are getting, [that] anyone who comes closer to you gets it too. That is where we see the two forces recorded in Galatians 5: 19-25.[11] We see that the Bible tells about this combination.' The danger is, he emphasises, that people end up confusing the two. Therefore, he states, 'we have to be very careful that we do not possess the bad spirit and call it a good one. Because when we have a spirit that hates people, it sees to it that what you have built is brought down. In that case we possess a spirit that envies others, or we possess a spirit that sees to it that no one progresses besides ourselves: those cannot be called a spirit from God. These are the differences', he concludes. 'If we do not take care and Satan puts that kind of spirit in you and tells you to be arrogant and boastful, to hate everybody, to see to it that nobody smiles, and you say: "that spirit is good", you *must* know that that spirit does not belong to God. It is very necessary for the Christians of this modern day to decipher the difference and also hold on to the true spirit, which is: walk in goodness, see to it that forgiveness comes from the heart.'

Although Himmans is acutely aware of the danger involved in exposing someone as a witch, he insists, like most of his fellow-Africans, that witches do exist. Not only does the Bible make clear, according to him and other African pastors, that witches have existed from the very beginning[12] but, more importantly, that there are gifted people who can handle them in a responsible and humane manner. These, in his view, are people with a special calling whom he refers to as the anointed, 'people who are prepared to be selfless.' It is with the help of such persons, he observes, 'that you can lead them [i.e witches] out and say: this person is like us, he can be saved'. But, he emphasises, you have to work on it spiritually, because 'these things only come about prayerfully. If you are spiritually endowed with foresight, you can easily identify the person as possessing a spirit that does not belong to good'. To avoid any misunderstanding concerning his own spiritual powers, he explains further: 'I am not trying to say that I have [the] power to detect witchcraft. I am trying to tell you that these things [witchcraft powers] exist. And upon the power of the Lord, when He wants you to see them, you will see them, and then save the person who is carrying such a heavy load.' From such a perspective, witches are not simply evil-doers, as they are often depicted. Their possession of witchcraft powers poses a pastoral problem that needs the full attention of the Church which, in Himmans's view, is in the unique position to help those burdened in this way.

Himmans knows from his own experience how many Ghanaians, whether they are Christian or not, seek the services of certain traditional healers who enjoy a wide reputation for their spiritual powers. There are even Christian pastors, he says, who go to them to protect themselves against witchcraft and other types of evil. They do so, in his view, because these pastors are unable to cast out demons in their own churches and they lack the ability to 'see' who is evil. Having no spiritual eye, they lack spiritual vision and insight. Relying on traditional healers in these matters is a dangerous path to follow, in his view, because they always demand 'their pound of flesh', as he puts it, wanting something in return. Himmans is convinced that in the long run a strategy of seeking solutions outside the Church will backfire. He does believe that there are powers in the universe, and that other people may use those powers to heal. But as a Christian he regards those powers as offering only a temporary solution. 'If you want a permanent solution, [you have to] seek for the infinite', he explicates. 'The infinite is the Almighty. If you are an instrument of the infinite, who is the Almighty, why go for temporary gods?' People should be encouraged to look for a permanent, rather than a temporary, solution to their problems, in his view. Spiritual healing, therefore, should be accepted by all churches as part of the Christian programme. If that were the case, he believes, it would be an enormous step forward: 'then we are half-way to heaven'.

Clearly, as a church minister Himmans is strongly in favour of a pastoral approach to the problem of witchcraft. He knows of pastors who themselves make random accusations of witchcraft and have personally participated in the inhumane treatment of the accused. To him, this seems not only wrong but also unnecessary, because he is convinced that 'genuine' churches—defined as 'those that follow the example of Jesus'—have the power to cast out evil, including witchcraft powers. There is no need to seek out such powers, in his view; they can be assumed whenever the problem of witchcraft arises. 'Jesus was not going around looking for such powers to be cast out', he says, 'but when he met them and they were blocking his way,[then] he would cast them out'. Similarly, he argues, when witchcraft powers threaten people in the church, all that is required is to cast them out with the power of the Holy Spirit. 'Why go about chasing somebody and burning his property whom you can easily stop in his track when he confronts you? Why go about accusing somebody when you know that the power in you is stronger than his?', he wonders. In this respect, he feels, most churches fail in their task, since they often fail to use the supreme spiritual power at their disposal.[13]

We may observe in this context that the proposed strategy of confronting witchcraft powers only when they manifest themselves conforms to the belief that a person born with such power—for example through inheritance (see below)—may actually live and die without it ever manifesting itself. It is only during particular times and at circumstances conducive to the creation of a 'witch-craze', that such powers are perceived by many Africans to become active. In many anthropological works on witchcraft, these are often described as times of crisis.[14]

WITCHCRAFT POWERS AND EVIL SPIRITS

Since Africans generally recognise various kinds and degrees of evil, it is relevant to the present discussion to distinguish between witchcraft powers, as one category of evil, and evil spirits, as another. Both are considered evil by many Africans. But there is a marked difference between the two. Witchcraft powers are a type of evil that is either inherent in the person or has become part of a person of his own free will, while evil spirits enter a person involuntarily, taking control of body and mind. Witchcraft represents a power that is contained inside people, an internal force. Evil spirits, on the other hand, represent an external force, one believed to come from outside to torment people. Evil spirits are considered able to lead a person into committing crimes unintentionally. 'Good people can be motivated by such spirits', says Himmans. 'These are the powers that disturb people and make them do wrong things. There are people who murder, and when they are finished they don't even remember they have done it! Those are the people who need deliverance. This is the work of evil spirits.'

Hence, a different logic is at work. In a case of witchcraft, a person is supposed to take control of evil powers. A case of possession by evil spirits works the other way around: the human subject is believed to be no longer in control, but to have been taken over by an evil spirit. The difference manifests itself in the type of behaviour that is subsequently displayed. Evil spirits torment the person they take possession of, while in the case of a person possessing witchcraft powers the process is reversed, as he or she is deemed in control of these sinister powers and able to manipulate them. One important consequence of this analysis is that, as an external force, evil spirits are considered easier to deal with, as they take up only temporary residence in a person. Witchcraft, however, is seen as an inherent force of a permanent character. Witchcraft power is often believed to reside in a fiery substance that resides inside a person and escapes during the night to join others with similar powers. Among the Akan, the largest ethnic group of Ghana, these witch-forces are believed to stay in the tops of trees. It is quite common in Ghana to hear people claim to have witnessed such spirits.

In spite of the differences between witchcraft powers and evil spirits, their common characteristic of evil causes many Africans to seek liberation from them. The effects of witchcraft powers go deeper than those of evil spirits, to the extent that, according to Reverend Himmans, the person who performs evil deeds needs to be saved, and not just have the evil power expelled. In both cases, confession is considered a necessary condition for effective healing, because without confession an exorcist would not have the power to cast out evil and would merely be doing something 'speculative', in his view. A person who seeks liberation from a troublesome spirit has to admit that he or she is in trouble in order for the spiritual treatment to be effective.[15] Thus, the evil power that needs to be cast out must be proven to be evil through the person himself. Further, the person who needs to be delivered has to be doctored or taught that there are certain evils leading them into danger that need to be delivered.

Confession, then, implies an admission that something is wrong. Himmans bases the need for confession on the biblical example of Jesus, who cast out evil only from those who confessed to being possessed by its spirit. 'You cannot go about it', he states, 'and say: "you are a witch, let me cast you out". The person has to confess before you can say: "this is a witch"'. It is the individual who knows whether the accusation is true. Hence, if confession takes place, this should proceed from self-awareness, and not an admission coerced after accusation by others. Witchcraft accusations, in Himmans's view, go entirely against the spirit of Christian belief. He particularly scorns pastors who perpetrate physical violence against suspected witches. 'If you possess the true spirit, why do you have to beat the truth out of somebody like a policeman?', he wonders. 'That is the African problem', he sighs. 'Africans accuse [each other] on the strength of what you do is not normal to him, [but] which could be normal to somebody else. I personally believe it is very unnecessary to go about accusing of witchcraft those who possess these powers, provided that you, in your church, know that when they come to challenge you, you can cast them out. Why go to the extent of accusing them and bringing them to court and burning their properties, unless you are afraid and *believe* they can harm you.' Christian believers, in his view, should be so convinced of the supreme power of the Holy Spirit that there is no need for them to be afraid of evil powers that can harm them, and they should certainly not retaliate by engaging in acts of violence.

In Ghana as in other parts of the world, witchcraft powers are often ascribed to women.[16] Among Ghanaians in the Netherlands, too, women are believed to be particularly susceptible to such powers. This view may be strengthened by biblical teachings, starting with Adam blaming his misery on Eve. 'And that is how it has come to stay', says Himmans. 'Everyone who possesses a power and wants a culprit, or he wants an assistant or messenger, he goes straight for the woman'. While witches are usually considered to be female and believed to have dealings with evil spirits or the devil, he states, their male counterparts are usually seen as wizards, who use their powers for constructive purposes. Witches, on the other hand, are considered to use their powers exclusively for destructive purposes. In Akan tradition, witches are believed to live a shadow life resembling that of normal human beings. They are believed to have their chiefs, queen mothers, courtiers, drummers and so on. It is also believed that they feed on human flesh and that each of them has to take their turn in supplying this.[17]

In Ghana, witchcraft powers are believed to be acquired in several ways. One important conduit, which distinguishes witchcraft powers from possession by an evil spirit, is through inheritance. Witchcraft powers, as Himmans explains, according to traditional belief in Ghana, are inherited in the context of the extended family system. They are not necessarily passed on from a mother to her daughter, or from a father to his son. An uncle can give them to a nephew or an aunt can pass it to a niece, a mother to her son, or a brother to his sister. The person who inherits witchcraft power in this way can hardly be blamed for it, in the same way as it not somebody's fault to be born with blue rather than with brown eyes. But by the same token, the involuntary character of inherited witchcraft makes it easier for a person to do something about it. As Himmans explains, it becomes a witch's own choice to decide that he does not wish to retain this power. He can have it removed in the church.

But there are also other ways of acquiring witchcraft powers. One way is simply by buying them. While women are generally believed to be more liable to inherit witchcraft powers, men are believed to be more disposed to purchase them. A person who wants to enrich himself may consult a healer known for his occult spiritual powers, who will accept to help a client for a price, as Himmans explains. He will say, for example: 'I'll give you a power by which you can be rich, but I will need human blood.

I will need a newly born child, and I will need seventeen goats. What I need, is what you have to provide. If you provide all that, you will become rich. So, the person buys the power. And when he buys it and becomes rich, there comes a time that he cannot provide the things that are required to keep the power. Then he becomes poorly and himself bewitched. He becomes tormented, to the point whereby he needs redemption. But he cannot get redemption, because he has sold his soul to the devil.'[18]

WITCHCRAFT AND MIGRATION

Witchcraft beliefs are clearly very strong in Ghana and among Ghanaians elsewhere. It is normally believed that a bewitched person is the victim of a close relative. According to Peter Sarpong, one of Ghana's Catholic Bishops and an anthropologist who has written on the subject, the effect of the belief in witchcraft on people's social life is considerable. For example, Sarpong says, the belief that somebody can give you a gift that contains witchcraft substance makes parents warn their children not to receive gifts from old people especially. When people are sick, they will not stay near their home because it is believed that witches strike at short range but cannot attack someone who is far from home. So it happens that when somebody is going to have a medical operation, they will either not inform anybody in their immediate circle for fear that witches may use the opportunity to attack, or else will travel far away for treatment.[19]

However, this last counter-witchcraft measure may no longer be considered effective, as I learned during my work among Ghanaian immigrant communities in the Netherlands. Ghanaians living in Amsterdam believe that 'witches' now also travel overseas to strike their victims there. Just as in Ghana—and other parts of Africa for that matter—witches are often believed to be able to make themselves disappear to evade capture. One such tactic that allows an alleged witch to escape is by transformation into a bird. Both in Ghana and in the Netherlands people have described their personal experiences of a witch's transformation into a bird. 'If a person wants to transform himself', says Reverend Himmans, 'he always will like to transform himself in an environment that is conducive to his powers. Some people would like to have a tree, some would prefer something else'. Such experiences of transformation have also been recorded with regard to powerful African politicians, such as Samuel Doe, former President of Liberia, for example, shortly before his violent death,[20] but similar beliefs are held about powerful marabouts, such as Malian-born 'Djinne' Cissé, reputed to have made a pact with the devil.[21] These beliefs conform to Himmans's comments that transformative powers are often ascribed to 'real' criminals, who in most cases find a way to escape.

Although people may retain witchcraft beliefs when they migrate, they may respond differently to such beliefs in their new environment. Himmans has noticed this during his years in Europe. 'When people travel overseas', he says, 'they still hold on to witchcraft belief. But they do not become as aggressive as they used to be when they were in Africa. What I have found in my European experiences [is that] angry people, to prove that they are right and others are wrong have to call him or her a "witch". They still peddle with the word witchcraft, but they don't do anything with it. They do not become so aggressive as is often the case in Ghana, but they see to it that you lose as many friends as possible and become isolated.' But there are always exceptions, as he knows from his experiences in the Bijlmer district where he lives. 'There are always people who will go all the way to harm a person when they discover that the person is a witch, even in Europe'.

To illustrate his point, he relates the story of a woman selling *kenkey*[22] in the Bijlmer to make a living. She was accused of being a witch and her vending-stall was overturned. Such actions also implicate African Christians in Europe who, in Himmans's view, should have no fear of witchcraft and therefore refrain from engaging in any violent actions against alleged witches. He blames church leaders for their lack of spiritual guidance in this and for not depending entirely on the spiritual power available in the church. He is proud that in his own church, the True Teachings of Christ's Temple, there is no fear of witchcraft. According to him, his parishioners are not afraid that witches can harm them. 'Every African knows that witches exist', he says, 'but the church [TTCT] does not believe in them as being powerful over their

God. So we don't care about them [the witches] flying from Africa or coming in their great numbers, we care very little about those kind of things. Because we know Jesus has the power, and with that kind of power we can cast out any challenging forces that come. Whether other people like it or not, that is our stand'.

It thus appears that the social conditions in which Ghanaians find themselves in Europe have brought about certain changes in the way people deal with the phenomenon of witchcraft in actual practice, though the basic conception of witchcraft has remained unaltered. The context of migration may cause new anxieties, but at the same time it tends to limit violent action on the basis of witchcraft fears. The social integration of African migrants into Western society, Himmans believes, will help a great deal to reduce their fear of witchcraft. 'The issue of witchcraft may always be at the back of their minds, but it will not be operational', he believes. In the Bijlmer district of Amsterdam that is home to so many Ghanaians, most of them by necessity live as closely together as they used to do in their country of origin. This creates a situation conducive to witchcraft accusations, as it is virtually impossible to escape from the social pressures of this new-type African village community. This often changes when people get the chance to move to another part of town, where their neighbours are mostly Dutch. If Ghanaian Christians in the Netherlands had the opportunity to interact and share their experiences with Dutch Christians, Himmans believes, this would have a positive impact on their behaviour and reduce the risk of witchcraft violence.

There are three lines of policy that he would consider helpful in this respect. The first is what he refers to as 'integration based on equality'. By this he means that the Dutch government should not accept every cultural tradition that Ghanaian migrants have brought with them. For example, allowing 'fetish priests' into the country, pouring libation and generally engaging in what he sees as traditional practices that hamper progress, will encourage Ghanaians to stick to what they know rather than encouraging them to embrace constructive change. He is aware that he may be accused of being too westernised in thinking this way because, as he says, 'when you talk like this, they will say, you are not a Ghanaian, you don't love your culture. But what is the use of pouring liquid onto the ground and the ground just swallows it? Just because it was inherited it must continue.' Moreover, Westerners ridicule such aspects of Ghanaian culture, in his view, rather than respecting them. He criticises what he considers the sense of hypocrisy of the West allowing Ghanaian cultural traditions in their own countries, but at the same time ridiculing them when they comment on them. 'Culture', he states, lies in 'displaying those things that are beneficial to the West, and not those that the West laughs about.' These are aspects that bind Ghanaians with their new home. In the case of the Netherlands, Ghanaian culture has something to offer to all, not just to Ghanaians, he argues, but for this to be effective, Ghanaians should not retain aspects of their tradition that are unnecessary and that set them apart from the Dutch.

Himmans's comments concerning social integration are also instigated by current race relations in Western Europe, which has generally become more hostile to foreigners. Therefore he believes it is necessary for integration to be followed by 'combination', his second proposed line of policy, in the sense 'that black and white exist hand in hand'. Such combination will be based on mutual assistance and sharing on a basis of equality. Such co-existence of black and white people, he believes, will promote constructive habits. 'Because you see polished things, the other sees polished things from you'. This process can be furthered by a third policy, 'social associationship'. With this he means that all social organs, including the police and military, should be open to immigrants. Because, as he points out, if a Ghanaian immigrant gets frustrated due to the lack of social opportunities in spite of his educational background, he will resort to those believed to have witchcraft powers in order to get the money he needs.

Himmans is convinced that if the three areas of integration, combination and social association are addressed, the phenomenon of witchcraft will eventually disappear among Ghanaian immigrants. 'Because when you open the person's mind with intelligible things, he can do many things'. Similarly, he believes that if socio-economic conditions improve witchcraft practices may disappear, in spite of the continuation of the belief in witchcraft. The need to identify and eliminate witches as the carriers of evil, which motivates people into the use of violence, may then also disappear, even if the belief continues.

Notes

1. Centraal Bureau voor de Statistiek, Voorburg/Heerlen, 2005-08-28 (CBS Statline). Situation as per 1 January 2004.
2. At the time of writing, most of these were being demolished as part of a social renovation project.
3. See notably Gerrie ter Haar, *Halfway to Paradise: African Christians in Europe*, Cardiff Academic Press, 1998.
4. To avoid any misunderstanding: this does not mean that I share the same views, only that it helps me towards an understanding of Africans' belief in the spirit world. Cf. also Stephen Ellis and Gerrie ter Haar, *Worlds of Power: Religious thought and political practice in Africa*, London: Hurst & Co./New York: Oxford University Press, 2004, notably pp. 17-18.
5. All quotations in the present chapter are taken from personal interviews with Rev. Himmans-Arday, unless otherwise stated.
6. D. Himmans-Arday, *And the Truth Shall Set You Free*, London: Janus Publishing Company, 1996, p. 28.
7. The following information on the life of Rev. Himmans-Arday has been largely taken from Gerrie ter Haar, *Halfway to Paradise,* pp. 30-2.
8. 2 Kings 20:7.
9. John 9.
10. Cf. David Cumes, *Africa in My Bones: A surgeon's odyssee into the spirit world of African healing*, Claremont: Spearhead, 2004.
11. These verses concern the contrast between the Spirit and human nature, representing the forces of good and evil respectively.
12. See Old Testament references to 1 Sam. 28 and Book of Deuteronomy 18, notably verses 9-13, and New Testament reference Galatians 5:20.
13. The same point has been argued by the Roman Catholic Archbishop Emmanuel Milingo, former Archbishop of Lusaka: see Gerrie ter Haar, *Spirit of Africa: The Healing Ministry of Zambian Archbishop Milingo of Zambia*, London: C. Hurst & Co./Trenton, NJ: Africa World Press, 1992.

14. This is one of the conventional explanations for witch-hunting in Africa that requires criticism. See e.g. the introduction to Mary Douglas (ed), *Witchcraft, Confessions and Accusations*, London: Tavistock, 1970.

15. For the importance of confession as part of the healing process, see also Danfulani in the present volume, pp. Cf. also Mbambo, p. 202.

16. See the previous chapters by Abraham Akrong and Elom Dovlo.

17. Peter Sarpong, *Ghana in Retrospect: Some aspects of Ghanaian culture*, Accra/Tema: Ghana Publishing Corporation, 1974, p. 46.

18. Cf. Ter Haar, *Spirit of Africa*, pp. 143-5; also Ellis and Ter Haar, *Worlds of Power*, notably pp. 84, 92-3.

19. Sarpong, *Ghana in Retrospect*, pp. 46-7.

20. See e.g. Stephen Ellis, *The Mask of Anarchy: The destruction of Liberia and the religious dimension of an African civil war*, London: Hurst & Co., 1999, p. 10.

21. Ellis and Ter Haar, *Worlds of Power*, p. 86.

22. Cooked maize flour.

6

WITCHCRAFT AND THE CHRISTIAN CHURCH: ETHICAL IMPLICATIONS*

Elias K. Bongmba

INTRODUCTION

Studies of witchcraft and the occult in Africa continue to be a fascinating and disturbing subject. It is fascinating because scholars and general observers find it difficult to ignore a subject matter that is rooted in the very fabric and thought of many African people. It is disturbing because the subject of witchcraft deals with complex problems in social and communal relations. There is a strong conviction that witchcraft is real and effective. Many people still process misfortune through a logic that is based on the effectiveness of witchcraft.

In the Wimbum area in the northwest of Cameroon, where I grew up, witchcraft is called *tfu*[1] The term *tfu* is related to other terms such as *bri* and *bfui*, both of which refer to the ability to do extraordinary things. These powers can be used in a positive or negative manner. In this essay, I discuss witchcraft, which the Wimbum generally call *tfu*, as a belief system and a practice that has ethical implications. As a scholar interested in the claims people make that some members of the community practice *tfu* negatively, I must confess that I do not understand the real nature of *tfu*. I follow the general description of the phenomenon as a special ability that some people possess and which enables them to accomplish certain things.

The literature on African witchcraft reports that at the core of witchcraft dialogues and confrontation is the belief and claim that some people have abilities and powers that allows them to do extraordinary things. The discourse about witchcraft in many ways is a debate about a belief system as well as these alleged activities.

Very little has been done to actually understand the nature of the supposed power, as it is difficult for anyone who does not believe in mystical power to understand it. Hence, much discussion and writing on witchcraft remains elusive. General descriptions offer us information about the perceived effects of witchcraft power, such as the ability to fly at night, or the ability to bring wealth to a community or to protect people from danger, or the ability to see things that are to happen in the future. These descriptions are sometimes neutral and reflect understandings of power that remains at best elusive. However, most understandings of such power are negative. Those who are alleged to possess them are often accused of causing the death of someone, or making it difficult for a co-wife to get pregnant, and of hindering someone from making progress in business or in school.

In trying to understand the phenomenon, I have focused on the discourse of witchcraft and its alleged practices to highlight certain ethical issues. My interactions and studies carried our among the Wimbum people have convinced me that *tfu* discourse and practice remain not only a search for the cause of misfortune, but that they also constitute a moral discourse. Scholarly research on the subject in Africa continues to highlight the moral dimensions of witchcraft, even when the goal of such study is not ethics. Sir Edward Evans-Pritchard's magnum opus, *Witchcraft, Oracles, and Magic Among the Azande*, inaugurated studies of African witchcraft by mapping not only the conceptualisation of witchcraft but also the social dynamics and responses to the negative use of witchcraft. Thirty years after publication, Evans-Pritchard argued: 'Envy, jealousy, hatred, are the drive behind witchcraft, and hence the cause of failure, misfortune, and above all sickness and death. Witchcraft beliefs may thus be said to provide Azande not only with a theory of causation for particular events but also with a moral philosophy.'[2] Admittedly, those who talk about witchcraft in their communities do not formulate their questions and concerns in the same manner that philosophers and moral theorists formulate theirs. However, when people gather in the village and allege that someone has used witchcraft negatively, they are engaged in a moral discourse.

Ethnographic materials continue to unmask contemporary understandings of witchcraft in Africa, covering the social dynamics, economic aspects, religious dimensions, gender, and political dimensions.[3] I have argued elsewhere that ethnographic materials provide us with enough information to begin a meta-critical analysis of the moral terrain that is opened by witchcraft discourse.[4] However, such meta-critical analysis cannot replace other ways of studying the phenomenon. While the ethnographic approach is not the only method of studying the moral implications of witchcraft thought and practice, I must also state that philosophical and theological approaches alone cannot treat the phenomenon conclusively. In a previous study, I have taken an ethical approach to the matter and argued that it is important to focus on the individual and highlight individuality.[5] My commitment to individuality does not deny the importance of community. Ignoring the social dimensions of life would frustrate any attempts to articulate an ethical perspective, because the personal stands out only in a social context, which includes family, extended family and other social groups, as well as the community. Personal disorders only become social disorders, or vice versa, when we understand that the personal and social are interwoven in the social fabric that we call society.[6]

I return to the study of the phenomenon, focusing on ethics and social relations because witchcraft has been associated with certain dispositions. In his discussion of some of these dispositions, Evans-Pritchard referred to the concept of *sanza*. The Roman Catholic priest and missionary who worked among the Azande, Mgr. S. R. Lagae, translated *sanza* as 'animosité, haine, jalousie'.[7] Later translations by Canon and Mrs. Gore, missionaries who worked among the Azande before the arrival of Evans-Pritchard in the region, gave two meanings to the word. First, they indicated that the word *sanza* was often employed as a proverb. Second, when *sanza* was used in combination with a verb, it meant 'spite, hate, envy, jealousy... a meaning look, a wink, a scornful or disdainful look'.[8] After discussing the different ways in which the proverb *sanza* is employed, Evans-Pritchard pointed out that as oblique speech, *sanza* is also related to *mangu*, witchcraft, and people generally believe that those who employ *sanza* are witches. My point here is that the different meanings conveyed by terms associated with the term 'witchcraft' underscore the fact that witchcraft involves dispositions and actions taken by individuals for specific reasons. It is the belief that witches act in a purposive manner that forces an ethical reflection. Diane Lyons has argued that people in different African societies believe that witches act with intent. 'This behaviour', she writes, 'is purposive: it is a strategy used within a particular set of social relations and contexts of interaction. Indeed most accusations of witchcraft in Africa are between those who are on intimate terms, especially peers, kin and co-wives (…) suggesting the domestic contexts are potential loci for witchcraft practices.'[9]

This perspective strengthens my contention that witchcraft is often not a benign spiritual force, as some people think it is. In this chapter, I am concerned mainly with the negative use of witchcraft power, because negative use of such power raises ethical questions. It is crucial that those who engage in the study of witchcraft today continue to explore the ethical dimensions in dialogue with members of different African communities. Below, I carry out such an exploration of ethical solutions from within the Christian tradition in Africa.

Those who practise indigenous African religions have no problems with the concept of witchcraft, and they do not tend to question the validity of the claims that someone is using a mystical force that is not available to others. In African religions, deities, spirits, and ancestors are all attributed power. People believe that there are good and evil spirits, and that the latter can provide people with negative power. Thus, when certain people are seen as possessing negative power, members of the community are inclined to think that these powers derive from bad spirits. In African communities, people traditionally turn to certain ways of dealing with witchcraft, either by using 'magic', as Evans-Pritchard suggested the Azande did, or by performing cleansing rituals, or by sanctioning those considered guilty of practising witchcraft.

However, in the Christian tradition the issue is often not addressed as regularly as one would have expected Christian churches to focus on it, since witchcraft is such an important subject in the lives of many Africans. In the rest of this chapter, therefore, I will discuss the neglect of the subject of witchcraft in the Christian Church and suggest ways through which the Church, which has great influence on many Africans, can contribute to a new ethics concerning witchcraft. The material that I use derives from two approaches: a critical reflection on the subject based on published materials, or a hermeneutical approach; and personal interviews that stem from an on-going project on gender and witchcraft in contemporary Cameroonian society.

THE CHRISTIAN TRADITION AND WITCHCRAFT IN AFRICA

The mainline missionary churches devoted some attention to the problem of witchcraft in Africa during the 1970s,[10] but such efforts did not go very far. Leny Lagerwerf argues that the African churches focused on sorcery, witchcraft, and spirit possession at several conferences, including a Colloquium on Faith and Healing in Yaounde from 10-13 September 1972. Some of the papers presented there were published in *Croyance et guéri-son*, 1973. The Episcopal Conference of Africa and Madagascar (SECAM) met in Rome in 1975, calling attention to the problem of witchcraft and sorcery. Participants at the World Council of Churches colloquium on 'Religious Experience of Man in his Relations with Nature' recommended that the churches should study the beliefs and practices related to witchcraft and sorcery in Africa. Religious leaders attending a conference organised by the Episcopal Committee of traditional and syncretic religions in Bobo Dioulasso in Burkina Faso spent a great deal of time debating Father Hebga's book *Sorcellerie: Chimère dangereuse*, published in 1979.[11] The National Committee for research on African Culture and the Expression of the Christian Message in Tanzania met in 1980 to consider 'Witchcraft, traditional healing methods, and their impact on the Christian'. The Faculty of Theology in Yaounde organised interdisciplinary discussions on theology and witchcraft in 1984.[12] Despite these efforts in the 1970s and the 1980s, the mainline missionary churches in Africa still need to take up the challenge and address problems arising from the belief in witchcraft.

Christianity has had a very difficult relationship with the subject of witchcraft. In the history of Europe, people accused of being witches were persecuted and burned by Christians or with the complicity of Christians.[13] Alongside with palmist, astrologers, and fortune-tellers, the mainline missionary churches have taken a critical stance against witchcraft. In Africa, missionary theology taught a triumphalist christology that proclaimed the supremacy of Christ in the African context, ignoring the realities of the African context.[14] Trained in an intellectual climate dominated by Enlightenment epistemology and modernist assumptions of progress, many missionaries were impatient with beliefs in spirits and spiritual forces other than the Holy Spirit. Christianity was presented to Africans as a primarily textual religion, with Christian leaders preaching both the Hebrew Bible and the New Testament. Africans believed in the Bible and often held it in high regard, treating it sometimes as if it were a fetish or magical text.

In reading the Bible, Africans also found passages that talked about the belief in witchcraft. They found out that King Saul consulted witches when he faced a difficult battle.[15] However, the majority of references that many African Christians quote today are passages which indicate that witches would have their place in hell-fire with other evil-doers. Missionaries and pastors have not done very much about these passages because their modernist ethos, which rejected belief in witchcraft as irrational, convinced them that such beliefs would disappear with the advance of the gospel.[16] In an earlier critique of this ethos, Sam Erivwo argued that missionaries followed the path of the Anglican Bishop Hutchinson, who rejected witchcraft beliefs.[17] Writing about the South African scene, Gerhardus Oosthuizen has underscored the fact that the early preachers in Africa ignored a key component of the African thought system:[18]

> Witchcraft and sorcery have been largely ignored by the missionaries in Africa because of their deep-seated westernized disposition on these matters. Their highly intellectualized disposition on witchcraft, sorcery, magic, spirit possessions and the reality of demons (with the exception of Satan) has made

them turn a blind eye to these forces, which are considered to be out of bounds to any one associated with
Christianity and thus to be totally ignored, whatever
their influences might be.

Missionaries did normally not engage with the phenomenon,
and thus failed to interact with a thought and belief system that
affected people across the continent. Those missionaries and
African pastors who did engage with witchcraft saw it largely as
a confrontation with the devil, often represented in the person of
the so-called witch doctor or the rainmaker. In southern Africa,
Robert Moffat claimed that the rainmaker was the main opponent of Christianity and a pillar of Satan.[19] This approach further
complicated issues, because a negative approach to witchcraft also
led to missionary hostility towards traditional healing practices in
Africa.[20] In general, there was no attempt to carry out a dialogue
with indigenous worldviews. M. L. Daneel has argued that in Zimbabwe 'the general trend was towards elimination and a measure
of negation of Shona beliefs, rather than a sympathetic interaction
and dialogue (...) The implication of this policy was that the good
news of the missionaries seldom addressed the full range of existentially significant issues in a rural subsistence economy.'[21]

In recent years the journal *Missiology* published an article
entitled 'Witchcraft and the gospel: insights from Africa'. The
author, Harriet Hill, argues that when Christianity was introduced to the Adioukrou people in Côte d'Ivoire, many people
burned their fetishes and converted to Christianity. However,
seventy years later, witchcraft accusations and practices are rife
even among members of the church.[22] Hill argues: 'Missionaries
to Africa cannot afford to underestimate the place that witchcraft holds in African societies and in the African Church. We
cannot ignore it or hope that it will disappear with moderniza-
tion. I have found it to be the aspect of African worldview that is
the most difficult to understand (...) The idea that the Bible does
not address witchcraft and offers no solution for the problem is
the result of an imported theology.'[23]

Twenty years earlier, the same journal published another
article on witchcraft, which highlighted the dilemmas of witchcraft for the African Church. Jacob A. Loewen, who served as a

missionary in Zambia, reported that members of a Zambian congregation had gone to a missionary to ask him for permission to 'de-witch' a young woman who had accidentally become a witch.[24] She had married a junior government worker, who worked in the capital city of Lusaka. She could not stand the pressures of life in the city and wanted him to seek transfer to a rural area. Her husband did not like the idea, because he thought he would have a better chance of advancing in his profession if he stayed and worked in the city. His wife continued to be frustrated with city life. She fled the city and returned to her parents. Back at her parents' home she expressed in frustration that she wished she could get a divorce. Three days later her husband was killed in a car accident. The woman cried and felt bad, because she believed her husband had died because she had expressed a desire to be divorced from him. In expressing this desire out of frustration, the woman as well as others reasoned, she had become accidentally a witch. It is for this reason that the community sought permission from the missionary to 'de-witch' her. But the missionary, who worked for the United Church of Zambia that the couple attended, advised them to go to an independent church.

Belief in witchcraft has grown steadily, but mainline churches have ignored this growth in their training programmes, thus failing to prepare the leadership to deal with the problems associated with it. African Christians continue to deal with the crisis posed by belief in witchcraft. Although there is a steady discussion of the problem in the literature on African religions, some Christian churches continue to shy away from engaging systematically with this thought pattern. Members of Christian churches sometimes look up to the church, their pastors, and priest to help them deal with the phenomenon of witchcraft accusations and counter-accusations, but Christian leadership has often fallen short. In some communities, Christian leaders compete with traditional leaders for the control of the minds of the masses on these issues. When they do, Christian leaders tend to dismiss witchcraft powers while the traditional leaders and healers take these seriously. As a result, people tend to listen more to the traditional leaders and healers than to the Christian leaders.[25] This situation calls for a new reckoning, as the Church in Africa continues to wrestle with the human condition in the context of an African worldview. African Christian leaders, especially in the mainline missionary churches, need a critical appreciation of African values, belief in the occult and belief in spiritual forces, which they constantly affirm, quoting biblical texts to make their case about the existence of these forces.

Some theologians and religious leaders have paid attention to the problems caused by witchcraft. For example, Eric de Rosny, who worked as a Catholic priest in Douala, was initiated as a *nganga* (traditional healer).[26] During his many years in Cameroon, he learned to take witchcraft accusations seriously. The Cameroonian priest M.P. Hebga argues that we should see witchcraft as a symbolic language, especially when people talk of witches flying at night and doing all kinds of things. He believes the phenomena of magic and witches are real, although he does not demonstrate what makes him believe this.[27] Recognition of these forces by Christian leaders and theologians is also reflected in the work of Jean Masamba ma Mpolo of the Democratic Republic of Congo (DRC). In 1972, Masamba Mpolo defended a doctoral dissertation at the School of Theology at Claremont in California on a topic dealing with bewitched persons.[28] He later published works on *kindoki*, a term used in DRC to refer to various forces related to the abilities (both good and bad) that are often associated with witchcraft. He argues that *kindoki* as a belief and practice is used to diagnose and deal with misfortune.[29]

However, discussion of witchcraft has been, and still is, regarded with a great deal of suspicion in the mainline churches. It is the African-initiated churches (AIC's),[30] such as the Zionist churches in South Africa, that not only recognise the African reality of the widespread belief in witchcraft and witches, but also try to respond to it.[31] Many AIC leaders recognise the problems posed by the belief in good and bad spirits. For that reason they take witchcraft beliefs and practices seriously. Many of them believe that their calling includes not only preaching the gospel, but also to provide healing and deliverance from all oppressive forces. They pray and lay hands on people oppressed by witchcraft, proclaiming liberty from such forces. Oosthuizen argues that the prophet who helps people in need also takes up the task of 'taking personal interest in the sick, especially those who have problems with illnesses related to the African cosmology like sorcery and witchcraft-diseases which are associated with the activities of evil spirits'.[32]

Most AIC congregations also believe that prophets have the ability to see beyond the ordinary.[33] In that sense, prophets are claiming a mystical power, similar to that claimed by people who are believed to have an extra pair of eyes. Prophets thus claim that they are able to see what witches are planning, and they use this knowledge to warn people about these nefarious activities. Oosthuizen has argued that in South Africa prophets claim that they use the power of the Holy Spirit to detect misfortune and illness, and to bring healing to people affected by it. He observes that the belief in spiritual agency is more prevalent in economically marginalised areas.[34] It would be a mistake, however, to conclude that it is only the poor in Africa who believe in the existence of witches. Witchcraft belief cuts across class and gender. Recent scholarship has demonstrated that members of the political elite, who exploit these beliefs for their own ambitions, take the world of the occult very seriously.[35]

Given the tenacity of such beliefs, there is a pressing need for the Church in Africa to address these issues.[36] Other observers of the African scene argue that the Church has other priorities to deal with. Harry Hoeben, a Dutch Catholic priest, has argued in the past that '[w]e do not claim it [witchcraft] is Africa's most burning issue nor the one with which churchmen should be primarily concerned. There are sociopolitical matters of far greater moment than magic, black or white.'[37] I agree with Hoeben that there are important socio-political issues that the Church in Africa needs to focus on. However, he made a more appropriate point later when he argued: 'For the moment we simply want to show, thanks to a test-case from West Africa, that, for the time being at least, the matter warrants pastoral attention as well as theological reflection.'[38]

We have arrived at a point in Africa where witchcraft can no longer be dismissed as an exotic idea that continues to fascinate anthropologists and Africanists, who ignore other realities. How can theologians ignore an issue that continues to divide families and drive a wedge between communities, as it has among the Wimbum of the Northwest Province of Cameroon, where at least two people suspected of being witches were beaten to death in 1999 and 2000. In the same region, several people were exiled from their homes because they were suspected of being witches. In Cameroon many deaths, even the ones that result from HIV complications, are believed to be caused by witchcraft. One of the most extreme cases of witchcraft violence in recent years comes from the Limpopo Province in South Africa, where between 1994 and 1995 about 200 people accused of being witches were burned to death.[39] It seems to me that the Church in Africa, in addition to its numerous responsibilities at a time of social upheaval, needs to continue to wrestle with the theological implications of witchcraft beliefs, and design responses to the commonly held belief that certain members possess a power that can be deployed against another person, causing that individual injury. Such an inquiry should continue to ask questions about the background of such beliefs, yet offer prospects for a harmonious relationship anchored in mutual respect and reconciliation in cases where the dignity of another person has been violated and has led to broken relationships.

ETHICAL IMPERATIVES ON WITCHCRAFT

African churchmen and women of different backgrounds who have offered suggestions for dealing with the problem of witchcraft have emphasised the view that addressing needs raised by witchcraft ought to be an integral part of pastoral care. This was the central thrust of the work of Jean Masamba ma Mpolo of the Democratic Republic of Congo, as well as of M. Hebga of Cameroon. The charismatic ministry of Zambian Archbishop Emmanuel Milingo focused on ways of healing people from all oppressive forces, including witchcraft.[40] The missiologist Stephen Hayes argues that others have also emphasised the proclamation of the authority of God over all evil forces as a suitable approach. In this regard Bishop Nyasha of the Pentecostal Church in Zimbabwe has argued that God is powerful and can overcome all evil forces. 'All wizards can in fact be cured completely through the mercy and power of the Christian God, irrespective of the degree of their involvement with evil.'[41] The Zionist churches of South Africa regard witchcraft powers as evil, and try to weaken these in their healing ministry.[42] Other churches have used exorcism as a means of dealing with witchcraft powers.[43] Hoeben informs us of a Tanzanian priest who gave a crucifix to a parishioner who claimed to be threatened by *utamaduni*.[44] Yet other responses have called on people to practice love, as a force that can counter the forces of evil.[45]

In his 1976 essay, Loewen pointed out that religious communities ought to consider creating safe spaces, such as 'cities of refuge'. He envisioned these as places where persons who fear to be victims of witchcraft, as well as those accused of practising it, could go for healing. 'The city of refuge not only provides safety from whatever is in the process of overwhelming the individual, it also provides the environment in which the person can become strong enough to expel his 'demons' and ultimately go into the world healed and with a new courage.'[46] Such places might serve a good purpose by removing both the accused, who faces brutality and vigilante actions, and the accusers from the community, and provide shelter for them.

However, there are certain problems associated with this approach. Like the 'witch villages' that exist in northern Ghana, there is they the possibility that such a place might just be a place for the community to dispose itself of members whose presence they consider undesirable. The other set-back with this approach is that while a move to a 'city of refuge' might indeed provide a cooling period, people may not create other ways to deal with the problems involved. The bad feelings about the use of witchcraft, and the possibility that someone whom you know well has tried to apply this force to harm you, do not go away easily. Removing a person to a city of refuge might only postpone an opportunity to deal with the problems of witchcraft and seek reconciliation at the actual time of crisis. Yet, it is worth rethinking the subject in view of certain practices that have long existed in Wimbum culture. For instance, individuals accused of a heinous crime would often escape to the home of their mother. The maternal home served as a kind of refuge and provided shelter. At the same time, in the home of an uncle one had the privilege of consult his diviner and determine whether the accusations were true or false. Maternal uncles also served as intermediaries between the accused and the accusers, as they tried to resolve the dispute.

Hill suggested in her essay that missionaries and the Church as a whole ought to take a new position on witchcraft. In the past most missionaries denied the existence of witchcraft, while others described it as demonic and called for deliverance.[47] Hill suggests a third approach. Missionaries should recognise that witchcraft is a neutral power, and urge people to live a pure life. 'The key message, then, is love thy neighbor, live a pure life, and remove evil in all its forms. Do not give Satan a foothold.'[48] She developed a chart of ten points, in which she contrasts what she calls the 'witchcraft worldview postulate' versus the 'Christian worldview postulate'. This is her scheme:[49]

Witchcraft worldview postulates	Christian worldview postulates
1. A perfect world	1. A fallen world
2. Misfortune must be explained	2. We know we are in God's hands
3. Seeking revenge	3. Trusting God for justice
4. Do not talk about evil	4. Expose darkness
5. Human beings as victims	5. Human beings in control
6. Fear	6. Peace and protection
7. Managing relationships through witchcraft accusations	7. Speaking the truth in love
8. Group equality through jealousy	8. Group equality through love
9. Kindness out of fear	9. Kindness due to love
10. Guilt projection	10. Acceptance of responsibility

While one may agree with Hill that people ought to live a life of love, purity and seek to remove evil, the problem with her approach is that she restricts the argument to a witchcraft versus a Christian worldview. Other perspectives are missing, including that of African indigenous religions and the many rituals of healing and reconciliation that Africans traditionally practice. One could also argue that her scheme ignores what, for lack of a better term, might be called a secular worldview, meaning a worldview that is not grounded in any religious belief, and that may or may not believe in the validity of witchcraft. Even if one accepts her postulation of the witchcraft outlook versus the Christian outlook, there are some critical questions to raise about the positions Hill assigns to each group. One may wonder whether point 4 actually reflects the views of those who believe in witchcraft. Most Africans talk about witchcraft, rather than keeping quiet about it. They may not know all the details, because it is considered a spiritual activity, but they do have some opinion about what they think it is; and where they are in doubt, they will consult a diviner. In general, I find that the contrast depicted in points 6 to 10 more promising, because it presents these contrasting worldviews suggesting that the Christian worldview offers ways through which one could use interpersonal relationships to empower people to deal with problems associated with witchcraft belief.

In an earlier critique of the phenomenon of witchcraft, I have called for a theological response to it on the grounds that witchcraft belief presents a number of ethical issues, regardless of whether one considers it from a religious perspective or not.[50] Witchcraft belief gives rise to a particular discourse, and witchcraft allegations claim that a person has hurt somebody or done something that compromises the well-being of the community. In this regard, the accusations, charges, and counter-charges offer contested perspectives on human relations in the community. They deal with how others perceive what certain people are doing. The emphasis here is on the doing, because people often accuse others of using their alleged power in a purposeful manner with a view to hurting someone else. Central to my approach is that—at least for those who believe in it—witchcraft is something concrete. 'Witchcraft is not simply an imaginative idiom', Jean Comaroff and John Comaroff argue, 'it is chillingly concrete, its micropolitics all-too-real.'[51] However, the procedure to design an ethical path does not call for tacit proof that witchcraft is indeed a reality. What is needed, is a phenomenology of social relations that allows us to understand the multiple dynamics of the language and practice of witchcraft, so that we can raise questions about the negative impact such practices have on other people. As a discourse and a way of configuring the world, witchcraft then reveals ethical dilemmas, because it is alleged that through such practices some people use mystical power for their personal advantage at the expense of other members of the community.

It is possible for theologians to revisit the claims made about witchcraft in different contexts and interrogate the dialogues and texts that scholars have produced from their research to highlight the ethical problems raised by them. The use of spiritual power in ways perceived by the community as negative constitutes an abuse of power and a violation of other people's dignity. In this sense, what is ethically problematic is not the supposed possession of the ability to do the type of things that people claim witches do, but the employment of such power for negative purposes. What religious congregations are thus confronted with, is a claim that someone in the community is abusing power. However, far more critical is that, from a believer's perspective, witches abuse their power by diminishing what in the Christian tradition is known as the *imago Dei*. This is what calls for theological scrutiny.

In light of this, I have argued with reference to Cameroon that the theological motive that is needed to deal with *tfu* is *eros*, understood and stipulated by the French philosopher Emmanuel Levinas as a metaphysical desire.[52] In my view, his philosophical approach holds promise for a cross-cultural ethical discourse that can be applied in Africa as well as other places in the world. However, I must add here that many African Christians who engage in confrontational dialogues and disputes on witchcraft organise their world according to a theology that is not grounded philosophical premises but on the text of the Hebrew Bible and the New Testament. The Bible has played, and continues to play, a key role in the lives of Africans, and is for many an important source of ethics. Any ethical perspective on witchcraft, therefore, must take into consideration a theological perspective that holds the Bible in high regard.

Studies of the reception of the Bible in Malawi, both in the mainline churches and African-initiated churches, demonstrate that Africans read the Bible and preach it regularly. The main emphases in preaching are themes that deal with morality, which is often limited to 'adultery, promiscuity, drunkenness, and theft.'[53] This approach to the biblical text is widespread in Africa today, and I must add that they are important especially at a time when AIDS is killing many people. However, even in cases when witchcraft accusations are rife after the death of an individual, there is often no attempt to address this issue from a theological or biblical perspective. During a recent conversation with Cameroonian pastors, several told me that there is no such thing like witchcraft and that they cannot waste their time talking about it. Some told me that they believe witchcraft exists, but has no power over the 'child of God.' This calls for a new appreciation and a new reading of the Bible in the African context.

READING THE BIBLE TO UNDERSTAND WITCH-CRAFT

Biblical theology in Africa is growing. Following John Mbiti's book *Bible and Theology in African Christianity*,[54] theologians such as Itumeleng Mosala and Gerald West have published a number of scholarly works on the biblical theology and interpretation.[55] Central to recent scholarship is the idea that people read the Bible in context, and that such a context cannot be taken to mean the context of the world of the Bible alone, but also includes the particular context of the reader.[56] There is a growing consensus among African biblical scholars that the Bible should be read as a text which offers a world whose message and meaning confront the readers' world; hence, readers should appropriate its message as a 'fusion of horizons', to borrow Hans Georg Gadamer's familiar phrase.[57] Such a reading brings together the worlds of the biblical text and the African context. To accomplish this, scholars must continue to wrestle with 'a variety of ways that link the biblical text to the African context such that the main focus of interpretation is on the communities that receive the text rather than on those that produced it or on the text itself. . .', as Justin Ukpong states.[58]

A critical, contextual reading of the Bible in Africa is also important in the light of the widespread belief in witchcraft in relation to women. Many women are not only active members of religious communities, but also frequent targets of witchcraft accusations that may result in lynching. African women today challenge conventional readings of the Bible because of their male bias.[59] According to Mercy Oduyoye, women continue to be blamed for causing evil, and Pauline texts on subjection are constantly applied to women since there is no critical engagement with these texts in the African context.[60] She calls for an 'African Testament', which will focus on the lives of African women, who have been taught to love their husbands and honour them. Yet, they live under suspicion and the scourge of a mob that is ready to beat, kill, or exile them if it suspects that they have anything to do with the illness or death of their husbands. Such a Testament will create a text that forces Christian churches to read the Bible from a perspective that promotes justice in the community.

One such story would be that of Nancy Tawong, a wife and mother, and a faithful member of the Baptist Church in the Wimbum area of Cameroon.[61] She was suspected of using *tfu* powers to kill her husband and fellow Baptist Christian of many years, Mr. Peter Tawong. The details of the circumstances of Mr. Tawong's death are terse, but typical, like most of the narratives involving *tfu* accusations. People claimed that he was in good health on June 5 1998, but fell ill the next day. He was transported from his house at the school where he taught as a Baptist teacher to a local Baptist health centre. His condition deteriorated and he was moved to the Baptist hospital, but he died on the way. His body was returned to his home town for burial.

The community was visibly shaken, since Mr. Tawong's death was the fifteenth that had occurred in the village in two weeks' time. Some of the youths of his area, who suspected that something was wrong, told the elders of the village that they should find out who was responsible for his death, before they could bury the deceased. According to reports that circulated in the Wimbum area, the diviners accused four people, including the wife of Mr. Tawong, of being responsible for his death. They further revealed that the suspected individuals were also planning to kill one of the pastors of the area.[62] This prompted the *Fon* (chief) of the area to send runner masks of the *nwarong* society (a regulatory society in the Northwest Province of Cameroon) to the area to exile the suspected people, including Nancy Tawong. She was tortured by the members of the *nwarong* society and the youth who made the accusations, and sent into exile.

If Nancy Tawong were to write her own Testament, this would be her story. Because of fears and unfounded accusations, she was stripped of all she had and sent into exile, back to her parents' home. My contention is that situations like this continue to cry out for a critical understanding of the discourse on witchcraft. Biblical images do not always reflect local situations so clearly; for that reason the text and context of the reader must be studied in a fresh way. Such a study must take into consideration the mental ideas of members of religious communities whom Gerald West calls 'ordinary readers'.[63] They must become new partners in Bible interpretation, since the Bible cannot be read as if the lives of those who are lynched due to witchcraft accusations do not matter.

Reading the Bible in such a manner would not imply a less critical reading of the Bible. In his book *Circles of Dignity*, James Cochrane argues that the African Church should engage in a critical contextual reading of the Christian tradition in a theological practice that stresses social intelligibility rooted in local knowledge.[64] Members who read the Bible together, in community, should be willing to use what Jürgen Habermas has called 'mundane reasoning'.[65] Cochrane developed this perspective of reading the Bible in community on the basis of his long-time intellectual and practical engagement with the Amawoti Base Ecclesial Community in the Kwazulu Natal region of South Africa. Members of this congregation read the Bible in the light of their daily struggle, their worldview, and the socio-political struggles of South Africa in order to gain new ideas on social responsibility.[66] Though not every community needs to follow the same approach, it is likely to open up new ways of understanding biblical texts and their ethical implications.

TOWARDS A NEW ETHICS OF THE WITCHCRAFT PHENOMENON IN AFRICA

In view of the realities posed by witchcraft, the Christian community in Africa—which is growing at an exponential rate—should adopt a new, critical appreciation of the Bible. Such a turn will have profound implications for a new ethics concerning the issue of witchcraft. There are several implications for such a project, and I will only mention a few here.

First, a new critical reading should treat the texts of the Bible as cultural products, which should be studied in light of their historical contexts, as well as the various contexts of Africa. As cultural products, the questions that the Bible addresses cannot be read in isolation from the present culture in Africa. The African worldview thus becomes important to those who seek to appropriate the message of the Bible. My claim in this respect is that African culture, and its belief that certain people possess witchcraft power, cannot and should not be dismissed as devilish. Therefore, Bible-reading should involve a theological *epochè*, which suspends hasty condemnation of beliefs such as witchcraft. For example, the Wimbum people belief that possessing special powers to see what witches do is not bad. If a person has such powers and uses it to bring good things to the community, no one would complain about the use of them. It is therefore important that a new reading of the Bible and the proposed theological *epochè* advance a new appreciation for the logic of witchcraft, which offers contested ideological premises in a vast world of power and influence. This does not mean that African churches should share the ideological landscape that witchcraft beliefs offer. It simply means that religious communities must find creative ways of dealing with witchcraft accusations. Reading the Bible with such views in mind could be the beginning of a new understanding of the phenomenon of witchcraft.

The approach I am suggesting is important for a number of reasons. It takes the reader of the Bible out of the quagmire and futile debate concerning the rationality or believability of witchcraft beliefs. It recognises those beliefs as contested ideals and tools that individuals and communities use to make sense of the real world. Furthermore, it avoids the slippery path to the demonisation of individuals, and opens up the opportunity for raising questions about the usefulness of the witchcraft ideology to both the individual and the community. Since witchcraft accusations are often contested, there is at least some common ground, in that members of the community often find the ideology of witchcraft problematic. I must emphasise that much of the Christian literature that articulates the belief that witchcraft exists, does not observe the theological *epochè* that I am calling for, because the authors are convinced that the practice originates from the devil. To give one example, Sam Erivwo declares:[67]

> '... Christians ought to recognise that there is witch-craft, and that it is both a subjective and objective reality emanating from the devil; but having recognised this, like Paul when combating the Colossian error, they must proclaim the pre-eminence and uniqueness of Christ. His all-embracing love is able to draw all 'men' to himself, and his infinite power can liberate all held in the bondage of sin and Satan. This should be driven home into the hearts of all men, accused of witchcraft or not.'

It is precisely this approach that I contest, because its proposed path to deliverance might ignore aspects of the discourse on witchcraft, which a large section of the African community is not willing to concede as emanating from the devil. Africans must look beyond the literature of demonisation to include perspectives that argue that, when referring to 'witchcraft', individuals and communities deal with a complex system of thought that conceptualises and categorises social arrangements and strategies of interaction in a variety of ways, which cannot be summarily ascribed to the devil. In this respect, Hoeben was correct when he asserted: 'it must be recognised that witchcraft belief is part and parcel of a fundamental outlook on, and a basic option about, life in the world and in society. It is not just an ugly excrescence that can be excised without jeopardizing the whole. Remove witch-craft, and a substantially sound edifice could crumble.'[68]

It is therefore important that, in reading passages in the Bible that deal with witchcraft, readers keep in mind the various African outlooks on *tfu* and *kindoki* etc., which describe the phenomenon in terms of a conflictual relationship. This may then allow members of the community to focus on interpersonal relations. One way to do so would be to carry on a dialogue that offers members of a community an opportunity to enquire about the question why certain persons think or believe they need witchcraft power. Furthermore, these members can then also engage in a critical dialogue about the alleged uses of witchcraft powers in view of present circumstances in the modern world. This is important because people claim that some persons employ witchcraft power for their personal gain, while others use them for the benefit of the community. Reading the Bible in community invites the readers to reconsider biblical claims about how to relate to others and live like neighbours—a biblical concept that does not always refer to proximity. This might reveal to the readers that while cultivating vertical relations with the divine may be important, cultivating horizontal relations with other community members is equally important. To recognise this, and act accordingly, means to take an ethical stance that provides one with the strength to relate to others in a way that does not require the use of excessive hidden power.

A second *epochè* calls for reading biblical texts that address witchcraft powers but suspend judgement on what should happen to supposed witches. Instead, such reading should focus on creative ways of understanding the concept of witchcraft and its various meanings in different African communities. What is needed here is for members of local Christian communities to study the Bible together and reflect on texts that discuss witchcraft and witches with an open mind. Since such a reading would take into consideration the present circumstances and the understanding that the reader brings to the message of the text, it could provoke debate and discussion on the different meanings of witchcraft.

A third step in contextual Bible-reading calls for a critical appropriation of biblical teachings that emphasise certain themes, dispositions and ways of relating to one another. This calls for the practice of certain dispositions that reflect what we may call, after Fabien Eboussi-Boulaga, the Christic model, or, in the language of St Paul, 'the mind of Christ'.[69] This has several implications, and I will only highlight here a few theological motives that are relevant to the ethical problems posed by witchcraft, namely hospitality, love, freedom, and reconciliation. I will explore these ideas briefly below.

Hospitality is an important New Testament motive that has not been explored as well as it should, even though it has a strong grounding in African thought. The New Testament exhorts hospitality to strangers—to be read as another person, someone different. In their work on narrative theology, Joseph Healey and Donald Sybertz have explored African aspects of hospitality.[70] They argue that the Eucharist symbolises the presence of Christ, offering an inclusive spirit of celebration and sharing. They argue that the Luyia (Kenya) proverb, 'friendship is in the stomach, and you should prepare food for a person even if the person pretends not to be hungry', indicates hospitality and calls for a 'guest christology' or a 'theology of welcoming'.[71] The idea of hospitality, they argue, invites people to address the issue of discrimination.

Witchcraft often involves discrimination against the person designated as a witch, who is regarded by members of the community as an anti-social individual. However, a much greater problem is the claim that these anti-social individuals use their powers to force others to comply with their wishes and, when they cannot compel them, may kill them and consume their flesh. The problem here is 'totalisation'. Witchcraft powers can be used to totalise and neutralise difference. Hospitality to the other person, on the other hand, is an invitation to recognise and respect difference. Practising hospitality requires an open spirit towards other people. The practice of hospitality affirms their freedom to live and act independently of all forces that might be used to control them. In family relations, it means that people cannot use witchcraft to compel family members to share their wealth with those who have no means, as is often claimed witches do.

Hospitality involves more than providing food and clothing to those in need. It involves a radical 'de-centering' in the face of the 'other' who may be part of the community but yet remains a distinct individual. Hospitality in a general sense involves the cultivation of openness towards others, resisting the temptation to assume the worst, such as suggesting that they are successful because they are witches. Furthermore, such hospitality avoids false accusations, for which there might be no other basis than the fear of others. However, people who believe that witchcraft exist may argue that one cannot always be sure that witchcraft claims are not true. In that case, we may extend our understanding of hospitality further by insisting that being hospitable also implies being generous and resisting the temptation to use witchcraft powers in a negative manner. In this respect, where such power is believed to exist even in abundance, a new hospitality should involve the attitude that St Paul encouraged to the churches of Galatia, admonishing the communities to serve one another and bear each other's burdens.[72]

This is important for the Church in Africa, because the discourse on witchcraft implies accusations of neglect and abandonment. In the 1980s, in Ntumbaw village in the Northwest Province of Cameroon, a sub-chief had been accused of causing the illness of an elite member of his extended family. He did not refuse the charge, nor did he accept that he was guilty. His only answer was that he had wanted his relative to buy him a vehicle. In other words, he wanted to be served by this elite member of his family. No doubt there would have been much better ways for this relative to serve him other than by buying him a car, but this was his desire. In such cases, the Church could work with people to help define their needs, in such a way that others can be of service in meeting those needs.

Secondly, the Church in Africa ought to continue teaching a biblical theology of love, as a way of combatting the difficulties imposed by alleged witchcraft practices. One text that communities can ponder seriously in this regard, is what many refer to as the distinguishing mark of membership in the Christian community. In the gospel of John, the apostle recalls the following words of Jesus to his disciples: 'A new commandment I give you, love one another. As I have loved you, so you must love one another. . . All men [sic] will know that you are my disciples if you love one another'.[73] For a Christian community that claims to follow the example of Jesus, this is an important commission, because Jesus himself commanded it. It is the only way in which members of a Christian community can demonstrate to the world that they are followers of Jesus. At a time when suspicion continues to grow and fears abound that people are using witchcraft, the Christian community needs to return to such texts and seek to understand the teaching of love, so that they can urge their members to desist from acts of violence when faced with witchcraft accusations.

Thirdly, the African Church ought to recover the idea of freedom. Following the New Testament, the Christian tradition proclaims that one of the basic ingredients of salvation is freedom. The idea of freedom is the basic message of the gospel, because it is believed that the Son of God sets people free. This is not to suggest that in the quest for such freedom one should resort to the language and discourse of witchcraft and the occult to demonise other people or claim that they are eradicating the devil in order to free them. It is much more subtle than that, especially if we think of freedom at a personal level. I have suggested above that, from the perspective of those who believe in it, witchcraft involves certain actions that are undertaken after careful deliberation. Since this involves reflection, making choices and setting goals, it is important to underscore here that one way of understanding freedom is that a person also has the freedom to choose *not* to do certain things. In other words, to be free in a Christian sense is not only to be free from sin or from the control of external forces, but also to be free from one's own negative ambitions that do not promote the good within the community.

Finally, the Church in Africa ought to recover the horizontal dimension of liberation and reconciliation. According to St Paul, a person is reconciled to God through Jesus Christ. However, this reconciliation is not restricted to the vertical relationship with God in the divine-human encounter. It also involves establishing horizontal relations among people here on earth, who, according to St Paul, are part of one community by virtue of the faith they share in Christ. J. Christian Beker has argued that this social message includes liberation, justification, and reconciliation.[74] The idea of liberation in the letters of St Paul does not only mean liberation from sin, but also liberation from principalities and powers. Anyone who makes a commitment to Christ, from Paul's understanding, is liberated from *all* forces that might establish control over an individual. Such an approach does not deny that those forces exist; it simply emphasises that those who have taken that faith stance have agreed to be subject to a new authority, with other forces having no control over them. Liberation, then, is also liberation from forces that are believed to exercise an undue influence over the individual, such as witchcraft powers. The New

Testament also encourages Christians to restore broken relations with one another. There are many families in Wimbum land of the Northwest Province of Cameroon that have gone through separation because of witchcraft accusations. A dialogue that promotes hospitality, love, and freedom could be instrumental in reconciling these families.

CONCLUSION

I have argued in this chapter that studies of witchcraft in Africa continue to emphasise that the idea of witchcraft reflects a complex thought system which involves ways of dealing with uncertainties and misfortune in the concrete world. I have also indicated that while many people in African communities have no problems accepting the logic of witchcraft, some people in the Christian tradition have not always acknowledged the phenomenon, or where they have accepted it, have dismissed it as the work of the devil. During the 1970s and 1980s, a number of African theologians addressed problems associated with witchcraft, but there is still a need for the Christian Church in Africa to rethink their approach to the issue of witchcraft. In order to do this, the Church, which has been influenced greatly by the text of the Hebrew Bible and the New Testament, ought to begin reading these texts together in the local communities as they struggle to figure out how to enable members of their communities to deal with witchcraft-related problems. I have argued that such a reading of the Bible in the community will offer an opportunity to emphasise hospitality, love, and reconciliation. I do not presume that these ideas would work in non-Christian contexts. Even within the Christian context, each community must develop its own ethics and theological understanding of problems posed by witchcraft.

Notes

* I am thankful to Gerrie ter Haar for reading the original draft and giving me critical feedback.
1. See Elias Kifon Bongmba, *African Witchcraft and Otherness: A philosophical and theological critique of intersubjective relations,*

Albany: SUNY Press, 2001. See also Ibid., 'Toward a hermeneutics of Wimbus *tfu*', *African Studies Review*, vol. 41, nr. 3, pp. 165-91.

2. Edward E. Evans-Pritchard, *The Zande Trickster*, Oxford: Clarendon Press, 1967, p. 12.

3. For recent work on the social dynamics of witchcraft, see Peter Geschiere, *The Modernity of Witchcraft: Politics and the occult in postcolonial Africa*, Charlottesville: University Press of Virginia, 1997; for works that address gender issues, see Diane Lyons, 'Witchcraft, gender, power, and intimate relations in Mura compounds in Dela, Northern Cameroon', *World Archeology*, vol. 29, nr. 3, 1998, pp. 344-62; Mark Auslander,'"Open the wombs!" The symbolic politics of modern Ngoni witchfinding', in Jean Comaroff and John Comaroff (eds), *Modernity and its Malcontents: Ritual and power in postcolonial Africa*, University of Chicago Press, 1993, pp. 167-92; Pamela Schmoll, 'Black stomachs, beautiful stones: soul-eating among Hausa in Niger', in Ibid., pp. 193-220. For religious perspectives, see John Mburu, 'Witchcraft among the Wimbum', BA thesis, Regional Major Seminary, Bambui, Cameroon, 1979; Jean Masamba ma Mpolo, *La libération des envoûtés*, Yaounde: Éditions CLE, 1976; Ibid., 'Psychotherapeutic Dynamics in African Bewitched Patients: Towards a multi-dimensional therapy in social psychiatry', Th.D. diss., The School of Theology at Claremont, 1975.

4. Elias K. Bongmba, *African Witchcraft and Otherness*. See also Ibid., 'African witchcraft: from ethnography to critique', in George Clement Bond and Diane M. Ciekawy (eds), *Witchcraft Dialogues: Anthropological and philosophical exchanges*, Athens: Ohio University Press, 2001, pp. 39-79.

5. Bongmba, *African Witchcraft and Otherness*.

6. See Michael Jackson, 'Thinking through the body', *Social Analysis*, vol. 14, 1983, pp. 127-49.

7. Edward E. Evans-Pritchard, *Social Anthropology and Other Essays*, New York: Free Press, 1962, pp. 330 ff.

8. Ibid.

9. Lyons, 'Witchcraft, gender, power', pp. 344-5.

10. See Leny Lagerwerf, 'Witchcraft, Sorcery, and Spirit Possession: Pastoral responses in Africa', *Exchange*, vol. XIV, nr. 41, 1985, pp. 1-2.

11. Meinrad P. Hebga, *Sorcellerie: chimère dangereuse?*, Abidjan: Inades, 1979.

12. Lagerwerf, 'Witchcraft, Sorcery, and Spirit Possession', p. 3.

13. Norman Cohn, *Europe's Inner Demons: An inquiry inspired by the great witch-hunt*, London: Sussex University Press, 1975; William Charles, *Witchcraft*, New York: Meridian, 1959; Ronald Hutton, *The Pagan Religions of the Ancient British Isles*, London: Blackwell, 1991; Charles Stewart, *Demons and the Devil*, Princeton, NJ: Princeton University Press, 1991.

14. Gerhardus C. Oosthuizen, *The Healer-Prophet in Afro-Christian Churches*, Leiden: E.J. Brill, 1992, p. 18.

15. 1 Samuel 28.

16. Some Europeans thought that the introduction of electric lights would dispel fears of witchcraft.

17. Sam U. Erivwo, 'Christian attitude to witchcraft', *AFER*, nr. 17, 1975, pp. 23-31.

18. Oosthuizen, *The Healer-Prophet*, p. 120.

19. See the discussion by Adrian Hastings, *The Church in Africa, 1450-1950*, Oxford: Clarendon Press, 1994, pp. 313-7; See also some missionary writings, including R. Moffat, *Missionary Labours and Scenes in southern Africa*, 1842, p. 305, quoted in Hastings, p. 314.

20. See James McCord, *My Patients Were Zulus*, New York: Rinehart, 1951.

21. Marthinus L. Daneel, *African Earthkeepers*. Vol 2: *Environmental Mission and Liberation in Christian Perspective*, Pretoria: University of South Africa Press, 1999, pp. 99-100.

22. Harriet Hill, 'Witchcraft and the gospel: insights from Africa', *Missiology*, vol. 24, nr. 3, 1996, pp. 323-44.

23. Ibid. p. 325.

24. Jacob A. Loewen, 'Mission churches, independent churches and felt needs in Africa', *Missiology*, vol. 4 nr. 4, 1976, p. 406.

25. See Mathew Schoffeleers, 'Christ as the medicine-man and the medicine-man as Christ: a tentative history of African christological thought', *Man and Life*, vol. 8, nr. 1/2, 1982, pp. 11-28. See also Aylward Shorter, 'Folk Christianity and functional christology', *AFER*, vol. 24, nr. 3, 1982, pp. 133-67. Ibid., *Jesus and the Witchdoctor: An approach to healing and wholeness*, Maryknoll, NY: Orbis Books, 1985.

26. Eric de Rosny, *L' Afrique des guérisons*, Paris: Karthala, 1992; see also *Healers in the Night*, Maryknoll, NY: Orbis Books, 1985.

27. M. P. Hebga, *Sorcellerie*, pp. 219 and 251.

28. See Mpolo, 'Psychotherapeutic Dynamics in African Bewitched Patients'.

29. Ibid, *La libération des envoûtés*. See also his numerous publications on the subject, including *Pastoral Care and Counselling in Africa Today* (ed. with Daisy Nwachuku), Frankfurt/M: Peter Lang, 1991; *The Risks of Growth: Counselling and pastoral theology in the African context* (ed. with Wilhelmina Kalu), Geneva: WCC, 1985.

30. In the present essay I use the terminology African Initiated Churches to refer to religious independency in African Christianity.

31. Stephen Hayes has argued: 'It was the Zionists who re-contextualized the Christian message for a pre-Enlightenment culture in which witchcraft and sorcery are part of the prevalent world view'. See Stephen Hayes, 'Christian responses to witchcraft and sorcery', *Missionalia*, vol. 23, nr. 3, 1995, pp. 339-54, notably p. 34.

32. Oosthuizen, *The Healer-Prophet*, p. 19. Oosthuizen argues that the prophet deals with spiritual as well as physical healing. Many of the Zionists who responded to witchcraft as a need that ought to be met also stayed away from 'traditional medicine' and emphasised instead healing through prayers. See James P. Kiernan, 'The role of the adversary in Zulu Zionist Churches', *Religion in southern Africa*, vol. 8, nr. 1, 1987, pp. 3-14; also B.M.G. Sundkler, *Bantu Prophets in South Africa*, London: Oxford University Press, 1961, p. 226.

33. Ibid., p. 33.

34. Ibid, p. 117.

35. See Geschiere, *The Modernity of Witchcraft;* Stephen Ellis and Gerrie ter Haar, 'Religion and politics in sub-Saharan Africa', *Journal of Modern African Studies*, vol. 36, nr. 2, 1998, pp. 175-201.

36. See the many writings of M. Hebga, including *Croyance et guérison,* Yaounde: Éditions CLE, 1973; *Émancipation d'églises sous tutelle,* Paris: Présence Africaine, 1976; 'Sorcellerie et maladie en Afrique noire: jalons pour un approche catéchétique et pastorale', *Telema*, vol. 8, nr. 32, 1982, pp. 5-48; *Sorcellerie et prière de délivrance,* Paris/Abidjan: Presence Africaine/Inades, 1982.

37. H. Hoeben, 'Who is who in African witchcraft?', *Pro Mundi Vita Dossiers*, 1980, p. 2.

38. Ibid., pp. 2-3.

39. Hayes, 'Christian responses to witchcraft and sorcery', p. 1 in the online version. See also S. T. Kgatla et al., *Crossing Witchcraft Barriers in South Africa*, 2003.

40. For a discussion of Archbishop Milingo's work, see E. Milingo, *The World In-Between: Christian healing and the struggle for spiritual survival* (edited with introduction, commentary and epilogue by Mona Macmillan), London: Hurst& Co./Maryknoll, NY: Orbis Books, 1984; Gerrie ter Haar, *Spirit of Africa: The healing ministry of Archbishop Milingo of Zambia*, London: Hurst & Co./Trenton, NJ: Africa World Press, 1992.

41. Quoted by Hayes, 'Christian responses', p. 11. See also M. L. Daneel, 'Exorcism as a means of combating wizardry: liberation or enslavement?', *Missionalia*, vol. 18, nr. 1, 1990, at p. 238.

42. Kiernan, 'The role of the adversary in Zulu Zionist Churches', p. 11.

43. Daneel, 'Exorcism as a means of combating wizardry', pp. 220-47.

44. Hoeben, 'Who is who in African witchcraft?', p. 13.

45. See Luakale Mukundi Mubengayi, 'La sorcellerie: problème et fléau', *Telema*, vol. 9, nr. 34, 1983, pp. 19-24 (Reference originally in Lagerwerf, 'Witchcraft, sorcery, and spirit possession', p. 79).

46. Loewen, 'Mission churches, independent churches and felt needs', p. 416.

47. Hill, 'Witchcraft and the gospel', p. 337.

48. Ibid.

49. Taken from Hill, 'Witchcraft and the gospel', pp. 338-40.

50. See Bongmba, 'African witchcraft'.

51. Comaroff and Comaroff, *Modernity and Its Malcontents*, p. xxvii.

52. Emmanuel Levinas, *Totality and Infinity: An essay on exteriority*, Pittsburgh, Penn: Duquesne University Press, 1969. Ibid., *Time and the Other*, Pittsburgh, Penn: Duquesne University Press, 1987.

53. Hilary B.P. Mijoga, 'The Bible in Malawi: a brief survey of its impact on society', in Gerald O. West and Musa W. Dube (eds), *The Bible in Africa: Transactions, trajectories, and trends*, Leiden: Brill, 2001, at pp. 378-9.

54. John S. Mbiti, *Bible and Theology in African Christianity*, Nairobi: Oxford University Press, 1986.

55. Itumeleng J. Mosala, *Biblical Hermeneutics and Black Theology in southern Africa*, Grand Rapids: W. B. Eerdmans, 1989; Gerald West, *Biblical Hermeneutics of Liberation: Modes of reading the Bible in the South African context*, Maryknoll, NY: Orbis Books, 1995.

56. See West and Dube, *The Bible in Africa*; Vincent L. Wimbush, *African Americans and the Bible: Sacred texts and social textures*, New York: Continuum, 2000.

57. Hans Georg Gadamer, *Truth and Method*, New York: Crossroad, 1989, p. 306; see also Anthony C. Thiselton, *The Two Horizons: New Testament hermeneutics and philosophical description*, Grand Rapids: W. B. Eerdmans, 1980; Ibid., *New Horizons in Hermeneutics: The theory and practice of transforming biblical reading*, Grand Rapids: Zondervan, 1992.

58. Justin S. Ukpong, 'Developments in biblical interpretation in Africa: historical and hermeneutical directions', in West and Dube, *The Bible in Africa*, pp. 11-28, notably p. 11.

59. Mercy Amba Oduyoye, *Daughters of Anowa: African women and patriarchy*, Maryknoll, NY: Orbis Books, 1995.

60. Ibid., pp. 189-90.

61. The names I have used in this account are not people's actual names.

62. My informants in the Wimbum area did not know the identity of that pastor.

63. West, *Biblical Hermeneutics*.

64. James R. Cochrane, *Circles of Dignity: Community wisdom and theological reflection*, Minneapolis: Fortress Press, 1999.

65. Ibid. at p. 127. See Jürgen Habermas, *The Theory of Communicative Action: Reason and rationalization of society*, vol. 1, Boston: Beacon Press, 1984.

66. Cochrane, *Circles of Dignity*, p. 128.

67. Erivwo, 'Christian attitude to witchcraft', p. 31.

68. Hoeben, 'Who is who in African witchcraft?', p. 31.

69. Fabien Eboussi-Boulaga, *Christianity Without Fetishes: An African critique and recapture of Christianity*, Maryknoll, NY: Orbis Books, 1981.

70. Joseph Healey and Donald Sybertz, *Towards an African Narrative Theology*, Maryknoll, NY: Orbis Books, 1996.

71. Ibid., p. 133.

72. Galatians 5:13 and 6:10.

73. John 13:34-5.

74. J. Christian Beker, *Paul the Apostle: The triumph of God in life and thought*, Philadelphia: Fortress Press, 1980, p. 259.

7

ANGER AS A METAPHOR OF WITCH-CRAFT: THE RELATION BETWEEN MAGIC, WITCHCRAFT AND DIVI-NATION AMONG THE MUPUN OF NIGERIA*

Umar Habila Dadem Danfulani

INTRODUCTION

This paper is as much about *sot* witchcraft as it is about *dor* anger. Among Mupun people of the Jos Plateau in the Middle Belt of Nigeria *sot* witchcraft is a real threat to individuals and society at large. For the Mupun, the danger of *dor* anger is not as great as that of wilful *sot* witchcraft in terms of the deliberate intention to wreck havoc on the lives of individuals and the community. However, the injury *dor* anger is believed to unwittingly render on its victims is considered equally lethal as that wrought by *sot-mo* witches.

In the following, I use three case studies to illustrate the consequences of *dor* anger on its victims. These cases were collected during fieldwork from Mupun diviners and are used to examine and compare Mupun concepts of both *sot* witchcraft and *dor* anger. I have come to the conclusion that anger and witchcraft in Mupun belief cause similar pains to their victims, with the slight difference that *sot* witchcraft is believed to do so deliberately and on a wider scale than *dor* anger.

I will start by providing background information on the Mupun as a people, including their location, language family group and brief history. I then describe Mupun cosmology, establishing the place of mystical forces—particularly the belief in magic, witchcraft and divination—within their worldview. I then give an analysis of how the Mupun traditionally try to demystify mystical forces, even including concepts they consider dangerous, such as *sot* witchcraft. The ambivalent roles of *dor* anger and *sot* witchcraft are then examined, followed by the role of divination in revealing witchcraft. I then discuss the consequences of *dor* anger, and the role of rites of confession as a form of healing in *Pa* divination, by reversing *dor* anger and preserving the life of the self-confessed *sot* witch.

THE MUPUN

The Mupun ethnic group is one among more than a dozen Chadic-speaking ethnic groups living in the eastern part of the Jos Plateau in Central Nigeria. The Jos Plateau is home to many ethnic groups varying in numbers of more or less 500,000, occupying small areas often centered around rocky defensible sites, preserving their own languages and dialects, shrines and festivals, and a fascinating variety of houses, implements, ritual equipment and decorative clothing.[1] The Jos Plateau is situated approximately in the centre of Nigeria, forming a hydrographic centre for northern Nigeria. Though within the tropics, the Jos Plateau has the most temperate climate in Nigeria due to its height above sea level. Standing at an average height of 1220 metres (circa 4000 ft) with peaks reaching 1766 (5829 feet), it enjoys a moderate and pleasant climate throughout the year.[2]

In the Jos Plateau region, languages from two of Africa's major language families meet. These are the Niger-Congo and the Afro-Asiatic language families.[3] The sub-family of the Afro-Asiatic language spoken on the Jos Plateau is Chadic. The Hausa language cluster of northern Nigeria belongs to this group too. The immediate neighbours of the Mupun include the Mwaghavul, who live to their immediate north and the Miship, who are found to the south. The Ngas, Fier, Tambes, Gung (Ngung) and Kor are located to the east, and the Kofyar group of Jipal and Chakfem, both members of the Chadic-speaking family, are found to their west. The Mupun and their neighbours form a single continuum with numerous other Chadic-speaking ethnic groups stretching eastwards to the Chad-Borno basin. In the 1980s, the Mupun numbered circa 500,000, a great increase on the 1963 census figures.[4]

MUPUN WORLDVIEW, MYSTICAL FORCES AND DIVI-NATION

Mupun traditional religion came into contact with Christianity, which has now eroded virtually most of it, from the 1920s. The first Christian missionary outpost was established in Mupun land as recently as 1935. This means we can study Mupun traditional religious ways of life with more precision than is the case with ethnic groups that have been in contact with monotheistic religions for a much longer time. I therefore set the time-frame for the discussion in this article at a period in Mupun history from 1935—when Christianity was established in Mupun land—to the early 1970s, a period when the agents of change were becoming too strong for the traditional structures to bear.

Mupun traditional religion divides the world into three sections, the visible *terra firma,* which they call *yil gurum* —the human world; the invisible or unseen world which they call *yil nji*—the spirit world or literally the land of the ancestors;[5] and a third world, which is the world of mystical forces. With the exception of what is known as *baak ka* magic, mystical forces are conceived according to their utility, that is whether they are seen as positive or negative agents. This duality depends on who is handling or feeling the impact of the particular mystical force being manipulated. Further, negativity or positivity here is highly dependable on the question whether a mystical force possesses ambivalent characteristics or not. *Baak ka* magic, as I will show, is considered a neutral force, which possesses ambivalent characteristics enabling it to be used either for good or for evil.

Basically, believed mystical forces and the experts that control them—such as magic and magicians, the art of rain-making and rain-makers, medicine and medicine-men and women, witchcraft and witches, sorcery and sorcerers—are supposed to help *gurum-mo*, human beings, to relate with the spirit world in positive, negative or neutral ways. They are the media of interaction and channels of communication between *yil nji*, the spirit world, and *yil gurum*, the world of human beings. *Yil gurum*, solid earth, is populated by human beings, animals, plants and mineral life. The invisible world forms their spiritual realm and is populated by a horde of invisible spirits. The most important of these spirit beings that live in *yil gurum*, close to human beings, are the *Kum-mo* deities and *nji-mo* ancestors who live inside the ground. Other important spirit beings include *Naan* Mother, the supreme deity (God), *riin-mo*, wandering free spirits or *jinns*, and *shon-mo*, ghosts.

Yil, the earth (world) that is populated by *gurum-mo* (human beings), *luwa-mo* (animals), *shitmo ki kompe-mo* (plants) and *mbi-mo* (mineral organisms) is conceived as a flat disc with two sides suspended in the universe. A Mupun picture of the world therefore spans in two opposite directions. Firstly, the abode of *Naan* Mother, the creator deity, which is located somewhere in the sky (beyond eye level). Secondly, *yil nji*, the land of the ancestors is located somewhere inside the ground, which is in the opposite direction from that of *Naan* Mother deity. By implication, the ancestors are believed to occupy the other side of the flat disc, which is the exact replica of the human side of the world. *Kum-mo* deities live with human beings on earth and serve as the channel of communication between *Naan* Mother and *gurum-mo* human beings.

The *Kum-mo* deities, the *riin-mo* free spirits and *shon-mo* ghostly spirits roam freely between the sky and the earth, being at home on mountains, out-crop rocks, in the air, in caves, groves, streams, lakes, ponds and trees. The physical human world is different only in theory from the invisible spiritual realm of the ancestors, but in practice one is a continuation of the other. Hence, when an old man or woman is about to die, the person may say, 'I am going home'. When an old person dies, people very often remark, '*war/wur ki yo wa* ', 's/he has gone home'. But if a baby dies, they usually exclaim, '*nih ki ba nber (nbir)*', 'it has gone back'; and in the case of an adult, '*wur kih wen* ', 'he has gone (disappeared)', or '*war do set nber*', 'she went away yesterday'.

The Mupun hold that all beings in their universe, at least in their capacity as mediators, possess the potential of initiating, increasing and enhancing the health, welfare and progress of *gurum-mo* (human beings), who are the most important occupants of the cosmos, together with their life-giving environment. They equally possess the quality and capacity to cause and afflict the human world with diseases, epidemics and other catastrophes, both on individuals and the community. It is such anomalies that the Mupun refer to as *mu'ut*, ill-health, which is exactly the same word used for death. Thus for the Mupun, any abnormal situation in society, whether it affects an individual or the whole community, an animate or an inanimate object, is referred to as *mu'ut*, ill-health, since it is capable of diminishing strength, vibrant life-force and causing death. *Sot* witchcraft is believed to be one such agent that is capable of frustrating or constituting a threat to health and well-being.

THE PLACE OF WITCHCRAFT WITHIN THE REALM OF MYSTICAL FORCES

The Mupun of the Jos Plateau recognise the existence of a number of mysterious forces in their cosmos, and *sot* witchcraft is one of them. The existence of these forces is known to all, and they are exploited by religious specialists and the whole community to achieve variant goals and in varying degrees. These forces are categorised into positive, ambivalent, and negative forces, with rather blurry dividing lines between them. Though the lines of demarcation are thin, Mupun people clearly know and differentiate between them.

The positive elements of the mystical world consist of *yen* (medicines) and the knowledge of their application in treatment and therapy, and *ya fwan* (lit. 'catching rain') and the art of rain-making. *Zari*, outstanding wisdom and supernatural knowledge, and *jyom* (lit. long jaw), a gift that is exhibited in the display of a sharp mind, presentiment, foreknowledge, intuitive knowledge, prophecy and revelation of secrets, all form part of positive aspects of the Mupun mystical world. Other mystical forces include *kos pa*, the casting of divination pebbles, and numerous other types of *pa* mantic practices, *baak ka* (lit. 'to split one's head') magic and *sot* witchcraft, which are all considered ambivalent. However, the type of mystical forces that play completely negative roles are found in the practice of *lom* (lit. 'leprosy') sorcery and *fwo tom* (lit. 'spilling blood'), the evil eye. Males and females can possess any of these mystical and spiritual gifts, except the gift of *kos pa*, a professional knowledge of how to cast the divination pebbles and other forms of mantic practices, and the arduous task of preparing *lom*, that is sorcerous substances. Elsewhere I have made the point that although *Pa* divination is open to every male, the gift is usually only pursued professionally by a few, who usually go on to become household heads or political heads and therefore chief priests of their respective extended families.[6] As for sorcerous substances, women may apply these only as accomplices of their husbands or male counterparts who own them and sanction their application by women.

BAAK KA MAGIC

Dhavamony's definition and taxonomy of magic tends to agree with Mupun belief concerning the category of mystical forces referred to as *baak ka*. Dhavamony asserts that,

> Magic is a belief and practice according to which men are convinced that they may directly affect natural powers and each other among themselves either for good or for evil by their own efforts in manipulating the superior powers. Those who possess the necessary secrets can know the unseen powers that govern the world and hence control these powers in the interest of the operator.[7]

Dhavamony discerns three forms of magic – productive, protective and destructive. The Mupun add a fourth type – *yen ndaat* entertaining magic. The Mupun concept of magic *baak ka* means 'to split or splitting one's head', and the magician is known as the *ngu baak ka*, 'one who has split his head'. The secrets of magic amongst Mupun people are usually controlled by separate extended families because of the role of magic in handling crisis situations. Such crisis periods include the appearance of a *shon* (ghost) in the village, an attack by locusts, the appearance of certain species of caterpillars that attack crops on the farm, drought and epidemics. It is also interesting to note that the onset of such a crisis is usually associated with a witchcraft attack on the community.

The potency and efficacy of *baak ka* magic rites reside in the ability of the magician to strictly observe certain food, sex, and other such *waar* (taboos), and the correct recitation of certain words or spells, accompanied by some ritual acts or formulae and *yen* medicine. The latter are composed of *waar*, the taboos that the *ngu baak ka* must observe— and the mystical objects he normally uses. They also include the acts he normally performs—the magical rites and the words he speaks—the magical spells. All these are usually accompanied by other traditions, which differ depending on the type of magic being performed.[8] The Mupun use *baak ka* to assert control over nature, by manipulating supernatural powers believed to pervade the universe either for good or evil.[9] Thus the strongest differentiating characteristic of *baak ka* is its neutral nature, unlike *lom* sorcery which is considered wholly evil, and *sot* witchcraft which is believed to contain a great deal of evil. As part of *baak ka* magic, *lom* sorcery, which involves the magical and anti-sociable application of poisonous substances that are injurious to human health, negates the purpose of *yen* medicine. *Yen* medicine is believed to possess a positively portent and orderly character, demonstrated in effecting healing. Thus there is a sense in which *lom* sorcery may be referred to as the manipulative use of knowledge of *yen* medicine and *baak ka* magic. Though the Mupun use magic for entertainment as exhibited in the cult of *yen ndaat*, which can be found, for example, in Akong Village of the Jipari section of Mupunland, its primary purpose is set more towards the production of abundance, and to the promotion and protection of the well-being of society. Hence, *baak ka* magic is employed in *ya kapwan/shon*, ghost-hunting, and in *ya sot*, witch-hunting. It is also needed in the acquisition of useful skills, such as physical macho strength needed for farming, or the strength to carry milling or grinding-stones for women, for the hunting of animals at a time of paucity of game, or for travelling long distances within a short period, as well as drumming skills among others. Moreover magical means are used in combination with medicines to render hunters and warriors invisible in the bush, and in rites of *ba ndaas*, 'which bring warriors killed in battle back to life', and generally for protection against danger.

ZARI OUTSTANDING WISDOM AND *JYOM* FORE-KNOWLEDGE AND THE GIFT OF PROPHECY

Among the Mupun, certain individuals are believed to possess positive intuitive powers, the gift of prophecy, presentiment, foreknowledge or great wisdom. Such persons, usually both male and female, are categorised differently. The owner of *zari* (lit. meaning 'obscure') is usually male and considered to possess outstanding wisdom and exceeding intelligence, the equivalent of a genius. Such knowledgeable and wise persons are only found in a few clans, some of them are *deskom*, extended family heads. The owner of *zari* is usually a *mishkom* (lit. 'the man who does not feel/show pain'), the first among warriors (brave males), a priest chief with his *kum lu* compound deity and *Pa* divination pebbles. However, the office of chief does not make him *nguzari*, the owner of *zari*, unless he possesses the qualities described above; moreover, *zari* is also found among commoners. The owner of *zari* uses his qualities to lead justly. Among Mupun people, the signs of *zari* qualities of outstanding wisdom and exceeding knowledge in a young man show that he has been chosen and destined by the ancestors and the deities for a life of greatness and bravery, and a lifestyle that will make him a popular leader among his people. This is important among a people who possess no central government and pride themselves on the importance of freedom, justice and fair play, to the extent that the position of *mishkom*, priest-chief, the highest political office that translates as clan head, was never an enviable one. Prospective candidates, therefore, had to be forced into accepting the office after the demise of a ruling priest-chief.

There are also those believed to possess *jyom/pitur* (lit. 'jaw/chest'), normally composed of both males and females. They are regarded as persons who possess knowledge of things or are owners of extra-ordinary knowledge, since like the owners of *zari*, they can foretell and prophesy future events. A man possessing such powers is referred to as *ngujyom*, 'the male owner of the long jaw', while his female counterpart is called *matjyom*, 'the female owner of the long jaw'. The concept of 'the long jaw' here should be interpreted more in symbolic than in literal terms. It symbolises the ability to see things and warn the community long before the events are likely to occur. The Ngas, who are neighbours to the Mupun, for instance, refer to owners of *jyom* as *jeprit/jepritmwa*, that is 'the good children'.

In the case of an epidemic such as smallpox or a drought, the role of owners of *zari* earnestly comes into play. Chief priests or owners of respective shrines consult with the *mishkom*, preferably one who owns *zari*, and directs them to the owners of *jyom* after making prophecies. Twelve owners of *jyom* (six males and six females) are selected to prepare themselves for a ritual cleansing of the land. Several *Pa* diviners are then invited to start casting the stones that are to uncover various moral *shikbish*, wrong-doings of the people, according to extended families and clans. The main duty of the *nyem jyommo*, owners of the long jaw, at this juncture is to keep the *sot-mo* (witches) at bay while the job of cleansing the land commences. This is born out of the belief that calamities, epidemics, drought, mildew, and ill-health are caused mostly by *sotmo* witches. These same categories of religious experts also assist during *ya sot* ('catching the witch') or *chyan sot* ('sizzling/burning the witch') witch-hunting sessions.

Some element of *baak ka* is needed in making *yen* medicine, *ya fwan* (lit. 'catching rain') rain-making, *yendek* (lit. 'thunder') magical macho strength received from thunder, the casting of the pebbles in divination, the use of *zari* and *jyom*, and indeed in the use of all mystical powers. However, *baak ka* magic or mystical power also possesses the potential for evil usage. Its use in *yen*, *Pa* divination, *zari* and *jyom*, however, borders more on the miraculous than on the actual use of magical procedures.

For the Mupun, the matter does not end here. The possessors of mystical powers who use them positively, such as the *ngu* or *nyem zarimo* (owners of outstanding wisdom) and *nyem jyommo* (persons who possess knowledge of things unknown to others), are also believed to possess every potential power available and technique known to the *sot* (witch). For them, the difference between the two lies only in the fact the *sot* has chosen to use his or her knowledge in a dangerous manner, while the *nguzari* and *nyem jyommo* have decided to use theirs for the good of society. These two positive mystical gifts (*zari* and *jyom*) are seen as masculine and are passed through the patrilineal line of descent, since it is believed that only men can pass them on through their *chilem* (totems). Owners of *zari* bequeath the gift to male descendants, while owners of *jyom* pass it on to both male and female siblings, depending on choice. However, only the male child is believed to possess the capability of passing on his powers of *zari* or *jyom* to one of his siblings, while the female child dies with her own.

The possessors of these positive mystical powers are the protectors of society, including its customs, norms, values, medicines, deities and other secrets of the land. They symbolise the opposite of *sot* witches, *nyem lommo* sorcerers and *nyem fwo tommo*, the possessors of the evil eye examined below. This group of wise men and women, who may well represent the intelligentsia and philosopher class in pre-modern Mupun society, are believed to possess powers of astral projection, like the *sotmo* witches, but use their powers for benevolent purposes. Many characteristics associated with witchcraft world-wide, such as the use of animal forms and the symbolic sharing of victims' blood and flesh within a circle of witches' guilds, represent beliefs also held by the Mupun.

SOT WITCHCRAFT

Sot, witchcraft, is a term used both popularly and loosely among the Mupun to describe all sorts of evil and the secret employment of spiritual forces, mystical powers, or life-forces to destroy other persons' life-force[10] or what Tempels describes as the *force vitale* among the Bantu.[11] Whereas the Azande believe that a man can transmit witchcraft only to his sons, and a woman only to her daughters,[12] for the Mupun witchcraft is feminine, but a craft that incorporates both male and female members. The male witch is called *ngu sot*, male owner of witchcraft ability, while his female counterpart is called *mat sot*, female owner of witchcraft ability. However, only female members are believed to be capable of passing on the craft to their children. So, while a Mupun man is said to pass on the knowledge of sorcery and positive mystical forces such as *baak ka* magic and *jyom* foreknowledge and the gift of prophecy, a Mupun woman is believed to pass on the witchcraft ability.[13]

This explanation is important, since not all persons with a witchcraft ability are believed to participate in the so-called 'eating of human flesh' and 'drinking of human blood'. This is because a few may not intentionally have become witches, but once trapped into the craft, the witchcraft potential remains dormant. The Mupun use the term *sot* to mean both witch and witchcraft, and they consider both as inherently evil. Their Ngas neighbours refer to witches as *goshekbesmwa*, 'suckers of blood and other body fluids'. However, unlike sorcery, the patterns of *sot* witchcraft among the Mupun follow kinship lines only, both maternal and agnatic. Victims of witchcraft are supposed to emanate from the blood relations of a *sot* witch. Hence, the presentation of victims is believed to be done serially within a witches' guild system. This point is driven home by the Mupun saying: '*Sot kih put a ndir paal*', meaning 'the witch usually emerges (comes out) from under the (or one's) sleeping mat'. This is another way of saying that a victim of witchcraft must seek for the alleged witch within the blood kin group, since a witch does not seek for its victims outside the kin group. *Dir paal* (lit. 'the bottom side of the sleeping mat') symbolises the kin group.

It is believed, however, that since the witch has given away a blood kin, they must confess their guilt openly in a public witch-confession rite known as *ser sot,* narrating the guilt of witchcraft, otherwise the witch will die. Unlike *lom* sorcery, which will 'catch' even the owner of the substance if s/he mistakenly takes it along with food or drink, *sot* witchcraft does not harm the owner. *Lom* sorcery is a learned craft, while, once acquired, *sot* witchcraft becomes an innate tendency. *Sot* can be acquired in one of four ways: inheritance from a parent or relation who is a witch, by purchase, from one's conjugal partner, or unconsciously. Furthermore, there is a belief that unchecked greediness, gluttony, and selfishness in children may lead to the acquisition or purchase of witchcraft later in life. A deity known as *Hime* is, however, employed to control greediness in children.

The Mupun thus hold that one may deliberately choose to become a *sot* witch, in which case witchcraft becomes an innate power that can be used by its owner to do harm to others. In the same vein, a person may unconsciously become one without initially realising its potential. This notion agrees with the Azande construct which, according to Evans-Pritchard, holds that 'I may not know that I am a witch until, in a fit of anger, I say "I wish X were dead"; and X dies. Making this discovery, I may be horrified and try to get rid of the power. On the other hand, I may welcome it and begin to associate with other witches. This association may take place only in immaterial form.'[14] *Sot* witchcraft destroys its owner only in cases where the witch is incapable of finding a victim when it is his or her turn to supply one to the guild. In such a case the guild turns upon a colleague, devouring the person because of the flesh debt incurred that must be paid for in human life.

It may be concluded in this section, therefore, that the Mupun hold that calamities such as droughts, epidemics and personal ill-health are caused in the human world by, among others, a number of mystical agents manipulated by human beings. *Sot* witchcraft is by far the most volatile of these human agents. However, the Mupun equally acknowledge possessors of other mystical powers that may keep witchcraft in check, including the owners of *zari* (outstanding wisdom) and *jyom* (foreknowledge), the casters of *Pa* divination pebbles, and the operators of various other mantic systems. *Pa* divination, therefore, is a mystical force that provides human beings with hidden and expert knowledge to discover the cause of ill-health in society, and how to appease the spiritual agents that can avert and ameliorate the affliction caused by the agents mentioned above. The Mupun use *Pa* divination for the diagnosis of diseases and their causal agents, for the prescription of drugs, and for the treatment and rehabilitation of victims of affliction arising from the punishment of benevolent spirit beings or the malevolent acts of evil spirits and human agents.[15]

DEMYSTIFYING NEGATIVE MYSTICAL FORCES

The Mupun demystify *sot* witchcraft when they playfully and appreciatively praise an outstanding or extraordinary achievement in witchcraft terms. They thus exclaim, *La si a sot*! 'This boy is a witch'! This is similar to the way it is said of a specialist that s/he is an ace, a wizard, a genie or genius in a particular field. *Sot* as a terminology is, however, usually not ascribed verbally to a person, unless in positive terms denoting the witch as genie or genius. Although such a use is permitted, it is rarely employed. Mupun very often substitute the term *sot* (witch) in this positive sense with the term *baak kaa* ('the person who has split his/her head'), which is more fitting. *Baak kaa* is associated with outstanding performance and extraordinary events, particularly something bordering on the miraculous or when one makes an almost impossible thing to happen. In this case the elders exclaim in praise and with pride: '*ha lah sih a bhak kaa bah*', meaning 'You this boy, you have split your head [very well]', or '*wun jep simo wu baak kaa bah*', 'You children, you have split your heads [very well]'. Yet the Mupun hold that only a genie or genius can 'split his head'. However, one may attain the same feat due to good luck, after one has accidentally ran into a fair-complexioned *riin*, which is a good or benevolent wandering spirit, or after a meeting with the totem spirit of a departed parent who was the owner of *zari* or *jyom*. A chanced meeting with a good or benevolent spirit usually results in the blessing of a well-mannered person with temporary or permanent gifts of *baak ka* magic. The achievement of an extraordinary feat indicates that the person has acquired *zari* outstanding wisdom or *jyom*, the gift of foreknowledge or both.

It is pertinent to note that while *sot* witchcraft for the Mupun is mystifying and carries with it a stigmatising effect in many areas, it has also been demystified in its association with achievement, where it is regarded as a commendable feat worth emulating by society. By the same token, they associate magic with *baak kaa*, splitting one's head, particularly because magic is supposed to deal with the realms of the cunning, the unexpected, dexterity and craftiness in manipulating the secrets of everyday natural phenomena through long and arduous practices. Those activities that fall in the category of *sot* witchcraft or *baak kaa* magic in this positive sense usually include hunting and war heroes, and macho men who carry grinding mills from the bush to the village house for use by the women. Others include medicine-men who exorcise notorious spirits, winners of archery competitions (particularly target-shooting experts), wrestling and stick-fighting champions, and magicians who utilise their art for entertainment and for chasing away or catching dangerous ghosts.

The Mupun also reason that Europeans use their witchcraft abilities positively in the manufacturing industry where they fabricate cars, aeroplanes and weapons, build overhead bridges or fly-overs, etc. The first Mupun who observed 'frog men', who entered the water of the river Niger with scuba-diving equipment and stayed there for a long time at a stretch when the Niger bridge was under construction during colonial times, promptly reported that Europeans used their witchcraft positively.

DOR ANGER, *SOT* WITCHCRAFT AND AMBIVALENT USE OF MYSTICAL POWER

There is a relationship between *dor* anger and *sot* witchcraft in a different sense, from which the Mupun understand witchcraft both as a positive and negative force. The Mupun word for anger, *dor*, is the same as for scorpion. They only differ in the context of usage. The analogy derives from the pain, sorrow and sadness that both cause. The sting of the scorpion is as painful as the surging discomfort one gets when mistakenly stepping on a small piece of burning charcoal. Thus Mupun children, when experiencing the sting of a scorpion for the first time, cry out: '*wus-eh wus-eh!*', 'fire, fire!' when stung in the dark by a scorpion. Given its rocky and stony terrain, scorpions are common in Mupun land, especially during the first half of the rainy season. Thus, *dor* anger is synonymous with *dor* the scorpion, and vice versa.

Dor anger, however, generates and invokes deeper painful sensations and distressful emotions than the suffering and pain caused by the fiery sting of a scorpion. The Mupun conceive the scorpion as a reptile that is always angry, because it walks around with its tail held high up, ready to sting at the slightest opportunity, even without any provocation. And when provoked, the scorpion scurries around frantically and angrily stinging everything it comes into immediate contact with. It is the opposite of *dakur*, the tortoise (in Mupun imagery a figure of patience, wisdom and divination), which under attack withdraws harmlessly into its shell, which serves as a fortress and a last line of defence.[16]

The scorpion thus represents *dor*, mere anger, which can be displayed by both human beings and animals. Furthermore, wherever it goes the scorpion carries anger with it to remind human beings of the reality of *dor* anger. This serves as a subtle warning that humans should avoid anger in their interpersonal relationships, because anger can be lethal in its destruction of human relationships that have taken years to build. Embedded in this reality is the fact that human beings should also be reminded that some types of anger are more dangerous and permanently destructive than others. Such forms of anger unwittingly stimulate and invoke the release of unseen forces which can profoundly and negatively affect the lives and destinies of others if they are not reversed. It is this type of *dor* anger that destroys in the same way as *sot* witchcraft.

The Mupun hold the belief that deep *dor* anger emanates from the stomach, similar to the scorpion's anger. The same is believed to be true of the source of *sot* witchcraft, and the reason why both are considered feminine. Both are believed to emanate from the same uterine source. However, while *sot* witchcraft is believed to be generated by factors such as greed, envy, jealousy, rivalry, competition and affinity, which is said to cause disdain and breed contempt, *dor* deep anger is believed to begotten by deep love. Both however translate into hatred and may breed deep anger and destruction. In *sot* witchcraft, anger leads to a witchcraft attack on the victim of hate, whereas *dor* deep anger, once expressed, stimulates the release of mystical forces to effect damage on the person at whom it is directed. This is, however, only possible when a sibling or more junior person is the victim of *dor* anger and a parent or elder person is the one who has been angered. This is *dor*, the anger that curses, and this *dor* anger is equated to witchcraft. In the following we will examine some cases involving deep anger.

THE ANGER OF THE DEITIES

The *Kum-mo* deities are often angry at human beings. At such occasions they demonstrate their *dor* anger through malevolent and malignant behaviour towards humans, until these seek redress in appeasement rites. This is also true of *njimo*, the departed fathers or ancestors. In both cases, human beings are afflicted by all manners of ill-health, either as individuals, as a family or extended family, as a clan or an ethnic group. The calamity, crisis or illness meted against human society can be redressed after *Pa* divination rituals have revealed the cause of ill-health. The same *Pa* divination system prescribes the type of redressive rituals and the venue needed for the rites, usually a grove, a house or a bush shrine, within rocks, or amongst bamboo plants. *Pa* divination also prescribes the type of sacrifice to be made and the time. It describes even the colour of its skin or feathers, the manner of its slaughtering, the preparation of the meat, and who partakes in the consumption of what part of the meat. This is what the Mupun refer to as *tok kum*, a concept that is at the heart of Mupun religious tradition, culture and customs. The term variously denotes religion (*kum*), deities (*kum-mo*), praying (*tok kum*), making sacrifices (*tok kum*), divination (*tok kum*), judging in the traditional way (*tok kum*) and trial by ordeal (*shuwa kum*). It is inclusive of virtually all rituals and festivals associated with the cult of the ancestors, deities and Mupun religion in general.

In some cases, the Mupun feel that the malignant behaviour expressed towards them by their deities or ancestors may be a completely misplaced injustice, in which case they feel forced to accept such cruel verdict and injustice as the voice of the spirit realm. They may, however, protest in subtle ways, such as in the names they give to children born around the time of the event. Such names include *Kumbish*, 'the deities are bad or wicked', *Kumben* (lit. 'religion has been postponed'), 'the deities are unreliable', (or: 'religion is no longer useful and should be put aside'), and *Kumdor*, 'the deities are angry'. Such names express a human dilemma, the frustration and protest against injustice before the spiritual and human worlds. *Kum dor* also refers to the redressive and appeasement rites for 'cooling the anger' of the deities. Such rites usually involve a sacrifice. The magnitude and reason for the provocation determines the type of sacrificial victim to be used. However, in all rites of *Kum dor*, both human beings and the spirit realm are invited to come and partake of the sacrificial food, meat and drinks.

Dor anger is so central in Mupun thought that it has a deity called *Kufwor*, the deity of *dor* anger. This deity is invoked when a victim of theft or treachery and conspiracy lodges a formal complaint with the deity to grant him or her justice. In such a case s/he requests the priest to invoke the deity in a ritual known as *pak kum,* which means 'to suppress', 'to cool' or 'close' their anger. It also means 'to suppress anger by transferring its lethal effect back to the culprit'. This is a quest for vengeance. In order to launch a formal complaint before the deity, the victim provides a hen and some *fonio,* flour, for performing the complaint rites. Thereafter it is believed that a swollen stomach, an affliction that gradually spreads to the rest of the body, will afflict the culprit. The person may die if s/he refuses to recant and provide animal victims for redressive rites after consultation of the *Pa* diviner. In order to be freed from this divine affliction, the culprit must provide three goats for the rituals. The redressive rites in cases concerning the deity of anger must take place in a forested area covered with tuffs of grass and bamboo. Again *Pa* divination plays a central role in determining the cause of oedema in the culprit and in soliciting voluntary confession, after which the appeasement rites are performed to allow health to gradually return. If the culprit accepts his fault, the *dor* anger is taken away.

In other words, the gods can be angry with humans, and their *dor* anger carries with it consequences that are lethal to humans, even if the human beings so malevolently punished cannot find any justifiable premise for such a punishment. Furthermore, when such happens, for the affliction to be reversed human beings must consult the *Pa* diviner to find out causes for the malignant acts of the gods. It also follows that justifiable deep human *dor* anger can be dangerous to fellow-human beings, particularly juniors (not mates or seniors), since compared to the deities human beings are in a position of dependency. *Pa* divination can discover the causes of human anger and reverse ill-health caused by *dor* anger through respective rites. We will turn to that below.

PA DIVINATION AS REVEALER OF *DOR* ANGER AND *SOT* WITCHCRAFT

The most common sources of affliction emanating from human agents, put forward by Mupun *Pa* diviners, are *dor* anger, which leads to loss of parental blessing, *sot* witchcraft, *lom* sorcery, and *fwo tom*, the evil eye. Of all these, the last one is the least common as a source of affliction. In all cases, *Pa* divination acts as a checking, balancing and controlling agent. During ordinary divination sessions, most afflictions are blamed on *dor* anger and *sot* witchcraft, and very seldom on sorcery. In whatever form, *dor* anger is considered dangerous; thus children are implored not to anger their parents and elderly relatives. Likewise, elders are told that they should be humble enough to ask their children and younger kinsfolk for forgiveness if they have wronged them. Thus the saying, '*ngunan kih mak lap bish pih la*', 'the elder can accept rebuke from the child'.

Dor anger comes from the stomach, and when it comes into the heart it can kill. The Mupun distinguish between *tup*, ordinary anger, which may not last long, and *dor*, intense anger, which can never be forgotten or forgiven unless through ritual intervention. The word *tup* is also used for the human heart, but *dor*, 'burning anger', as noted above, is similar to the sting of the scorpion. The type of anger called *dor*, however, is only seen as dangerous when a parent or relative is enraged at a child, but not the reverse. If there is no reconciliation, children will suffer as a result because *dor* will turn into a curse, similar to witchcraft, that has been placed on somebody's head. It manifests itself in the form of a loss of blessing, and the victim may become insane, impotent or barren and materially poor, demonstrating that s/he is searching for that lost blessing. The most regular form this takes is as *jyer*, 'the matter of the dry tree' – barrenness in women and impotency in men. The patient may not be aware of it until s/he visits a diviner. In this way rituals make explicit and conscious those powerful and dangerous thoughts that are liable to become repressed.[17] Monica Wilson has stressed in her work that this notion of anger is found in many African societies:

Anger was feared, the anger of *nji-mo* the living dead, of kinsmen and neighbours, and above all, anger that was unadmitted and was fostering in a man's heart. The only cure was for the angry man to 'speak out', to confess, to admit this anger and express goodwill. This idea occurs right down Africa, from the Sudan down to the Cape, and the same symbols of confession recur also. The commonest is blowing water which Nyakyusa interpret thus, 'if a father is angry with his son or daughter, he may say some day, "I forgive you now' and spit on the ground, all the anger that is in him comes out like spit"'.[18]

Welbourn illustrates the same issue in case of a curse by a father or his sister. A curse must be justified—that is to say, the cursed person must have done genuine harm or shown disrespect to the curser. If the curse is unjustified, it will have no effect on the cursed one and may rebound on the curser or his relations. If the curse is justified, it may cause illness or even the death of the cursed one, and the curse may be active even after the death of the curser. Thus, one who knows that he has been justly cursed will try and have the curse removed before the curser dies. After that, there is no hope.[19]

Fwo tom, the evil eye, too tends to run in families. Its owner has only to look on someone without answering their greetings for that person to become ill. Even though such a power may be used for evil purposes, its possession is often regarded as a misfortune. Among the Mupun, people take precaution to see that *ngu fwo toom*, 'the person who drains blood from the body', that is, the owner of the evil eye, answers their greetings. When this does not happen, he will be pursued by his victim and greeted over and over again. If he still does not answer the salutations, he will be challenged to do so.

The three case studies below underscore the relationship between divination and anger as a witchcraft metaphor. A careful examination of the cases reveals that *Pa* diviners very often make allusions to *dor* anger when they mention witchcraft, and vice versa. In most cases, the issue of witchcraft was raised when the overriding consequences of *dor* anger were pointed out.

CASE 1: A CASE OF DOR ANGER FROM BWONPE [20]

The patient, Narum, who hails from Bwonpe in Amkwe, had not given birth in five years of marriage. Her husband, who comes from Kowel in Kagu Village, consulted the diviner on behalf of his wife. The diviner asked, 'what is her name'? The husband answered, 'Narum'. The diviner then started to cast his pebbles, murmuring and writing down the divination symbols on the divination tray. While casting the pebbles the diviner narrated the situation as follows:

> 'Narum, Rumdi, Rum [the name of the patient is used in the divination process] is from Kukwen country. Reveal to me about Narum, [the] deities are divining, they are speaking. Taken by youth, youth, on her own [she got married at a very early age, probably through the rite of wife-stealing]. Do not tell lies [referring to the divining pebbles], reveal all, reveal all. Reveal accordingly, reveal everything, even if she will die, tell me all, reveal all forever, even if she is innocent, tell me all.
>
> Human life [the business of living] is difficult. When you become an elder, then children will call you 'father', then just keep quiet [take things easy, behave yourself]. When you started growing, children already say the same to your fathers, and it ends there [that is life]. But you want to be *angry* over a matter! This is not fighting you old man! [uttered in a rebuking tone].
>
> Tell me all about her [the patient]. You keep quiet divinities? To keep quiet is bad [indicates a serious problem: *witchcraft*], tell me all about her, tell me all. I say many lies bring plenty redness [troubles]. I cannot touch this forever. I see the shadow of the fair man, it spoiled the totem. Here comes the fair woman, then the dark man, he has a tail (sits on his tail) in the totem form. The syrup of the oil [*sorcery*?] has gone and spoiled it in its totem form. The fair woman, the dark woman, reveal to me, you spoiled [kill] the person in the totem form![allusions to an unborn child] You spoiled [killed] her totem![21]

The fair man [forever], the fair woman and the dark man gave some medicine [sorcery] to her [patient]. It killed her child and it eats us all [*in the form of witchcraft*]. We ran away from the dark man. Tell all, all [reference to divining pebbles]. It eats just like [*witchcraft*] from Ampang. It steals, but he has his blood [mother's blood nurtures the seed of the man]. It has stolen their child, it is lost forever, forever. The sun (day) searches for the child of man, the fair man and the dark man also searched for the child. The sun [phallic (fertilising semen), day] refused the married woman, refused the married woman [allusions to childlessness].

The deity *Kumpaal*, the deity *Kumpaal*, the deity *Kumpaal*, the deity *Kumpaal*, come and tell all [prayer for information]. The ancestor of the gorge: tell all, the ancestor of the gorge: tell all. See the fair man, the owner of the ancestor of the gorge. He searched for her child still. He said, 'I-saw-it-with-my-eyes!' The ancestor of the gorge saw the thing of the fair man, he saw the mountain of the fair man and the mountain of the dark man too.

Tell me all, tell me all. Hunger has killed their child; hunger killed their child strapped on the mother's back. Then I see *matpa* (the female *Pa*), *mishpa* (the male *Pa*), you women and *mishpa* (the male *Pa*). But quietness is bad [*allusions to witchcraft*]. That the name of this *Pa* is *chon*, it means he will stand on his feet. Then *chon chon*, *lusu giri* and the female *Pa* appear. Oh no, it is not anger! *Kam* appears, then we meet *shi*, we meet *kapla* and *nwa*. Oh, their guilt [*wrongdoing which causes anger*] is like dust? We meet *gene* and *kapla*, then we cry out, 'oh!' Then we walk for a while; we meet with *matpa* (the female *Pa*)...she takes medicinal syrup. Again we see the female *Pa*, the male *Pa*. This is the thing that the dark man has eaten [allusions to witchcraft].

Just take it like that. The day [she] repairs quietly [passage of time]. We meet *bere*, oh no!...We meet *kapla*. The ancestors will repair it, the patient, Narum, will repair it [recovery takes time through the help of the deities and ancestors, depending on the will of the patient]. Then we meet with *matpa* (the female *Pa*), *shi* and *kwere*. Then you coil up [*with anger*]. It is the thing of the male. We ask (him) for *fonio* (ritual crop), he keeps quiet [allusion to *tok kum*—redressive rites]. You, have you eaten me already, already in your mouth, ah? [*allusions to witchcraft*]. The leg (*shi*) sits [stays] in one place. On the day of the ancestors, then you [feminine] just stood up, because you saw that he stood up [you thought you have recovered]. Then you fell down *kirip*! [with a thud, indicating a relapse?]. Your husband is fair; I know [the diviner hisses]...'

The verdict given by the diviner emanating from the casting above

In interpreting his castings, the diviner first talked about miscarriages in the life of the patient when he said, 'why do you give birth and the child "comes and goes, comes and goes"'? (hissing in the process). The husband [client] confirmed this revelation [of miscarriages]. The diviner then asked the question, 'Is her mother alive'? He answered by himself, 'yes, she is alive'. He asked again, 'Is the problem located around *anger* (*dor*)?' Again he answered himself: 'Yes it is *anger* (*dor*)'. He then passed the verdict in the following narration.

> It shows that the client has two wives. We must say it, so that even if we die, we shall have told you what is wrong, and it shall be remembered of us that we told you [since he perceived that the client is a Christian and should under normal circumstances not be polygamous]. *The mother is angry with her daughter, the daughter knows why*. Ask her, she will tell you. *Ke*, a fowl, is needed for the reconciliation rites. She must take the fowl to her mother by herself.'

The patient, it seems, did something shameful at home before marriage, perhaps by giving birth to a baby at home out of wedlock. It is also almost certain that she ran off with her husband through a secret elopement (allusions to 'taken by youth' above). As a consequence of these events, her maternal relatives are now angry with her mother. The mother is in turn angry with her daughter Narum, and this *dor* anger has made her barren. It should be noted that even though some allusions are made to witchcraft and sorcery, the diviner kept these to himself. He would surely have preferred to discuss such matters with the husband in private, since these are rather sensitive issues that possess the potential for gossip, rumour-mongering and stigmatisation. The *Pa* diviner clearly and constantly compared the effect of *dor* anger with *sot* witchcraft. The patient is advised to visit her mother with *ke dor*, a chicken or fowl of anger (usually a goat), from her husband to perform reconciliation rites with her and her relatives.

In the case below, *dor* anger resulted in barrenness, because a daughter deliberately married outside the ethnic group against her parents' wishes.

CASE 2: A NARRATIVE ABOUT DOR ANGER FROM AMPANG-WEST[22]

The name of the client and patient is Naandi Shemack from Ampang-West. She has been married for ten years but has had no children because she has been suffering from *jyer,* 'the matter of the dry tree' (barrenness). After diagnosis, the *Pa* diviner revealed that the cause of her barrenness is *dor* anger that stems from her father. The father hails from Jiblik, one of the five major Mupun villages, but his daughter got married to a Mwaghavul man from Ampang. Her grandfather and agnatic kinsmen accused her father of giving his daughter away to another ethnic group. Her father was angry, because this was in spite of the fact that he had given his father and kinsmen their full bride-wealth. Why then should he be so hated by his kin?, he asked himself. He reasoned that it was because his daughter Naandi had decided to marry outside her own ethnic group while she could have married within the ethnic group, and peace would have reigned between him and his kinsmen. So he was angry, and this annoyance was considered to have caused *jyer*, 'the matter of the dry tree', in his daughter.

The diviner suggested that the daughter should *ya ke*, 'catch' a fowl (actually, provide a goat) for her father and his relatives, and a *ke* fowl (not a goat) for her mother and her relatives. According to Mupun tradition, these items (the goat and chicken of anger) are understood to be provided by the patient's husband and his relatives for causing so much anger and hatred in the family of their in-laws. The diviner directed that the problem must be discussed by all the paternal and maternal relations, including the siblings and their spouses, in order to uncover and confess other hidden causes of *dor* anger. They would meet at a big family reunion to reconcile with one another and with their Mwaghavul in-laws, because *dyik* marriage is supposed to build new extended families and not to break down contractual existing ones. After this ritual, the daughter would be pregnant in a year's time, and some medicinal herbs were given to the patient for further treatment at home. The diviner constantly asserted that 'the problem is in your father's stomach', and 'the problem is in your mother's stomach', thus pointing to the reality of *dor* anger.

CASE 3: A CASE OF DOR ANGER FROM MANGU[23]

This is a case according to the diviner, which again refers to *jyer* 'the matter of the dry tree', that is, barrenness, resulting from parental *dor* anger, though here the diviner does not tell us why the parents are sorely angry with their married daughter. The diviner starts his narrative as he casts the divination pebbles by mentioning the name of the client (the husband who consulted the diviner) and the patient (the wife of the client).

Name of Client: Bitrust Tokma from Mangu town
Name of Patient: Naandi Bitrus Tokma
Relationship of client to patient: husband
Condition of patient: Critical insanity

The Narrative:

> **Diviner** (casting the divining pebbles and chanting): Ahhh! I stand up and start the journey. You [feminine] *Pa*, reveal to me. You reveal to me quietly about Tokma, that is your own, about Naandi, Naandi (turning to the client), is that the name?

> **Client**: Yes, Naandi.

Diviner: Yes, Naandi. That is, *Naan dyi* [meaning, 'There is God'] Tokma. You [referring to divination apparatus] reveal all, in the land of Mangu. If it takes a maiden [wife stealing] and then she refuses, but then she just follows like that, then reveal to me [the diviner coughs]. *It is beginning to make him angry in his stomach* [!] that is it. Then you [feminine] should reveal. You should not speak lies, I will scratch [search] the lies, all, all, you see, I search, the divinity searches lies, I search on, and that is it. It pulls it from the roots, and shakes it, with my youthfulness (*shi zilang*), that is it. Then it will soon be taken, suddenly but quietly. Have you arrived old maid? [Referring to a particular *Pa* divination symbol]. Our journey has reached it end. I cannot hide it. Our journey has ended 'by head' [through the use of intuitive powers]. Reveal it all, all, so that Naandi does not sit amongst other people with lack of confidence. You see, knowledge of truth is [hidden] with the Supreme Being. You see, they discussed among themselves. It is the Supreme Deity [hisses]. Oh no! no! oh! This divinity, no...If you see mourning, we know you are a human being. If the divinity has the deities, [and He does] then [we know] you are human beings...reveal to me, reveal all, all, I scratch, I search for the truth.

Translating the castings:

Poetry: Oh, journeying, journey, the journey has begun. Yes, journey, the journey has began. We are on the journey.

Prose: From *Kaapla*, then we see *Lusu, Mishpa*. You, the thing of the woman [the thing that belongs to the woman], keep quiet [your thing]! I am speaking with the dark-complexioned man. Then *Kaapla, Saa* and you [woman], you refused to stand up. Is this *Saa*? And you woman, you spoke with the light-complexioned man. You [feminine] *Saa, Kaapla* ha! ha! ha! Have you spoken good to each other? [Did you settle your differences?] When it started, you woman, spoke with the dark man and the light man, why?

That we built the earth so that we can settle our differences. Did you settle your differences? But he sat down quietly. He said nothing at all, old man/father. He keeps quiet, so quiet, his mind is in a far country. Oh oh! Do you see Naandi, that the divinity exists, isn't it? Since the divinity exists, then all is well! Then all is well? Naandi, yes there is the Supreme Deity. You [feminine] bring peace in the land of Mangu, down and all over the land of Mangu [the way a dying or shot bird flaps around]. Free, peaceful [cool] from judgement and free, peaceful [cool] from illness. There is *Kaapla*, and is there *Ke*? *Ke*, *Shi* [leg for walking] comes by *Kaapla*. The light-complexioned people had a talk [over a matter], so also did the diseases, then *Ke*, *Toro*. And he coils up unexpectedly [a relapse in patient's condition?] You belittle me. Then *Mat Pa*, *Mish Pa*. Do I then sit down quietly, sit quietly by *Mish Pa*? Are you speaking [quarrelling]? *Kaapla*, *Bere*, they started hunting [hunting is feminine] and *Shi*, does she just sit down [her own]? If they go for hunting, do you, do you [stammering by the diviner] take us for invalids? Did you create me, or did She the Divinity create me Naandi an invalid, or is it you yourself who is an invalid?

Poetry: Anger takes it, oh. It is anger that we drink; it is anger that we drink, oh! Anger, anger of the mother, anger of the father. Anger is in the stomach of Naandi [the patient]. Anger is in the stomach of her father. There is anger in the stomach of her mother...it stands on her, it makes her dizzy, when she meets it.

Prose: Then we meet *Kaapla*, the light-complexioned man, *Bere*, *Saa*, how did they go out that she slept there for the night? The dark woman, *Lete*, *Lete*, *Shi*, the dark man said [shouted] *Koi*, *Koi!* My elders [colleagues], why do you keep quiet? He suddenly decided to come up [northwards—indicating that all hope is not lost] like this [he speaks saying], by *Shi* [the leg] then I started to walk little by little [recovery]. Is it youuurrss? [stammering again]. I see, why is she angry? You, Naandi's father, you begin to walk in this place, then you deny each other? Then you walk in your totemic animal double (*chilem*), the totem of the light man, of the dark man, of the light woman, of the light woman. He spoiled her, that is, Naandi. The maternal uterine kin (*jep mwel*, indicating unity), the children of the co-wives (*jep mal*, pointing to disunity), you made her condition worst, then darkness (*jibit*), oh no, we leave this one in the hands of the Supreme Deity. Then *Shi,* it is ill [damaged]. If I come up, then the owners, [the people who own me—the maternal uncles], then they will come and meet me. You [feminine], you walk, you climb into the Supreme Divinity [the sky, heaven], then when I come down, oh did you think I will stay there in the sky, *Kaapla, Lete,* have I seen? But if my illness becomes worse [I cannot survive] it becomes worse! Mmm! Naandi, about the fathers, they talk aimlessly, if it becomes worse for me on this issue, then me, I... You see, the deity of the light man, is about to come. *Mat Pa, Gine,* ohhh! If I keep it in my totemic spirit, then where shall I turn and go to? If it becomes difficult for me over the rest, then I find Bere here. It is my spirit, my totemic spirit which is hidden in the thing of the past.

Poetry: Going out on a journey, going out on a journey. Somebody takes it, the person takes wealth. Prepared medicine [*yen*, sorcery] for Naandi. Is it Naandi? Naandi only in the land of Mangu, a particular road hits the light man, the dark woman, the light woman. If they prepared some medicine [sorcery] for her, then you divining pebbles, then you reveal all to me, reveal all about Naandi.

Prose: *Kam* oh, *Mish Pa* oh, oh no! *Lusu, Kwere* oh, no! [The diviner hisses and shakes his head]... Then later we were able to speak. The dark man just speaking and speaking on *Kaapla,* what is it? If it is postponed, then I will walk by my totemic spirit by licking the ground. That's all. Do you find something wrong with me? Do you find out that I came out by my totemic spirit? Who has poisoned [charmed] me? [Sorcery is suspected here]. *Gine*, girl oh, no, he started behaving like a malnourished child, we women, that is, will it not be better later? Has disease [*muut* death] descended on me? It will be better [later]. I am sure! They all say 'Oh it will be good for me'.

Poetry: Journeying, journeying on. O journeying, o something [the diviner coughs], meets [hits] her on her own [just] like that. It hits the light man, the dark man, then [I say] Naandi, Naandi, ihh [the sound of screeching wheels made by brakes] Tokma [husbands name] is in front, yes Bitrus is in front.

Prose: Then we meet *Mish Pa*, *Ke* ummh, in the past, the dark man came and made a useless talk, then you [people] inquired about the matter from the deities, what have I stolen from them? Then Gine came, the dark one consulted the deities (*tok kum*), and they revealed [to him] that it is anger (*dor*), but did they come and tell you? They talked, they said that you ate, mmm, that you ate, that you eh eh [stammering] you ate Naandi [allusion to witchcraft, diviner is reluctant to mention it by name], the dark man came and told him, [that] you ate Naandi secretly, you little boy! Then the dark man sat down, falling [*kirip*], he shouted oh! But who has poisoned mmm me? [Stammering]. *Gine*, *Chon*, count, count, my mother, did she, did she catch it there, where did I walk to, that they prepared poison for me? We *Toro*, *Lusu* [the diviner hisses], they poisoned me, why? [Diviner said this in a wailing tone and blows his nose as if crying]. Allah! [The diviner swears by the name of the Divinity], whether it is *Bere*, I am on *Chon*, then it falls back, then I go and rest on *Giri*.

Poetry: Oh! We are journeying on. Some dance the dance of the deity, *Kumpaal*. Oh, the dance of *Kumpaal*, the dark man, oh the dance of *Kumpaal*, the light man, oh. It remains with Naandi, touch [move] the leg of the girl, then he sat down [on his own], Tokma oh, so that it will disturb her in front of Bitrus. Oh *Chon, Chon, Chon*, the deity *Kumpaal*, they guard the place, then am I the one who will go there?

Prose: *Nwa, Saa, Bere*, what taboo is this? It falls on this light man. If falls on him, falls, falls on his own deity *Kumpaal*, so you should go and touch some for him. *Nwa, Shi*, see! See! He has his own stick of the deities, he has started walking on his own. *Bere, Giri*, yeeh [diviner shouts, then hisses]. If it is quiet, and it is not touched, then it is good. Put it down. Hoi, hoi, hoi, hoi! [The diviner shouts], Naandi, not here!

Poetry: Walking, just journeying in the dust [reference to the divining powder]. The dust of the light man, the dust of the dark man, she, she, she Naandi touches it in the hand, in front of him, in front of Mangu, in front of Bitrus.

Prose: Then we meet *Kaapla, Lite*, but what is this that we walk on? [diviner hisses, blows his nose]. Oh! Mmm! You [female], stand up that we shall judge [by invoking the deities?] so that we find what is wrong, then we shall, then we shall see. You man, you, you, you [stammering] this light man, you should stand up and go and see your thing. *Lite, Gine*, the dark man judges his thing, do we come? *Kwere, Lusu*, or if, if I sit down in darkness, am I dark, very dark? Oh people, the light complexion! Uh! You [feminine] see, you have become a man, have you? Cast *Nwa, Bere*, my mother. That [small anger], there is small anger, isn't it? No! [diviner hisses]. We see clearly, we wait [see] on the Divinity alone. No, no, no! This small anger, disturbing, disturbing. I will not hide it. What is revealed, the Supreme Deity made it possible for you to return to Him, *haba*! You see, wait so that I will reveal it to you. The day of anger, then you see, this is [also] the healing [feminine] oh. It is you [plural], you who [decided to] talk, this is [her] healing, then you told each other. Very often, you you you, sit there quietly, oh oh oh! Then you hold yourself and coil up and sit there, yes your wife is of dark complexion, and you see, she decided to shut her mouth and talk to the dark man. The next day then you said no. The next day you stood up and it disturbed you [your ears], but what will you do now? Then the big men, up till now, still that anger. The day she gets better [is healed] then you can see, then I will see clearly, yes then, then her anger, the anger that produces guilt, then I left the place, anger still, then we met, yes the thing the dark woman told you, yes, the thing of the dark woman, she turns there still, it is in the preparation [work], but like of old, oh! The dark man eh! Perhaps he is here? No [my] people, the dark man suddenly decided to come upwards, upwards, the dark man, then he started running, he decided to come upwards, upwards, you see, you see. The dark man denies this man, but he has seen the Supreme Divinity eh! Naandi is sitting here and she walks slowly [in an unsteady manner]. The dark man searches, searches here, you [woman] be careful [warning!]... You see, you dark man, *haba*! She is the one. Something, it should guard Naandi, but it doesn't, it is he who came out through his totemic spirit. See her here, your Naandi is here [you], see [for yourself]! It is Naandi, you know her, she is dark-complexioned. You see, it is this Naandi, she left climbing northwards, you see, she is here in the sky [in the deity]. You see Naandi, do you? See her here, she is walking on her own. You see, you, you have some talk [unknown] on your mind [unexpressed anger or guilt]. Like your father, then you hang yourself [get very angry]. You left, later when you [plural] go and you sit down and you fight in the [beer] drinking house, then you hang yourself [you are mad/livid with anger], isn't it? You see, if you see the small dark one, will you see Naandi? Her totemic spirit is somewhere [herself] in hiding.

I cannot hide it from you. I say I will not give you a long story. I will not start far away. Am I not the one who placed your divining dust? [Am I not the one who divine for you?].

I placed her mother, then I am the one, you see, who came and placed the deity [*Kumpaal*]. Then Naandi, she took, you see *Kumpaal* is for catching human beings, you see *Kumpaal* then falls on children, you see things, then you see these, you see the things of *Kumpaal* are standing here. Naandi went there, you see. You see here, you see. It is the light man, it was in him who used to perform the rituals of *tok Kumpaal*. He has his own stick of *Kumpaal*. He plants his own deity. He plants it [his own deity]. Naandi oho! She touched it, you see. He suddenly came up, he placed his own deity. You see Naandi, she is sitting [her thing] here, in darkness. My father's [ancestors] how do you see this? There is guilt, cold cold guilt, then we shall see, that's all, *haba*! If you [masculine], kill him with mouth [much talk], you see, it is the light man, he stood up and jumped, he just spoke and the dark man said, mmmh [that is, I know what's happening]. Emm, that the in-law is dark, it is he who is light-complexioned, no no, and the dark man kept very quiet, performing his judgement rituals of the deities, do you hear? And he passes the verdict by himself, you see Naandi [the diviner hisses].

Naandi's husband [Birus the client], I will place [reveal] your own anger [which is] in your own stomach so that I will see what has spoiled this [brought about the problem]. I will place it in her mother's stomach, then I will leave and go and pull it out of her father's stomach; yes, Naandi's father from his stomach. It can be done.

This last case shows that Naandi, the wife of Bitrus, was suffering from insanity (madness) and the 'matter of the dry tree' barrenness because her parents were angry with her. The exact reason, however, remains unknown. In all three cases a reunion meal was prescribed by the diviner as a ritual process of healing.

These three *Pa* case studies above examine possible causes of afflictions and their remedies. They mention deities and their symbols, ancestors, and human causal agents of affliction. Human agents of *sot* witchcraft and *lom* sorcery are mentioned in veiled language. For instance, the phrases 'eating a human being' and 'medicine' refer to witchcraft and sorcery respectively, though in the latter, one has to examine the context in which the word 'medicine' (*yen*) is used, since it refers to both sorcerous and medicinal usage. *Dor* anger is often mentioned directly as a causal agent. The deity is frequently named as an aide in *Pa* divination.

As the Mupun do not have any formal marriage ceremonies except elopement, wife-theft and wife-capture, a type of events that usually brings about *dor* anger, daughters easily incur the anger of parents. And, as shown above, the *dor* anger of a parent against their child carries malevolent effects, though they may not be consciously applied. The most common consequences of *dor* anger from Mupun parents appear to be afflictions causing *jyer*, that is, disease of the dry tree and *dip* (lit. penis) impotency.

DOR ANGER AS A CURSE FROM 'UGLY OLD WITCHES'

Dor anger can also manifest itself in the form of a curse on arrogant and disrespectful youngsters when such persons mock and laugh at decrepit, toothless old people with wrinkled skins, poor sight and grey or white hair. Many folk tales discourage the youth from showing disrespect to elders and strangers, for fear of incurring *dor* anger and related curses. For instance, in Mupun and Miship, *jirap nen bi˘m-mo*, the laughing maidens (lit. 'lost girls'), are a group of three tall stones, said to have been three beautiful maidens who were petrified because they laughed at an old woman and refused to help her. The fourth maiden escaped this curse because she helped in carrying the old woman's load and treated her respectfully. A rhyme is sung in their memory:

Mupun:
Jirap nen bi˘m mo oh, yak wu wa pak kih puus,
ka ba ko kih ta be, ka wu gwar doh nƏka lar.
meaning:
the maidens of the people of *bi˘m*, [later] you should go home early,
[so that] before darkness comes, then you can stand on the rocks and shout.

The Mupun take disrespect for elders seriously. They believe that such acts of disrespect are capable of causing drought and calamities, since neither the gods nor the ancestors sanction it. Hence, the first query a *mishkom* (priest-chief or sacred ruler) puts to a diviner searching for causal factors of any calamity, particularly drought, includes the phrase 'maybe the youth abused an old man, saying that he is nothing, and he went away angry.'[24]

I showed above that some human agents may unwittingly cause affliction, as is the case with *dor* anger. I also demonstrated in the *Pa* divination narratives above that in most cases affliction is reversed or removed, and health and well-being are restored in reconciliation between a child and its parents. This is achieved through a family reunion feast, accompanied by redressive sacrificial rites where ancestral spirits are duly informed.

CONFESSION OF *DOR* ANGER AND *SOT* WITCHCRAFT

In the three case studies above it was demonstrated that confession is necessary to restore health and well-being in *dor* anger-related cases. The need for confession as a part of the healing process is exemplified in *Pa* divination rites. It is also exhibited in the cases of *dor*, deep anger, where concerned parties bury the hatchet over a ritual reunion meal. In association with witchcraft, however, it assumes the rather shameful public rite of *ser sot*, confession of witchcraft, after the death of a believed victim of the craft. Below I will examine the role of rites of confession involving *Pa* divination, *dor* anger and *sot* witchcraft.

CONFESSION AS HEALING IN THE RITES OF *PA* DIVINATION

The *Pa* diviner is expected to ascertain the cause of anomalies in individual and societal life, and the spiritual and human forces involved. However, in the case of personal illness, it is not his duty to inform the patient of the cause of ill health, even though he must reveal it to the relatives of the sick person. Patients who may witness the casting sessions for their own sake are asked to leave before the interpretation session starts. A trusted relation or a friend whom the patient can 'talk to', that is, reveal intimate secrets to, will urge him or her gently to confess guilt after the *Pa* divination session is concluded. Together, they will probe all possible wrongdoings by the patient until he makes the correct confession. This trusted friend has to witness the divination sessions from the beginning to the very end, including the redressive sacrificial rites that follow. When the sacrificial victim is a fowl, it will be waved over the head or body of the patient; if it is an animal, the patient will be asked to lay his or her hands on it. This signifies the process of transferring guilt from the guilty patient to the innocent sacrificial victim. The victim is then sacrificed and dies in the place of the patient.

The *Pa* divination sessions, together with rites of confession, the sacrificial rites and prayers offered for the removal of guilt are all regarded as important to ensure healing and well-being.[25] The *Pa* diviner ascertains the cause of illness by revealing the spiritual force(s) and human agents involved. However, the efficacy of the sacrificial rites to remove affliction lies in the power and accuracy of the confession of guilt and the reconciliatory rites that follow. The redressive rites may be properly carried out and the diviner may be reliable and truthful. However, if the patient does not confess all 'with one mind', it is believed that the affliction will persist.

CONFESSION AS HEALING IN THE RITES OF REVERSING *DOR* ANGER

The importance of confessing *dor* anger and seeking for reconciliation, which the Mupun find in sacrificial rituals, is similarly underscored in the work quoted above by Monica Wilson on the Nyakyusa.[26] She states that anger may render rituals ineffective. Rites of reconciliation between subjects of various categories are important. 'So repeatedly in the rituals, there is confession of anger, of quarrels and of rejection of anger, symbolised...by blowing out of water, sharing of meals between shades and the warring human parties.'[27] Axel-Ivar Berglund makes the same point about the importance of confession among the Zulu of South Africa.[28]

The Mupun express parental blessing, which is absolutely vital for personal well-being, as the rite of *bwet zel n-ka laa*, 'spitting on the child', or 'anointing the child with spittle'. Thus an elder may tell his son, 'come, let us get reconciled, so that I may spit on you before I die'. In most cases, however, the diviner—as seen in the cases above—advises the affected child to visit its parents with the prescribed gifts of *dor* anger. In the reunion rites that follow, the child openly apologises and confesses guilt throughout the time of the festival, showing remorse, while parents may restrain the child or tell it to forget the past; friends, husbands and wives who are also invited participate fully in the rites. The process of healing begins already when the son or daughter returns home and begins working together with the parents towards the reunion service. In some cases, where the events that led to *dor* anger involved heated arguments, other family elders may intervene to see that peace and reconciliation are attained and *dor* anger is made harmless and completely averted.

The Mupun also express rejection of *dor* anger and the reconciliation of warring parties in public and private songs. They further demonstrate it in the culture of *kaat mwes*, a rite in which the reconciled parties share the same meal and drink beer in pairs (or in threes). In *kaat mwes*, two or three persons drink simultaneously from the same calabash, with their mouths lined up side by side, (with one touching the other), along one edge of a calabash. This rite is call *mukaat*, 'let us join together'. In this way the warring parties not only eat, but drink simultaneously from the same calabash. The confession of guilt and of *dor* anger thus becomes the essence of *tok kum* sacrificial rites. In the morning before departure, the parent calls the affected child and spits to the ground in their presence, uttering phrases such as 'Go in peace and progress in your place of work' or 'Go in peace and give birth to many children'. They may utter the following as they throw out spittle, 'See, I have nothing against you. If I was the cause of your childlessness, go now and let us hear the cry of a child in your house by this time next year. You will be a mother of many children.' Or simply, 'Go in peace, our daughter. Don't worry, when you visit us by this time next year, you will have a baby strapped on your back.' In all three cases described above, the women gave birth to a baby a year after performing reconciliation rites with their parents, as predicted by the diviners.

THE RITE OF *SER SOT* CONFESSING WITCHCRAFT AS A MEANS OF ESCAPING DEATH FOR THE ALLEGED WITCH

The rite of *ser sot* confessing witchcraft however, is not a pleasant one. It is a shameful rite, in which a *sot* witch, in desperation to live, confesses his or her alleged evil deeds in public. The rite of *ser sot* confessing witchcraft is determined through standard codes and oracular speech. This is based on the belief that the *sot* witch has performed an anti-social act by killing a blood kin. Affliction and ill-health are believed to 'catch' the *sot* witch because (s)he has killed through *sot* witchcraft and has refused to perform the ritual of *ser sot*, public confession. Thus *ni bih ya wur/war mmut*, 'it will catch him/her in the form of illness'. It is to avoid such that the accused witch, in a public place, most commonly in a drinking place, on a festival day, while working with others on a farm or with friends in the market place, assumes a prophetic voice and narrates his or her evil deeds. At other times, they may talk as if in possession trance, but still in full control of their senses. The *sot* witch may say, 'You know we killed so-and-so and his meat is so sweet, it will last up to seven years', or 'You know I killed so-and-so because I was envious of his progress.'

Provided a confession is procured during a divination session, no fines are asked, nor are any punishments administered after the rites of *ser sot* public confession. But this does not prevent the public from responding with malicious gossips, rumours and stigmatisation of such persons through songs and popular *longkat*, moon light song-dances of the maidens, that spread from village to village like wild fire on dry harmattan grass. In pre-colonial times, those who confessed too frequently to such witchcraft activities became targetted for elimination during witch-hunts. They were gradually sizzled to death on large bonfires in a valley designated for this purpose, with adults and children standing on surrounding hills to watch the disgraceful event to deter others, even children, from becoming witches.

In Mupun land, when the verdict of a *Pa* diviner indicates *sot* unconfessed witchcraft attacks, in which case the afflicted experiences mild insanity, the victim is expected to give two goats and polished *fonio* as fines. Here the divination for uncovering cause of affliction is referred to as *Pa kyËr*, and witchcraft itself is called *kyËr*, for fear of incurring pollution of divination paraphernalia from the mere mention of *sot* witchcraft by name.

SOME CONCLUSIONS

It is clear from this article that unlike some other African groups, the Mupun differentiate *sot* (witchcraft) from *baak ka* (magic) and *lom* (sorcery). They attribute magic and sorcery to males, while witchcraft is regarded as a feminine activity. However, some women are believed to connive with male sorcerers, while, though considered a feminine craft, any number of males could engage in witchcraft activities as long as they belong to a 'guild'. People believe that in some guilds men are predominant, while others consist overwhelmingly of women. These guilds may not necessarily be organised along kinship lines, but their meeting places conform to certain societal structures; for instance, it is believed that witchcraft guilds are still organised along the traditional compound structure of Mupun society. Victims are however provided, bewitched and killed in turns along kinship lines.

Pa divination, which, strictly speaking, belongs to the world of mystical forces, provides the key to understanding the patterns of interaction between human beings and mystical forces in the cosmos. For example, all spirit beings are believed to possess the potential to cause ill-health. Mystical forces such as *baak ka* magic, *lom* sorcery and *sot* witchcraft have the same potential, and so does *dor* anger. *Pa* divination, however, operates as a mediator between *yil nji*, the spirit world, and *yil gurum*, the human world. It reveals to human beings what they should do to appease *yil nji*, the spirit world, and how to avert evil plans by fellow human beings in *yil gurum*, the human world.

Certain traditional causal factors such as drought, famine, epidemics and diseases associated with the deities and ancestors have greatly diminished in importance and are only relevant today to a few active traditional religionists. Yet other traditional causal factors, such as evil spirits, *dor* anger, *sot* witchcraft and *lom* sorcery, are still very much accepted, as are the believed sources of modern sorcery. In a consumer capitalist economy, where an effective civil society is lacking and where the economy has been devastated by massive corruption, with few facilities operating, and where a stupendously large population is competing for scarce resources, *lom* sorcery and *sot* witchcraft beliefs are given a new leash of life. New types of witchcraft beliefs that cut across blood kin, and sorcerous practices believed to kill victims quickly, with portents of even more devastating consequences, have emerged. It is no longer held that witches can only harm their kin or blood relations.

Under British colonial rule in Africa, practices related to witchcraft and sorcery were made illegal. The problem encountered with the ban, which still exists in Nigeria, is the difficulty of proving alleged witchcraft crimes to the satisfaction of a court of law, which may then punish the culprits under the appropriate sections of the law. Here, three developments have come to the surface. First, many people do not press charges of witchcraft accusations beyond the level of gossip because of fear for the witches, since the legal system is not capable of dealing with them. Secondly, only self-confessed witches are really liable to any legal punishment in by a law court. Thirdly, many people are not satisfied with the current legal situation, which prohibits people from accusing others of witchcraft since it can hardly be proven in a court of law. Finally, this has created greater fear of witchcraft in people's minds. As a result, modern witch-hunters and anti-witchcraft movements have become popular in both the urban areas and the countryside. This is itself an important issue, discussion of which goes beyond the scope of this article.

Although not the only factor, it is the candid opinion of this author that witchcraft beliefs persist in Africa today largely because of the failure of African states to establish sustainable civil society groups. Massive poverty, large debt burdens, weak national and individual economies, and the inability of most governments to provide adequate social welfare, housing schemes, medical and other health facilities, a proper learning environment for children, and the absence of most social amenities, tend to make witchcraft, sorcery and other cultic practices popular. If and when African governments were to provide adequate social, health and educational amenities to their citizens, reduce corruption to the barest minimum, and begin to establish civil society groups that focus on the development of the human person, some of these practices will become less pronounced than they are today.

The inability of most African nations generally to establish civil societies has resulted in very little change in African cosmologies concerning witchcraft beliefs. In my view, a change in the popular cosmology that underlies witchcraft beliefs, sorcery and other cultic practices will adversely effect changes within the African belief system concerning such issues. The cosmological changes experienced have only been widened to include more sophisticated beliefs and practices from other ethnic groups. Thus, ethnic groups such as the Bache (Rukuba) and Berom of the Jos Plateau, who had no knowledge of witchcraft before colonial times, today believe to have witches in their midst. So far, the type of change that have taken place in African societies as a result of colonialism, including Western capitalist and industrial economy and consumer patterns, education, politics and social patterns of interaction, have not succeeded in changing people's beliefs concerning these mystical forces. When such African nations are able to develop fairly stable civil societies with highly developed social, educational, health, economic and social amenities, people's picture of the cosmos will change drastically. This will consequently reduce the practice of witchcraft, sorcery and other cultic practices that seem rather to be on the increase in many African societies today.

Finally, I have established in this article that *dor* anger can be understood in both ordinary and witchcraft parlance. The scene of ordinary anger is *tup*, which is not harmful to anyone, whereas the scenario for *dor* anger is a much deeper and burning type of anger that transforms unwittingly into witchcraft intentions and attacks, loss of parental blessing and lack of progress for its victims. It is in this regard, according to Mupun thought, that anger metaphorically leads to witchcraft attacks. I further established in this article that though *dor* anger could be regarded as a metaphor of witchcraft, there is a clear sense in which *sot* witchcraft is different from *dor* anger.

Notes

* The author is grateful to Professor David Westerlund for inviting him to the University of Uppsala as a guest researcher and to Professor Gerrie ter Haar for soliciting funds from Utrecht University, which made it possible for him to present the original draft of this article as a paper at the IAHR Congress in Durban, South Africa in August 2000.

1. C.P. Grove, *Africa South of the Sahara*, London: Lutherwirth, 1970, p. 148. It is estimated that the various peoples, languages and dialects of the Jos Plateau number circa 150; see Marie de Paul Neiers, *The Peoples of the Jos Plateau, Nigeria: Their philosophy, manners and customs,* Frankfurt/M: Peter Lang, 1979, p. 17.

2. Cyril Imo, 'Religion and Social Stratification in Jos, Nigeria', Ph.D. thesis, University of Ibadan, 1989, p. 19.

3. See H. Crozier and Roger M. Blench (eds), *An Index of Nigerian languages*, Dallas: Summer Institute of Linguistics, 1992; C. Hoffman, 'Provisional Check List of Chadic languages (by Language Family)', Ibadan: Ibadan University Press; Hermann Jungraithmayr (ed), 'Die Sprache der Sura (Mwaghavul) in Nordnigerien', *Afrika und Ubersee*, vol. 47, nr 1, 1963, pp. 8-89; and Paul Newman, 'Chadic classification and reconstructions', *Afroasiatic Linguistics*, vol. 5, nr. 1, 1977, pp. 1-42; Ibid., *Nominal and Verbal Plurality in Chadic*, Publications in African Languages and Linguistics, Dordrecht and Providence: Foris Publications, 1990.

4. Umar H.D. Danfulani, 'A historico-missiological analysis of fifty years of COCIN in Mupunland', MA diss. University of Jos, 1986, pp. xxvi-xxvii.

5. *Nji* used in this context means spirits, but in the strict sense of the word it translates 'spirits' or 'souls of the ancestors'. *Yil* denotes 'world', and is also used for earth, ground and soil. Thus *yil nji* means 'spirit world' or 'world of spirit forces' believed to be located somewhere in the ground.

6. Umar H.D. Danfulani, *Pebbles and Deities: Pa divination patterns among the Ngas, Mupun and Mwaghavul in Nigeria*, Peter Lang: Frankfurt/M, 1995, pp. 117-9.

7. M. Dhavamony, *Phenomenology of Religion*, Rome: Gregorian University Press, 1973, p. 30.

8. Cf. Paul Radin, *Primitive Religion: Its nature and origin*, London and New York: Dover Publications, 1957, p. 57; E.E. Evans-

Pritchard, *Witchcraft, Oracles and Magic among the Azande,* Oxford: Clarendon Press, 1976, pp. 176 ff.

9. Cf. Ade Dopamu, 'Magic and Medicine in Yoruba Traditional Religion', Ph.D. thesis, University of Ibadan, 1977, p. 11.

10. Cf. C.L. Temple (ed), *Notes on the Tribes, Provinces, Emirates and States of the Northern Provinces of Northern Nigeria,* London: Frank Cass, 1965; J.S. Mbiti, *African Religions and Philosophy,* London: Heinemann, 1969, p. 202; Umar H.D. Danfulani, 'Islam, Christianity and traditional religion in a changing Nigerian society: case study of the Ngas of Plateau State', BA long essay, University of Jos, 1982, pp. 36 ff.

11. Tempels, Placide, *Bantu Philosophy,* Paris: Présence Africaine, 1959.

12. Evans-Pritchard, *Witchcraft, Oracles and Magic among the Azande.*

13. Cf. Danfulani, *Pebbles and Deities;* Daniel N. Wambutda, *A study of conversion among the Angas of Plateau State, with Emphasis on Christianity,* Frankfurt/M: Peter Lang, 1991.

14. Cf. Evans-Pritchard, *Witchcraft, Oracles and Magic among the Azande.*

15. See Danfulani, *Pebbles and Deities.*

16. The tortoise is the divination symbol of the majority of Chadic-speakers found on the eastern Jos Plateau in central Nigeria or the Nigerian Middle Belt.

17. Cf. Victor Turner, *The Ritual Process: Structure and anti-stucture,* Chicago: Aldine, 1969, p. 23.

18. Monica Wilson, *Communal Rituals of the Nyakyusa,* London: Oxford University Press, 1970, pp. 28 ff.

19. Cf. F.B. Welbourn, *Atoms and Ancestors,* London, 1968.

20. Danfulani, *Pebbles and Deities.*

21. The Mupun hold the belief that unborn children choose their totemic forms, which become the hiding places of their spirit-double. To kill the totemic animal in whatever form is to cause the death of its owner.

22. See Danfulani, *Pebbles and Deities,* pp. 149 ff.

23. Ibid., pp. 179 ff.

24. Ibid., p. 138.

25. Ibid., pp. 130 ff., 144 ff.

26. Wilson, *Communal Rituals.*

27. Ibid., pp. 28 ff; cf. Susan Whyte, 'Uncertain persons in Nyole divination', *Journal of Religion in Africa*, vol. 20, nr.1, 1990, pp. 41-8.

28. Axel-Ivar Berglund, *Zulu Thought-Patterns and Symbolism*, London: Hurst, 1976; Ibid., 'Confessions of guilt and restoration to health: some illustrative Zulu examples', in: Anita Jacobson-Widding and David Westerlund (eds), *Culture, Experience and Pluralism: Essays on African ideas of illness and healing,* Uppsala: Almqvist and Wiksell, 1989, pp. 109-24.

8

THE *MBAMBI* BROUGHT THE MESSAGE: *SHITERA*, WITCHCRAFT OF REVENGE

Samuel Kaveto Mbambo

INTRODUCTION

It is a common belief among the Vagciriku of Kavango Region in the north of Namibia that some witchcraft-related illnesses are caused by *shitera*(revenge). Such a step is believed to be taken when a family member is hurt or killed and no compensation is paid. The relatives of the deceased or injured person will pay a *nganga*(healer) to execute *shitera*.

A good example of this practice is what happened in Dosa village at the beginning of 1998, when eleven people of the same household and the same clan and totem died within a very short period. The people who were affected believe that this was the work of a person who uses witchcraft as a means of revenge. The tragic incident was widely reported in the mass media. The Namibian Broadcasting Corporation (its radio as well as its television section) and two newspapers in Namibia described the incident as a mystery.[2]

Mysterious or not, the Dosa tragedy is a real story, in which real people were involved. It is a story that did not happen centuries or even decades ago, but only a few years ago. The homestead where it happened still exists and the graves of the victims are still fresh. In the village of Dosa, it became once again clear that witchcraft practices in Namibia are much alive and continue to do what they are known for: killing people. Witchcraft beliefs and practices are alive in the modern world of the Internet and cell-phones, at least in Africa. If one were to go to an African graveyard to look for the grave of witchcraft, the warden would probably ask the person:[3] Why are you looking for the living among the dead?'[3] Witchcraft in Africa has survived despite Western-Christian cultural denial and rejection. In Africa, witchcraft is a reality today as it was in the past. It is a life-style, a totally different view of life and of the universe, another cosmology. It is a world with its own rules, morals and ethics.

My objective in this article is to show that witchcraft plays a dominant role in the life of the people in the Kavango Region, particularly the Vagciriku. It constitutes a reality which needs to be taken seriously by anybody who wants to interact with them.[4]

THE DOSA TRAGEDY

The witchcraft incident took place in a small village called Dosa in Kavango Region of Namibia, where everybody knows everybody. The village is situated about 50 km south of Nyangana Catholic Mission station and falls under the Nyangana health district. On 15 January 1998, seven death cases were reported from Dosa village within 24 hours. According to Mr. Kapirika, the councillor of Ndiyona Constituency under which Dosa village falls, these deaths affected three generations within the same family, from the great-grandmother to the great-grand children, ranging in age from a four years' old child to an elderly woman of seventy-five years. The incident took place during the summer season, when people were busy working in their *mahangu* fields.[5] The following provides a detailed account of what happened.

According to the councillor, the sequence of events started with the death of a four years' old boy called Haingura, whose mother was Numba. The boy died within few hours after the appearance of *mbambi*, the messenger, on Sunday 14 January 1998. That same day Haingura's grandmother, Shidona (55 years) became very sick. She went to the clinic in Kandjara, a neighbouring village, but the nurse at the clinic advised her to go to Nyangana Hospital. The following day, on her way to the hospital, she died. Meanwhile Rukunde (75), the mother of Shidona and the great-grandmother of Haingura also got sick. She went to the clinic, where she died on the same day, January 15th.

During the course of the very same day, 15 January 1998, Namutenya (45), the younger sister of Shidona and the third daughter of Rukunde, took her two years' old grand-daughter

Matumbo to the clinic. When she arrived at the clinic in Kand-jara, her grand-child Matumbo died. In the meantime Nam-utenya also fell ill. She was taken to Nyangana hospital, where she died on the same day.

On that day, the Nyangana hospital decided to send a medical team to investigate the cause of these deaths at Dosa village. When they arrived in Dosa they found two boys dead: ten years' old Kamonga and eight years' old Shikongo. These two boys were the children of Matumbo senior (51 years old), the daughter of Rukunde and a sister of Shidona and Namutenya.

The Nyangana hospital staff brought nine people to the hospital for treatment and closer monitoring. Five of them were under treatment, while four were under observation only. The four who were under observation were discharged within two days without any problem. But three of the five who were under observation and treatment died. This included Wayera, a nine years' old girl who died on 16 January 1998, Muku (10) who died on 17 January 1998, and Mudumbi (12) who died on 18 January 1998.

The actual cause of the deaths could not be determined either by the police or the hospital's medical staff. Various speculations were made regarding the incident by the different sources from which I collected the information, including the Namibian Police, the Nyangana and the Rundu Medical Staff, the councillor of Ndiyona Constituency, surviving relatives and the people in the Nyangana area. The preliminary police report stated that 'the cause of death is still unknown and the case is under investigation. A post-mortem will be held on the bodies to determine the actual cause of death'.[6] The Ministry of Health and Social Services (Kavango Directorate) compiled two reports on the incident. The first report was compiled immediately after the tragic events on 15 January 1998. It concluded that most likely the disease that led to the deaths was due to food poisoning (toxin) and might have started in the home where four members of the same family died.[7] This conclusion was drawn despite the fact that the surviving relatives denied eating any poisoned or contaminated food. On 19 January 1998 the Ministry of Health and Social Services compiled a second report, after senior medical staff members of Rundu State Hospital had been despatched to Nyangana Hospital. This report concluded that the aetiology did not look clear from the signs and symptoms present and did not support infectious agents such as bacterial, viral or parasitic ones at that stage. However, from the fact that all members of the same family got sick and died, as well as from findings of distended tender abdomen and vomiting, it could be assumed that the most likely cause was food poisoning.[8]

In an interview with Stefan Kuit, a Dutch student who was doing research in Nyangana area at the time of the incident, Numba, one of the survivors and the mother of Haingura, the boy who died first, claimed that the deaths had been caused by a paid *nganga*. Numba was convinced that these were not ordinary deaths but the result of *shitera* (revenge). She affirmed her allegation with reference to an event that preceded the incident. She claimed that three days before the tragedy started, something unusual happened. Numba called this unusual incident *shipo* (a bad omen). She related the incident as follows:[9]

> That day, most of the people went to the *mahangu* fields. I stayed behind with my four years' old son Haingura. While I was washing dishes in front of my mother's house, a *mbambi* [bush buck] entered the compound and stood between the house of my mother and my younger brother's house. Kamonga, my younger brother, was also present while the *mbambi* stood on that spot for a long time. He instructed the dogs to catch the *mbambi*, but to our surprise they did nothing. I think the *mbambi* stood there for at least half an hour. We called our grandfather, whose compound was close to ours. He came with our cousin Steffa Kamonga, who brought his dogs with him. He instructed the dogs to catch the *mbambi*. The dogs chased the *mbambi*, but they could not catch it and it got away. We talked about this strange encounter with the *mbambi*. Steffa was worried, saying: 'I have never seen such a thing in my life. This *mbambi* is a *shipo*' [a bad omen, a messenger of bad news].

Three days later the problem began. My son, Haingura, complained about pain in his chest and said that
he wanted to vomit. The stuff he vomited was yellow.
Haingura was an asthma patient. When the problem
started, I thought it was the same old problem that
started again. All of a sudden he stopped breathing.
The colour of his urine was also very yellow, like
someone who is suffering from liver disease.

Just after the boy had stopped breathing, my mother
arrived from the *mahangu* fields. When she saw the
boy, she became weak and collapsed. Her last words
were: 'I have no power in my body, otherwise I could
have helped you to take the child to the hospital'.
After these words my mother slept. I tried to wake
her up but she did not wake up again. Meanwhile
my grandfather and grandmother also came to our
compound. They took my mother to Kandjara clinic,
but the nurse referred her to the hospital. On the
way to the hospital she died. From there, many other
members of the family died within a very short time.
I therefore believe that this was *shitera* [revenge].

Like Numba, many people in the area believed that the cause
of the deaths was not food poisoning as the medical staff and
the police claimed, but that the cause must be *shitera* (revenge)
since all the people who died belonged to the same clan of the
Vakandjadi (hawk clan). Although there were other people in the
homestead who belonged to another clan known as Vakankora
(toad-frog clan), they were not affected. This seemingly 'selective
death' made the Vakandjadi clan believe that these deaths were
witchcraft-related. They suspected the Vakangombe clan (cattle
clan) to be the culprit.

Their suspicion was based on an incident that had occurred
two years earlier, in 1996. One of the members of the Vakangombe clan (Nico Haingura) died in 1996 while he was under
treatment of a traditional healer called Thadeus Murorwa.
Murorwa is the only son of Rukunde, one of the victims of the
Dosa tragedy. When Nico Haingura died, the Vakangombe clan
accused Murorwa of killing him. The police arrested Murorwa
on charges of poisoning, but after investigating the matter they

found him innocent. The Vakangombe clan was not happy with the outcome of the police investigation, alleging that Murorwa had bribed the police. They demanded compensation for the death of their relative. The Vakandjadi were waiting for the heads of the families of the Vakangombe clan to invite them to discuss the issue. But there was reluctance on the side of the elders of the Vakangombe clan. Some people thought that the headman of the area was also to be blamed because he was informed about the incident but did not do anything about it. According to Kapirika, the councillor of Ndiyona Constituency, it was this delay that angered some members of the Vakangombe clan, especially the young people. They decided to take up the issue without informing and consulting the elders of the clan. Rumours went around that one of Nico Haingura's brothers went to Botswana or Zambia to engage a *nganga* to take revenge.

People believe that it is only *nganga's* from outside Kavango Region who possess the witchcraft power to do these things. Sicknesses caused by *shitera* or *shipo* are considered difficult to heal. It takes a lot of money and time to treat such sickness, with or without drums.

URODI (WITCHCRAFT) BELIEFS

The Dosa tragedy is seen by the Vagciriku as the result of witchcraft, caused by *shitera* (revenge). The event raises a number of questions: What precisely do the Vagciriku mean when they refer to witchcraft (*urodi*)? Who is considered a *murodi* (witch)? What does a *murodi* use? Who can be affected by *urodi*? Why and when are people believed to bewitch others? Does *urodi* serve any purpose in the community? Or, in short: how does the Dosa incident contribute to our understanding of witchcraft (*urodi*) among the Vagciriku?

This section seeks to know what do the Vagciriku mean when they are talking about witchcraft (*urodi*). When a Mugciriku hears the word *murodi*, his reaction is one of fear. He or she is frightened because *urodi* is considered as dangerous by the Vagciriku. Whether a person is accused of being a *murodi* or threatened with *urodi*, in both cases the consequences are deemed catastrophic.

To define the term *urodi* has proven to be a difficult task. Although feared by many, *urodi* is also not well-known to many people. This is clear from the answers of some interviewees:

> I hear about *urodi*, but I have never seen it. The only people who know about *urodi* are the *murodi* and the *nganga*.

> I have heard about these things, but up to now I do not know what *urodi* looks like, whether it is black, red or white.

> Yes, I know that *urodi* exists, although I have not seen it. I believe that the lives of many people have been destroyed by *urodi*.

Some respondents claimed to have seen *urodi*, especially when it was exposed by the *nganga*. Some *vanganga* confirmed to me the existence of *urodi* by narrating their personal experience of it.

The concept of *urodi* has various meanings. The user of the term can imply various connotations, from those of a believed 'real' witch to those of a man who only occasionally uses harmful magic on provocation, or perhaps even simply a tendency to act secretly.[10] In general, in the social context of the Vacgiriku, *urodi* may be defined as a belief in a metaphysical power that can be acquired from evil spirits with the sole purpose of destroying people's life and property. It may also include the use of poisonous substances from plants or animals:

> *Urodi* is a way to kill a person by using mysterious objects and hypnotising techniques.

> *Urodi* is poison and it is very dangerous.

> *Urodi* is the power possessed and used by some people to execute their evil plans. The aim of this practice is harmful. There is nothing good in *urodi*. Everything about it is evil. People tend to look down on *urodi*.

> *Urodi* is the use of poisonous plants. There are plants that are poisonous in the field, just as you get plants

that have the power to cure. These plants can kill people when used. People who use such plants with the aim of killing others are *varodi*.

Urodi is a sensitive subject to discuss in public, especially among adults, because no one wants to be associated with this phenomenon. *Urodi* is perceived as a destructive power in the community. In the field research it was my experience that people did not openly talk about it. One interviewee said:

> It is not safe to talk openly about *urodi* for fear that people will think that you are a *murodi*. The question everybody fears is: How do you know about these things if you are not a *murodi*? We believe that it is only those who have *urodi* who ought to know something about it.

TYPES OF *URODI*

Among the Vagciriku *urodi* is classified in different categories. These categories are determined by the kind of *urodi* possessed by that person. There are many types of *urodi*, of which *shitera* (witchcraft of revenge) is only one. Some of the most well-known ones are discussed below.

Urodi wa likiti (witchcraft of an ogre)

It is believed that there are some *varodi* (witches) who use a goblin to kill their victim. A goblin is said to be invisible and can only be seen by a *murodi* or a *nganga*. People were not able to give me a physical description of this phenomenon. They believe that when *likiti* witchcraft is used the victim will not live long but will die after a short illness. Such sickness will only last for one or two days. *Likiti* witchcraft is believed to be one of the fastest killing witchcrafts. The symptoms of this type of witchcraft are headache and fever. Later the victim will have hallucinations. He claims to see things that other people do not see.

Urodi wavirumbarumba (witchcraft of spooks)

Some *varodi* are believed to use *urumba* (spooks) as their assistants. These spooks are spirits of people whom the *murodi* bewitched. They are believed to be partially invisible, independent phenomena. These creatures are sent to people to make them sick or even kill them. *Urumba* are also used to destroy other people's properties. One interviewee told me that this kind of *urodi* is very unusual today because *urumba* are too demanding. They eat too much like pigs and a person has to work hard to sustain them. *Urumba* are also used to work in the fields of *mahangu*. They are sent by the owner to collect *mahangu* (millet) from other people's fields. There are many stories about people who have been bewitched and turned into *urumba*. This type of witchcraft bears a relation to *rututa* or witchcraft of collection.

Rututa (witchcraft of collection)

The term *rututa* is derived from the verb *kututa* that means 'to collect.' It is believed that *rututa* is a way in which a *murodi* collects crops from other people's *mahangu* fields and barns. This happens when a person commits a ritual murder (*kupitita*) and puts some parts of this victim in the *mahangu* barn. It is alleged that a person who has *rututa* does not need to work very hard in his *mahangu* field, because his *urumba* will collect *mahangu* from other people's fields. The collectors of *mahangu* are believed to be those victims who have been bewitched and changed into *urumba*. People say that they are not really killed, but kept in a secret place where only the *nganga* and some who are specially treated by the *vanganga* can see them.

Rututa is not the type of *urodi* which people are often accused of. But when it happens it becomes a serious issue to the point that it may divide entire communities. When such accusations occur in a family, the only way to solve the problem is for the members to separate, as it is very difficult or almost impossible to reconcile them. On the other hand, family members who have this bad relationship sometimes use witchcraft accusations to express their deteriorating relations and use the excuse of witchcraft to separate from each other.

Muterembe (witchcraft of lightning)

Muterembe can be translated as lightning or thunder. The Vagciriku believe that some *varodi* use *muterembe* to strike their enemies. This means that in the witchcraft discourse people consider the *murodi* as someone with the ability to manipulate nature, in this case the ability to cause lightning. Many interviewees told me that originally the Vagciriku did not know *muterembe*, but that it is something they learned from their Angolan neighbours, the Vanyemba.

It is believed that *muterembe* can be successful when the targetted person is guilty. It is sent to the victim's house and strikes like lightning. People will think that this is just natural lightning and nobody will be suspected of being responsible for this destructive act. People consider *muterembe* as a type of *urodi* possessed by very few people. *Muterembe* is used in many cases for revenge purposes.

Kata, bwakama and *wandjongoka* witchcraft (types of witchcraft used by women)

Kata and *bwakama* are other types of *urodi*. The first type is called *kata*, which can be translated as a 'small bow', because it is a small bow made of the rib of a snake called *lihuko* (a frog-snake) and a hair taken from the sexual area of a man. *Kata* is believed to be an effective mechanism for women to control their husbands' sex life. When the husband leaves the house, his wife unties the small bow. This means that the man will not have an erection and therefore be unable to have sex with other women. When he comes back home, the wife ties the small bow, and the man becomes normal again.

Bwakama is another type of *urodi* believed to be used by women to control their husbands. *Bwakama* means 'to seat down'. It is believed that when *bwakama* works effectively, a wife will have control over her husband. The husband will be mentally disabled in such a way that he will only act on the instructions of his wife. One informant told me that when a man is bewitched with *bwakama* he becomes like a puppet of his wife. When he, for instance, comes from the bush with a bunch of wood, he will have to wait for his wife to tell him to put it down. It is said that *bwakama* is put in the husband's food.

A third type of *urodi* considered to be used by women is *wandjongoka* (softener). *Wandjongoka* influences a man in such a way that he will follow his wife wherever she goes. It is said that when a man is bewitched with *wandjongoka*, he will follow his wife even when she is going to fetch water or collect firewood. He will only stop following his wife when she tells him not to do so. A person who is bewitched with *wandjongoka* or *bwakama* is said not to be able to think for himself. He is also seen as a person who does not like his own relatives.

The urge to control that manifests itself in *kata*, *bwakama* and *wandjongoka*, is believed to have the capacity to develop into fully-fledged *urodi*. Sometimes the *mutondo* or medicine that a woman may obtain from a healer does not function as it should. This may prompt her to look for additional means to get her husband under her control, and she may eventually become a *murodi*.

Upure and matura

Upure and *matura* are two more types of *urodi*. It is difficult to distinguish the two from each other as they are believed to have more or less similar functions. When people make a distinction they say that *upure* is a kind of power that is used to protect a person or his property. In the past people used *upure* to protect their household against their enemies during the war. When, for example, an enemy were to come close to a household, this would be surrounded by water or a jungle. The enemy would only hear people talking and women pounding *mahangu*, but would not be able to see them. In this respect *mutondo* is used in a positive way.

Matura, on the other hand, is a *mutondo* that is used to harm other people. A person who has *matura* is believed to have the ability to adopt the form of an animal. He can change himself into a lion or crocodile in order to catch other people's cattle or even to attack other people. Such a person is also believed to be in possession of dangerous animals, such as lions, hyenas, crocodiles, snakes, and dogs and cats, as his familiars. These familiars are used to destroy other people's lives and properties.

One informant explained the difference between *upure* and *matura* as follows:

> *Upure* is used for protective and defensive purposes, while *matura* is used to cause harm and destruction.

Although *matura* is used for an individual's self-defence it is considered more negative than *upure*. Both *upure* and *matura* are powers which only people with high positions in the community can posses. These people use this power to protect themselves, their families and their people. *Upure* gives a person a kind of high status and respect. It is not just anybody who can posses this power. A person who has *upure* can change into an animal such as a lion, elephant or a crocodile if need be. Others have the ability to change a bunch of grass into a snake in order to catch a thief in the field or garden. It is also believed that such people can use this power to change a homestead into a lake of water, especially when enemies attack it.

The Vagciriku believe that most of the people in high positions in the community, such as chiefs, posses one or another type of *upure* to protect themselves and their people against enemies. One particular type of *upure* used by the *vahompa*(chiefs) of the Vagciriku is called *peku*. *Peku* is believed to have the power to change an angry person's heart and mind. Someone who comes with anger to a person who possesses *peku* will not do any harm. He will just stand outside the homestead and pass urine. After passing urine, the anger is gone and he may even forget what he actually wanted.

Lingowore

Lingowore is a type of plant believed to be grown by certain people to strengthen their status and their position in the community. This plant is found in the *mahangu* fields or hidden somewhere inside or outside the homestead. *Vahompa* (chiefs), *vanganga* (healers), and big cattle and *mahangu* farmers are believed to be people who use *lingowore*. *Lingowore* has to be kept alive, lest the owner will get sick or the cattle will start to die. People believe that *lingowore* is kept alive with human blood. That is why from time to time the owner of *lingowore* will sacrifice a person, especially a member of the family. The *hompa* (chief) has a small branch or a leaf of *lingowore* tied on his belt, which he wears around his waist. It is said that whenever the leaves of *lingowore* begin to wither, human blood is needed to feed it. Therefore, the Vagciriku consider *lingowore* as another type of *urodi,* as it destroys people's lives.

Some people who own many heads of cattle or large *mahangu* fields are also believed to have *lingowore.* In the first few months of obtaining the plant, a particular ritual is done. The person is expected to wash his body in an old calabash with medicine. The washing continues until the content of the calabash becomes rotten. The worms that appear in the calabash are taken out and squeezed on the backs of the cattle, whereafter the calabash is smashed into pieces in the cattle kraal. The person is expected to observe sexual abstinence for the duration of the ritual. When such a person dies, one of his cattle is slaughtered and buried in the kraal without eating any part of it to prevent his cattle from 'following' him. It is further believed that people who possess *lingowore* use it to collect crops from other people's fields. In such a case *lingowore* is planted in the middle of the field. While the *mahangu* are growing, *lingowore* also grows. It is said that when the crops are ripe the possessor of *lingowore* collects *mahangu* from other people's fields, especially during the night.

Some *vanganga* are also believed to have *lingowore.* The ceremony of obtaining *lingowore* takes place early in the morning, while other people are still asleep. The old *nganga* will takes an aspiring *nganga* into the bush, where he is instructed to cut one of the roots of a particular plant. When the root is cut, a person whom the novice wants to kill is believed to die, because the root represents an individual's throat. A piece of this root is cooked for the whole night. The next morning *lingowore* is planted somewhere in the homestead of the new *nganga.* Although *lingowore* is considered to be evil, it provides the *nganga* with a special authority. Like chiefs, *vanganga* too are considered to be mysterious and untouchable.

Lingowore is considered to be one of the most dangerous types of *urodi,* because it kills people every year. In 1996 there was a case at Shighuru village, where a man was accused of possessing *lingowore.* This was a big case, which was brought to the traditional court. The man was accused of sacrificing two of his children to *lingowore.* The man agreed that he had bought it from a *nganga* in Angola to strengthen his medicine, since he was also a *nganga*. After he had been exposed, his wife divorced him and he was fined five head of cattle to pay the relatives of his wife for the death of the children.

THE CONCEPT OF *MURODI* (WITCH)

So far we have dealt with the concept of *urodi* (witchcraft). In the following I will focus more on the *murodi*, the person who is believed to practice witchcraft. A *murodi* is believed to have the ability to harm others with inherent or acquired mysterious power. He or she may or may not be aware that (s)he possesses such power. Some respondents described a *murodi* this way:

> A *murodi* is someone who possesses evil powers with the aim to harm others. The community regards a *murodi* as an evil person. There is nothing good about a *murodi* and people tend to dissociate themselves from such a person.

> A *murodi* is an evil person who only seeks to kill other people. During the day he looks normal. But in the night he changes completely and sees other people like animals. Even his own child looks like an antelope. What comes up in his mind when he sees another person in the night is to kill him.

Those who were interviewed on the matter stated that there is nothing good about a *murodi*. One *nganga* put it this way:

> There is always anger and hatred in the heart of a *murodi*. He pretends to be happy and friendly, but in reality his heart is always boiling with anger.

Another *nganga* described a *murodi* as a person who is 'more cruel than a murderer, because a murderer gives you signs that he is angry with you or that he does not like you. But a *murodi* never shows you any sign but in the night he bewitches you.'

The Vagciriku describe a *murodi* in different ways: as someone who likes to walk alone, or who does not want to eat with other people. They have a proverbial saying: 'Whoever does not drink even a cup of water in the home of another person is a *murodi*'.

But also somebody who walks during the night or someone who likes to speak to himself can be considered a *murodi*. In that sense, every unusual mannerism is considered tantamount to *urodi*. When a person behaves differently from the accepted norm he is liable to be accused of *urodi*.

I got various answers to the question: how does a person become a *murodi*? Some said that a person could become a *murodi* through inheritance (*urodi wakupinga*). Witchcraft by inheritance means that a person inherits *urodi* from his parents, especially from a mother to a daughter. The common term used for this phenomenon is *urodi wakuyamwenena*, which literally means: 'witchcraft obtained through the sucking of milk'. But it includes more than that. The same term is used when *mutondo* (medicine) is put on the food of the child or rubbed on the breasts of the mother. Generally, every type of *urodi* obtained during childhood is known as *urodi wakuyamwenena*. Because of this perception, people believe that a child of a *murodi* is a potential *murodi*. The reason for giving the child this medicine is to protect it from *varodi* and other evil spirits.

It is also believed that a person can become a *murodi* through the services of a *nganga*. There is a general belief that those who like to consult healers regularly end up being *varodi*. This happens sometimes during the process of healing. It is said that some *vanganga* tell their patients that they could give them *mutondo* (medicine) to protect them against the *varodi*. This medicine comes in different forms. It can be a kind of liquid that must be drunk or used in the bath; an ointment that a person should smear on his body; or an object called *mpero*, which has to be swallowed. *Mpero* consists of the wax of the honeybee, the blood of an antelope, and the powder of medicinal herbs.[11] It is believed that this *mutondo* often turns out to be *urodi*. The *mpero*, especially, is a substance commonly believed to have the potential for turning a person into a *murodi*. It is this substance that enables a *murodi* to kill people.

People may also buy *urodi*. This type of *urodi* is believed to come from South Africa. It is said that many people who used to work in the gold-mines in Johannesburg bought there *mutondo*, which later turned out to be *urodi*. People buy this to protect themselves or their property against evil powers. Nobody will go to a *murodi* and ask to buy *urodi*. A person will go to a *nganga,* or any other person whom he considers as an expert in medicine, and offer to buy medicine from him.

It is generally believed that no person has the intention of becoming a *murodi*. The process starts by looking for medicine that may help solve a particular problem. Sometimes a person looks for medicine to solve marriage problems. Or he may look for medicine to help him with his agricultural activities. Others might want medicine for their business to improve. The medicine might work well in the initial stage, but at a later stage, it is alleged, such medicine might develop into *urodi*. It is believed that when such a stage is reached, a person will become a *murodi*. Such people are sometimes exposed by the *nganga* or they make a confession and seek help.

FAMILIARS OF MURODI

It is believed that a *murodi* uses a variety of animals and objects as his familiars to harm people. These objects are taken from people, animals and plants or derived from supernatural powers.

Pieces of human flesh are considered to be the most common and feared substance of *urodi*. The most popular substances used by *varodi* are pubic hair, menstruation blood, semen and the human brain. It is believed that these things are given to, or forced upon, a victim before they can work effectively.[12] A victim of witchcraft may, for example, be forced to eat human flesh during the night; later this becomes a problem for the rest of that person's life. It is also said that an entire corpse can be used by a *murodi* as a familiar. In other words, not only may the flesh of a corpse be used in bad medicine, but also the dead themselves may be captured and used. One *nganga* described how the *murodi* is believed to do this:

> When a person dies because he is bewitched, he is not really dead. He stops breathing because the *murodi* has sucked out his soul and keeps it in a pipe for the time being. After the burial the *murodi* goes to the graveyard to exhume the body. When taking

out the body he cleanses the person with cold water. At the same time he tries to put back the spirit, which is kept in the pipe. When the person starts to move the witch gives him medicine to drink. This medicine changes the mind of the victim. He will become like a puppet in the hands of a *murodi*. From there this person becomes an *urumba* [ghost] which the witch uses to harass other people.

Animals are equally considered useful instruments or familiars of the *varodi*. Animals such as snakes, cats, dogs, crocodiles, hyenas and lions are common familiars that are believed to work for them. It is also believed that some *varodi* have the power of meta-morphosis and can change themselves into animals such as lions. Such lions are known as *mangwangwa* among the Vagciriku. It is said that when such lions are injured, the *murodi* who possesses the power is also injured. It is further believed that the *varodi* use certain animals, such as hyenas, as means of transport, because they are reliable and fast.

In addition to *urumba,* animals and birds, the *varodi* are believed to use other objects such as the poison of snakes, the gall of a crocodile or the brain of an anteater. A *murodi* is believed to be capable of using any object such as *mahangu*, corn, a piece of human flesh or a piece of human bone to hurt other people. A person would be careful not to leave hair clippings or nail parings lying around for fear that someone might use them against him. Every time a person has a hair-cut, all the hair is carefully col-lected so that it should not end up in the wrong hands.

Another known method used by *varodi* to harm others is *likova* (a witchcraft object). *Varodi* specialised in the use of *likova* may order their ghosts to shoot *likova* at the person they want to harm. Or they may bury *likova* under the threshold of a person's house or in the middle of a path that he or she frequently uses. The instructions are given to the *likova* as if it could hear and see the targetted person and attack him in a particular way. *Likova* is believed to contain human skin or other parts removed from a child that has been recently killed for the intended purpose. *Likova* can only be removed from the victim by a *nganga* by sucking it out of the patient.

Generally speaking, it is believed that *varodi* involve themselves in activities which are considered the reverse of normal values and behaviour. They act secretly at night, instead of openly by day as honest people do, and they operate with the assistance of familiar animals of the night. They are associated with death and are often presumed to desecrate graves, to eat human flesh, and to kill people either for fun or to further their own powers. They are believed to have special powers, often through the help of evil spirits. Moreover, *varodi* reject kinship loyalties, and the kin of *varodi* are believed to be in as much danger as anybody else. One interviewee expressed this as follows:

> The *varodi* become vicious like wild beasts during the night. They become like lions and wild dogs. Other people become like bucks and gazelles in their eyes. When they see people they only want to kill and eat them. *Varodi* are cruel people, they do not have mercy for anyone. They kill and eat even their own children.

It is generally believed among the Vagciriku that once a person is a *murodi* he will be a *murodi* forever, although there are differing opinions about the question whether a *murodi* could get rid of his *urodi*. Particularly if such a person acquired it through the sucking of the mother's milk, it is believed not to be possible to get rid of it. Others are of the opinion that it is possible to get rid of *urodi* if the person were to confess, show the substance he has hidden, and destroy it with fire. Thereafter he should drink a medicine, called *kuhamba*, which takes away every possibility of further effectiveness.

CONCLUSION

From the above it appears that witchcraft beliefs and accusations are pervasive among the Vagciriku. There are many reasons why witchcraft is believed to be used to harm other people, such as jealousy, hatred and revenge. The Dosa case is a good example of *shitera* or witchcraft of revenge. *Shitera* (revenge witchcraft) becomes operative when an innocent family member is hurt or killed and the relatives feel or believe that justice is not done to them.

The Vagciriku believe that revenge is one important reason that forces a person to use *urodi*. For example, when a weak or poor person has a dispute with a powerful or influential person in society the former is usually disadvantaged. His case is not treated well or fairly, as it ought to be. This is expressed in the saying: *Ushi wamutighona kughulya nakashoni* ('The honey of a poor man is eaten with a piece of grass'). *Shitera* starts when such things happen. People in Nyangana believe that the Dosa incident, in which more than ten people died within 48 hours, is a clear example of *shitera*. The general perception among the Vagciriku is that this incident was the result of revenge.

The Vagciriku believe that when witchcraft is practiced, it affects all members of the family and neighbours. When an individual is affected, the community is also affected and the social organisation disrupted. In the Dosa case, all those who died from *shitera* belonged to one particular clan—the hawk clan. Although only one clan was directly hurt, the rest of the community was also affected. The mistrust and distrust caused in the process will take long to overcome, especially between the hawk clan and the cattle clan in the village. And more importantly even, Dosa village will never be the same again.

Notes

1. A *mbambi* is a bush buck.
2. *Die Republikein*, 22 and 29 January 1998, and *The Namibian*, 2 February 1998.
3. A reference to the New Testament story of the resurrection of Jesus. See Lk. 24:5.
4. See Samuel K. Mbambo, *'Heal with God': Indigenous healing and religion among the Vagciriku of Kavango Region, Namibia*, on which the present article is based (Utrecht University, 2002), notably chapter 5 on witchcraft beliefs and accusations.
5. *Mahangu* is a traditional crop cultivated by and considered as a staple food of the Vakavango.
6. Police report: Regional Commander, Kavango Region, 16 January 1998.

7. Nyangana District Epidemic Preliminary Report, 15 January 1998.

8. Nyangana District Epidemic Second Report, 19 January 1998.

9. Cf. Stefan Kuit, '"Witchcraft is African technology": vertalingen van hekserij in de antropologische literatuur en in Gciriku, Namibia', MA thesis, University of Amsterdam, 2000, pp. 66-7.

10. Samuel K. Mbambo, 'Magie 'n struikelblok? 'n Ondersoek na die vraag of magie enighe negatiewe uitwerking het op die verkondiging en die uitlewing van die evangelie onder die Vakavango', MA diss., University of the North, 1990, p. 193.

11. See also Kuit, 'Witchcraft is African technology', p. 45.

12. Mbambo, 'Magie 'n struikelblok?', 1990, p. 42.

9

WITCHCRAFT AS A CHALLENGE TO BATSWANA IDEAS OF COMMUNITY AND RELATIONSHIPS

Gomang Seratwa Ntloedibe-Kuswani

INTRODUCTION

> Witchcraft, as a form of Evil, has become a bother and a serious embarrassment for any philosophy of life, whether atheistic or religious. It threatens to destroy all but silently' [Unknown].

Kenneth Kaunda, former President of Zambia, once said that Europe is famous for its technology, Asia for its mysticism, and Africa for its ideas about relationships. Yet, Africa faces a challenge from within, due to the witchcraft beliefs that are so dominant on the continent. Witchcraft beliefs and practices have been recorded from various parts of Africa, including, for example, former Rhodesia, present day-Zimbabwe[1], Tanzania,[2] and the Nile-Congo area[3]; as well as from other parts of the world, such as the blood-sucking witches of South-Central Mexico.[4]

When I was first asked to take part in a symposium on the issue of witchcraft, known as *boloi* in Setswana, I had to think hard about the subject, especially knowing that *boloi* is discussed as an abstract subject in my society. It is abstract in the sense that, in Botswana, no one can come out and declare him- or herself a 'witch', and in many instances people are called witches behind their backs. Immediately after accepting to participate in the symposium, I started to ask some people to be my research assistants. None of them agreed, arguing that witchcraft is an untouchable topic. Instead they wanted to know where I got the courage to research such a topic. As for them, they did not want to be associated with *boloi*.

One time, when I was searching information on the Internet, I came across an article entitled 'Earth-Spirit'. As I read through, I found an interview by Theodore Mills from Massachusetts in the United States, published in 1989 in *Fire-heart* magazine. It recorded that Mills has been an influential figure in modern American witchcraft and a mentor to hundreds of witches, from Massachusetts to Arizona. The statement confirms that witchcraft is not to be considered an African phenomenon only; it is a worldwide phenomenon, especially since the Mills interview mentions that most of the witches are in England and some in Italy. So one assumes that it is deliberate for Europeans, Americans and Asians not to be represented in the symposium. American and European witches seem free to declare their witchcraft publicly and are considered as normal part of society,[5] unlike in my country Botswana and probably the continent of Africa at large.

Apart from the *Fire-heart* magazine story, some time in 1999 a drama was shown on South African television called *Ke Bona Boloi*. In Setswana this phrase can be interpreted differently, either as: 'I see witchcraft', or as: 'It is witchcraft', depending on the dialect and tone that are used. I followed the drama with interest because I had already started working on this paper. But what I discovered was that, relatively, the drama was a bit exaggerated. However, I assumed that it was intended to share with the viewers how witchcraft-related problems cause unrest in some South African communities.

In addition, in early 2000 several newspapers in Botswana were carrying a story about witchcraft reported from Swaziland. The story was entitled: 'Swaziland Apart', and discussed the phenomenon of witchcraft in the context of the small southern African kingdom of Swaziland. It was reported that King Mswati's inner circle was leading a campaign to have the Speaker of Parliament expelled from the House for alleged stealing of cowdung from the royal kraal during an annual thanksgiving ceremony on Christmas day.[6] The same story was reported on Radio Botswana. It was said that the campaign against the Speaker happened because the Swazi believe that unauthorised taking of cow-dung from the royal kraal is associated with attempts to bewitch the king.

Witchcraft, in other words, is a subject much debated in African societies, including in Botswana where many believe in the reality of it. In my contribution I will examine witchcraft beliefs among the Batswana and the challenge that such beliefs pose to their traditional ideas of community. In the following, I will first discuss the complex witchcraft beliefs that exist among some communities in Botswana. I will then trace the type of problems found in contemporary Batswana communities as a result of witchcraft beliefs. Finally, I will investigate how these problems pose as a challenge to Batswana ideas of community and relationships.

WITCHCRAFT BELIEFS AMONG THE BATSWANA

Below I intend to discuss witchcraft beliefs among the Batswana. First, I will reflect on my own experience as a Motswana child and woman. Second, I will discuss the concept of witchcraft as it is understood among Batswana by addressing its different types.

I grew up in Botswana as a school-going girl and spent most of my time in the same country as an adult teacher, working in many different villages of Botswana. I noticed that there are always talks about witchcraft. People discuss witchcraft either as a joke or as a serious matter. Witchcraft talks take place at all levels of Batswana society: individually or at the family or community level; at work or sports, in school or in any other group that one identifies with. For instance, after my father lost his first wife my mother was married to him as a second wife. All her married life the children from her husband's first marriage accused her of witchcraft. Whatever goes wrong in the first house, my family (the second house) is blamed for it. In most cases witchcraft accusations dominate second marriages, and are inherent in polygamous relations in Botswana. Though husbands may claim social status from a polygamous marriage, that same relationship hurts many wives and children. This becomes even worse in cases where husbands die before their wives. But it becomes a paradox when one learns that children from these marriages are expected by the community to relate to each other as members of the same clan, venerating the same ancestors who are to bless them, provided they are living together in harmony. The latter is often not that easy. I recall one incident in my village where we attended a burial ceremony, only to witness a fight between relatives because the wife of the deceased believed that her eldest sister had bewitched her husband. After the burial ceremony, the matter was taken to the ward *kgotla* (court), where those found guilty—not of witchcraft but of fighting at the ceremony—were given punishment. In spite of that, the two families are still accusing each other of practising witchcraft and refuse to carry out family activities and rituals together. In other words, the relationship is broken.

These individual and family experiences reflect upon the Batswana communal framework of thinking. For example, according to Batswana beliefs, when there is drought or any natural disaster, traditionally a ritual of purification is conducted. The ritual is done because the Batswana believe that either something unpleasant might be happening in the community, or that some neighbouring *merafe* (peoples) might have placed *dibeela*[7]in their territory so that the community will suffer misfortune. This is generally explained as witchcraft. For that reason every year the Batswana perform a ploughing ritual, known as *Go Ntsha Letsema*, to mark the beginning of the ploughing season. The ritual is performed to purify and heal the land, regardless of whether *dibeela* has been discovered or not. The ritual is meant to take care of people's shortcomings and to neutralise the working of some *dibeela* that may have remained undiscovered.

Below, I will discuss the concept of witchcraft as understood by the Batswana.

Boloi (witchcraft)

The English words sorcery and witchcraft have come to be translated in Setswana as *boloi*. Collins Dictionary (1993) translates 'witchcraft' and 'sorcery' as enchantment, magic, necromancy, incantation, occultism, sorcery, sortilege, spell, black magic, voodoo, charm, and divination. Some of the words used to translate the term witchcraft here cannot be translated as *boloi* in the Setswana language. In Setswana, the term *boloi* refers to a system of evil, the effect of bad relations or disharmony among the living. In most cases *boloi* incidents are reported when there are feelings of contention, jealousy and hatred. Two examples may illustrate the point.

Recently, a certain Mokgalagadi Sechele died in Botswana as a result of a car accident. His death came at a time when he had a filed a case against the Bakwena (one of the ethnic groups in Botswana) and the government of Botswana concerning how his father Kgosi Sebele II had been exiled to Gantsi from Molepolole by the British colonial administration in 1931 and lost both his kingship and his property.[8] Sebele II was exiled because he believed in his own Setswana culture, especially in the importance of witchcraft and initiation schools. His exile resulted in a conflict among the Bakwena, who are still divided about their kingship. The death of Mokgalagadi Sechele, Sebele II's son, might be considered by some the result of witchcraft from those Bakwena who opposed his case.

A second example concerns the death of Diana, Princess of Wales, in 1997. According to Batswana witchcraft beliefs, due to her conflictuous marriage, her death would be explained as the result of witchcraft performed by those who were in conflict with her or who were against a divorce.

One other situation that makes Batswana people talk about witchcraft or sorcery is when a member of the society performs 'abnormally', either extremely poorly or excellently. In most cases the one who performs excellently will be thought of as a sorcerer, that is, as a person with extraordinary or spiritual powers which he or she exploits to perform beyond expectation. On the other hand, if somebody performs extremely poorly, that is, below the social standard or expectation, he or she is thought of as being bewitched, that is, certain evil powers are believed to have been used to work against the person. This belief can be understood within the Batswana myth of origin.[9] The Batswana myth of origin holds that people were enabled to populate the world as a community—not as individuals—and on equal basis. Modimo (the Batswana divinity) enabled the Batswana people to come out and occupy the world as children, women and men. No one came out as a result of the other. They were all brought out to occupy the land with property, especially livestock, and no one was given more than the other. Land and livestock were for all of them to share.

The lack of justification for inequality forced Batswana traditional societies into a moral obligation to the poor in their community. Pre-colonial Batswana societies used the *mafisa* system to cater for the poor. This is a traditional system whereby the poor were given some livestock to take care of and use it for their daily needs. Once a year they would be given one beast as a way of helping them eventually to own their own livestock. Living above or below the expected standard was considered abnormal and called for a moral obligation or an explanation. The most common explanation was one associated with witchcraft, and this is still the case today. The Batswana trace both physical and spiritual sources of problems. For instance, though it is common knowledge that one might be poor because he or she has lost all their cattle, a spiritual reason has to be investigated in order to find out why this happened.

Boloi, or witchcraft, is thus a complex subject among the Batswana, who distinguish several types. The types of *boloi* that the Batswana recognise are known as heart, mouth, night and day witchcraft. These different types are discussed next.

Heart witchcraft

This type of witchcraft is thought to exist when one is not happy about what another person has done or said to him or her. By feeling offended, the attention of the ancestors is called to the offence. They respond by withdrawing their protection from the offender, who then remains exposed to harmful forces that cause the person to feel ill. Usually the offender does not suffer from any physical illness, and in case a physical illness manifests itself it appears as a symptom. In most cases the illness manifests itself in the form of misfortune: infertility of one's fields or livestock, sickness or death of children, or failure to progress at work. In all areas of life things hardly go well. A ritual of reconciliation is needed to heal the condition. The *ngaka* (healer) will let the offender know why he or she suffers and advises them to reconcile with the offended. A sacrificial offering may be required to pacify both the offended and the ancestors. The ritual provides a way of restoring the disturbed relationships, so that the sufferer can enjoy the protection of the ancestors again.

There is another, similar condition, called *phutso* (curse), which is believed to be caused by serious cases of heart witchcraft. This *bolwetse* (illness or disease) is usually caused by an offence against the poor or disabled, against strangers, children or very old people; in short, against the powerless: those who do not have any means to justice. Any ill-treatment of such people will direct misfortune at the offender. Since the powerless have no means to justice, such people will appeal to the ancestors and to Modimo. They may do so in many ways, even by being quiet. The ancestors will then intervene by withdrawing their protection from the offender. In this way the ancestors make sure that the powerless are treated justly. This illustrates that the disadvantaged groups in society deserve to be treated well, so that they will have no ill feelings against others. Some of the food and meals that characterise the Batswana rituals are more than a thanksgiving to the ancestors; they are also meant to share with the disadvantaged in society, so that all may eat and be happy.

Mouth witchcraft

There is a Setswana proverb: '*Lefoko ga le boe go boa monwana*'. This means that it is much better to point a finger than to pronounce a negative word against a person, for a finger pointing can literally be withdrawn but not a word pronounced. 'Mouth witchcraft' is slightly different from heart witchcraft. The difference is that in heart witchcraft the offended retains the offence in the heart, while in mouth or word witchcraft the offended speaks (casts a spell) out of bitterness. It is an open call for the ancestors' and Modimo's attention to restore a broken relationship. The offender's attention and repentance has to be sought through withdrawal of ancestral protection. As a result of his suffering the offender has to take steps toward reconciliation. No statement can be withdrawn without a ritual of cleansing.

From the two types of witchcraft discussed so far, it appears that from a Batswana perspective anyone can be a witch. If a person is not happy about somebody else, or unhappy about you, anything bad can happen to that person or to yourself. Both heart and mouth witchcraft relate closely to ancestral wrath. The effects can harm more people than the offender alone. Heart and mouth witchcraft are common types of witchcraft in Botswana, and people involved will easily come out for reconciliation, for the good of the community, of nature and the land.

Night witchcraft

As the name implies, this type of witchcraft is related to night activities. In most cases night witchcraft is believed to take place in social groups that visit each other at different and far away places at night. These groups of people are believed to go around at night dressed in special costumes. They can open locked doors without using keys, enter houses and make people oversleep while busy with their business. It is believed that they can suck milk from cows and goats, that they can open graves and restore the dead to life and use them for their night transport in different forms: as zombie, *thokolosi* and *setotwane*.[10] They are believed to use even living people for their transport at night just for fun, as well as other things such as needles, blankets and winnowing trays. This type of witchcraft has its own, special type of music. Some people claim that night witchcraft can be dangerous, depending on whom is involved and for what reason. Night witchcraft is associated with women, especially elderly women in society. Paradoxically, Batswana believe that women and men become ancestors or start their ancestorhood status at the same time: at old age.

In Batswana traditional society the day was for formal work, while the evenings were for leisure. In the early evenings, it was common to find groups of children singing, dancing, and playing games. Traditionally, Batswana communities are characterised by youth social activities, such as *redi, diketo, mokomelo, koi, mmiliki, dibeke,* and *mmalebonye*, which are all traditional sporting games, and by traditional dances such as *dikoma, borankana,* and *marabi.* Most of these activities used to take place in the evenings, after a busy day of work. Some of them involved the preparation of formal ritual presentations such as marriage celebrations, while others were just for the sake of leisure and relaxation. Youth groups were not supposed to carry on till late or throughout the night, because the night was believed to be the time for 'night witches' to start their socialisation. Night witchcraft was seen as a secret institution, or a private-style socialisation.

Day witchcraft

Many writings reflect on this type of witchcraft.[11] Strong hatred, malice, greed and envy are believed to motivate this type of witchcraft. The purpose of day witchcraft is believed to injure and kill.

Day witchcraft can happen in different ways. First, some people believe that one can be poisoned through food. The poison may develop into something else when it gets into the stomach and trouble the victim for a period of time before causing their death. This is called *sejeso*, meaning 'something that one has been given to eat with the intention to harm'. *Sejeso* is not poison in the English sense of the word. It is not a 'poison' that can be tested in a laboratory. However, some Western medical doctors in Botswana refer to it as 'Setswana poison'. Second, it is believed that 'day witches' may place harmful herbs in one's compound to cause evil to the family. These herbs are believed to counter those used by *dingaka* (healers) when they fortify their homesteads. While *dingaka* are considered to use their powers to keep evil away, this type of witches are believed to use theirs to invite evil. Third, it is also believed that a particular thing might be set on others in order to cause their death. In most cases this is something that the person in question is attached to. For instance, an alcoholic person may be seen as someone on whom beer has been 'set' in order to destroy his life. Any excessive use can be explained in that sense.

Witchcraft-related problems in the colonial period

Many witchcraft talks circulate in the villages and towns of Botswana, but few of them go through courts and get recorded. Below, I will give a few examples that were recorded during the colonial era. Most of these concern witchcraft accusations at *bogosi* (kingship or political) level.

In 1927, among the Bakwena, Kgosi Sebele II accused his cousins and councillors, Kebohula and Moiteelasilo, of bewitching him. His argument was that the cousins intended to weaken him so that they could gain strong control over their wards or locations. As a result, the councillors and their *ngaka* (healer), who was called Zulu, were banished from the village of Molepolole. Eventually, as mentioned above, Kgosi Sebele II himself was also banished, in this case by the British colonial administration, which was opposed to the witchcraft beliefs held by the *kgosi*.[12] The banishment of Kgosi Sebele II took place when Charles Ray was the British Resident Commissioner (1927-37). Ray did not like Sebele II, whom he considered more of a 'ruffian' than a king. He was of the opinion that the natives were utterly out of hand and that their respect for white men was diminishing. He concluded that this was because there had never been any legal definition of the chief's power, as a result of which chiefs could do as they like, to the extent of 'playing hell'. He started a plan to discipline the 'natives and make them realise the moral superiority of the whites. One of the intentions of his plan was to depose Kgosi Sebele II, which he eventually did on 2nd June 1931.

Cases of witchcraft accusations similar to those among the Bakwena are found among the Bakgatla, Bangwato and other *merafe* (groups). For example, the families of Kgosi Isang and Kgosi Molefi among the Bakgatla accused each other of witchcraft after both had lost children. The problem started when, in the late nineteenth century, Kgosi Isang was a regent on behalf of Kgosi Molefi and people feared that Isang would not hand over *bogosi* (kingship). Among the Bangwato, Kgosi Sekgoma accused headman Phetu Mpoeleng, his own cousin, of practising witchcraft with the intention to oust the present *kgosi* and have one installed of his own choice, if not himself. As a result, Mpoeleng was imprisoned and later banished from what was then still known as Bangwato reserve. This took place in the 1880s and was done by the colonial administration with the help of Kgosi Sekgoma himself.

Around the same time, in 1889, a witchcraft case was brought against two women by their husbands at Molepolole. It is not known how the case was resolved, because the colonial administration strongly warned the Bakwena *kgosi* to stop the proceedings.[13] Due to frequent witchcraft accusations, the

British colonial administration issued in 1927 the Bechuanaland Witchcraft Proclamation Act.[14] The Act failed to stop witchcraft accusations, however, up till today, because it was mainly targeting at the activities of Motswana healers (*dingaka*), who posed a serious threat to the activities of the colonial administration. A Motswana healer or *ngaka*, just as a Motswana *kgosi*, held a position of power in Batswana society, which undermined the power of the colonial administration. For the Batswana the *ngaka* is undoubtedly a healer and a saviour.[15]

Witchcraft-related problems in contemporary society

No information exists concerning witchcraft cases tried in court during the post-independence era. None of such cases can be found in the national archives, while some of the *dikgosi* whom I interviewed on the subject were recently enthroned and did nor try any witchcraft cases. However, I have made every attempt to find out from ordinary Batswana people how they understand the concept of witchcraft and the problems associated with it. For that purpose I designed and distributed sample questionnaires among students at a Senior Secondary school and two Colleges of Education, as well as among some students at the University of Botswana. I deliberately chose this age group in order to discover the understanding of contemporary youth regarding witchcraft, and their views on the subject. All of them responded to the questionnaires, and the respondents came from different parts of the country. A total of 93 questionnaires were filled out and returned by individuals between 17 and 28 years old.

The respondents, though based in no more than four different institutions, came and reported witchcraft cases from the towns and villages in various parts of the country. Most of them defined witchcraft as something evil, and as a form of abuse of medicines and herbs with a view to harm or to kill. They named *dingaka* (healers) and women as categories of people that are commonly accused of witchcraft. *Dingaka* because they are knowledgeable in the use of herbs and usually the ones who tell people that they are bewitched; and women because they are associated with jealousy and gossip.

But there was another group of respondents who said that everyone can be a witch or be bewitched, whether old or young, male or female, poor or rich, indigenous or foreign. Such people may include the following—and even contrasting—categories:

- The wealthy, because people are jealous of their riches.
- The educated, as education is associated with wealth. Those educated get well-paid jobs and therefore live better.
- The poor, who are associated with lack of education and unemployment, for they have nothing on which to survive.
- The irresponsible and lazy people, who fail to meet their targets.
- Those who do not attend church, because they are not protected by God.
- Youth who fail at home or at school.
- Those who suffer frequent misfortune, such as sickness, madness, deaths and accidents.
- Those who believe in and make use of indigenous healing practices.
- Churches may also be suspected of practising witchcraft, because some churches conduct their services only at night. According to some respondents, if it is one's first time to attend, one is asked questions such as: 'If you are given ten bottles, where will you keep them?' If one fails to give the answer they expect, the person is not allowed to the service. They regard this as witchcraft.

Several reasons were given to justify the Batswana's witchcraft beliefs: Batswana are jealous of one another's wealth; witchcraft accusations result from poor living standards, or result from the misfortune that people suffer in their lives; or they were ascribed to a belief in indigenous healing. All respondents acknowledged that there are different causes of events or misfortunes, including witchcraft, ancestral wrath and divine will. Events believed to be caused by witchcraft include fire, the death of a child, lightning, the death of livestock, not being promoted at work, the neglect of parents, continuous miscarriage or abortion, and long illness. Events believed to be caused by ancestral wrath included: bad dreams and visions; failure in life; death of livestock or crops; long illness; and misfortunes that affect the whole community, such as floods, droughts and storms. One may note the overlap that is often found between witchcraft and ancestral wrath. Finally, the following type of events were believed to be caused by divine will: the death of very old people; the death of a long-suffering disabled person; death after long illness; failure due to arrogance about one's success; a personal tragedy that does not affect the person himself but their livestock or property.

The respondents further noted that people accuse each other of witchcraft in situations where there are broken relationships, where there is jealousy or conflict, or competition for a position at home, at work or in society, or where a disparity or wider gap exists in living standards. Some respondents said they did not believe that witchcraft exists, ascribing such beliefs to jealousy. They stated that it is natural to experience both good and bad things in life.

However, a majority of 65% said they believed that witchcraft exists because:

- *Dingaka* have identified many events caused by witchcraft.
- They themselves have witnessed or experienced witchcraft activities.
- They have seen witches and heard about incidents where witches have been caught and tried at courts (*dikgotla*).
- Batswana still believe in their Setswana type of healing (*bongaka*), which reflects a lot on witchcraft.
- The Bible talks about witchcraft (Daniel 2:2, and 5:11). In Daniel 5:11 of the Setswana Bible soothsayers are equated with witches (which may be criticised as a colonial translation).
- There are harmful herbs that can be abused.
- There is still jealousy among people.
- Some people have testified that they once were witches.
- *Boloi* represents a type of belief that is part of Batswana culture.
- There are certain tragedies or mysteries that happen in Botswana without any normal or scientific cause. Despite

media coverage, these respondents argued, no one has been able to explain incidents such as the 'Segametsi Murder' case at Mochudi, which was even investigated by Scotland Yard; the fire that haunted some families at Mochudi and Gumare; the case of the northeast *thokolosi* that sexually abused some female civil servants; or the Molepolole lightning that killed many people, destroyed livestock and burned down houses.

Most respondents mentioned some form of transport believed to be used by *baloi*: winnowing trays, needles, blankets, loafs of bread, baboons, hyenas and humans. Most of them also argued that '*Moloi ga a utswe, e seng jalo o ka timelelwa ke boloi*' ('A witch does not steal especially during witchcraft activities, or else she/he will lose the art of witchcraft'). They also argued that some *baloi* are not out to enrich themselves, but only to harm or kill. Further, *boloi* is something that is not easily given up once one has seen the secrecy of *baloi*. Many *baloi* prefer using other people in witchcraft activities, especially other people's children, so that where there are side-effects, it is not they themselves but someone else who will be affected.

Witchcraft stories

Whether they themselves believed in witchcraft or not, all respondents had some witchcraft stories to tell. Some of these are reproduced below. They are classified according to where they took place, not to whom was telling the story or where the story was told. For example, some stories from Gaborone were told by students at Moshopa and Tlokweng villages.

Gaborone (Broadhurst suburb):

> One day, when my mother woke up in the morning to sweep the yard, my father and I heard her shouting. We went out only to find a woman near the gate wearing terrifying clothes and bracelets made out of nails. She was holding a tin full of blood. My parents asked me not to talk to her till sunrise, so that other people would come and see her. After sunrise people came to see her, and that is when we started talking to her and she suddenly disappeared. [It is a

general belief found among the Batswana that if you
see a *moloi* during the early hours of the morning (*a
setswe*) and you do not talk to them, the *moloi* will
remain there till whatever time you talk to him or her
and then disappear suddenly].

(19yr. student High School, Moshopa)

A female witch went out one night. She returned a
little bit late and found school children already up,
preparing to go to school. She arrived still dressed in
her witchcraft attire. One of the children met her in
the yard. The woman immediately turned her back
and stooped towards the child (*a mo kgonamela*),
who got a shock and fainted. The child was taken to
the hospital to be treated for shock, and up till this
day does not look normal.

(19yr. student High School, Moshopa)

My cousin told me that one day, as he was sitting
outside the house, he heard a lot of noise and strug-
gling inside the house. He stood up to open the door,
and a dog came running out of the house. As he tried
to shout at the dog, his arm got broken.

(19yr. student High School, Moshopa)

A male witch was working at the Ministry of Agriculture in Gaborone, who had his lunch every day
at Francistown, 450 kilometres away, between 12.30
and 13.45 hrs. There is a rumour that one day a friend
invited him for lunch. As they went out he asked
his friend to close his eyes (till he would tell him to
open them again), for that is what he does when he
goes for lunch. His friend closed his eyes as he had
been asked, and when asked to open them again, it
was ten minutes later and they were already sitting
at Thapama lodge in Francistown. Lunch was ready
there for the two to eat. At 13.30 hrs. they left the
lodge. The friend was again told to close his eyes as
they departed. But this time he decided to open his
eyes immediately again in order to see what was happening. This time he found himself at Pilane, sitting

under a tree, some thirty kilometres away from their work place, Gaborone. He took a bus from Pilane to Gaborone, where he arrived late for work. He told this story to explain why he was late for work in the afternoon.

(25yr. student, College of Education, Serowe)

Moshopa (village 60 km southwest of Gaborone):

In 1993, after my grandmother's death, the family consulted a *ngaka*. The *ngaka* told the family that my grandmother had been bewitched by her sister in-law. He promised the family that the culprit would be dead by the end of the funeral. And indeed, it happened.

(20yr. student, High School, Moshopa)

Gantsi (a small town in the far west of Botswana):

At Itekeng Community Junior Secondary School in Gantsi, there was a group of witches consisting of a night watchman and some industrial staff workers. The group used some students to bewitch their teachers. They were found out and eventually dismissed from work. [The informant was a student at the school at the time of the incident, but told the story after she had graduated from that school and become a student at a College of Education in Tlokweng].

(28yr. student Tlokweng College of Education)

Maun (a small town in the far northwest of Botswana):

In 1992, after writing my Junior Secondary examinations, I went to my uncle's cattle-post while I was awaiting the results. When at the cattle-post I received a message that the results were out and I had obtained a second-class degree. I informed my uncle and his wife, and asked for money to go to school and confirm the results. They first refused, and only gave me the money two days later. When I arrived at the village I started having an aching finger. After a few days the finger deteriorated. My mother then took

me to a *ngaka*, who told us that my uncle's wife had
bewitched me because she was jealous of my passing
the examinations. Since that day I am afraid of my
uncle's wife.

(21yr. student, Serowe College of Education)

In general the argument of the respondents is that witchcraft
brings hatred, mistrust and fear, and causes bad relationships
among close relatives and within communities. Gabriel Setiloane
has argued that a breakdown of relationships implies that the
whole of society is ill.[16] This is also relevant to Batswana ideas
of community and relationships, which remain at stake. In addition, the informants mentioned underdevelopment in Batswana
communities as a witchcraft-related problem, since many people
fear that they will be bewitched for any new developments they
introduce. They noted that some Batswana migrate to towns and
cities for fear that their relatives will bewitch them at home or
in the village. According to the respondents, HIV/AIDS is also
attributed to witchcraft by some people, who associate it with
that because it resembles a long illness. Many people remain care-
less regarding the spread of HIV/AIDS, as they tend to blame
witchcraft for it.

WITCHCRAFT: A CHALLENGE TO BATSWANA IDEAS OF COMMUNITY AND RELATIONSHIPS

As quoted at the beginning of this article, Kenneth Kaunda,
former president of Zambia, once said that, unlike other continents, Africa is known for its strong relationships. This appears
also true of Botswana, where the idea of community and relationship is strong in the local communities. Botswana society
is centered upon the belief in ancestors; a belief that focuses on
the idea of community and relationships. By venerating ancestors people maintain relationships between the living and the
dead, between humanity and nature, and between human beings
themselves.[17] The objective behind all these types of relationship
is to live in harmony with all. Nevertheless, Batswana communities are characterised by all sorts of conflicts, at a personal,
family, and community level. The cause of these conflicts is often

ascribed to witchcraft. Witchcraft-related problems disturb relationships between African men and women, between young and old people, and between relatives and neighbours.

Gender, power and witchcraft

The last two types of witchcraft mentioned above—day and night witchcraft—are mainly associated with women, especially those in old age. This becomes a paradox in the sense that at an age that women should be respected as ancestors-to-be, they are blamed for the occurrence of evil in their community. In Batswana society, women are generally associated with witchcraft because of their place in the community as housewives, cooks, child caretakers and midwives. Since day and night witchcraft are generally associated with women, one suspects that this is so because Batswana patriarchal society hardly appreciates what women can do without male involvement. Their involvement in midwifery has led men to think that women use the afterbirth (placenta) to strengthen their own position in the community. The stronger a woman's position in society, the more threatened the position is of the man. Consequently, male-dominated societies as the Batswana communities tend to denounce women as witches.

The association of women with witchcraft results from a patriarchal ideology that seeks to distance women from social power.[18] In fact, it creates myths that belittle the achievements of women. Such a myth, for example, was created about a pioneering business woman in Botswana who became successful in the village of Molepolole. She was subsequently labelled a witch. One of her businesses was a bar. Many people around the village were made to believe that the woman was involved in ritual murders to help her business prosper. If a customer got killed after quarrels or fights at his bar, like in any other bar, as a result of drunkenness, the following morning news would be circulating around the village that she had killed that person for ritual purposes. Many people were warned not to go into her places of business, for they were rumoured to have large invisible holes in the floor that were meant to capture victims of ritual murders.[19] Remarkably, whereas men associated with witchcraft are usually presented as powerful witches, in patriarchal societies women associated with witchcraft are hardly ever identified with powerful and empowering roles.

There is reason to believe that 'night witchcraft' has been labelled 'witchcraft' simply because it is associated with women. Melissa Raphael speaks of 'feminist witchcraft', following Mary Daly's argument, that any woman who has spiritually liberated herself from a patriarchal worldview is essentially considered a 'witch'.[20] In Batswana patriarchal society, many women have no power of their own and few of them have the freedom to organise themselves as a social group. Whenever an individual woman or a group of women meets independently, the male-dominated community becomes sceptical. This is probably the reason why women's night activities are dismissed as witchcraft.

There is a general belief among the Batswana that women with mystical powers are witches, while men are healers.[21] This belief is especially held among male diviner-healers. I interviewed several of these on the subject, who forwarded a number of reasons to support the argument. First, they argued, women are short-tempered and quick at taking decisions, including wrong decisions. Second, socially, women are considered as cooks, and it is believed that women can poison people through food, especially—if married—their husbands. Third, traditionally women are midwives, who are thought of as people who have access to human flesh, especially the after-births. There is a general belief among the Batswana that afterbirths are used to produce harmful medicine for witchcraft purposes. Women in Batswana society tend to be labelled as witches in marriage by their husbands, in-laws and the community at large in cases where the man does not perform his social roles. The blame is largely put on his wife, who is accused of having turned the husband into another woman by means of witchcraft.

Accusations of witchcraft have been used in the patriarchal society of the Batswana to keep women, as a group, from effectively competing in male-dominated areas such as divination and healing, and other prestigious fields. However, there are women who have succeeded on their own and asserted a role for themselves as single parents, community leaders, business women and *dingaka*. They are usually thought to have achieved their position by manipulating natural powers through witchcraft. Because of the dominant ideology, they are not easily accepted in their powerful positions. They are often severely criticised and dismissed as 'witches'.

Relatives and neighbours

Witchcraft talks and rumours normally involve close relatives, by blood and by marriage. Many Batswana suspect that it is especially their relatives who are out to bewitch them, and many *dingaka* confirm these suspicions and beliefs when they are consulted. Relatives are the first suspects because they come closest in the network of relationships. Another immediate group of suspects are neighbours in the community, with whom one relates on a daily basis. In most Setswana villages neighbours often end up as members of one's extended family. The concept of neighbourhood can be further extended to those with whom an individual relates at work, school and in other social groups.

The paradox of relationships is that the same people that one is expected to relate to in harmony are the same people that one suspects of witchcraft. To explain that paradox, it is important to understand witchcraft among the Batswana within the Batswana framework of thought: a framework that constantly seeks to explain experiences of evil, pain, mystery, abnormality and misfortune. Second, witchcraft accusations underline the fact that the Batswana are indeed related and interconnected. Therefore, Batswana people are responsible for each other's wellbeing. When a misfortune occurs, a relative or neighbour has to account for it and take the blame. Thirdly, witchcraft accusations also underline a philosophy of hope and a sense of being in control, instead of being left hopelessness. For eventually all the pain, evil or misfortune that the Batswana may suffer and experience can be contained, controlled, reversed or stopped. Even in cases where witchcraft is deemed to be the cause of misfortune, *dingaka* are seen as able to handle it effectively. The *ngaka* is the only figure in Batswana communities who is expected to find a solution to all problems. These are presented to him in the form of illnesses or disease. The *ngaka* diagnoses the cause, gives advice and finds a suitable treatment, prescribing preventive and protective measures.[22] By so doing, the *ngaka* endorses popular sentiments and inspires not only healing, but also a sense of liberation, life-giving, justice and security among people, thus assuming a stabilising role in society.[23] At the same time, however, as noted above, by endorsing popular sentiments regarding witchcraft the *ngaka* is responsible for the harmful consequences of witchcraft accusations.

CONCLUSION

In conclusion, I would like to state that witchcraft is a complex subject among the Batswana. Though witchcraft can be classified as a form of evil, it is difficult to define that form of evil precisely or exemplify it clearly in isolation from the idea of jealousy. This difficulty can be traced through the types of witchcraft discussed in this chapter and the witchcraft stories that were related. One might be tempted to classify or dismiss such stories as 'gossip'. However, all the stories told regarding witchcraft, no matter how nonsensical they sound, they make a lot of sense to a believer in witchcraft.

Witchcraft stories and witchcraft accusations, regardless of whether they make sense or not, pose a challenge to Batswana communities and relationships. It is unfortunate that these communities are made up of men and women who strongly believe that they are expected to relate well and respect each other in order to receive the ancestors' blessings. These are the same persons who continue to accuse each other of the use of witchcraft and create an environment that is not conducive for harmonious relationships. Hence, I would say, witchcraft accusations have become a serious concern and are an embarrassment to any Batswana ideas of community and relationships. Witchcraft accusations have destroyed community life in Botswana, though often silently. In Botswana, there are women who have been divorced as a result of witchcraft accusations, and there are relatives and neighbours who do not see and talk to each other because of witchcraft accusations. This mars up the idea of community and relationships among the Batswana.

However, witchcraft-related problems have to be fought within their own context in order to defeat them. Even though in daily practice witchcraft beliefs prove a challenge to Batswana ideas of community and relationships, the Batswana framework of thought remains the context in which witchcraft-related problems have to be resolved. If there is need for any change in beliefs, such change cannot be expected to come from outside, through the imposition of a foreign frame of mind. Such change has to happen at its own pace and as a result of experiences of the Batswana people themselves. It has happened before in some Batswana communities that, out of personal experiences, people have come to realise that witchcraft beliefs and accusations destroy the harmony in their communities and break human relations. As a result of their own awareness, they took it upon themselves to reconcile and live well together. It does not help if foreign ideas are imposed to try and solve the problem of witch-craft accusations, as has been the case with the Proclamation Act that was introduced by the British colonists in 1927. Apart from stopping the Batswana from believing in witchcraft and accusing each other of witchcraft, the Act was mainly intended to paralyse the role of the indigenous Motswana diviner-healer or *ngaka*. In spite of the fact that the Act was designed by the colonists for colonial purposes, the post-colonial administration of Botswana has continued to use the Act.

Notes

1. J.R. Crawford, *Witchcraft and Sorcery in Rhodesia*, Oxford: International African Institute, 1967.

2. R. G. Abrahams (ed), *Witchcraft in Contemporary Tanzania*, Cambridge: African Studies Centre, 1994.

3. E.E. Evans-Pritchard, *Witchcraft, Oracles and Magic Among the Azande*, Oxford: Clarendon Press, 1976.

4. H.G. Nutini and J.M. Roberts, *Blood-sucking Witchcraft*: An epistemological study of anthropomorphic supernaturalism in rural Tlaxcala, Tucson: University of Arizona Press, 1993.

5. Melissa Raphael, *Introducing Thealogy: Discourses on the goddess*, Sheffield Academic Press, 1999.

6. *Mmegi Newspaper (The Reporter)*, vol. 17, no. 1, 7-13 Jan. 2000, p. 8.

7. *Dibeela* means something that has been placed in order to cause harm.

8. J. Ramsay, 'The neo-traditionalist: Sebele II of the Bakwena', in F. Morton and J. Ramsay (eds), *The Birth of Botswana: A history of the Bechuanaland Protectorate from 1910 to 1966*, Gaborone: Longman, 1987, pp. 30-44. See also p. 214 of the present article.

9. W.F. Lye and C. Murray, *Transformations on the Highveld: The Tswana and Southern Sotho*, Cape Town: David Philip, 1980.

10. *Thokolosi* and *setotwane* are zombie-like creatures. Zombie is a Zulu word, while the other two are Sotho-Tswana names for the same phenomenon.

11. See e.g. R. Bocock and K. Thompson (eds), *Religion and Ideology: A reader*, Manchester University Press, 1985.

12. Ramsay, 'The neo-traditionalist'.

13. HC. 44/14, Despatch, Secretary of State for the Colonies (Lord Knutsford) to Sir Hercules Robinson, concerning accusation of witchcraft brought against two Bechuanaland women by their husbands at Molepolole, 26 February, 1889.

14. See Sandra Anderson and Frants Staugard, *Traditional Healers*, Gaborone: Ipelegeng, 1985, pp. 227-8.

15. G.S. Ntloedibe-Kuswani, 'Ngaka and Jesus as liberators: a comparative reading', in Gerald O. West and Musa W. Dube (eds), *The Bible in Africa: Transactions, trajectories and trends*, Leiden: Brill, 2001, pp. 498-510.

16. Gabriel Setiloane, *The Image of God among the Sotho Tswana*, Rotterdam: Balkema, 1976.

17. Andrew Linzey, *Animal Theology*, London: SCM Press, 1994. Linzey argues that humanity and nature might be carrying equal weight.

18. M.B. McGuire, *Religion: The social context*, London: Wadsworth, 1997, pp. 93-140.

19. Gomang Seratwa Ntloedibe-Kuswani, 1999, 'Bongaka, women and witchcraft', paper presented at the 7th International Conference on Women, 20-26 June 1999, Tromsø, Norway.

20. Raphael, *Introducing Thealogy*; Mary Daly, *Pure Lust: Elemental Feminist Philosophy*, London: Women's Press, 1984.

21. Ntloedibe-Kuswani, 'Bongaka'.

22. Ibid.

23. Anderson and Staugard, *Traditional Healers*.

10

WITCH-HUNTING IN ZAMBIA AND INTERNATIONAL ILLEGAL TRADE

Hugo F. Hinfelaar

INTRODUCTION

I have lived in Zambia since 1958, working as a Catholic priest (WF), and the problem of witch-hunting has always been there. I cannot say whether these days the problem is worse than it was in the past. Communications have improved to the effect that we have a wider knowledge of its implications.

The belief in witchcraft is widespread in Zambia. Both people in the villages and highly placed officials in the public and private sector believe that witchcraft exists and needs to be dealt with. In this article I do not wish to go into an argument of the veracity of witchcraft belief, nor will I discuss the dark machinations of magical practices. People believe in the presence of witchcraft, and the consequences of this belief are real. One of them is that both in the past and present the development of Zambia was and is impaired by continuous accusations of witchcraft. Unless this reality is faced, many projects and investments, especially in the rural areas, are bound to fail.

In the following I will argue that people who believe in the existence of witchcraft can easily be manipulated by those who do not share this belief, that in many ways people's humanity is being impaired by witchcraft belief, and that in the past Zambia suffered damage because of such belief. I hope to demonstrate this with data from the mercantile times, when Africa came first into contact with international trade, up till the present day. In the conclusion I will present some suggestions concerning how to cope with the situation as it poses itself today.

HISTORY

Mercantile times

Zambia is a landlocked country, mostly situated in the centre of the continent on the high plateau, with a watershed to both the Atlantic and the Indian Oceans. International trade came relatively late. At the beginning of the eighteenth century there were markets in Feira in the western part of the country, and in Kazembe in the east of Zambia. Both of these trade-centres emerged because of Portuguese presence in Angola and Congo, as well as Mozambique. The traces of the commercial slave trade, as practiced from the beginning of the sixteenth century in many parts of Africa, appear to be fewer in what is now Zambia than, for example, in West Africa. Nevertheless slave-rading was known and disrupted the precarious way of living of the interior peoples. Some ethnic groups moved away from more coastal regions towards the centre, while other groups enriched themselves by colluding with the traders, who not only dealt in slaves but also in a great variety of materials. There was a constant demand for precious stones, for natural resources such as gold, silver and copper, for ivory, and for exotic perfumes. Trade caravans were organised from the coast. Distances were huge, and the only and cheapest means of transport were human beings who acted as porters. When it became known that these porters could have commercial value, the trade increased. Porters and carriers, men and women alike, were appointed or recruited by the local authorities—the chiefs—and their councillors who, as part of the local judiciary, also had to dispose of criminal elements among the population. The alleged wrongdoers included people suspected of practising witchcraft. One of the known ways of getting rid of criminals and those accused of witchcraft was condemning them to slavery and porterage. Historical records show that witchcraft accusations were rife as the international trade increased.[1] Some chiefly families that intermarried with the traders were only too tempted to have difficult, outspoken subjects accused of witchcraft in order to get rid of them. Zambia may well have lost that way many of its most creative and independent-minded people.

Colonial times

The new power, the British Administration, together with the missionaries, came to abolish slavery in the 1890s. But they could not abolish witchcraft beliefs and practices; instead they simply denied that witchcraft existed and forbade the local judiciary to deal with witchcraft-related cases. This caused the problem to break out of its traditional constraints, no matter what the administration said or thought about it. The local people felt that they had to defend themselves against witches and therefore took the law into their own hands. From the beginning of the 1920s therefore we see the emergence of uncontrolled, illegal witchcraft accusations and punishments meted out to the accused by the so-called *Ba-mucapi*, gangs of witch-hunters. In Zambia it was also the time of the beginning of heavy industrialisation and urbanisation. Capital punishment or being sent into slavery were no longer possible as means of eliminating those accused or suspected of practising witchcraft. Taking the matter into their own hands, the one way to rid society of such people was for the populace to confiscate the property of alleged witches and allow them to disappear forever into the anonymity of the urban compounds.

The colonial and federal administration allowed for a tremendous mobility. People could move practically all over southern Africa and present themselves as part of migrant labour force, never to return to their home village. In those days the far-flung provinces of Zambia were kept poorly developed and only seen as potential barns of cheap labour for the mines. In this case too, be it indirectly, the harassment by witch-hunters may be seen as having contributed to the international trade in cheap labour, with people from Zambia (at that time still known as Northern Rhodesia) moving to another part of the same territory, or still further afield into other colonies in the region.

Post-independence

The issue of witchcraft, and the different ways of dealing with it, appears not to have been addressed by the post-colonial administration. In some ways this new group, the so-called *apamwamba* (the high class) raised over and above the local chiefs in terms of power. Due to their position as well-paid bureaucrats, civil servants or party officials they were believed to be immune to the believed evil influence of rural witches. Also, they lived in the low-density areas of the towns in Zambia. In many ways they had become *basungu*, Europeans, who were not considered to be affected by rural witchcraft. Yet they had to defend and protect themselves against subordinates who were jealous enough to try and harm their superiors with magic in an attempt to displace them and take over their lucrative employment. But this was seen as part of the necessary magic that chiefs had always practiced in order to remain in power. And, just like the old chiefs, the new *apamwamba* could not easily be harassed in any way or be accused of being witches.

In conclusion we can say that it is evident that in the past and more recent history of Zambia there has always been a sharp divide, a kind of stratification in the world of witchcraft and its believed nefarious effects on individual people. It is clear that the commoners, the ordinary people, who have less power to protect themselves, are more vulnerable to charges of witchcraft than the elite who exercises power, whether they be the *apamwamba* ('big men') or the witch-finders themselves. The commoners refer to themselves as *bantu bafye* (in Bemba) or *antu a chabe* (in Chewa), meaning 'only people', while the elite is placed in a higher category. The latter are considered special people, who have special powers or privileges, which immunise them from the effects of rural magic. Since colonial times, in the mind of many, such special people are associated with the *basungu,* the Europeans, the lucky group that has more power over, and immunity from, 'African magic' than any other.

WITCHCRAFT IN MODERN TIMES

From 1996 till the year 2000 the Justice and Peace Department of the Catholic Secretariat of the Zambia Episcopal Conference conducted a series of seminars on the occurrence of witchcraft accusations in most of the Zambian provinces. The Catholic bishops were of the opinion that many witch-hunters operated outside the law and that they posed a threat to the development of the country, especially of the rural areas. They decided to collect some hard facts concerning the issue in order to draw public attention to this scourge of uncontrolled witch-hunting. Some of the results are given below.[2]

In the northern provinces, most districts are regularly visited by *shi-nganga*, healers or herbalists. Most of these receive permission for their work from the gazetted association of traditional healers called THEPAZ (Traditional Health Practitioners Association of Zambia) and from the local authorities. They have a certificate that indicates the cures in which they are known to be specialised. A good number of them, however, are inclined to go beyond the well-defined limits of their profession. It appeared that sixty percent of the herbalists were prepared to exceed the limits of their professional competence, due to pressure of their clients who not only asked them to diagnose and heal, but also to indicate through divination *who* had caused a particular disease, ailment or misfortune. This had led to constant witch-hunting.

To limit ourselves to some examples, here are first some facts taken from a report by the Catholic Justice and Peace Commission in the Serenje district, an area 300 km to the north of Lusaka and more than half the size of Belgium. In July 1997 Serenje district in Central Province had a total of 176 witch-finders. They move around, do not stay long in one chieftaincy, and are in constant demand by some local chiefs and headmen. The fees that are charged to victims of witchcraft accusations are exorbitant. Almost everything that the accused possesses is grabbed by the witch-finder and his assistants, who sometimes resemble a gang of hooligans. Furniture, sewing machines, bicycles, all sorts of cattle, and anything movable is taken away. These items, it was discovered, are quickly resold in another area or in the nearby district *boma* (headquarters). Sometimes the victim's house is burned down or, in other cases, confiscated and given to the headman and his family. Very often the accused is driven out of the village, losing his right to any trust land, that is, land allocated by the local chief. Similar data have been obtained from Petauke district in Zambia's Eastern Province. It can be proved that a number of chiefs are in collusion with the witch-finders, attracted by the promise of financial returns up to forty-five percent of the loot.[3]

In their dealings with witchcraft-related cases, the police go by the law currently on the Zambian statute books. When victims of witch-finders report to the police on the harm they have suffered, the police take action if they have the means to do so. In such cases, following up on the reports of the victims, the police will apprehend the witch-finder. However, this is not always the case as fuel or proper transport are often lacking, preventing the police from catching the culprit. In actual fact, many instances of witch-finding are never taken to the police at all. The victims are usually under heavy emotional and physical strain, and not always inclined or able to report the harm done to them. They experience sorrow and misery after the humiliation inflicted on them. They are forced to payment of a heavy fine in cash and property, go through the physical pain of ritual cleansing, or are in fear of family members and neighbours. Fearing their revenge, they end up in terrible isolation. In the end they are in doubt about their own dignity and even inclined to agree to plead guilty to any accusation, however wild. They are in constant danger of being murdered.[4]

In one area of chieftainess Chiawa, situated south of Lusaka, research was conducted by C. Bawa Yamba.[5] In 1994-95 a witch-finder, called Chaka Zulu, was hired by the village headman because of the high number of deaths that had occurred as a result of accidents and AIDS, which needed an explanation. By February 1995, sixteen people had died as a result of an poison ordeal, imposed by the witch-finder. The suspected persons were forced to drink a concoction called 'tea'; the ones who died were accused of being witches. Partly as a result of Yamba's research, the case became widely known in Zambia and the witch-finder was put behind bars. However, after some time he was seen to have returned and re-started his witch-finding activities in nearby area. It was rumoured that the prison guards were afraid of him.

In the Luapula and Northern Provinces, Catholic missionaries have been waging a war against witch-finders from the early 1930s onwards. In their diaries are regular entries on this subject, and some of the expatriate priests became almost obsessed by the phenomenon.[6] Their main frustration was that even fervent and strong Christians holding leadership positions in the wider community would give in to employ witch-finders in order to cleanse their area of witches. Those few who had the courage to refuse to take part in the rituals would be duly accused of practising witch-craft themselves and subsequently lose their status as leaders, not only in the village but also in the Christian community. If they were to overcome the severe beatings, punishments and isolation, they would then usually depart for the mines or one of the towns along the line of rail, where they could escape into anonymity and avoid further persecution.

During my own doctoral research carried out in 1988 in an area of chief Mukupa Kaoma, some 200 kms to the west of the provincial capital Kasama (Northern Province), a particular case of injustice by a local witch-finder was followed up and brought to the notice first of the local police and then all the way up to the Provincial Commissioner of Police himself.[7] I observed that although all these police officers, from the highest to the lowest, complained about the lack of transport to follow up cases of severe beatings and forceful and illegal removal of property, the available cars, usually landrovers, were always destined for other purposes. It was a period when people were being constantly harassed by the military with endless traffic road blocks put in place under the cloak of national security. The powers-that-be had no serious interest in controlling witch-finders, since witch-craft accusation and eradication seemed to be a convenient and welcome part of this harassment.[8]

From the 1990s up to today there has been a continuous series of witch-hunts in the Western Province of Zambia, especially along the border with Angola, where the witch-hunters are called *karavinas*. Here the situation is even more blatant and crude, as in the Kalahari sands of these remote areas transport and normal communications have become prohibitive, notably due to the high price of fuel. Regular policing is well-nigh impossible. Those who participated in a seminar on the issue of witchcraft, organised by the Catholic Church and conducted in Mongu in August 1999, reported that a number of people had been accused of witchcraft and summarily executed by hired assassins recruited from across the border.

Some witchcraft cases may end up in the national newspaper published in Lusaka, on the page dedicated to 'local news'. The following, for instance, is taken from a report published in the *Times of Zambia* in 1999:[9]

> A man yesterday told a Ndola local court that his father used a muzzle-loading gun for hunting human beings instead of animals through witchcraft. 'He could just breathe into the gun's chamber once and his mere breath became the ammunition. Before he pulled the trigger he first called the name of his victim.' (...) Justice Kakonkanya ruled that the court could not order that Mr. Kasongo be cleansed against his will because he might die. But he ordered Mr. Kasongo to destroy or throw away the witchcraft and warned him he would be responsible if one of his relatives died in the next year.

Besides reporting specific cases, newspapers sometimes publish insightful analyses of witch-finding. 'Why is it that most workers dread retirement?' was the question asked by Charles Simengwa in the *Times of Zambia*. 'Retiring, going back home, has become a risky business! The spectre of witch-cleansing is haunting villages across Zambia and pensioners are the main targets. Some village leaders are believed to be conspiring with witch-finders in schemes to implicate pensioners and their families in sorcery in order to strip them of their assets they have acquired over the years. Victims of witch-finding are made to pay huge sums of money in the absence of which they are compelled to pay in kind, usually in the form of cattle.'[10] The same article went on to quote cases reported in the newspaper since 1995 from all parts of the country. The author finished by writing: 'Sadly, the practice will not only discourage pensioners from settling in places of their choice, but it will hamper the much-need improvement of rural areas as potential developers are scared off.'

Unfortunately these well-researched articles are not given enough prominence and are too infrequent as to gather momentum for mounting a national campaign against witch-finding. Cases against witch-finders are rarely followed up, allegedly due to shortages of finance, which sounds like an excuse rather than the real reason.

Sometimes victims of witchcraft accusations have been reported to be released due to pressure from the Catholic Justice and Peace Commission,[11] but in other instances people were reported to be jailed for professing and practising witchcraft.[12] Even the London-based *News from Zambia* wrote, in 1999, that (of all people) a Kaoma court justice had been jailed for professing to practice witchcraft and owning charms. His house was consequently burned down.[13]

'Time to stop terror of witch finders', wrote Charles Chisala in March 2000 in the *Times of Zambia*.[14] The article noted that witch-finders were not empowered by any law to name witches, beat them up, and detain them or confiscate their property. The problem is considered to be complex and to be resolved by patience, tact and money. One of the biggest culprits seems to be the law itself, the Witchcraft Ordinance of 1914, which was enacted in 1914 and amended in 1963, shortly before Zambia received political independence. The law should be amended again, in my view, to suit the current social demands, especially now that democracy appears to be taking root in Zambia, but there are no signs yet of this to happen. There is a great need to turn the current anti-witchfinding legislation into a truly Zambian law, rather than a hangover from colonial times. This should be made part of a national debate via radio and television. It should also be the daily concern of the churches, and figure in the manifesto's of the political parties. The notion of democracy goes hand in hand with that of equal rights for all, without any discrimination.

Meanwhile witch-hunting in Zambia continues unabated. In the current era of uncontrolled 'market forces' as preached by the present government and other supporters of neo-liberalism, confiscating land and other forms of property has taken on a more sinister dimension. It has been noted that witchcraft accusations and cleansing rituals are particularly rife in areas that have been earmarked for game management and game ranching, for tourism, and for occupation by potential big landowners.[15] Hard and fast proof that witchcraft accusations are deliberately manipulated in order to destroy normal village life can as yet not be procured, but the suspicion appears not to be unreasonable. Some chiefs and headmen profit from selling considerable portions of their domain to international investors, and fomenting social disruption in the villages facilitates such transactions. A divided village will not have the power to unite and oppose attempts to having the land they cultivate being taken over by someone else. As a matter of fact, the villagers are at times so engaged in accusing one another of practising witchcraft that they hardly notice that they are being dispossessed and that they have turned into squatters on their own ancestral land.

It has also been noted that the same chiefs and village headmen travel regularly to town to contact their family, many of whom often appear sharp businessmen who know how to change weak *kwachas* (the Zambian currency) into hard dollars.[16] Indeed, the question remains, where does all this stolen and confiscated property end up? In general, though witch-finders themselves seem to remain poor, they may be agents, knowingly or unknowingly, of wider networks to whom they pass on much of their profits, or who capitalise on the havoc they wreak. These wider networks may be criminal, semi-criminal, or entirely liberal-capitalist in their intentions, being involved in the 'land grabs' that both the previous and present government have let loose, and which is likely to transform the small peasant farmer of today into the landless labourer of tomorrow. Some people's intentions might even be genuine, such as those fostered by an ecological concern or the wish to preserve Zambian wildlife. Whatever the case might be, a national debate on the issue of land rights should be part and parcel of good governance of any future administration.

WHAT IS DONE TO TACKLE THE PROBLEM?

Gradually people in Zambia have become aware that something must be done to counteract the grave injustices done against persons suspected of practising witchcraft, and the enormous loss of property and money involved. The accusers of today may become the accused of tomorrow, and nobody who owns something of value seems really safe.

The following is an example of a strategy adopted in one parish in Serenje district, where a programme was launched that proved to be rather successful.[17] The programme focused on identifying the victims of witchcraft accusations by helping them to report to the police in order to claim justice for the harm done. According to the law of Zambia and the recommendations of local police officers, this was the quickest way to have a witch-finder arrested. At first such arrests led to a direct confrontation with the chief and his councillors, since they had given the witch-finder permission cleanse their chieftainship. The various parties were therefore summoned to the local court. This proved to be an excellent occasion to present to them the law of Zambia on the issue of witchcraft and witch-finders. It was also explained that the authority of the chief was not challenged this way, but rather that the purpose was to have the law respected and unjust practices stopped. This led in turn to an agreement to hold a seminar on witchcraft and its legalities, at which the chief, the police officers, a representative of the Office of the President, as well as a representative of THEPAZ would all be present.

Much of the discussions during these subsequent seminars revolved around the role of traditional health practitioners. As long as they kept to their own profession of healing by traditional means they were seen to be natural allies in the struggle against the unjust practices of witch-finders. The problem emerged if and when they went beyond their herbal skills and took up witch-finding themselves. In 1999 a number of young men, who had been part of the entourage of witch-finders and come to realise the cruelty and unjustice of their practices, revealed their tricks, including the forms of intimidation and the way in which charms are planted in the homes of those already suspected of witchcraft, even before the witch-finder had arrived. This proved very revealing and removed a considerable part of the mysterious and eso-teric dimension of the entire cleansing procedure. In the same year, two video's were made on the subject, which were shown on on national television.[18] All this helped to 'objectify' the issue and to draw widespread attention to the miseries of people in the rural areas.

I have come to the conclusion that much more research has to be done in this field. Helping the victims and bringing the witch-finders to justice does not do away with the harsh reality of witchcraft as experienced by so many people. Though Zambia is in the fortunate position of having—relatively speaking—plenty of space and arable land, the majority of its inhabitants prefer to stay in the ever-growing urban towns. One of the the main reasons for this is the fear of witchcraft.

More research is currently undertaken by the local churches in Zambia, and data are being collected during seminars that are conducted all over the country. Victims are asked and helped to write down a statement in order to make them more confident during court cases and remove fear and intimidation. However, this does not solve all problems. Most people remain convinced that witchcraft exists and is used out of jealousy, greed or hatred. Some have therefore asked the question: 'If all these witch-finders will be caught and brought to justice, who will protect us against witchcraft?'

It is also clear that people are being manipulated into accusing their neighbours, in many cases members of their own family, while the real root of the evil they experience should be found elsewhere. They are often 'barking up the wrong tree' in their desire to see immediate results by endless cleansing ceremonies that give instant satisfaction, but for a short time only.

The issue of witchcraft must be broadened and seen in relation with other forms of injustices. One of these is the reluctance of the government to help people acquire a title-deed to their small holdings. Access to the land was traditionally vested in the hands of local chiefs and headmen. People could not own the land in the Western sense of the word, as land was seen as belonging to God the Creator. Usufruct was given to each family as long as a household made regular and good use of the assigned portion of land. During colonial times a large amount of land was taken away from the jurisdiction of the chiefs, but a good portion remained in their hands as 'native trust land'. After independence, and in particular in 1996, all land rights were given to the new administration and allocation by title-deeds was centralised in the Department of Lands in Lusaka.

The manner in which title-deeds are obtained is extremely unfriendly towards the poor and in practice discriminates against them. The amount of money to be paid to the Department, and to surveyors and lawyers, is almost the same for a huge tract of land as it is for a small holding of a few hectares. These days this can amount to more than one thousand US dollars, a sum of money that poor villagers simply cannot pay. Even if prices would be within their reach, they are often not aware of all the implications and regulations of the Land Department in the capital city of Lusaka, which is hundreds of kilometers away. The villagers are not properly informed of the changes taking place around them, and the villages are too small to organise or defend themselves appropriately.[19]

Another injustice lies in that government officials are not particularly concerned about the frequent witchcraft accusations: they keep the people harrassed and divided among themselves. In the meantime land is being offered to investors from abroad, notably from South Africa, for farming and game ranching. The title-deeds of these huge areas are signed in far-away Lusaka, while the local people unaware of the loss of their ancestral land, wrapped up as they are in witchcraft accusations.

During the many church seminars held on the issue of witch-craft, it was repeatedly argued that an easier and less costly way of obtaining firm possession of a piece of land would be one of the ways to counteract the belief in witchcraft and the accom-panying wild accusations. If a person were to have a firm title on his piece of land, which would then remain in the name of his wife and children after his death, the temptation to dispossess him by unproven accusations would no longer be attractive to anyone outside his nuclear family. Neither the accuser himself, nor anyone else, would profit from a witchcraft accusation, for a person's land and property would be passed on automatically to the heir or next of kin.

THE ROLE OF THE CHURCH

The Justice and Peace Commission of the Catholic Church in Zambia, as mentioned above, initiated a series of seminars in the various dioceses which were held in the period 1996-2000 as part of its strategy to combat witchcraft accusations and the social injustices emerging from these. During these seminars representatives of all small Christian communities in Zambia, including both Catholics and Protestants, were invited, together with members of the police, the local judiciary and the district administration. Dependent on the size of the parish some forty to seventy people participated in the seminars. All participants agreed that there was a marked increase of witchcraft practices in the area, but also on the fact that witchcraft accusations had to be proved in a court case. Catching illegal witch-hunters and bringing them to justice proved a more difficult problem to solve. It was evident that many people feared to imprison witch-hunters because of their believed magical powers, while the chiefs and the police complained about the lack of transport and other means to facilitate their work. It was then decided in these seminars that the Catholic Church and the other mainline churches would assist people in the communtity by providing transport to the police and initiating a court case against witch-hunters.

This initiative proved to be such a success that in later years the people concerned began to report themselves cases to the police, as they were no longer afraid to take action against a witch-finder. During the seminars the various conjuring tricks of the witch-finder were exposed, such as the changing of water into 'blood' by adding permanganate, or discovering the 'witch' by the use of invisible chemicals with which the name of the accused is claimed to be written, or the use of simple card-tricks, etc. Witch-finding ceremonies were re-enacted so as to 'objectify' the ritual and disperse the fear with some humour and plenty of laughter, which had a liberating effect.

Witchcraft beliefs and witch-hunting are rife because many people are left harassed and uncertain about the rightful claims they can make. They are being manipulated by national and international capital, which may have come from dubious sources.

Finally, there is also an important human rights element involved, given the inhumane treatment of alleged witches. As long as normal human rights are not seen to be applicable to certain people, the *anthu a cabe*, this group of the voiceless can be manipulated by those who both claim and exercise more power.

The right to be judged by an impartial judiciary, and not by the 'instant justice' of a village mob, is enshrined in the Universal Declaration of Human Rights.

Here a cultural factor might well have crept in, which seems not yet to have been properly discerned. This is based on the distinction that is made between two ways of being human, as expressed by the opposition between the Bantu concepts of *muntu* and *musungu*. The deeper meaning of *mu-ntu* is a person who is cosmologically positioned in the centre of the life circle, a 'within-being'. The *mu-ntu* is situated in the middle of human existence. The *mu-sungu*, on the other hand, is not really involved. He is a person who is placed slightly away from the centre and seems to be above the exigencies of life. Being positioned around the centre, such a person is nearer to the spirit and animal world. As such he cannot be touched by evil coming from the human world or the community. This applies also to those people who have been 'set apart', or rather are considered to have 'moved on' to an outer circle of life, such as local priests and religious sisters. They too are deemed untouchable by the evil stemming from the inner circle of life, as they have cosmologically moved from the *muntu* to the *musungu* position.

The distinction between *muntu* and *musungu* might well be exacerbated by the opposition between rural and urban. This needs some explanation. When one lives in an urban, or peri-urban area, in comparative anonymity and and as part of a multi-ethnic society, the international rights of the Western world, that is, of the *basungu*, seem to apply. But when a person returns to the village, for example after retirement, he loses the status of *musungu*. He is reduced to the lower status of being only human, that is, to the status of *muntu*. In that position he becomes vulnerable again to witchcraft accusations. This is the case when people arrive in the village with their pensions, or have been given a lump sum when they are made redundant. They are not able to invest the money in productive property since they run a great risk of being accused of witchcraft. They are at the mercy of a vague set of unwritten traditional laws that can easily be manipulated by those who hold the rein of local power.

The participants of the seminars expressed their concern about this situation by recommending that slowly but surely the rural areas should be 'urbanised and humanised' and upgraded to legality, providing people with the possibility of title of possession (title-deeds). This has successfully been done—and continues to be done—in the peri-urban compounds of the city and the towns. The first group to be reaffirmed in their human dignity, in their view, would be the traditional chiefs themselves. They should be the first to be given a considerable piece of land, if possible around their chiefly residences. The income from land tax should not go entirely into the salaries of the Department of Lands in Lusaka, but part of it should benefit chiefs and other local rulers with a view to enhancing their income and status. If they are reasonably well established, the temptation to resort to witchcraft practices or to make unproven accusations in order to acquire property will be less strong.[20]

On the religious-cultural side, the fact that many Zambians have adopted Christianity as a preferential option may be a mainstay for counteracting the strength of the evil forces that people experience in their life. The Church holds that a steady faith in Christ as the Son of God is incompatible with an equal belief in the power of evil spirits. It preaches the message of St Paul that Christ has been placed above all principalities and powers. In the opinion of the Church, faith in Christ makes the presence in a hidden, let alone stronger, power irrelevant.[21]

Notes

1. See White Father diaries 1890-1895, e.g. White Fathers' Archives Lusaka, 5-ZWF-MD 56 (The Ubemba— Kayambi Diary 1895-1899), translated (from French) and edited by Fr. Louis Oger.
2. See also Catholic Commission for Justice and Peace-Zambia, National Office Strategic Plan 2000-2003, prepared by the National Office together with diocesan coordinators 20th to 23rd July, 1999, which provides an analysis of the socio-economic and political situation in Zambia, including 'witchcraft injustices' (p. 9) (http//www.ccjp.org.zm/Documents/strategic-plan.doc).

3. Information drawn from the *bulozi* or witchcraft seminars organised by the Catholic Church in Zambia, see pp. 241-4 of the present article.

4. Ibid.

5. C. Bawa Yamba, 'Cosmologies in turmoil: witchfinding and AIDS in Chiawa, Zambia', *Africa*, vol. 67, nr. 2, 1997, pp.183-209.

6. For examples, see White Fathers' Archives Lusaka, 5-ZWF-MD 66 (Chalabesa Mission Diary 1934-1978) or 5-ZWF-MD 63 (Ilondola Mission Diary 1934-1993).

7. Personal observation.

8. Lubushi, 1988, as recorded in Mukupa Kaoma, by author and priest Fr. Damian Musonda. Correspondence to, and conversation with, the Commissioner of Police, Kasama. White Fathers' Archives, Lusaka.

9. *Times of Zambia*, 22 July 1999, p 3.

10. *Times of Zambia*, 15 January 2000, p. 8.

11. See e.g. *Times of Zambia*, 9 March 1999, p 2.

12. *Times of Zambia*, 17 February 2000, p. 3.

13. *News from Zambia*, 21 October 1999.

14. *Times of Zambia*, 9 March 2000, p. 2.

15. This is based on research carried out by Andrew Long in North Luangwa Valley in the 1990s.

16. Data from the Project History and Research, Catholic Church, National Pastoral Office, Catholic Secretariat, Lusaka, May 2000, carried out by a committee including the author of the present article.

17. St Peter's Catholic Parish, Serenje, 'Report to National Commission of Justice and Peace, July 1997-98', and 'Evaluation' in June 2000.

18. Weekly television programme of the Communications Department of the Catholic Secretariat, entitled *Lumen 2000*.

19. Information from Rev. Dr. Jo Komakoma, Office of Justice and Peace, Catholic Secretariat, Lusaka, February 2000.

20. Recommendations from the seminars in Livingstone, Mongu, Kasama, and Chipata,1998-99.

21. Letter of St Paul to the Ephesians, Ch.1: 21-2. This is not the same as saying that powers of evil do not exist, only that they have been overpowered and chained up by Christ's victory.

11

THE IMPACT OF WITCHCRAFT BELIEFS AND PRACTICES ON THE SOCIO-ECONOMIC DEVELOPMENT OF THE ABAKWAYA IN MUSOMA-RURAL DISTRICT, TANZANIA

Stephen Nyoka Nyaga

INTRODUCTION

This article discusses some aspects of witchcraft beliefs and practices among the Abakwaya, one of the Bantu communities in Musoma-Rural District in Mara Region of Tanzania. The term witchcraft is used to refer to perceived practices of manipulating mystical powers with the aim of causing harm to, or disturbing the peace of, certain people by so-called sorcerers and *waturutumbi* or night runners. Witchcraft practices also justify the activities of diviners and indigenous medicine experts, who are believed to possess the ability to manipulate greater mystical forces as they try to neutralise the powers of sorcery. From an African perspective, the belief in witchcraft powers does not contradict belief in the powers of God.[1] The Bakwaya, for example, believe that while sorcerers manipulate evil spirits to cause harm to other people, diviners and medicinemen derive their powers from God to neutralise evil spirits or other destructive forces. In other words, for them the belief in powers of witchcraft goes hand in hand with a belief in the—greater—powers of God.

The article explores traditional Bakwaya concepts of God, and of ancestral and remote spirits, showing the influence of such ideas on the community today. There appears to be a close relationship between the belief in the powers of Nyamhanga, as God is traditionally known among the Bakwaya, and their belief in spirits and witchcraft powers. These beliefs and subsequent practices continue to influence the way in which people relate to each other in society, as well as their concept of development.

The article is based on my personal observation and primary data that I collected between January and June 1999. The research was carried out in a predominantly Christian region. However, some views of Muslims were also taken into consideration. I conducted oral interviews in 11 out of the 13 villages in Musoma-Rural District. These were conducted among the elders, aged between 70 and 100 years old, middle-aged men and women, and youth and religious leaders. The religious leaders consisted of priests, nuns and catechists in the Catholic Church, pastors of Protestant churches, and a number of imams among the Muslims. All together, some 100 people were interviewed, either individually or as a group. Most of the interviews were based on a discussion guide. Individuals and groups were interviewed at various places. Answers were sought to basic questions concerning the history of the Bakwaya, their traditional ways of worship, the history and influence of modernity in the community, and traditional as well as current perceptions on the influence of witchcraft beliefs and practices on socio-economic development programmes in Bukwaya.[2] The overall purpose was to investigate people's own understanding of their identity, and to base the contemporary socio-economic reality of the Bakwaya on their historical perspectives. Hence, the following is based on people's religious history as perceived and told by themselves. The concept of socio-economic development is used in this context to refer to the process of acquiring a more effective and efficient means of transport and communication, the construction of more spacious and permanent living houses, the extension of water sources closer to the homesteads, the construction of modern medical and education facilities, and the acquisition of the necessary skills to enable people to use modern technology in their daily life.

THE BAKWAYA

Bakwaya community is one of the few matrilineal societies in East Africa, which migrated from Sudan/Egypt region around the fourteenth century. Following the reconstruction made on the basis of the narratives by Bakwaya elders, the ancestors of the Bakwaya passed along the shores of Lake Victoria in Uganda and

Kenya, to settle in the north-western parts of Tanzania about two centuries later. The Bakwaya now live in Musoma-Rural District in Mara Region, Tanzania. The community is made up of subsistence farmers who grow mainly cassava, finger millet, sorghum, ground-nuts, beans, sweet potatoes, besides rearing goats and poultry. Fishing is an important economic activity, due to the proximity of Lake Victoria. The Bakwaya are predominant in their district, but there are other communities too, including the Wakiroba, Wazanaki, Wakerewe, and Wakabwa, who arrived as immigrants as a result of the *ujamaa* policy (policy of villagisation) that was implemented in 1972 by the government of Tanzania.[3]

The community, which is one of the egalitarian communities in Mara Region, traditionally adhered to a matrilineal system.[4] This implied that children were entitled to inherit property from their maternal uncles. Hence, they would move to their maternal uncles' homes after the death of their father, or even on reaching maturity. In this type of system, parents tended to have a higher regard for their nephews and nieces than for their own children. The Roman Catholic missionaries from Germany and France, who came to the region around 1897, discouraged matrilinealism and even applied coercion to implement their principles. For example, they used colonial government policies to enforce the payment of dowry and other patrilineal customs among the Bakwaya.

The Bakwaya elders did not take kindly the missionaries' negative attitude towards their traditional beliefs and practices. They were convinced that the powers of their god Nyamhanga and their ancestral spirits could strike anybody who showed contempt for what they traditionally valued. For instance, when around 1909 two of the three White Fathers, who were the first Christian missionaries in Bukwaya, died of unknown causes in the same year, Bakwaya elders are said to have rejoiced over their death. They observed that Nyamhanga and the ancestral spirits had been enraged by the presence of foreigners displaying abhor-rence of Abakwaya religious beliefs and practices. They told the remaining White Father that the indigenous mystical powers derived from Nyamhanga were working against Christianity. The latter advised his colleagues to look for an alternative area of settling. Generally, the Bakwaya proved inimical towards the new faith and its methods of worship. Their religious specialists incited the community against the missionaries, arguing that they were undermining traditional Bakwaya values and practices that had guided them for many centuries.[5]

Available statistical data from the Catholic Secretariat in Musoma Diocese show that about 55% of the Bakwaya profess Catholic Christianity. Data obtained by Magesa and Nyaga indicate that about 35% are listed as traditionalists, while close to 5% belong to Protestant churches, and another 5% are Muslims.[6] Nevertheless, Bakwaya of various religious persuasions have continued to adhere to traditional values, particularly those associated with a belief in the powers of evil spirits and in the magical powers of traditional medicines, both for healing purposes and in social relationships.

THE CONCEPT OF GOD AND MYSTICAL POWERS

Traditionally, the Bakwaya had no objective definition of their God. People used to worship Nyamhanga, who was given the same name as the sun.[7] The Bakwaya believed that Nyamhanga was a universal God, who gave them the power to work and to acquire all they needed for their sustenance. He was not feared but ascribed with attributes such as kindness, love, utmost goodness, provision, and sustenance of all living things.

The belief in the universality and omnipresence of Nyamhanga caused the Bakwaya to provide him with the same name they used for the sun. Just as the sun illuminates every corner on earth, they believed that Nyamhanga sees every part of Bukwaya and is above all things.[8] The Bakwaya believed that Nyamhanga lives in the spirit world. After the death of a person, his or her spirit was believed to join Nyamhanga in the invisible world. No one could exactly tell where Nyamhanga was staying, although most elders described his resting-place to be in the sky. This appears to be based on the fact that they associated him with the sun, and other natural phenomena, such as rain, winds, and lightening. People, however, did not associate their suffering with Nyamhanga. Such a concept of God and the associated beliefs are still common among the contemporary Bakwaya.

Every clan had its own sacred place in the bush where members conducted ritual activities as a means of communicating with God. But the Bakwaya also believed that there were other, less powerful forces, that affected their lives more directly. These notably included ancestral spirits, of whom the Bakwaya had a clear conception. Most worship practices were directed to these ancestral spirits.

THE WORSHIP OF NYAMHANGA AND ANCESTRAL SPIRITS

The worship of Nyamhanga took place in specific places, which were mainly around the wells and other water sources, and in bushy areas, particularly on top of the hills. This phenomenon is not peculiar to the Abakwaya. It has been reported in other African communities across Africa.[9] Traditionally, the main place of worship was around Buramba hill. The Buramba shrine is located where the early ancestors of the Bakwaya had settled before dispersing to present-day Bukwaya. The people believed that the ancestral spirits that inhabit their sacred places, though invisible, made their powers felt. They could be silent, hence harmless, or active, causing harm when annoyed by their descendants.

The Bakwaya also prayed in other places that were regarded as sacred. All clan members know such places. Non-Christians and many Christians, including religious leaders such as priests, members of parish councils, catechists, pastors, and also Muslims within Bukwaya continue to believe in the existence of supernatural powers which can only be controlled through traditional ways of worship.[10] Many traditional religious leaders and elders still visit sacred groves for prayers and to offer sacrifices to Nyamhanga in times of calamity, misfortune, and when they fear impending danger such as prolonged drought, epidemic disease, or the mysterious death of livestock or people.[11] Such places can be found in Kigera village, where I conducted some of the interviews, at Kumgongo hill, and near a natural well in Nyakatende village, among other places. It became apparent during the research that most Christians attend Sunday services while at the same time participating in traditional rituals. In cases where the rains delay or floods continue to cause devastation, the

Christians not only conduct prayers in the church but also join the traditionalist believers in their rituals to alleviate impending calamities. In view of this, Magesa and Nyaga contend that the phenomenon of dual religiosity is still prevalent among Abakwaya Christians.[12] The local priests and members of parish councils make little effort to discourage this type of syncretism among Bakwaya Christians. In congregations where the priest appears to be very strict on Christian principles, they secretly conduct their traditional worship activities. I was told how Muslims and Christians, including even members of the parish councils, contribute animals for sacrificial purposes in the traditional shrines.[13]

Some mysterious activities and attributes are ascribed to certain objects that are found around the sacred places. In Kigera-Etuma shrine, people believe that a small black stone that is found there is inhabited by spirits. It is seen as a magic stone, that is found where they believe the spirits of the progenitors of Abakwaya society, known as 'Nyere-tuma', or the mother of Etuma, to reside. This black magic stone, which weighs about ten kilograms, is immovable. Attempts to move it by those who doubt its magical powers has always been futile. Stories are told of how on occasion people tried to move the stone to another place, but without success. The stone always returns to its original position at night in a mysterious manner. Those who try to move the stone are struck by its magical powers. Some become insane or terminally ill, others lose their properties or their livestock and children through mysterious deaths. When I appeared curious and asked for permission to move the stone, I was advised not to engage in such an act in view of incidences in the past, such as those cited above.

The sacred bushes are also believed to be inhabited by snakes. Snakes are said to have a special place in the religious beliefs of the Bakwaya. In addition, there is a belief that certain species of snakes are embodiments of ancestral or nature spirits. The most common such snake is *chatu*, the python, which is greatly revered by the Bakwaya. Traditionally, the Bakwaya believe that the snake has received special powers from Nyamhanga; for example, it can cause certain spirits to take revenge on humans. Killing this snake is therefore a taboo. Instead it is handled very carefully, and nobody will dare to kill it, even if it appears in people's home-steads.

During worship and sacrificial ceremonies, the animals offered to Nyamhanga and the ancestral spirits are usually a white or black chicken, a goat or a cow. A decision on which animal to offer is made with the assistance of the diviners, who are respected because of their role in interpreting the causes of mysterious phenomena. They are also important in advising local healers, who treat all sorts of diseases and health problems. During ritual worship, the elders say prayers, slaughter the goats or cows, sacrificing some of the meat, and eat and drink beer in the sacred bush as a way of partaking with their god Nyamhanga and the ancestral spirits. They also present offerings in the form of money, tobacco or snuff, meat, honey, millet, beer, and other forms of food. Bibi Nyang'oko of Kigera village recited the words that are used in Kikwaya. Translated into English, the recitation involves praising the spirits in the bush, stating the purpose of the prayers, and making the sacrifice as a way of appeasing the offended spirit.[14] Missionaries and others foreign to the Bakwaya ways of worship tended to regard these practices as evil, while some described these practices as satanic or a form of devil worship.

The elders argue that sacrificial foods and drinks are also made to *chatu*, the python, on behalf of certain spirits. According to them, *chatu* is presented with honey and meat, and other food.[15] *Chatu* is fed by one elder, who will face backward and put some honey and sacrificial but roasted meat on the palms of their hands, which are positioned towards the back. The one feeding *chatu* is not supposed to see it. It is also a taboo to disclose the experience of the ritual feeding of *chatu*. In some instances, *chatu* may come to the sacred ground where the elders are gathered to prepare their sacrificial animal. In such instances, the elders believe that their grievances are taken directly from them, without mediation of a ritual leader. Not every elder is allowed to approach the most sacred parts of the bush-shrine. Requests are usually made to the *chatu* to withdraw its anger or wrath that is considered the cause of a particular suffering or misfortune.

MYSTICAL POWERS ASSOCIATED WITH ANCESTRAL AND REMOTE SPIRITS

The Bakwaya believe that the living have a duty to commemorate and show honour to their ancestors. Hence, nominal reincarnation is a common belief. People are obliged to name their newborn babies after their departed elders or are given the name of an ancestor as a sign of honour. The names given are usually accepted, or they may be rejected by the ancestors. Normally the father suggests the name of the child, but in most cases his parents or grandparents assist him. However, a child may be renamed, even several times. For example, when a baby cries for no particular reason, the parents will consult a diviner, who assist them in identifying the ancestor who might be complaining of being forgotten. In such a case, renaming is done under his guidance. The naming of some children is easier than that of others, particularly those who are born with a resemblance or certain birthmarks, similar to those of their deceased relatives. When this is the case, the child will be named after that person, and it will be known that the ancestor has reincarnated.[16] Such incidences are common in Bukwaya. One informant, who is a teacher by profession, provided an example of how his family determined who would be named after his grandfather, who died after he had been shot with an arrow in the chest.[17] Subsequently, every child that is born with a birthmark on the chest is given the name of that grandfather.

Failure to name the child after the right deceased person is believed to be a major cause of calamity and misfortune, which strikes children and their parents. The calamities range from frequent crying of the baby after birth or after the naming rite, and retardation in mental and physical growth, to different types of ailments, prolonged stomach-ache, headache, visual or hearing impairment, and other ailments. I came across many incidences of illness and clinical cases, including body deformities that were attributed to the wrong naming of the victims. This belief has made the profession of diviners to be very popular in Bukwaya. Medical officers find it difficult to convince people that health problems of the sort mentioned above have normally bacterial, viral, clinical or hereditary causes.

However, some exceptional cases were presented by certain people, explaining how diviners and traditional medicinemen diagnose and heal certain complicated problems. In Kiemba village, for instance, there was one married couple that got a baby which later became blind. This couple went to various hospitals where they were told that no medical remedy existed for the problem. Subsequently, the couple decided to visit a diviner to examine the child and be advised on what to do. The diviner told them that the cause of the problem was with one of their grand-parents, named Kagere, who fostered a complaint. During the divination process Kagere's spirit explained that the baby should be named after him. The ancestral spirit lamented that the couple had forgotten their grandfather.[18] Under the guidance of the diviner the couple changed the name of the baby, which regained its eyesight. Since that time, the baby grew into a mature man who has never lost his eyesight again.

Among the Bakwaya, diviners are believed to facilitate com-munication between the living and the dead. It is through the diviners that the ancestral spirits communicate with the living. They for example complain if the living appear to be abandon-ing them, particularly if the living forget to clear the bush on their graves and to organise the memorial ceremony commonly known as *mitambiko*. In these ceremonies, close clan elders are invited by family members. A cow is slaughtered, food and beer are prepared, and a ritual is conducted by the family head in the presence of close relatives. The bush around the grave is cleared, the family head or the ritual leader pours beer or honey on the grave of the departed elder. A communal prayer for peace and reconciliation is said during such a ritual. Those who participate in such rituals include family members and clan members of the deceased elder. Such rituals also enhance cooperation and cohe-sion among society members.

The Bakwaya believe that failure to honour the dead can make a woman to experience a stillbirth or to give birth to a child with physical or biological disorders. If a family buried an elderly person in a way contrary to their will, (s)he will complain. The ancestor's anger may cause sickness to children or misfortunes to family members, whose cause will be revealed by a diviner. In such incidences, unearthing the remains of the deceased and reburying them will instantly reverse the calamity. Elders from all over Bukwaya observed that although their people adhere to Christianity or Islam, they acknowledge the powers of ancestral spirits.[19] During the interviews they explained that the powers of ancestral spirits and the diviners cannot be doubted by anybody in Bukwaya.[20]

The Bakwaya believe also in powers of remote, non-ancestral spirits that can be manipulated by certain people. They have the ability to get possessed by them, neutralising their harmful effects. Those who are believed to possess such powers and to be able to use them, are mainly diviners, witches or sorcerers. As such, the Bakwaya do not have definite terms of differentiating witches and sorcerers. However, it became apparent that sorcerers are commonly associated with misuse of mystical powers in order to cause death or adversity to fellow human beings. Sorcerers are therefore seen as the worst enemies of the society (social misfits), as will discussed in the next section. On the other hand, witches are believed to manipulate mystical powers to work out magic. Some of their magical results may be positive, such as avenging the calamities or harm caused by those who hire the services of a sorcerer. This makes it difficult for most people to distinguish between positive and negative attributes of witches and sorcerers. Witches are sometimes associated with good attributes and at other times with bad ones, depending on the end results.

Some informants argued that remote spirits, usually known as *jinni* or *mashetani*, evil spirits, are responsible for most accidents and mysterious misfortunes that cause suffering in the society. This is a popular belief among the Bakwaya, who think that all accidents, including deaths, are usually caused by evil spirits. Before a conclusion is made on the actual cause of a particular calamity, a diviner will always be consulted.

The Bakwaya fear spirits, because they believe that sorcerers can use their powers to manipulate the spirit world. They can manipulate spirits to cause the death of children, livestock, failure of crops in the farm, the drying up of wells, sickness, loss of fertility, flopping of one's business, failure in examinations, unstable marriages, and many other problems at personal, family and even societal levels. When people suspect a spirit to be the cause of their misfortune, they will perform a ritual, using medicine to cleanse the affected person and neutralise the powers of sorcery or evil spirits. Only a ritual leader can preside over the ritual of appeasing the aggrieved spirit.

SORCERY

The Bakwaya have a strong belief that sorcerers can cause irrevocable physical, economic, social or psychological damage on a neighbour or relative. They are believed to cause harm through use of their medicine, which can control evil spirits. These medicines are either consumed, touched, inhaled, or crossed over. Some medicines used by sorcerers are believed to work in a remote sense, particularly when the sorcerer is given any product from the targeted person's body. Most of these products consist of anything that has been in contact with the body, for example, blood, urine, faeces, nails, clothes, saliva, foot or finger prints.[21] Their impact, after the medicine has been used, is deemed to cause death, poverty, madness, insanity, impotence, snake bites, heart diseases, divorce or separation, premature birth of a child, failure in exams in schools, failure in businesses, and all forms of body disorders, social, psychological or environmental instability. Sorcerers may act this way for several reasons: out of jealousy, or because they have been paid, to test their medicine, or to take revenge, or to destabilise peace in a society.

It is generally believed that more women than men are sorcerers. This, according to some elders, is because most women are more envious and jealous than men are. The present research revealed that more women are reported to use sorcery with a view to harming their enemies than men. Some informants argued that sorcery constitutes a women-dominated career, while divination is a men-dominated career. Powers of sorcery are believed to be inherited, taught or sold to interested people. Some clans are considered to have more powers of sorcery than others. Some sorcerers are deemed to be more powerful than their colleagues. Those are the ones whose powers are said to be derived from their medicine.

In view of the above, people fear becoming rich, highly educated, popular, beautiful or handsome, as this may attract the attention of potential enemies or competitors; hence, cause their death through sorcery.[22] The most famous villages concerning witchcraft practices are Kigera-Etuma, Nyasurura and Nyakatende. However, witchcraft beliefs and practices pervade the whole of Bukwaya society. Activities of sorcerers are seen as the opposite of those of normal society members, as well as of other specialists such as traditional priests, sincere diviners and medicine persons.

Sorcerers can be identified through the help of diviners, who will establish where they are: in the eastern, western, southern or northern side of the village. Some may give more detailed information by describing the appearance or the specific identity of a sorcerer. Without the help of a diviner, it is difficult to identify sorcerers. It is possible for someone to marry a sorceress without knowing.[23] This is because sorcerers' powers are used in a secretive manner. They fear exposing their powers to those who are not in the same business, knowing that once discovered, they may be publicly condemned or killed. Their activities are deemed to be anti-social, inasmuch they are believed to cause death, damage and suffering to innocent members of the society.

It is, however, difficult to tell whether the same diviners who identify sorcerers do not ignite hatred between neighbours, given that witchcraft activities are discussed in secret. When a rumour brands somebody a sorcerer, people become over-conscious in their dealings with that person. Some will cut all relationships with such people, while others may approach them to buy medicines or hire their services. Sorcerers are therefore both liked and hated among the Bakwaya.

The fear of being bewitched make most people fear being seen to prosper in business and to be able to educate their children up to a higher level. Parents with educated children often advise them to buy a piece of land far from home for fear that they might be bewitched if they develop their family land. Other parents refuse to have a decent house built by their children for fear that this might endanger their live.[24] This was quoted as one reason explaining the underdevelopment of the Musoma-Rural District compared to other districts in the Mara Region. Elders argue that the best lifestyle to maintain in order to ward off envy is that of modesty. This implies that most people will continue to rely on public water sources, living in a grass thatched hut, educating children up to primary school level, and wearing cheap clothes, particularly *mitumba* (second-hand clothes), while making a living through subsistence farming or fishing. Anybody who aspires to rise above others has to look for strong medicines, which are also expensive. These may be obtained from the neighbouring groups such as the Wakuria, Wajaluo, or Wakiroba. Others may get their protective medicines from the Wasukuma, or from coastal communities, and even from communities in neighbouring countries. Rich people and successful businessmen are always believed to be using medicines to attract customers to buy their merchandise. They are therefore associated with witchcraft practices.

WATURUTUMBI (NIGHT RUNNERS)

A different type of witches is that of the category commonly called *waturutumbi*, also referred to as 'night runners'. They are believed to enjoy disturbing people at night, running up and down in their homesteads in stiff nakedness. *Waturutumbi* knock or hit on people's doors, disturbing them while they are asleep. They run away as soon as they are detected. Sometimes, people believe, they throw soil, stones, leaves of trees and other objects against doors or on rooftops. Night running is believed to be a common practice, that most people claim to know about. Most people who hear movements at night readily associate it with night runners, rather than with robbers or thieves. Night runners are believed to be protected by their medicine from being seen, and it is said that cowards fear going out at night, especially when other people are asleep. Children in particular are cautioned against walking at night.

According to the Bakwaya, some witches possess powers to make use of other people at night. They maintain that they secretly visit people's houses, open the doors, eat their food and leave the house without being noticed, hardly stealing anything from the house. Others can enter the house, move around, sleep in a person's bed and wake up early in the morning and leave the house unnoticed. The most powerful witches are believed to be those who have medicines that enable them to go into people's houses, take the residents out of their bed, take them to their farms to work and return them in the morning. People believed to be taken to the farm to dig or harvest, particularly when there is moonlight, are considered to do this unconsciously. The only sign that causes them to suspect that they have been used by a witch is when they wake up in the morning feeling very tired, yet they do not suffer from any form of physical ailment or have any mental problem.[25] Some people, who wake up feeling tired and restless, may stay at home all day, because they believe that they worked for a witch during the night. Others will look for money to visit a diviner who may assist them in identifying the witch who misused them at night.

There are also school-going children who wake up and inform their parents that they are too tired to go to school. Such a feeling of mental and physical fatigue is usually associated with the work of *waturutumbi*. People argue that one can only see a night runner with the help of special medicines to be obtained from diviners and medicine persons, which provide them with the ability to effectively see and identify night runners and sorcerers. However, our informants argued that diviners and medicine persons have no power to eliminate sorcerers and *waturutumbi*. Some maintain that this reflects a conspiracy between diviners, medicine persons, and certain sorcerers and *waturutumbi* to safeguard each other's career as a way of maintaining their profession. Others, however, dispute this, arguing that while sorcerers engage in destructive activities, diviners and medicine persons' acts are basically constructive (or curative).

The incidences that were narrated by Bakwaya people suggest that belief in sorcery makes most people to desist from crime and other social immoralities such as stealing each other's property, adultery, harassing neighbours' children, showing contempt to elders, and other common offences. Witchcraft beliefs and practices, therefore, create complex social relationships among all the Bakwaya. Such beliefs and practices are enhanced by a failure to explain the causes of mysterious events or episodes, or of changes in people's bodies or in the social environment or of natural phenomena. Jealousy between co-wives in a polygamous household, or between clan members, students in schools and colleagues in workplaces in all sectors causes many to indulge in witchcraft practices.[26]

In some Bukwaya villages, people who are victimised for practising sorcery are simply scolded. In other places, particularly near shopping centres, they are killed. Most people, however, are afraid to kill sorcerers for fear that their colleagues might take revenge. The national government (provincial administration), through the village secretary and the police force, tries to protect those who are suspected of practising sorcery from being killed through mob justice. The laws in the Republic of Tanzania remain silent on the punishment to be accorded to those suspected of practising sorcery. The law actually discourages victimisation and harassing of those who are accused of such practice.

DIVINERS AND MEDICINE PERSONS

Belief in witchcraft goes hand in hand with belief in divination and in the powers of medicinemen, as highlighted above. Diviners are believed to possess powers to heal the sick, reveal the hidden, interpret the causes of problems such as sickness, friction between family members and other people in the society, etc. The knowledge of diviners and medicinemen is believed to be obtained in different ways. Some are said to inherit this or learn it from their parents who teach them from childhood; others are believed to learn it as a career from other diviners and medicinemen; yet others are believed to be born with a particular talent for divination. According to informants, those who are born with such a talent become a genius in the field of medicine if they attach themselves to practising diviners or medicinemen.[27]

The Bakwaya believe that other communities in Tanzania, such as those living along the Indian Ocean—for example, the Wakuria, Wajaluo, and Wazanaki within Mara region—have more efficient and powerful diviners and medicine persons than those from their own community. On the other hand, people from those communities often come to Bukwaya for divination services. In fact, people prefer to consult diviners from distant areas if they can. This enables them to trust the diagnosis of their problems as they believe that an interpretation offered by a diviner from other communities than their own is more reliable since it is free from local biases. This, however, does not stop people from visiting local diviners.

Some diviners are known to be liars. They get known with time and people try to avoid them. Insincere diviners cause people to clash, or to argue over trivial issues or without genuine reason. Some informants argued that insincere diviners and sorcerers work together to cause harm in order to protect their careers. Without people falling sick or having problems, the help of diviners would not be needed. Bakwaya diviners carry out their duties in their rural homes, in rental houses or rooms in residential estates in town, and near major shopping centres.

Bakwaya diviners are divided in to two categories. One category consists of those who can identify the causes of mysterious phenomena, but cannot heal the victims or rectify the course of events. Such specialists simply advice the victim on how to respond to their problems. The second category contains those who identify the cause of a particular problem and offer medicine to treat or rectify it. This category of diviners is small, and some Bakwaya rely on diviners from neighbouring groups, particularly on those who combine divination with the prescription of medicines. Certain problems may be diagnosed through divination as to require the victim to abstain from specific behaviour in order to be to healed.

One survey, carried out in 1999 to investigate the treatment of people in local health facilities, showed that over eighty percent of patients in Mkirira and Buhare villages in Bukwaya visit diviners and medicinemen before seeking treatment in government and private health facilities. This has led to the death of many victims of deadly diseases, such as meningitis and cerebral malaria, cancer, diabetes, AIDS, and strokes among other known cases.[28] A local medical officer underlined that Mara Region is one of the regions with the highest number of HIV/AIDS victims in Tanzania. He further underscored that Abakwaya is among the communities in Mara Region with a high number of HIV/AIDS victims who die while undergoing treatment in their rural homes. The majority of patients die while seeking a cure outside the hospitals.

Our research revealed that family heads generally spend much of their resources on divination in search of explanations for various problems at the family level. The charges of different diviners vary. Some ask for a goat or a cow. Others ask for several goats or cows depending on the nature of a problem. Modern diviners and medicine persons ask for money, ranging from 20,000 Tanzanian shilling to 100,000 or more.

It was noted above that witchcraft beliefs and practices cause people in Bukwaya to live with fear and suspicion. This fear and suspicion have persisted despite the presence of the Church and despite government policies, which do not recognise the alleged powers of sorcerers, *waturutumbi* and diviners.[29]

CONCLUDING OBSERVATIONS

If there is any positive side at all to witchcraft beliefs and practices among the Bakwaya, it may be that compared to neighbouring communities in Mara Region there is fewer crime and perceived immorality, as noted earlier. People fear stealing, because the offended person can use diviners to identify them as the culprit. Potential thieves, for example, fear the *waturutumbi* who are believed to move around at night and to be invisible. According to informants, this might explain why robbery or stealing of property among the Bakwaya was uncommon before the Tanzanian government implemented its policy of *ujamaa*, bringing people from other communities to Bukwaya.

It is implicit that in contemporary times witchcraft beliefs serve to reinforce moral values among the local community. Most people in Musoma-Rural District, including those working in the civil service or for NGOs, Christian and Muslim religious leaders, and schoolchildren, all believe in witchcraft. They are always cautious in carrying out their activities because they fear the mystical powers of sorcerers and *waturutumbi*. They are aware that such people can be hired to harm them, if they give reason for local people to hate or envy them. People try to be on good terms with each other as much as possible. When they quarrel or argue over a particular issue, they look for an arbitrator to help them sort out their differences. Personal enemies are seen to be potential collaborators of witches. Belief in witchcraft causes parents to discourage their children from eating in neighbours' houses and interacting with strangers. Children are also encouraged to look for marriage partners among families which have never been associated with witchcraft, particularly in harming a relative.

From the foregoing discussion it may be concluded that witchcraft beliefs and practices are used to explain the causes of various psychological, social, economic and even political challenges. Witchcraft beliefs foster a naive attitude among the members of Bakwaya society. They are passed from one generation to another in such a way that one might almost say they are part of Bakwaya heritage.

Witchcraft beliefs and the associated practices have led to underdevelopment of Bukwaya compared to areas occupied by other communities in Mara Region. The Bakwaya fear being seen to be prospering in education, business, and farming among other sectors. Parents are afraid to appear better off than their neighbours. Some prospective developers deliberately refuse to improve their rural homes by putting up permanent houses, installing electricity and telephone lines, among other modern facilities, to avoid igniting jealousy among fellow Abakwaya. In this regard jealousy is conceived to be a major cause of misfortunes and adversities commonly linked to witchcraft and sorcery as discussed in this chapter.

In some villages in Bukwaya, prominent fishermen and farmers still prefer living in low-cost grass-thatched huts. They contend that the safest life is that of a humble person and not that of those who try to work harder than others to be better off economically. Young and prosperous people buy land outside Bukwaya to start a home. They conspire with their parents to keep this a secret for fear of witchcraft accusations. This shows that, although belief in witchcraft appears to be more common among people without formal education, many people who have pursued higher studies as well as those living in urban centres still succumb to traditional values and the associated beliefs. They also tolerate witchcraft practices in that they do not make an effort to discourage reliance on diviners to solve social problems among their own family members. Some educated children send their parents money to pay for the costs of visiting a diviner or sorcerer.

Some business people from other parts of Tanzania, such as Wachagga and Washale, but also people from Kenya and Uganda, take advantage of the Bakwayas' fear for witchcraft and their reluctance to invest seriously in their own land to start a business there. It is people from outside Bukwaya, therefore, who make good money in Bukwaya, especially by selling consumer goods. Ironically, the Bakwaya do not attempt to use witchcraft powers on them. Visitors are protected against witchcraft by custom. Bakwaya customs prohibit the bewitching of visitors. Sorcerers decline from using their witchcraft powers on foreigners, given the popular belief that one does not know what type of medicine visitors may have used to protect themselves against the manipulation of evil powers.

At the social level, women from a polygamous marriage spend much of their resources on buying medicines to protect themselves and their children against being bewitched by their co-wives. In those families, our informants alleged, co-wives rely on medicines to 'strengthen' their marital relationship with their polygamous husbands. In such cases the diviners protect their clients against victimisation by ensuring confidentiality to both parties. When we sought to know the reason behind this secrecy, it was alleged that this is diviners' 'professional ethics'. Some diviners, however, thrive on their clients' special problems, ignorance and naive attitude to life.

Scientific knowledge denounces witchcraft beliefs and the belief in divination, due to a lack of verifiable explanations. Christian teachings equally do not support such belief. One of the biggest challenges of early Christian missionaries was how to discourage the belief in witchcraft. They were determined to use religious teachings and formal education to eliminate witchcraft practices among the Bakwaya. They built schools and dispensaries, teaching Christian principles and educating people who later served as catechists, teachers, clerks and mission workers. Although they managed to gradually change Bakwaya Christians' attitude towards witchcraft beliefs and practices, the belief in witchcraft is still widespread at all levels, including among those in formal employment as civil servants and teachers, religious leaders and business people in local towns and urban centres. This confirms the observation by certain scholars that some traditions take a long time to disappear, including belief in magic and witchcraft.[30]

In view of their attempts to further socio-economic development, one of the biggest challenges that the government and the Church face in Bukwaya is how to discourage the negative concepts associated with witchcraft beliefs and practices in the community, which hamper development programmes. The challenges are particularly critical in the areas of health and education, where the creation of awareness is required. Comparatively, the Bakwaya are regarded as amongst the poorest in Mara Region; yet their land has a higher potential than that of the neighbouring communities. I was told by several groups of informants that the Bakwaya are poor because they are bewitched.

The Bakwaya community needs to be sensitised, notably to be done by targeting social workers and community leaders. The ultimate aim should be to make them more open-minded, and appreciative to scientific and technological advancement. This would make them effective in their duties. The training of local social workers and religious leaders should take place in institutions that are located in other parts of the country, to give them some exposure. Christian and Muslim religious leaders from different parts of Tanzania should participate in sensitisation seminars.

Interaction of the Bakwaya people and their local leaders with people from other parts of Tanzania can help in minimising overreliance on witchcraft beliefs to explain social phenomena in the community. This should be encouraged in schools, higher institutions of learning, as well as in workplaces. Awareness seminars should be organised by NGO's, government departments, and educational institutions in Bukwaya, particularly by agriculture extension officers and health workers. The ultimate goal should be to enlighten the local population about modern scientific explanations of the causes of health problems.

Scholars in social sciences, educationists, social development officers and social workers in Bukwaya have a big task to develop appropriate programmes and techniques for changing people's attitudes and responses towards socio-economic development. People should be encouraged to appreciate the economic achievements of their fellow Bakwaya. This positive attitude would be a first step towards finding a solution to changing the slow pace of socio-economic development in Bukwaya, where witchcraft beliefs and practices pose serious constraints to community development.

LIST OF ORAL INFORMANTS (O. I.)

The under-mentioned are names of individual informants and groups of respondents who were interviewed in the course of the study. The list is not all-inclusive. It does not include the names of informants who sought anonymity.

Name of Informants/or Groups of Respondents	Village or Place of Interview	Date of Interview
Mzee Masanjara	Buramba/Nyegina	5/1/1999
Elders Group III	Nyegina	31/1/1999
Elders Group IV	Nyegina	8/2/1999
Elders Group II	Etaro	13/2/1999
Bibi Nyango'ka	Kigera -Etuma	20/2/1999
Elders Group I	Kiemba	21-2-1999
Elders Group II	Kiemba	22-2-1999
Mwalim Kiraka	Kiemba	22-2-1999
Elders Group II	Nyakatende	27-2-1999
Elders Group II	Mkirira	1-3-1999
Elders Group II	Nyasurura	13-3-1999
Mzee Mayomi	Nyasurura	13-4-1999
Mzee Majengo	Kigera	14-4-1999
Youth-Students	Buhare Inst. of Development	16-4-1999
Youth Group I	Kigera	16-5-1999
Youth Group I	Nyasurura	19-5-1999
Elders Seminar	Nyegina Parish	1-6-1999
Dr Rwagasira	Buhare Health Center	14-6-1999
Catechists Seminar	Nyegina Parish	23-6-1999

Notes

1. Laurenti Magesa, *African Religion:The moral traditions of abundant life*, Maryknoll, NY: Orbis Books, 1997, pp. 190-1.
2. The name Bukwaya is used to refer to the area occupied by Bakwaya community.
3. Laurenti Magesa and Stephen Nyaga, 'Telling their own story: report on history, state and prospects of Christian marriage and

family in Bukwaya, Musoma-Rural District, Tanzania', 1999 [research report]. See notably p. 18.

4. Ibid., p. 13.

5. Elders Seminar, Nyegina Parish, O.I. (List of Oral Informants) 1/6/1999.

6. Magesa and Nyaga, 'Telling their own story'.

7. Ibid.

8. Mzee Masanjara, Buramba/Nyegina Village, O.I. 5/1/1999.

9. For example, E.B. Idowu, *African Traditional Religion: A definition*, London: SCM Press, 1973; John S. Mbiti, *African Religions and Philosophy*, London: Heinemann Education Books, 1979; Magesa, *African Religion*.

10. Elders Seminar, Nyegina Parish, O.I. 1/6/1999.

11. Bibi Nyango'ka, Kigera-Etuma, O.I. 20/2/1999.

12. Magesa and Nyaga, 'Telling their own story'.

13. Mzee Mayomi, O.I. Nyasurura village, 13/4/1999.

14. Bibi Nyango'ka, Kigera-Etuma, O.I. 20/2/1999.

15. Elders Group II, Nyakatende, O.I. 27/2/1999.

16. Elders Group II, Kiemba, O.I. 22/2/1999.

17. Mzee Kiraka, Kiemba, O.I. 22/2/1999.

18. Elders Group I and II, Kiemba, O.I. 21 and 22/2/1999.

19. Magesa and Nyaga, 'Telling their own story', p. 46.

20. Elders Group I, Kiemba, O. I. 22/2/1999; and Elders Group II, Nyasurura, O.I. 13/3/1999.

21. Elders Group II, Etaro, O.I. 13/2/1999.

22. Kigera Youth, O.I. 16/5/1999, and Nyasurura Youth, O.I. 19/5/1999.

23. Bibi Nyango'ko, Kigera, O.I. 20/2/1999.

24. Catechists Seminar, O.I. 23/6/1999.

25. Elders Group II, Kiemba, O.I. 22/ 2/1999, and Elders Group IV, Nyegina, O.I. 8/2/1999.

26. Youth-Students, Buhare, O. I. 16/4/1999.

27. Mzee Majengo, Kigera, O.I. 14/4/1999.

28. Dr Rwagasira, Medical Officer, Buhare Health Centre, O.I. 14/6/1999.

29. Magesa and Nyaga, 'Telling their own story', p. 53.

30. W.R. Bascom and M.J. Herskovits, *Continuity and Change in African Cultures*, University of Chicago Press, 1962, pp. 3 and 295.

12
CONTAINMENT OF WITCHCRAFT ACCUSATIONS IN SOUTH AFRICA: A SEARCH FOR A TRANSFORMATIONAL APPROACH TO CURB THE PROBLEM[1]

Selaelo Thias Kgatla

INTRODUCTION

Witchcraft accusations and the resulting violence have become phenomenal of South Africa's Limpopo Province.[2] In the years 1996-2001 more than six hundred people have lost their lives because of witchcraft-related violence.[3] This poses serious problems that are economically, socially and politically disruptive and frustrate any attempt at self-development.[4] Hence, there is an urgent need to curb the violent elements of witchcraft accusations. Human weaknesses, including gossip and jealousy, or negative political and economic rivalries are at the centre of the accusations.

Most of these witchcraft accusations emanate from the 'home' and the family, where people spend much of their time together as kinsmen and friends, disrupting social harmony and relationships.[5] As a rule, the first people to be suspected of witchcraft are those living close to the complainant. People who are supposed to live communally and care for one another find themselves in antagonistic relationships, fighting where they were should be cooperating. Witchcraft accusations, therefore, underline the sad fact that jealousy, hatred and aggression exist within the intimate circle of the family, where solidarity and trust should reign supreme. The prevalence of this phenomenon puts a large degree of stress on everyone within close family circles, because the fear of being pointed out as a witch and the consequences that may follow from such an accusation keep people in a constant state of agony. Rumours, gossip and slanderous talk frustrate and render victims utterly helpless. Under these circumstances people never know who will be the next victim of witchcraft accusations, and are unsure about what to do to avoid being accused.

The potential of witchcraft accusations for selecting its victims among close relations also stifles development within South African society, as victims are often found among those who try to initiate development projects. Barendse and Dederen describe, for example, how witch-pointing frustrated a firm in Nelspruit in Mpumalanga Province of South Africa, which tried to promote hardworking employees. The whole system of performance appraisal was brought to a standstill because the employees who were promoted were accused by their colleagues of using witchcraft to bluff their supervisors.[6] Witchcraft belief can thus be used by members of a community as a subversive weapon to induce submissiveness.

The economically able and socially active are often restricted by witchcraft accusations to develop their potential to the full. The weak may use the weapon of witchcraft accusations in order to stop the powerful from broadening the development gap that exists between them. Where such fears exist, it is easy for jealous and irresponsible people to hold the hardworking and successful ones at ransom. At the same time, the capacity of the powerful to keep the community in a state of stagnation and submissiveness thrives where fear of the supernatural is great. Most Africans believe, for example, that witches can manipulate thunderstorms and create lightning out of these to strike their opponents.[7] It is primarily the poor and vulnerable who are affected by thunderstorms, and every year several people in the rural areas are killed by lightning. Due to their social circumstances and the weather conditions, they are kept in a situation of constant guess and fear concerning what will happen to them next.

For black South Africans to develop after the demise of apartheid, it is imperative to find an urgent and lasting solution to the carnage caused by witch-pointing. Below, an attempt is made to suggest certain measures to address the problem.

SUGGESTIONS TO CONTAIN WITCHCRAFT ACCUSATIONS IN SOUTH AFRICA

This article does not pretend to deal in detail with prevention strategies concerning witchcraft accusations, and the suggestions are limited to the fields of education and health care. In my opinion, all measures suggested to combat witchcraft accusations and the violence related to these should be informed by authentic and reliable analyses of the causes of the plague. Empirical research is needed to recommend any solutions to the problem. If the recommendations to contain witchcraft accusations are not grounded in sound research but of a merely theoretical nature, such recommendations will not address the problem adequately. On the other hand, we must note that if some reliable findings on causative factors of witchcraft accusations are established, this does not automatically mean that the recommendations flowing from them will curb the problem.

Social scientists, especially those working in the fields of religion, anthropology and sociology, have suggested various solutions to combat witchcraft accusations and the violence that is associated with them.[8] Their suggestions for the containment of the phenomenon are varied, and can be grouped into three broad categories: the education of those trapped in witchcraft beliefs, the control of witchcraft beliefs through legal instruments, and Christian influence. These remedies thus all refer to a humanisation of society that leads to the liberal and sceptical view that regards witchcraft as 'superstition'.

These three broad theories—concerning education, safety and security, and religious theories—on the containment of witchcraft accusations cannot all be fully analysed within the confinements of this paper.[9] I will pay specific attention to the education model, highlighting some shortcomings and suggesting possible solutions. I will also briefly touch on the contributions other departments can make towards the containment of the problem. My discussion of suggested measures leaves out the role and contribution the Department of Health could make. There is an ongoing debate in South Africa on the role of traditional healers on the one hand and Western medical doctors on the other. The controversy is about putting the traditional healers on a par with Western doctors. A discussion of the role of the Department of Health requires another paper because of the policy implications raised in the debate. In general, a good programme of medical service would do much to reduce the stress placed on communities by witchcraft accusations, but would not wipe out the problem as disease abounds in South Africa and may always be attributed to witches, as is the case with death itself. Similarly, better economic and agricultural conditions will go some way towards addressing the problem, but may not remove the family squabbles that often lead to witchcraft accusations.

Educationist model

The educationist model was clearly espoused by Advocate Seth Nthai, Member of the Executive Committee (MEC) for Safety and Security of the Northern Province, when he stated in 1995: 'The killing of people suspected of practising witchcraft portrays the northern Transvaal Province as still backward and inhabited by people trapped in beliefs belonging to the dark ages'.[10] In his view, remnants of witchcraft beliefs of the fifteen and sixteen centuries of Europe were still present in Africa. He believed that in Europe witchcraft had been exterminated by a rigorous process of education and civilisation. He therefore exhorted churches and educational institutions in the Northern Province to join the battle against witchcraft beliefs. At a political rally held at Bochum the year before, the MEC put it thus: 'We would like to use this opportunity to challenge the Church to make efforts to fulfill its historic mission, and embark on vigorous programmes aimed at educating our people and saving them from the belief in witchcraft which belongs to the dark ages'.[11] During other political rallies in the Province he challenged members of civil society to join him in this fight. As part of his campaign to wipe out witchcraft belief, the MEC eventually appointed a Commission of Enquiry to look into the causes of witchcraft beliefs (as well as ritual murders) in the Province. In 1996 the Commission submitted a lengthy report whose recommendations centered around the introduction of rigorous education and the revision of the Witchcraft Suppression Act of 1957.[12] None of the recommendations were implemented by the Provincial Government. In the general elections of 1999, Advocate Nthai stepped down as MEC of Safety and Security, returning to his practice as advocate of the High Court of South Africa.

The example shows how hard it is to introduce an educationist model to wipe out witchcraft beliefs. An educational solution requires concerted efforts by the government regarding a variety of programmes aimed at liberating people trapped in the belief.[13] Simply stated, the model suggests the organisation of workshops, political rallies, media programmes, and school curricula to address the situation.

People favouring such approach believe that the problem lies within African culture, which is closed to the outside world and civilisation. Here, education is viewed as a liberating tool that would change the African mentality to become receptive to civilised standards and belief systems of the West. Witchcraft beliefs, in their view, will disappear as soon as the African mind becomes saturated with Christian ideas and a Western way of life. They believe that the solution to the witchcraft problem is within the reach of agents of social change such as Christianity and the national government. The Western view of education is held up as a messianic model for African 'salvation'. The underlying assumption is that within African culture and religion there is nothing good that can be invoked to address the problem. Africans are perceived to be tied to a 'rock of ignorance'[14] from which they can only be released by education, which should deal with the realities of African socio-religious and economic life. According to some commentators, education should mainly deal with the improvement of agriculture and such conditions as would lead to the economic betterment of Africans.[15] Most of the literature on the efficacy of Western education for combatting witchcraft belief holds that an insight into the natural causes of diseases and other misfortunes will show Africans that their fear of witchcraft is unfounded.[16]

Modern technologies have also been recommended as a means of fighting 'outdated and backward beliefs'. Without going into details on how these should be employed in the process of education, the Ralushai Commission cited mass media—printed or electronic—workshops, symposia, and conferences as examples of mass education. Implicit in this point of view is the assumption that Western knowledge imparted to African children in school can systematically erode their 'superstitions', to the point where they will apply standard Western patterns of causality. This poses the question whether one should exclusively seek solutions for witchcraft accusations in Western logic and ignore African experience. The problem, however, is too complex to be addressed exclusively by Western education and civilisation.[17] Quick-fix solutions alleged to be provided by Western education are not sufficient to address the problem adequately. Most black South Africans, although many are well educated in Western culture and science, still believe in, and fear, witchcraft forces. They live and are socialised in a cultural milieu that provides them with a mind-set that structures their belief in supernatural forces that are accessed by evil people with the aim of harming others. These beliefs continue to control their lives despite the formal education they received.

There are numerous flaws in the suggested education model, although its intention is good. It is often falsely assumed that people who are sceptical about witchcraft are educated, while those who believe in it are not. Hence, the sceptical are seen as liberated and free, and the believers as primitive and backwards. Another false assumption inherent in the model is that, by its very nature, education is antithetical to witchcraft belief. Education is therefore often prescribed as a solution, without going into any finer details about how it should be planned and executed. The education model is normally given in concluding sections of books or articles written on the subject. Such books are frequently written in haste and thus often lack careful consideration of the solutions proposed. Details of how things should be done are normally not provided, not even in the footnotes. Sometimes these writers refer to education as a remedy for all problems faced by developing countries, without specifying how this is supposed to work.[18]

In the following sections some concrete steps are discussed on how to use the education approach. The list is potentially long, but I confine myself to a few examples.

The Departments of Education, Sport and Culture

An educational system that engenders healthy relationships with one's fellow human beings will go a long way towards addressing the social problems that arise from waning interpersonal relationships. Such an approach will serve as an important transformational factor. The majority of black people in South Africa have suffered from the disempowerment resulting from the apartheid system, which told them lies about themselves. This has brought the quality of relationships within the black communities under severe strain. One effect of this prolonged negative system has been a loss of self-esteem and the development of self-hatred. In order to change the negative image that was inculcated into people over the years, a well-planned educational system based on high-quality research is required.

In addition to the effects of the apartheid system, the worldview of black South Africans legitimises jealousy and reinforces hostility among individual people. For example, one oppressive dimension of this worldview is the belief that a successful farmer uses zombies to plough for him or her during the night. Zombies are people believed to be dead but having magically been transformed into slaves to serve witch-masters. The use of zombies is regarded as a form of witchcraft practiced by wealthy people.

It is mostly the youth that are instigated by the adults to carry out witchcraft violence. Since they are under eighteen years of age and therefore considered minors before the law, they are likely to receive sympathetic sentences from the courts. The youth are also ready to act before they consider the consequences of their action. They often operate in gangs, which makes it difficult to identify the individuals that are responsible for the actual killing of the alleged witch. They plan their actions against their victims at specific meeting places such as soccer fields, in the evenings after their sport, and at graveyards before and after burials. As soccer players playing for local teams, or village gravediggers, they often extend their role to include the guardianship of the community. If a perception arises that witches are tormenting innocent people in the community, they frequently take it upon themselves to identify them and bring them to book. In the process, the laws of the country are ignored and the rights of innocent people violated.[19]

Healing the divide between people occasioned by religious beliefs is critical to long-term change. This means that they need to recover what it is that makes them poor and miserable. Long-term educational programmes that are transformative in nature and compulsory to all learners should include the following competences and be introduced by the Department of Education to address the problem.

a) Knowledge of, and respect for, people's fundamental right to hold different views, values and beliefs

The right to differ from others and still remain their friend is one of the basic requirements for the peaceful coexistence of human beings. In a normal society people go beyond their personal boundaries to reach out to their neighbours in a spirit of acceptance. Individuals with opposing views or beliefs different from those held by mainstream society are respected, without being seen as adversaries. In South Africa, however, many years of apartheid and struggle against oppression have created an intolerant and even aggressive society. A gradual readjustment of perceptions and attitudes through sustainable training is therefore crucially important to replace aggression and rage with tolerance. To achieve true neighbourliness, one of the objectives set in a new educational plan should be creating a willingness to give oneself to others by realigning one's personal identity in such a way as to make space for them.

b) A comprehensive understanding of human relationships and coexistence

The first step in creating the right relationship with others is a healthy relationship with oneself. As suggested above, South Africans, both black and white, have suffered from the disempowerment that arose from the web of lies told about them, which still revolve in their minds. Black South Africans were told they were inferior, while the whites were inflated with lies of being superior. These daunting and conflicting voices inside themselves are the root of some of the conflicts that haunt the country today. Transformational education must, as a first step, start with the development of a new character that will make the learners accept and appreciate themselves for what they are. The second step in healing the relationships of people enmeshed in the web of self-hatred and aggression is to transcend historical racial, tribal and clan stereotypes, which cause tensions between people. The divide that separates them and puts some in the category of 'others' should be eliminated through a systematic and purposeful educational plan. Living in peace with those who constitute the 'other' implies their acceptance irrespective of who they are and what they have done. Healthy relationships can be built by developing values which enhance interpersonal relationships such as honesty, responsibility, and accountability. This should be embedded in educational programmes with a view to enabling people to relate better to one another, enjoying relations also with those seen as different.

c) Principle of totality in the learning process

The appropriate approach to learning is one that is characterised by the principles of totality, integrative mobility, and empowerment for coexistence. Such a comprehensive approach takes the development needs of learners, their home situation, as well as their school environment into consideration. The principle of totality opposes, protests against, and rejects the traditional approach to learning in which the learner's intellect, emotions and physical needs are separated from one another. Incorporating existential problems that face the learner at home, on the sports field, at school and in the veld with the herd of cattle, should decide the agenda for the type of education that may produce a society capable of handling conflicts. Totality in learning encompasses holistic educational programmes that include character formation, a better self-image, and improved family and community relationships. Similarly, education programmes should strive for more than intellectual learning. They should aim at creating a critical consciousness of societal structures and contribute to a holistic coexistence. They must stimulate social participation for total liberation from all oppressive conditions. Such education will clearly demonstrate the interrelatedness of home, school, and recreational life. Since the community should own the process of its development, people first need to be educated to realise their destiny, and subsequently how to get there.[20]

d) Developing life skills in the techniques of problem-solving or serving others

Learners should be exposed to a situation that can help them develop creative thinking and problem-solving methods. In the past, traditional education solved problems for learners instead of helping them to solve problems for themselves. The new approach in learning should assist and guide learners from an early stage to develop their own techniques to solve problems. This will enhance learners' ability to be less dependent on tribal myths and legends that normally provide them with stereotype solutions. By developing critical thinking, they will question those tribal stories that draw on supernatural explanations for physical occurrences. They will not automatically accept stories, for example, perpetuating the myth that witches use broomsticks to travel long distances, or that witches feed on human flesh and that this explains why they cannot change their behaviour.

e) Demonstrating the role and function of religion in promoting and discouraging conflicts in society

Religion by its very nature promotes values, beliefs and attitudes that may either be in conflict with those promoted by others, or may be in agreement with them. Where there are religious differences, often the equilibrium is reached through strife and violence. If these negative elements of religion are instilled in learners from tender ages, they are less likely to manage their religious differences when they occur later in their lives. On the other hand, most religions strive for peace, justice and eternal happiness. If these virtues are emphasised in education, learners may not be aware of the rivalry religions normally promote. Rather, they will be aware that religious virtues such as love, justice, fairness, reconciliation and righteousness can cement relations and promote peaceful coexistence.

f) Correcting and resolving social and economic disputes and conflicts

Nearly all disputes and conflicts leading to witchcraft accusations emanate from competition for scarce resources. Witchcraft accusations may become survival techniques, used by members of the community to address their plight. The 'haves' are indirectly reminded by the 'have-nots' to share their resources with them. On the other hand, the rich and powerful may use witchcraft accusations to absolve themselves from their responsibility towards the poor.[21] To address and correct the imbalances between the poor and the wealthy, education frameworks should be introduced that can gradually assist the learners to diagnose and analyse their problems and make them (learners) part of the solution from their early lives. Conflict-stricken communities will be able to minimise their disputes when they learn how to analyse a particular situation and to find their own solutions.[22]

Further, the Education Department should consider introducing compulsory education up to grade twelve which includes the areas mentioned above. Compulsory education is extremely expensive, but its benefits outweigh the effects of the high costs. Its introduction will go a long way to create a community that is at peace with itself. As argued above, authentic development can only take place effectively in a society that maintains peaceful relationships among its members. This can be achieved by an educational plan that is responsive to community needs as indicated by the people themselves.

Changing people's worldview is not easy. This also applies to the issue of witchcraft beliefs and accusations. It requires careful planning and a sustained effort by those responsible for designing policies. As part of a strategic intervention adult education could be introduced, that will aim at changing existing worldviews. This notably includes changing harmful beliefs, values and orientations, in such a way that that the community adopts a new way of life. Destructive elements within a culture should be removed and replaced with those that can empower and transform the community. Religious Education programmes on social conflict and management could be introduced at an early stage. If properly managed, these programmes could go a long way in their formative function and moulding of creative thought. They can lead people away from the scapegoating that takes place through witchcraft accusations.

Changing one's worldview begins with listening to, and learning from, the agent of change. The anti-life conflicts inherent in witchcraft accusations are not always visible, nor they can be anticipated. They strike when least expected. Listening and learning should therefore be based on good societal research. This means that educational programmes are needed that are informed by authentic research undertakings. Such education should be evaluated and its methods constantly reviewed. Its objectives and aims should be a direct response to real community needs. An African traditional approach involving the whole community under the leadership of the chief, blended with a Western one, modified for local conditions, could be introduced.[23] African children must discover their environment and experiences through such education. The learning process should address African children's aspirations and capture their imagination.

Compulsory education at school level, as well as adult education, should also involve economics. People must be taught how the economy of their country works, and what their role is in the creation of wealth for the country. They should all be taught how to participate (together with the rich) in the development of their country. They should be taught to reclaim, own and develop their own country. Such education will reorientate people and bring a sense of belonging to them. Human weaknesses like jealousy, selfish behaviour, aggression and laziness, and their consequences on the overall community development, should be addressed in the curriculum.

g) Retreating into fantasy as an educational strategy

One of the common ways for individuals to comes to terms with their problems is by retreating into fantasy.[24] They take flight into a world of imagination, where the facts are different and problems do not exist. When people are watching a football or rugby match, or in fact any game, they are taking a mental holiday that prevents preoccupation by evil. Films, television, radio, and other forms of entertainment help people to escape from the real world. They enter the world of fantasy for a while, and may find it hard to return again to the real world. Forms of entertainment such as sport, films and television programmes, transport people effectively, in their imagination, into situations remote from their normal ones, allowing them to redefine their character.

The Department of Education can take advantage of this scenario and insert structures that take care of the type of emotions that may generate conflicts. At present, sporting activities do not form part of an Education Ministry but are coordinated from the Departments of Sports and of Arts and Culture. If education and sports were under the coordination of one Ministry, this would be more effective. The provision of sport and entertainment to communities infected by witchcraft-related problems would go a long way to contain the problem. Through sport and other forms of entertainment pent-up emotions may be released. To yell support for a local football team playing against a foreign one cements social relations within the local community, since sport is a kind of ritualised combat that provides relief for aggressive instincts.[25] Sport helps to maintain the health of society by providing an outlet for harmful and dangerous emotions and tensions. South Africans love sport. They can forget all their differences and rally behind their players taking part in an international competitions. This has been shown with their national soccer, rugby and cricket players taking part in international competitions. If more of these competitions were arranged on a local front, especially in rural areas, it would help to keep the minds of people away from planning evil against each other.

The Department of Education could also introduce drama to the local community, for the same reason. A good drama invites people into the world of the imagination—away from idling and brewing evil. Through drama, people may be made to see their real problems clearly, especially as drama is designed to depict problems menacing them. By putting themselves in the shoes of the characters in the play, they learn something about their own lives. They feel with the characters; they feel sorry for them and understand why they act as they are doing. In understanding the characters, they understand themselves better. Drama can be utilised as a medium to change people's mind-set and readjust it in such a way as to channel human energies for social development.

Safety and security

Law enforcement agents should, in the first place, learn the basic principle that safety and security are not dependent on them. It is a negative and unproductive view for law-enforcing agents to think that the community has nothing to offer towards its own safety and security. They should strive to serve community needs on the basis of its own understanding of safety and security, including physical, mental, social, and religious stability, rather than on the basis of their own understanding.[26] Transformational development must enlist the cooperation of those it is intended to benefit. Too often law enforcement agents are seen as an impediment to development and security, because they have separated themselves from the rest of the community and adopted a top-to-bottom approach.

Much of this can be seen as the legacy of apartheid. Most members of the present police force were trained to serve the ideology of apartheid. The new ones, who joined the police force after the 1994 elections, are poorly trained, and some of them were promoted on political grounds through 'affirmative action'. Many competent members left the police force, and those who remained are often either despondent or corrupt. According to one informant who works at the Provincial Crime Analysis Centre in Limpopo Province, there is no longer effective policing and police morale is at its lowest ebb. Very few reported cases related to witchcraft accusations are successfully investigated. Some police members sympathise with those responsible for witch-pointing and related crime, because of their belief in the existence of witches. A careful reorientation of the police force is essential before proper policing can be restored.

Safety and security include such basic matters as life, food, water, health, and an environment that is conducive to conducting business. This means a sustainable agricultural environment where people have land to plough and graze their livestock, an adequate water supply and manageable health-care, so that they may utilise their local indigenous knowledge without any external threat. To be able to operate in this environment, law-enforcement agents should have full understanding of these basic needs. They must treat the people they serve with the dignity they deserve, and restore their psychological well-being where it has been interfered with. Community policing should develop from the bottom of the society to the top, and not the other way round. Change never percolates to the bottom, but when it starts from the bottom it is invariably felt at the top.[27] This is the approach to community policing that should be adopted and replace the old 'show-of-force' approach.

The role of the Church

I must sound a warning here about the role churches can play in the containment of violence occasioned by witchcraft belief. This includes all Christian communities, from mainstream orthodox traditions to African indigenous churches. A church can become a distraction or impediment to social transformation inasmuch as its members may separate themselves from the rest of society. They may understand themselves as being not of this world, but pilgrim people destined for another world. Sometimes the Church may regard development issues as not being part of its mandate, or it may unwittingly validate oppressive political and economic systems. Just social systems and political activism have not been squarely placed on the development agenda of the Church. In some circles public involvement is deemed 'too political'. While there is clear evidence that during the struggle against apartheid some church leaders did a stunning job in leading their congregation against the apartheid government, after the 1994 elections most of these leaders have been absorbed into the government structures. They are now defending the government arguing that the best way to help the government is to be in solidarity with it. Hence the Church has been robbed of its critical voice, and a once vocal Church has become a silent Church.

Church involvement in public affairs may also be deemed 'this world business'. The inclusion of a radical transformational agenda can easily be branded 'Marxist' or 'anti-Christ'. Looking at things from below, from the side of the downtrodden, and becoming creative sources of transformation does not always occupy the centre of the agenda of the Church. When it gets involved in the plight of the poor, the Church often tends to treat them somewhat romantically, playing the role of a messiah. It claims to know what the world needs.[28] Due to its missionary outreach, which is sometimes undertaken without introspection, there may be less or no room at all in the Church agenda the for the contribution of the poor.

At times the Church can, wittingly or unwittingly, become a stumbling-block to genuine holistic transformation. Churches operate from a particular stance of faith. It may therefore expect those whom it serves to embrace its faith before they are served as fellow human beings. Furthermore, the Church as a whole must be purged from any involvement in racism, especially in South Africa where it is just emerging from the bonds of legalised racism. The Church in South Africa is still painfully divided with white Christians closing their church buildings on Sundays to their black counterparts.[29] In a divided Church, very little can be achieved to assist those outside the churches who need guidance.

The Church can only lead through the service it is rendering to the community. If the Church were to initiate transformational development, it would be able to contribute meaningfully towards the containment of social violence. Its role in transformational development is that of a servant and a source of encouragement. As a servant of the Lord, the Church is able to make the hostile world of the victims of any form of social violence, including witchcraft accusations, more habitable. The role of the Church in building relationships can only be meaningful if its members radiate justice, peace and reconciliation, and if it is continually nourishing and sustaining the people it is serving.[30]

The Church can demonstrate the formation of positive values within the community. Through their radiant life of hope and faith, church members can be an inspiration to people trapped in witchcraft accusations. The Church can also serve as a sign of the values of the life to come and, therefore, bring peace into society. It must be a source of value formation within the community. It can act as a catalyst of justice, peace and hope. A

Christian presence in a community can enhance the process of changing a destructive worldview into one that shows care for human beings. The Church does not, and should not, exist for itself. It is not an inward-looking community but an outward-looking movement with a purpose in life.[31] It exists to give life to others, and through its witness it should spread the life of God's kingdom. The Church can inject love by challenging the delusional assumptions and lies created by witchcraft myths.

Non-governmental organisations

Communities have their own survival strategies. All communities have well-established patterns for making sense of the world and staying alive in it. It is only in crisis situations that they become dislocated and are unable to cope and survive. Understanding their existing survival strategies is critical to any attempt to help them in times of a disaster. It is important for those who assist the community from outside to view the world the way a particular community sees it. A community's survival strategies reveal its strengths, weaknesses, capabilities, resources, skills, and knowledge.[32] These qualities can serve as a foundation to build upon for further knowledge and assistance by non-governmental organisations. Others have argued that social sustainability must include establishing and developing local organisations with a social agenda. Furthermore, people need to develop a sense that, as part of a larger whole, they have rights which they should insist on. They have the right to expect that other people will respect their point of view. If this is ignored, any type of assistance creates a feeling of dependency and helplessness and will not work.[33]

A civil society is supposed to work for the social good. Non-governmental organisations refer to 'civil society' as a social system that includes a concern for building social fabrics on non-profit or voluntary services, such as development and self-help. It is only in places where civil society works effectively that the evil of witchcraft accusations can be curtailed.

Poverty and witchcraft accusations

Witchcraft accusations in South Africa are caused by many factors. They flourish where people experience mysterious natural phenomena or live through a social crisis. Enabling conditions include soured relationships, poverty, political uncertainty, psychological needs and social anxiety. The prolonged existence of these conditions leads to chronic frustration, which may give rise to violent behaviour. These factors are often driven by a dominant ideology and a desire to wield power over others. In an attempt to cope with the challenges of life, people often fall into the trap of bias and start blaming others for their own failures. To clear themselves from guilt they look for scapegoats. The dominant factor, however, that favours the escalation of witchcraft accusations is poverty. In addressing the problem of witchcraft violence, the government must also address the question of poverty.

Poverty is painful and frustrating. People who live in abject poverty feel helpless, disempowered and humiliated, having few options in life to improve their conditions. The world of the 'haves' slams the doors in front of them, so that their voices are not heard. The bottom line of poverty is hunger, which leads to a lack of energy and power of judgement. Having no say in matters affecting them directly, poor people fall victim to the circumstances and tend to rely on mystical forces for their protection and prediction of the future. Victims of poverty do not have the resources to access the judiciary system to protect their rights. Poverty engenders conditions of squalor and poor health, incurable diseases, disintegration of community norms, and religious fanaticism. The effects of these social conditions include a mistrust of people whose lives depend on the trust of others. The upshot of this situation is the disappearance of social cohesion as a survival link between members of communal societies.[34] Unemployment and lack of economic activity lead to idleness and rumour-making, especially among African people. Rumours can easily give rise to slanderous talk or talking falsely about one's neighbour. All these conditions favour witchcraft accusations.

In the containment of witchcraft accusations and their resultant conflicts the government and civil society must address the question of poverty. In South Africa, wealth is concentrated in the hands of few people. A distribution of wealth without allowing the poor to engage in the process of their upliftment will not bring about the desired development. Programmes that can help empower the poor, strengthen community-based development institutions and sustain the well-being of all are the way to go about it. Government institutions, the business sector and civil society must work closely together to address the problem of poverty, which will in turn lessen the escalation of witchcraft accusations.

CONCLUSION

In this article an attempt has been made to suggest some measures that can help contain the escalation of violence in South Africa that is occasioned by witchcraft beliefs and other precipitating factors, including poverty, failed interpersonal relationships and human weaknesses such as aggression, intolerance, gossip and an evil desire to hurt others. We have suggested an educational model that can lessen the negative effects of witchcraft accusations. Although these suggestions are based on the long term, a willingness to adopt and implement them is a step in the right direction to address the problem.

Education alone cannot reduce the negative impact of witchcraft beliefs. Other governmental departments should also take their share in uplifting the community. The legislature, the department of justice, and all law enforcement agents have a crucial role to play in creating stable conditions in the country. The laws that are formulated and passed to contain witchcraft violence should be based on rationality, and must aim at protecting all the citizens of the country without discrimination. The bill of human rights enshrined in the country's constitution should be upheld, irrespective of the persons involved. Gossip, hearsay and discourse premised on a personal vendetta should never form the principles on which the laws of the country are based. Community policing in South Africa should be overhauled and transformed to ensure the safety and security of all South African citizens. Fair standards in staff appraisal and reward for good work, rather than political preferences, should be upheld. The police force should serve the community and not a particular ideology, while the community should regard the police force as its ally rather than its adversary. The training of the police force to in order to serve the new order in South Africa should be treated as a matter of urgency.

In this article we have alluded to the fact that colonial Witchcraft Suppression Acts have not been able to curtail the destructive elements of witchcraft belief, primarily because these laws have not received public consent. Yet it would be irresponsible to lobby for their repeal purely on the grounds that they do not enjoy the support of the majority of the people. Some people may not voice their opinion for fear of being blamed as a witch: if they show their approval of the Witchcraft Suppression Act, this will be construed by others as an admission of being a witch. To reserve opinion in such a case is part of one's survival technique. Imperfect as they may appear, Witchcraft Suppression Acts protect many innocent lives as witch-hunters cannot freely accuse people of practising witchcraft without facing the wrath of the law.

Churches and non-governmental organisations have an explicit role to play in the transformation of South African society. Each of these organisations has a specific expert role to play in terms of its identity and vocation. The values they represent in their services should be lived to the full, so that people may emulate them. NGO's can be an embodiment of development action, where political empowerment and nurturing of social organisation take place. The Church can represent a true sign of passion for development, moving away from self-destructive tendencies like hatred and jealousy. The Church is only Church when 'it is inside out',[35] when it lives for the upliftment of the people it serves. The Church is the only society that is supposed to exist for the sake of those who are outside its borders—hence the Dietrich Bonhoeffer's coinage of it as 'the Church for others'.[36] The role of the Church in South Africa has been misunderstood, especially during the rule of apartheid, as servant of the State. The Church, as it responds to its faith in God, can offer a better faith than that of witchcraft. Relationships based on Christian love and morality will help people to cope with the strains of modern life, and can thus go a long way towards addressing witchcraft-related problems.

Education, we have argued, is certainly needed in the containment of witchcraft accusations. Educating people on how witchcraft accusations develop, as well as developing an understanding of the soil in which they flourish, are the first necessary steps to guide the process of remedying the problem, even though education alone cannot wipe out witchcraft accusations.

A transformational developmental approach that is informed by the principle of holistic character formation and the restoration of family relationships on a sustained basis, undersigned and coordinated by all governmental departments and non-governmental organisations, will effectively address the witchcraft conflict. This process may include the following six elements suggested by Myers:[37]

- walking with the victims of poverty
- a change in worldview concerning life, death, poverty, and justice
- development of a worldview based on hope in the future for everyone
- a vocation of service, encompassing community, leadership and solidarity
- a new ethical dimension to life, both private and public
- a holistic development that includes character formation, a better self-image, and improved community relationships.

Finally, true and lasting transformation occurs only when people discover each other and live in good relationships. In order for that to occur, a just distribution of life-sustaining resources must be achieved. Members of a particular society, therefore, should work for a common purpose in the spirit of shared vision and values.

Notes

1. This paper is based on research findings of a project funded by the South Africa-Netherlands Research Programme on Alternatives in Development (SANPAD). The author has benefitted from the research grant made available by SANPAD. The views expressed in this paper are not those of SANPAD but of the author.

2. The name of the province was recently changed from Northern Province to Limpopo Province on business grounds. There are many provinces in other countries called 'Northern Province',

which causes confusion among the tourist community. The name Limpopo, which is the name of the river demarcating the northern border between Botswana and Zimbabwe, is unique for tourism.

3. For the statistics of the people killed and displaced from their homes, see yearly police records made available by the Crime Analysis Centre in Pietersburg (now Polokwane).

4. S.S. Terblanche provides some examples in his book review of *To live in Fear* by Anthony Minnaar in the *South African Journal of Criminal Justice* (vol. 6, 1993, pp. 104-6). See also the Johannesburg daily newspaper *The Star* of 7 March 1995 for some details on the economic and social disruption of witchcraft accusations in the Northern Province of South Africa.

5. Anthony Giddens elaborates on the importance of healthy relationships in communities. If relationships collapse, social disintegration sets in, paving the way for a range of tensions and suspicions (*Sociology*, Cambridge: Polity Press, 1997).

6. E. Barendse and G. Dederen, 'Witchcraft in the workplace', *Productivity SA*, vol. 19, 1993, pp. 22-41.

7. *The Citizen* of 28 February 1995 gives a clear picture of what happens when a thunderstorm comes over the rural areas of the Northern Province of South Africa. K.R. Baholo provides some pictorial details on the subject ('A pictorial response to certain witchcraft beliefs within Northern Sotho communities', University of Cape Town, 1994).

8. A number of works are listed in the general bibliography in this volume, including Baroja (1961), Davies (1980), Evans-Pritchard (1937), Fadiman (1993), Gibson (1973), Maple (1973), Marwick (1970), Maxwell (1995), Mayer (1954), Niehaus (1997), Parrinder (1963), Rosen (1969) and Rush (1974).

9. Diane Ciekawy and Peter Geschiere, in analysing various scenarios in post-colonial Africa, have come up with some suggestions on how the negative impact of witchcraft beliefs can be minimised ('Containing witchcraft: conflicting scenarios in post-colonial Africa', *African Studies Review*, vol. 41, no. 3, 1998, pp. 1-14). With regard to Cameroon, Fisiy and Geschiere have provided some recommendations on how to curb the carnage ('Sorcery, witchcraft and accumulation: regional variations in South and West Cameroon', *Critique of Anthropology*, vol. 11, nr. 3, 1991, pp. 251-78). See also W.H. Wessel, 'Folk healers in South Africa: tradition cannot be ignored', *SALUS*, vol. 15, 1993, pp. 14-5.

10. *The Sowetan*, 10 March 1995.

11. *The Sowetan* of 10 March 1994 carried a report on the MEC remarks.

12. This is the report of the Ralushai Commission of Enquiry, entitled 'Report of the Commission of Inquiry into Witchcraft Violence and Ritual Murders in the Northern Province of the Republic of South Africa', published in 1996.

13. Ibid., p. 60.

14. Cf. Prof Van Rooyen, an emeritus professor of Old Testament at the University of Potchefstroom. Before he joined the university he worked for many years as a missionary among the Venda people of the Northern Province. He wrote some controversial articles, in which he alleged that poverty in Africa can be blamed on superstition and ignorance among Africans. In two articles in *Missionalia* (vol. 25, December 1997, pp. 633-46 and vol.27 of April 1999, pp. 131-7), the present author responded to Van Rooyen's views on African people and their religion.

15. Cf. Louw, 'Witchcraft among the Southern Bantu: facts, problems, policies', Ph.D. thesis submitted to Yale University, 1941, p. 252.

16. Ibid., p. 250.

17. Cf. E. Barendse and L. Best, 'A nightmare in Nelspruit: witchcraft in the workplace', *Indicator South Africa*, vol. 9, nr. 2, 1992, pp. 85-8.

18. Cf. Louw, 'Witchcraft among the Southern Bantu', p. 210.

19. Cf. Ineke van Kessel 1993, '"From confusion to Lusaka": the youth revolt in Sekhukhuneland', *Journal of Southern African Studies*, vol. 19, no 4, 1993, pp. 593-614; Ineke van Kessel en Barbara Oomen, '"One chief, one vote": the revival of traditional authorities in post-apartheid South Africa', *African Affairs*, vol. 96, nr. 385, 1997, pp. 561-85; and Jonathan Stadler, 'Witches and witch-hunters: witchcraft, generational relations and the life cycle in a lowveld village, *African Studies*, vol. 55, nr. 1, 1996, pp. 87-110.

20. M. Handa, 'The political economy of adult education', paper read at UNISA for the International Council for Adult Education, 1984.

21. Labelling the neighbour as responsible for one's demise is part of scapegoat behaviour. René Girard explores this phenomenon fully in his book *The Scapegoat* (Baltimore: John Hopkins University Press, 1982).

22. M.B. Anderson, in her *Development and Social Diversity* (1999), discusses humanitarian and development aid to people embroiled in conflict. She suggests a particular model to address the problem.

23. No process of human and social change can be entirely defined locally. Every community is part of a family of social systems that operate on regional, national and global levels. Cf. A. Fowler, *Striking a Balance: A guide to enhancing the effectiveness of non-governmental organisations in international development.* London: Earthscan Publications, 1997.

24. In his *Living with Guilt*, H. McKeating (London: SCM Press, 1970) discusses how fantasy as a recreational strategy works.

25. McKeating, *Living with Guilt*, p.81

26. B.L. Myers, *Walking with the Poor: Principles and practices of transformational development,* Maryknoll: Orbis Books, 1999, p. 126.

27. Handa, 'The political economy of adult education', pp. 16-7.

28. See Myers, *Walking with the Poor,* p. 126.

29. This was my personal experience when in 1999 we were refused permission to use a white members' church building in Pietersburg as black members of the Dutch Reformed Church.

30. Myers, *Walking with the Poor,* p. 127.

31. David Bosch put it aptly in his book *Transforming Mission: Paradigm shifts in theology of mission* (Maryknoll: Orbis Books, 1991), when he stated that 'the church is the church when it is the church for others'.

32. Cf. R. Chambers, *Rural Development: Putting the last first,* London: Longman Group, 1983, p. 46.

33. Cf. Myers, *Walking with the Poor,* p. 131.

34. See D. Narayan et al., *Can Anyone Hear Us? Voices of the poor,* Oxford University Press, 2000, p. 20.

35. Bosch, *Transforming Mission*, pp. 374-6.

36. Dietrich Bonhoeffer, *Letters and Papers from Prison,* London: SCM Press, 1971, pp. 382 ff.

37. Myers, *Walking with the Poor,* p. 219.

13

THE ESCALATION OF WITCHCRAFT ACCUSATIONS

Walter E.A. van Beek

INTRODUCTION: WITCHCRAFT AS A PROBLEM

Cultural anthropology has a long history of interest in witch-craft, especially in Africa. Both the classical studies of African witchcraft[1] and the recent resurgence of witchcraft studies[2] are situated at the core of the discipline. Throughout, anthropological studies have concentrated on the logic of witchcraft beliefs and discourses, on the reasons and processes, beliefs and accusations, and on the ways in which witchcraft has a place in both rural and urbanising African societies.[3] It is the sociologica of the witchcraft discourse that has been well revealed in this approach. As usual in anthropology, notions of judgement are pushed back as far as possible and the relativism that is dominant in anthropological thinking holds for the treatment of witchcraft discourses as well. Yet, there might be reasons to question the strict adherence to cultural relativism in this field, as both the witchcraft discourse of the people in question and the consequences of the accusations, trials and confessions often lie far beyond the borderline of quaint and curious customs. In other fields, such as head-hunting and cannibalism in colonial Melanesia and more recently the issue of female circumcision, anthropologists have clung less to relativism. Maybe in witchcraft studies the difference is one of belief: most anthropologists do not themselves believe in the existence of witches. The methodological atheism—or perhaps better: 'agnosticism'[4]—the profession uses in addressing witchcraft discourse separates the researcher from much of the actuality and brutality of the belief. Methodological agnosticism focuses our attention on social processes and internal logic, and thus leads to a sociological understanding of the strange beliefs and practices. On the other hand it does distract from the reality of belief and especially from the reality of suffering.[5]

And suffering is indeed included in the witchcraft discourse. Throughout the world, in Africa and elsewhere, witchcraft notions, accusations and persecutions have wreaked havoc on social relations and caused suffering to untold numbers of people. It has robbed them of their dignity, separated them from their kin and disowned them of rightful possessions. Harassment, torture, banishment and death have been disguised as 'cleansing', the individual accused standing no chance against the brutal force of the accusers. Witchcraft accusations have stripped away rights to defence, rights to a fair trial, rights to simple decency.[6]

Witchcraft, for all people within witchcraft discourse, is evil. Anthropology has long shied away from this notion, laden as it is with emotions. Parkin[7] opened up this Pandora's box but relatively few people have followed his lead.[8] Most anthropologists are ill at ease with the concept: it suggests a judgement that is not debatable, an absolute, which escapes relativism—a category that transcends cultural borders. As researchers bent on discovering variation, anthropologists start looking at exceptions to any absolute, to any universal. Evidently, in many African vernaculars, the notion of evil as such is difficult to translate[9] and, just as evidently, the notion is broken up into various evil agents, processes and acts. But in my view this does not invalidate the project Parkin started, on the contrary. Notions resembling evil can be easily found, and are recognised with great alacrity by people all over Africa. Symbols of evil, personifications of evil and names of evil agents circulate widely, ignoring cultural borders. In christianising Africa, the fame of Jesus has almost been eclipsed by the attention bestowed upon Satan.

One central notion of evil in the African context is, evidently, witchcraft. Not the only one, but definitely the dominant one. Witchcraft even bears the sign of the double evil. For those inside the belief system, witches are the epitome of evil, the embodiment of what is wrong with the whole world.[10] Witches, if people think they know them in person, are not to be tolerated but have to be cured, purged, evicted or killed, whatever measure is culturally acceptable. For those beyond the community of believers, accusations of witchcraft appear to lead only to turmoil, suffering, and death, and both the discourse on witchcraft and the techniques for detection-*cum*-persecution represent an extremely dark side of society. The argument that these accusations may serve as a social strain gauge, as put forward by, among others, Marwick for the Cewa,[11] may hold for some close-knit local communities. However, even then, the toll in suffering is such as to make this argument academic. Also, the positive function of witchcraft voicings depends quite heavily on the idea that society has few alternatives for its redressive mechanisms. And both comparative studies and the rapid changes African kin-based societies have experienced and coped with since the 1960s have belied that argument.[12] Societies without witchcraft accusations, or at least without witchcraft persecutions, are easy to find (as we shall see later), and both the witchcraft discourse and the way it operates in a given society have proved dynamic and open to change. New witchcraft notions arise[13] and witchcraft voicings find new arenas.

Witchcraft is a problem. For the believer, the eradication of witches may be a major concern, for the administrator (who often shares the belief in witchcraft notions) accusations and persecutions are a serious problem, and for the outside observer and the international community, accusations and persecutions express the ills of society through a major infringement of human rights. In this article I want to explore one particular aspect, namely the consequences of witchcraft accusations. Notions of witchcraft are widespread and can be found in various forms in different societies and cultures. But what people actually do with the accusations, what the follow-up is on the voicing of the suspicion of witchcraft is another matter. If suspicion can lead to accusation, and accusation to condemnation, conviction and execution, then where does this chain of violence end? For, even if a lot of pain is inflicted in the name of witchcraft eradication, not every suspected witch is killed. In fact, the ways of dealing with alleged witches vary more than the content of local witch beliefs. Witchcraft notions are repetitive and definitely translocal but the methods of dealing with alleged witches range from ignoring the matter, to humiliating an accused witch, to eventually killing alleged perpetrators.

So, our main question is: given the internal logic of witch beliefs, what processes stop people from pursuing witchcraft accusations to the very end, and finally from killing purported witches?[14] To discover the logic of these processes, I use a comparative approach, contrasting a few of Africa's many cases of witchcraft manipulation, to see where the slide towards escalation of violence halts in each of them. The choice of examples is deliberate, and follows a notion that developed during a workshop on combatting the increase in witchcraft accusations in South Africa's Northern Province (now Limpopo Province).[15] Following that, the thesis of this article is that several social prerequisites and belief elements are needed for witchcraft accusations to escalate from suspicion to execution. None of these prerequisites is self-evident in a given culture, even though they seem to be inescapable in every culture where they are present. These prerequisites hinge on the character of witchcraft notions, on the definition of personhood and social relations in the community, on divination techniques and the authority of the diviner and his techniques, on the social mechanism of consensus formation, and—of course—on the position and actions of national governments. But first we have to gain a perspective on not only the ubiquity of witchcraft discourses but also their relative homogeneity, which has to be rooted in their existential basis, in other words, in the experience of everyday life.

WITCHCRAFT: EXPERIENCE AND DISCOURSE

You can never get rid of all dirt in a house in a dense bush!
You can never get rid of all the witches in a big house!

Ovambo proverb

Witchcraft, in our treatment, is an experiential discourse with serious consequences. First, the experiential side. 'The Azande', according to Evans-Pritchard in his classic study of witchcraft, 'experience feelings about witchcraft, rather than ideas'.[16] At first glance this may sound strange from someone who has, more than anyone before him, shown the internal logic of witchcraft beliefs and actions. After all, his massive Azande monograph is replete with the logical correlates of witchcraft notions: the balance between accusations and redress, as well as the careful limitations between witchcraft beliefs and the realms of personal responsibility and expertise. The Zande distinguish clearly between the mistakes, stupidity and guilt of people on the one hand, and the influence of witchcraft on the other. At the heart of their reasoning is the difference between reasonable expectation and coincidence. If a potter has done his job well, mixed his clay properly, moulded the pot as he has done so often before, dried it thoroughly as he always does, in short applied his considerable and well-tested skill, if he on top of this has adhered to the principal taboo in firing and abstained from sexual inter-course the night before the firing ... if, after all this, the pot cracks in the fire, it must be witchcraft.[17] Of course ill-made pots crack, and just as evidently potters of loose morals see their wares spoil, but if everything has been done properly, things should go well. If not, it must be the work of a witch. Someone whose leg got burnt explained this by witchcraft. Of course, flames are hot but everyone sleeps near fires. 'It is a natural quality of fire to burn, but it is not a universal quality of fire to burn you'.[18] Even suicide can be explained as witchcraft: someone hanged himself when angry with his brothers. But 'if every one who was angry with his brothers committed suicide there would soon be no people left in the world'.[19] He must have been driven crazy to kill himself and someone did just that, drove him crazy with witchcraft.

Witchcraft answers the 'why' of the mishap, not the 'how'. Why does an unfortunate event interrupt the smooth flow of normal life? No different causality is needed but an additional explanation for what in other cultural areas is called chance or hazard. Since the time of the French philosopher Bergson, however, we have understood that the difference between the two is not that great. Bergson, in his analysis of the notion of hazard stressed the need for intentionality in humans.[20] The explanation of chance, hazard or coincidence is in fact not an explanation at all but a refusal to look for an explanation. It is a culturally learned 'halt' on the road towards an experiential explanation, for those events that address our immediate feelings. When we contract an illness it is bad luck, but when our child is hit in a car accident the notion of chance is no longer sufficient. Then we ask 'why?' and try to construct explanations; then the outer world is personified, chance becomes intention, and coincidence has a meaning for us. Trying to glean that meaning, we either turn to a supernatural world (the work of God) or to a human one. Similarly, when we win the lottery, it is luck (a similar notion), but if we really needed the money and were in dire straits, it is a 'blessing'. Most cultures offer these escapes from the limitations of the abstract notion of chance. Many of the written religions teach resignation in this area: 'the will of Allah', or 'The Lord has given, the Lord has taken, praised be the name of the Lord', as Job said after his first mishap. But in many cultures, including for example Islam and Christianity, a more personalised answer is given. Then witchcraft notions are used to answer these questions of 'why' and direct attention towards the human sphere. This is what is meant by witchcraft as a 'feeling': one is sensing the inadequacy of normal causality, sensing the intention the event has for oneself, feeling the existential meaning of the happening, and using culturally furnished symbols and notions to express these feelings.

Witchcraft notions and beliefs, even if they form a logical system in themselves, are part of a larger causal discourse that is existentially valid. Witchcraft notions hinge on 'experience in life': as researchers have found, one starts to think about witchcraft when experiencing it.[21] Of course, experience is socially constructed, and notions and concepts about witches are needed to experience it in this particular fashion. In case of bad luck, human causes add to the well-known physical causes, and the construction is called witchcraft. The main source of that construction is the social discourse. 'People say ...' and 'people talk about ...' are common clauses, often 'people whisper ...'. As it is experienced in actual and emotional situations, so is it talked about, the subject of intense and sometimes heated discourse. Sometimes muted, always between closely related people, often first in whispers, sometimes shouted out loud in the dark of the night as a suspicion, the experience of the witchcraft encounter finds a vocal expression, and a culturally accepted one at that.

So witchcraft is a way of talking about life, about mishaps, about illness and death, about differences between people, between rich and poor, between powerful and powerless. It is a discourse that complains about the state of the world and tries to find a culprit, a culprit of wrongs that are sometimes general: poverty, powerlessness, illness and death, rapid change or any type of insecurity. In doing so, the discourse brings world problems down to the local level, interprets the cosmos as ills inside the family and reduces the nation to kin relations. A witchcraft discourse is the 'inverted spy-glass': anything larger than human becomes humanised and anything larger than the local community becomes the neighbourhood. Thunder and lightning become the intent of someone next door, and the power of the national elite is reduced to witchcraft in the belly. Everything larger than life is reduced to human properties. This inverted spy-glass character is what makes the discourse as flexible as it is: it is by no means restricted to traditional settings or to classical kinship conflicts. The discourse easily enters the political sphere and finds its way between the dealings of elites and urbanites.[22] The mechanism of this reduction, the lens of the spy-glass, is human frailty, weaknesses that 'flesh is heir to': lack of information, the feeling of being excluded; in short the existential experience of not truly belonging to this world is translated into the not-so-laudable emotions of envy and greed.[23]

Any discourse feeds on three elements: the actual happening, the notions the culture has in its symbolic capital, and the society's ways of reaching consensus. The topic of this article is the interaction between these three, within the witchcraft discourse. Crucial in the witchcraft discourse is the fact that it is reactive, not proactive: the discourse zooms in on past happenings but only *post facto*, explaining the recent past by pointing at a more distant past. This reactive character of the discourse however is processual in kind: the discourse leads towards an explanation and in doing so to a reaction to the perceived actions. Witchcraft notions are positioned as a cause and may indicate a road towards redress. When the cause is known, one can do something about it. This is a logical corollary of the discourse but what action, by what means and to what ends, is part of the discourse and part of the particular culture. Thus, it differs between cultures.

Hence, the witchcraft discourse, with its notions and its ways of detection, is part of a social process, and has its own logic, social and mental. Thus, the actions taken on the basis of this discourse are social processes as well and can be expected to have their own logic. What are the modalities of witchcraft accusations and persecutions? What are the cultural and social prerequisites for accusations, what are the limits cultures impose on accusations and redress? To find out, we first have to delve into the characteristics of the discourse of witchcraft. This, of course, represents a generalised picture, but one that will receive some nuance later.

SPECIFIC CHARACTERISTICS OF WITCHCRAFT ACCUSATIONS[24]

Whoever wants to be believed, just has to whisper

Witchcraft is something people talk about: it is a common topic of conversation, of gossip, and a yardstick applied to their fellow men. As such, it constitutes a discourse, a coherent way of speaking about and looking at the world at large. Even if it is a covert domain of 'which one may not speak but can merely insinuate,'[25] it is a topic of intense communication. This discourse is flexible: it easily adapts to new surroundings, situations and changes in society. There is no problem so new that it cannot be interpreted in witchcraft terms. It can be used to contain the ambitious upstart or to condemn the non-conformist types in society, it may blame the weak in society or form a handy tool to eliminate competitors and rivals, or be a way to keep claims of poorer kinsmen at bay.

Witchcraft discourse is muted, frequently in the form of gossip and often hidden, taking place in whispered conversations. It only becomes vocal and public when a consensus has been reached. The discourse may become public, as has been the case in South Africa. A groundswell of gossip can lead to a public voicing of the accusations and a communal outcry; accusation and condemnation then easily blend. It is a debate-less discourse, where dissent provokes condemnation: whoever denies witchcraft must surely be a witch.

So the discourse is also self-perpetuating, where a minor indication leads to a chain of accusations. Stopping a witchcraft discourse seems to be extremely difficult and may first require major changes in society. One reason is that the discourse cannot be disproved. First, anyone opposing it or defending himself is prone to accusations. Second, any evidence to the contrary can be construed as the result of other more powerful witchcraft. The discourse allows no counter-evidence. Also, the witchcraft discourse claims to provide explanations in those realms of life where no clear-cut explanations of a more objective kind are available.

The social embeddedness of the witchcraft discourse has long been recognised in anthropological studies,[26] and even if the social environment of witchcraft dealings has expanded from the village and the tradition to the urban and the modern,[27] the basic approach is that witchcraft accusations are a social phenomenon. Even stronger, when unravelling concrete cases of witchcraft accusations, it becomes clear that the social explanation of these accusations is relatively transparent. The reasons why accusations flare up, and especially why specific people are accused, are easy to find. Accusations are motivated by envy, jealousy, greed, hatred, rivalry, vengeance, misunderstanding or a lack of information, feelings and factors that are usually easily recognised by the people themselves, or at least by bystanders, neighbours and kinsmen. Sometimes this transparency is reason enough to deny the validity of the witchcraft accusations: the community does not always agree with the voicing of the harmed individual. Details about relationships that went wrong and led to witchcraft accusations may be too obvious to allow the neighbourhood to take the allegations seriously.

The character of the witchcraft discourse, especially its hidden aspect, makes it hard for institutions to control. Also, these institutions are part and parcel of the same social problems that fuel the discourse itself. Administrators, the police, the judicial apparatus and also local elders and healers are thus hard put to contain incidences and especially the flaring-up of accusations. Native healers, who are part and parcel of the witchcraft discourse, cannot control accusations. The healers are themselves also frequently seen as being connected to the problem, either as people who are exempt from it or as people who are involved in it. But either way, they have a stake in the matter and cannot halt the accusations. Diviners are definitely part of the syndrome, and form a strategic element in witchcraft accusations. They depend on the discourse for their status and income, and cannot be expected to curb it. Geschiere talks of the circularity of witchcraft accusations: proof or disproof can only be given by people with vested interests, who in many cases (also among the Maka of Cameroon) have to be witches themselves.[28] The police, legal institutions and the political establishment partly share the discourse and partly deny it, an ambivalence that renders effective measures difficult. The muted character of the discourse keeps it easily beyond institutional control. At a more formal level, a witchcraft discourse cannot be countered directly. Anti-witchcraft measures, even social and religious anti-witchcraft movements, habitually run out of steam, in the end reinforcing witchcraft beliefs more than reducing them. As a Sotho academic remarked: 'We have caught all the students [in witchcraft], but the professors are still there'.

Witchcraft notions may be called the 'terror of closeness'. Witchcraft accusations mostly occur in the context of relational problems and people are usually only accused within close relationships, sometimes even within the family. In a society where close relationships should provide shelter against an oppressive outer world, witchcraft accusations form the reverse of this model of close relations. The alleged witch is the enemy within the gates, a situation sometimes shared with spirits in the invisible world. Witchcraft accusations create deep ruptures in the close relations of kin and community. They sometimes follow fission lines that already exist in social relations. But, as shown in the cases that have been the object of research by South African students, they tend to redirect themselves and create new oppositions in society. The need to explain misfortune does not stop at the traditional divisions in a given society but is used between new social categories as well. Thus, in the blaze of accusations, any close relationship seems prone to witchcraft accusations. Anyone may find him or herself being accused of witchcraft. In these situations the terror of closeness means that no close relationship is exempt, and every relationship is suspect. One consequence is the relative timelessness of accusations. Problems may lie dormant for a period of time with accusations re-emerging after a small incident or a minor misfortune. As tensions in social relations often lie at the heart of an accusation, witchcraft violence can simmer. It is almost never forgotten, and if seemingly so, can be revived in an instant.

FROM SUSPICION TO KILLING

What is needed for a witchcraft accusation to proceed from belief to killing? Six variables seem to form a logical chain, leading from one stage to the next on a scale of increasing witchcraft violence.[29] A comparison of African cultures in their different witchcraft discourses yields a series of logical and sociological prerequisites for a suspicion of witchcraft to turn into violence. In their logical sequence they form a ladder of escalation, each step leading towards increased danger for the accused.[30] The examples are taken from various cultures, showing the differences within Africa of witchcraft discourse and treatments of those accused. However, it must be borne in mind that in each of the societies mentioned, many suspicions never materialise into outright accusations, and many accusations never lead to convictions, let alone violence. So the options are always present to stop witchcraft violence before it reaches the ultimate form possible in that particular culture.

1) *Notions of evil*

Cultures differ in the way they attribute evil to human beings or to extra-human agents. In some traditions evil is part and parcel of the invisible world, influencing but not changing human beings (for example, evil spirits). In other traditions evil simply means a lack of success, dependent on an external factor. And in yet other traditions, evil is part of human beings, innate through inheritance, or achieved through character faults. Witchcraft beliefs result from a 'humanisation' of evil that is neither a common nor a self-evident theory. For instance, neither Islam nor Christianity recognises such a human power, at least not in their contemporary forms. But also quite a few traditional religions deny the validity of such a form of 'human evil'. For instance, the BaMbuti Pygmies in their Ituri forest harbour no notions of personal malevolent mystical power, or any belief reminiscent of witchcraft. Though they do know that their Bantu neighbours labour under such notions, the BaMbuti find these ideas quite ridiculous.[31]

2) Definition of internal relations

Witchcraft accusations result from stress, often within important relationships at the local level: kinship relations, neighbourhood relations, relations between old and young etc. The way in which these relations are defined, and how vulnerable they prove, are issues that shape witchcraft accusations. In effect, witchcraft accusations erupt when the need for explanation of personal mishap is larger than the linking relationship with the suspected witch. In a society with a strong orientation towards internal harmony, the common calm is valued over the release of individual frustration. Also, as has long been known in anthropology, some societal types generate more witchcraft accusations than others. Matrilineal systems have always been reported to be more accusation-prone than patrilineal ones. Though this difference is often explained by reference to the 'matrilineal puzzle', the structural clash between male-centered authority and female-centered inheritance, this association has been questioned too. Still, the difference between forest Africa (non-Pygmy, that is) and savannah societies with respect to witchcraft seems to be marked.[32]

3) Notions of agency

Cultural notions of personhood, especially of human agency, are an important factor. The position of the individual versus the group, the amount of leeway an individual has and the amount of peer control also shape witchcraft accusations. Witchcraft is, at its core, a theory of the person, of the many layers a person consists of. Beliefs are often incorporated, that is, witchcraft is associated with certain parts of the body: the stomach, neck, liver or whatever. But that corporality is always tied in with a section of the person on the spiritual plane: the shadow, the double, one of many spirits making up the person. These, in turn, relate to the other aspects of a personality, as experienced in that culture: other souls, volition, responsibility, accountability, distinctions between warm and cold people (or hot and cool), between genders, and between aspects of personhood and the supernatural world. They are also related to notions of pre-existence and post-existence that tie in with emic theories of conception and the intricate relation between bodies and souls. Here, agency is mentioned as a cover term for the relations between the constituent parts of a person, body, soul and personal characteristics, plus the consequences of those ideas for the personal accountability of mishaps.

Of importance is the specific character of the witchcraft substance. The idea of what exactly constitutes a witch varies, and an important aspect of the agency of the purported witch is curability. Can the witch be purified and cured? In many cultures witches may confess, purge themselves and be cured of their witchcraft. This offers an important escape from the escalation towards violence, and thus is a vital part of the group's ideology. A related matter is the notion of secrecy prevalent in the society. How well known are individuals? What notions of privacy and secrecy abound? What is the leeway for the individual to differ from the standard definitions of personhood?

4) Divination practices

Some societies purport to have the means to detect 'witches' and to be able to select between the guilty and the innocent. In such cases, the role of diviners is crucial—both as persons who are believed to embody power, and as people who depend on witchcraft violence for status and income. Other societies do not add names to accusations, as 'nobody saw the witch eat the heart of the victim'. Still others may whisper names but are not allowed to make the accusation public. This seems to be a distinguishing variable. The differences are huge. On the one hand the said BaMbuti brooked no nonsense when their Bantu-speaking hosts tried to discover who was responsible for the death of one of the Pygmies: they simply took off into the forest, having more important things to do than to try to establish a spurious guilt.[33] At the other extreme, many reports on the southern Bantu insist that all deaths lead to questions of why and who.[34] Also the Zande, Evans-Pritchard reported, invoke the oracle at each and every instance of misfortune.[35] The actual divination practices differ more widely than almost any comparison can cope with, as most natural processes imply that some hazard may be used: from rubbing board to poisoned oracle, from the crab to the fox, from a basket to a knife, from throwing tablets to listening to a dove, from ashes on the hand to the intricate calculations of Islamic geomancy. However, it is not the means but the authority and the scope of the practice that is at stake here: is the divination geared at discovering the fact of witchcraft, at pointing out and naming a culprit, and does it have the authority to make accusations stick? If so, do diviners have the means to escape the wrath of the accused and shape public opinion?

5) *Definition of inter-group power relations*

In cases of witchcraft accusations several social groups may face each other, within the community, or beyond its boundaries. The ways in which witchcraft accusations may serve in inter-group relations differ from one society to another. Relations of power have always played a major part in witchcraft accusations, in both their limitation and their credibility. In some instances witchcraft has been a weapon of the weak and forces the elite into the moulds of the larger population, stretching the reciprocity of kinship to its very limits. On the other hand, witchcraft can be used by the powerful to stave off demands from their kinfolk and to underline the special position of power. So, the larger situation of power relations extensively influences witchcraft discourse and accusations.

6) *Judicial situation*

The legal situation of witchcraft accusations forms an important context in the containment of witch scares. Not only the directives of police officers, judges and other legal officers are crucial but also the extent to which they share or do not share the witchcraft discourse is of vital importance. Although legal institutions may only have limited control over local incidences of witchcraft accusations, they may be in a position to clamp down on the public voicing of accusations, and in particular prevent the killing of alleged witches. Countries in Africa are increasingly differing in the legal approach they take to witchcraft accusations. The specific situation in Cameroon, where accusations of witchcraft have resulted in courtrooms full to bursting, is considered in the next section.

A MODEL OF ESCALATION IN 'ANTI-WITCH' VIOLENCE

Compounding the characteristics of the witchcraft discourse and the key variables identified above brings us to a model that depicts the logical and sociological sequences leading up to witchcraft violence. The basic idea is that tensions exist in any society. Every society, however, deals with these problems in its own way: societies can ignore the problems and tensions, they can recognise them but desist from acting, they can formulate suspicions or follow up on suspicions, they can make witchcraft accusations or they may pursue witchcraft accusations and finally kill. However, societies may also stop at any of those steps. For each step and for each option in halting the escalation, examples are given, from Africa and elsewhere. Again, two caveats: similar options exist within most societies as the majority of witchcraft whisperings never result in actual violence, and within any one society many different views on witchcraft coexist.

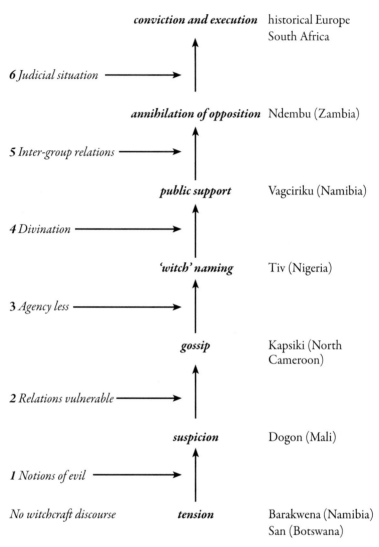

conviction and execution historical Europe
                               South Africa

6 Judicial situation ⟶

annihilation of opposition Ndembu (Zambia)

5 Inter-group relations ⟶

public support Vagciriku (Namibia)

4 Divination ⟶

'witch' naming Tiv (Nigeria)

3 Agency less ⟶

gossip Kapsiki (North
         Cameroon)

2 Relations vulnerable ⟶

suspicion Dogon (Mali)

1 Notions of evil ⟶

No witchcraft discourse **tension** Barakwena (Namibia)
                                         San (Botswana)

The model runs as follows. The figures correspond with the above-mentioned key variables. If the factor indicated is present, the level of witchcraft violence mounts one step on the ladder, to the next scale. On the right are examples of societies in which the new factor is not operative and where the witchcraft discourse and accusations halt. The examples are mainly taken from Africa and show that there are societies where the witchcraft discourse does not proceed beyond a certain point, halting before real harm has been done.

Starting at the bottom left-hand side, the model follows a logical sequence, a sociologica of witchcraft violence. Tensions exist everywhere. Where no notion of personal evil is present (*1*), witchcraft beliefs do not exist, as among the Khoisan peoples, like the Namibian Barakwena, the !Kung San, and the forest-dwelling BaMbuti of Congo and the Bakha of Cameroon. In general, hunters and gatherers have no witchcraft beliefs, harbour no witchcraft discourse (though they may be aware of the 'strange' Bantu beliefs in witchcraft),[36] and thus have at least one less problem in the world.

Some societies do have a witchcraft discourse, but a hidden one. When people die suddenly, without having suffered from a definite illness, suspicions arise. The Dogon of Mali are a case in point. Relations are dominant here (*2*), and the wish and need for harmony in close relationships is stronger than the need to identify witches or to do anything about them. So suspicions may crop up in one-to-one conversations but never develop into real gossip, let alone accusations. For the Dogon the most shameful (*dogo*) thing in the world would be to accuse a close relative wrongly, i.e. without overwhelming proof. This rules out accusations of witchcraft.[37]

If relations are deemed less sacrosanct, like those among the Cameroonian Kapsiki, people do gossip about witchcraft but the gossip will never develop into a public outcry. Occasionally someone might pick up a sick child—the purported victim of a witch's attack—and cry out in the night: 'let his heart go!', hoping that whoever is the culprit might show mercy or become scared. But it stops there: the social group in Kapsiki society has very little say over the wayward or headstrong individual, so against witchcraft only protection can be effective.[38] The agency of the individual is dominant (*3*), so there the escalation halts, and the society, though harbouring a definite witchcraft discourse (it is deemed an inherited trait and several forms are distinguished), is not 'witch-ridden'. This, curiously, is in a country, namely Cameroon, that allows jurisdiction over witchcraft accusations to formal courts.

If individual agency is less dominant, the gossip may become public, become voiced. The Nigerian Tiv serve as an example of a society in which the discourse over witches is quite public, at least in times of stress, and witches are considered a danger. Yet no methods of detection of individual witches are deemed sufficiently clear to warrant an accusation (*4*).[39] Witchcraft is something to talk about, complain about, to denounce and decry, but it stops there.

It seems to be especially among the Bantu-speaking groups in central and southern Africa that witchcraft beliefs escalate into more violent practices. The key factor is the belief in witch divination, a sure-fire method of detecting individual witches, as a means of generating public consensus over who is a witch and who is the culprit in question (*5*). The Kavango groups, such as the Vagciriku in northern Namibia, seem to exemplify this stage. Here, 'witchcraft' may be detected—or at least consensus over guilt may be reached—through divination and by an intense debate on the issue. So, here, witches may become known and be considered guilty but no action is taken. The groups in question, who oppose each other in witchcraft cases, have little hold over each other and cannot eliminate the opposing opinions of the other party, nor force their definition of the situation on them.[40] The fact that Namibian law prohibits any accusation of witchcraft reinforces the general feeling of helplessness versus the other group.

Finally, in cases where divination is considered a reliable method of sniffing out witches by all parties concerned, the naming of witches is possible. Sticking a name on a witch and creating a consensus on who is the culprit is in fact done. However, there too, the process may be halted. Among the Ndembu in Zambia, for example, the diviner may indicate the culprit but he usually does so in the presence of bodyguards and often makes a quick exit after naming somebody as a witch. The accused will often react strongly. They may also repent and promise to amend their ways, depending on the definition of the witchcraft substance. But no sentence follows (at least it has not in the past), although accused witches who keep denying their guilt and refuse to repent and make up for their alleged crime may be chased by the village.[41] Without a supporting juridical framework (*6*), or without a public consensus that alleged witches cannot repent and must be killed, the accusation sticks but without further sentence.

At the top, escalation is in full force: individuals are deemed guilty of external events, they can be named, they cannot repent, consensus can be reached and conviction follows. Whether the sentence is followed by actual execution depends on external factors in a particular society: the law, the implementation of the law by law enforcement agencies, the position of religious institutions, clashes between classes, ethnic groups or generations and the general level of violence within the society. This is the case in Limpopo Province of South Africa but was also the case in the historical witch trials in Western Europe. In the latter, the Church played a major role in fanning the accusations, providing an authoritative theological foundation and divination practices, and generating the means to ensure public support and to annihilate any opposition. It took a long time to heal the wounds that European society inflicted upon itself in those centuries.[42]

CONCLUSION

A model is just that: a model; that is, a model of reality. But models *of* reality have a tendency to convert into models *for* reality. There seems to be a sociological rationale in the escalation of witchcraft discourse, from belief to voicing, from voicing to naming, and from naming to persecution and execution. Of course, our cases have been generalisations in themselves. No society executes all accused or suspected witches, and witchcraft cases also in 'witch-executing societies' testify amply to the fact that not all accusations are taken seriously, that not all discourses are convincing and that some repentances are easily accepted. But in those societies with all the prerequisites for escalation no guarantees exist against this escalation. This has serious repercussions for individual safety and human rights and, as such, is the source of much human suffering. Witchcraft discourses cannot be viewed with the academic distance of cultural relativism. The relativist stance of academic researchers indeed leads to better explanations than the emic discourse itself, a fact that not only should be recognised but also generates responsibility. Similarly, if the logic of escalation has any relevance, then the same applies to this aspect of witchcraft research. Discovering processes in accusation deconstructs the emic discourse itself, translating from evil agents into societal woes plus personal experiences, and similarly the logic and pattern of escalation of persecution deconstructs the self-evident ways of dealing with alleged witches into patterns of belief, social relations and external authority that are understandable, predictable and may even be changeable. Indeed, witchcraft is the double evil, both for the accused and for the accusing society, and against such a double evil those who proclaim to understand it have also the duty to act accordingly.

Notes

1. E.E. Evans-Pritchard, *Witchcraft, Oracles and Magic among the Azande*, Oxford: Clarendon Press, 1937; M. Fortes and G. Dieterlen (eds), *African Systems of Thought*, London: Oxford University Press, 1965; S.F. Nadel, 'Witchcraft in four African societies: an essay in comparison', *American Anthropologist*, vol. 70, 1968, pp. 18-29; R.Willis, 'Kamcape: an anti-sorcery movement in southwest Tanzania', *Africa*, vol. 38, nr. 1, 1968, pp. 1-15; M. Douglas, M. (ed), *Witchcraft Confessions and Accusations*, London: Tavistock, 1970; M. Marwick (ed), *Witchcraft and Sorcery: Selected readings*, Harmondsworth: Penguin, 1970.

2. See e.g. I.M. Lewis, *Religion in Context: Cults and charisma*, Cambridge: Cambridge University Press, 1986; Ibid., *Ecstatic Religion: A study of shamanism and spirit possession*, London: Routledge, 1989; C. Fisiy and P. Geschiere, 'Judges and witches, or how is the State to deal with witchcraft: examples from southeast Cameroon', *Cahiers d'études africaines*, vol. 30, cah.18, 1990, pp. 135-56; J. Comaroff and J. Comaroff (eds), *Modernity and its Malcontents: Ritual and power in postcolonial Africa*, University of Chicago Press, 1993; P. Geschiere, *The Modernity of Witchcraft: Politics and the occult in postcolonial Africa*, Charlottesville: University Press of Virginia, 1997; M. Douglas, 'Sorcery accusations unleashed: the Lele revisited, 1987', *Africa*, vol. 69, nr. 2, 1999, pp. 177-93; A. Ashforth, 'Witchcraft, violence and democracy in the new South Africa', *Cahiers d'études africaines*, vol. 38, nr. 150/2, 1998, pp. 505-32; and I. Niehaus et al., *Witchcraft, Power and Politics: Exploring the occult in the South African lowveld*, London: Pluto Press, 2001.

3. Cf. J. van Baal and W.E.A. van Beek, *Symbols for Communication: Religion in anthropological theory*, Assen: Van Gorcum, 1984; Lewis, *Religion in Context*; B. Morris, *Anthropological Studies of Religion*, Cambridge University Press, 1987.

4. T. Blakely, W.E.A. van Beek and D.L. Thomson (eds), *Religion in Africa: Experience and expression*, London: James Currey, 1994.

5. Any confrontation with the brutal reality of witchcraft accusations suffices to dispel notions of relativism. The approach chosen in this article was greatly stimulated by encounters with victims of witchcraft accusations in South Africa during the SANPAD project 'Crossing Witchcraft Barriers in South Africa', jointly undertaken by the University of the North, Polokwane, and Utrecht University. For the final report of the project, see S.T. Kgatla, G. ter Haar, W.E.A. van Beek and J.J. de Wolf, *Crossing Witchcraft Barriers in South Africa. Exploring witchcraft accusations: causes and solutions*. Utrecht: Utrecht University, 2003.

6. Cf. A. Macfarlane, 'The root of all evil', in David Parkin (ed), *The Anthropology of Evil*, Oxford: Blackwell, 1985, pp. 57-76.

7. Parkin, *The Anthropology of Evil*.

8. W.E.A. van Beek, 'The innocent sorcerer: coping with evil in two African societies (Kapsiki and Dogon)', in Blakely et al., *Religion in Africa,* pp. 196-228.

9. R. Willis, 'Do the Fipa have a word for it?' in Parkin, *The Anthropology of Evil*, pp. 209-23.

10. Parkin, *The Anthropology of Evil*.

11. Marwick, *Witchcraft and Sorcery*.

12. Talal Asad, *Genealogies of Religion: Discipline and reasons of power in Christianity and Islam*, Baltimore: John Hopkins University Press, 1993.

13. Geschiere, *The Modernity of Witchcraft*, p. 67.

14. This was a central question emerging from the SANPAD project 'Crossing Witchcraft Barriers in South Africa'.

15. Both the comparison of African societies and the idea of the escalation ladder (see p. 308 of the present article) were generated during the SANPAD project and elaborated in one of the project workshops. I am especially indebted to the students of the University of the North (UNIN), who not only conducted most of the field research on which the present article is based, but who were also honest and explicit about the dilemmas they faced during their research on a topic they could not disengage from. The continuous

balancing act between being part of the witchcraft discourse on the one hand, and researching and analysing the discourse on the other, presented a challenge to which they rose with great courage and academic acumen.

16. Evans-Pritchard, *Witchcraft, Oracles and Magic,* p. 82.

17. Ibid., p. 67.

18. Ibid., p. 69.

19. Ibid., p. 71.

20. H. Bergson, *Les deux sources de la morale et de la religion*, Paris: Alcan, 1932.

21. S.K. Mbambo, *'Heal with God': Healing and religion among the Vagciriku of Kavango region, Namibia*, Utrecht University, 2002.

22. Geschiere, *The Modernity of Witchcraft.*

23. Van Baal and Van Beek, *Symbols for Communication*, p. 221.

24. See also Kgatla et al., *Crossing Witchcraft Barriers*, pp. 11-9.

25. Willis, 'Do the Fipa have a word for it?', p. 216.

26. Marwick, *Witchcraft and Sorcery*; Willis, 'Kamcape'; Nadel, 'Witchcraft in four African societies; Douglas, *Witchcraft Confessions.*

27. See e.g. Comaroff and Comaroff, *Modernity and its Malcontents;* Geschiere, *The Modernity of Witchcraft.*

28. Geschiere, *The Modernity of Witchcraft,* p. 207.

29. Cf. Kgatla et al., *Crossing Witchcraft Barriers*, pp.19-21.

30. Ibid., p. 23.

31. V.W. Turner, *The Drums of Affliction: A study of religious processes among the Ndembu of Zambia*, Oxford: Clarendon Press, 1968, p. 51.

32. See Geschiere, *The Modernity of Witchcraft.*

33. C. Turnbull, *The Forest People*, New York: Simon and Schuster, 1962, p. 51.

34. M. Hiltunen, *Witchcraft and Sorcery in Ovambo*, Helsinki: Finnish Anthropological Society, 1986.

35. Evans-Pritchard, *Witchcraft, Oracles and Magic*, p. 187.

36. Turnbull, *The Forest People.*

37. Van Beek, 'The innocent sorcerer'.

38. Ibid.

39. E. Smith-Bowen, *Return to Laughter*, New York: Doubleday, 1954; A. Dzurgba, 'The ethical dimension of Tiv religion', *Africana Marburgensia*, vol. 25, nr. 1/2, 1992, pp. 29-43; R.M. Downes, *Tiv Religion*, Ibadan University Press, 1971.

40. Mbambo, *'Heal with God'*. See also ch. 8 in the present volume.
41. Turner, *The Drums of Affliction*; Ibid., *Revelation and Divination in Ndembu Ritual*, Ithaca: Cornell University Press, 1975.
42. C. Larner, *Witchcraft and Religion: The politics of popular belief*, Oxford: Blackwell, 1984.

BIBLIOGRAPHY

Abrahams, R.G (ed), *Witchcraft in Contemporary Tanzania*. Cambridge: African Studies Centre, University of Cambridge, 1994.

Adams, Glen et al., 'The collective construction of friendship and enemyship in Ghana and the US: interview evidence and implications for development [note 1]'. Paper presented at the Tamale Institute of Cross-Cultural Studies (TICCS) seminar on 'ATRs and Development', 1-2 November, 1999.

Akrong, Abraham, 'An African philosophy of religion' [unpublished manuscript used for teaching, 1993].

——— 'Researching the phenomenon of witchcraft', *Journal of African Christian Thought*, vol. 2, nr. 2, 1999, pp. 44-6.

——— 'Neo-witchcraft mentality in popular Christianity', *Research Review, New Series*, vol. 16, nr. 1, 2000, pp. 1-12.

Amoah, Elisabeth, 'Women, witches and social change in Ghana', in Diana Eck and Devaki Jain (eds), *Speaking of Faith: Cross-cultural perspectives on women, religion and social change*. London: Women's Press/Delhi: Kali for Women, 1986, pp. 77-87.

Anderson, Mary B. et al., *Development and Social Diversity*. 1999. London: Oxfam, 1996.

Anderson, Sandra, and Frants Staugard, *Traditional Healers*. Gaborone: Ipelegeng Publishers, 1985 [Series: Traditional Medicine in Botswana].

Ankarloo, Bengt and Gustav Henningsen (eds), *Early Modern European Witchcraft: Centres and peripheries*. Oxford: Clarendon Press, 1990.

Apter, Andrew, 'Atinga revisited: Yoruba witchcraft and the cocoa economy, 1950-51', in Comaroff and Comaroff 1993, pp. 111-28.

Asad, Talal, *Genealogies of Religion: Discipline and reasons of power in Christianity and Islam*. Baltimore and London: John Hopkins University Press, 1993.

Ashforth, Adam, 'Witchcraft, violence and democracy in the new South Africa', *Cahiers d'études africaines*, vol. 38, cah.150/152, 1998, pp. 505-32.

———, *Witchcraft, Violence and Democracy in South Africa*. Chicago and London: University of Chicago Press, 2005.

Assimeng, Max, *Religion and Social Change in West Africa: An introduction to the sociology of religion*. Accra: Ghana Universities Press, 1989.

Auslander, Mark, '"Open the wombs!": the symbolic politics of modern Ngoni witchfinding', in Comaroff and Comaroff 1993, pp. 167-92.

Barendse, E. and L. Best, 'A nightmare in Nelspruit: witchcraft in the workplace', *Indicator South Africa*, vol. 9, nr. 2, 1992, pp. 85-8.

Barendse, E. and G. Dederen, 'Witchcraft in the workplace', *Productivity SA*, vol 19, 1993, pp. 22-41.

Baroja, J. C., *The World of the Witches*. London: Weidenfeld and Nicholson, 1961.

Barry, Jonathan, Marianne Hester and Gareth Roberts (eds), *Witchcraft in Early Modern Europe: Studies in culture and belief*. Cambridge: Cambridge University Press, 1996.

Bascom, William R. and Melville J. Herskovits (eds), *Continuity and Change in African Cultures*. Chicago: University of Chicago Press, 1962 [1959].

Behringer, Wolfgang, 'Witchcraft studies in Austria, Germany and Switzerland', in Barry et al. 1996, pp.64-95.

——— *Witchcraft Persecutions in Bavaria: Popular magic, religious zealotry and reason of state in early modern Europe*. Cambridge: Cambridge University Press, 1997 [originally published in German, 1987].

——— *Witches and Witch-Hunts: A global history*. Cambridge: Polity Press, 2004.

Beker, J. Christian, *Paul the Apostle: The triumph of God in life and thought*. Philadelphia: Fortress Press, 1980.

Berglund, Axel-Ivar, *Zulu Thought-Patterns and Symbolism*. London: Hurst, 1976 [Studia Missionalia Uppsaliensia 22].

——— 'Confessions of guilt and restoration to health: some illustrative Zulu examples', in Anita Jacobson-Widding and David Westerlund (eds), *Culture, Experience and Pluralism: Essays on African ideas of illness and healing*, Uppsala: Almqvist and Wiksell International, 1989, pp. 109-24.

Bergson, Henri, *Les deux sources de la morale et de la religion*. Paris: Alcan, 1932.

Blakely, Thomas D, Walter E.A. van Beek and Dennis L. Thomson (eds), *Religion in Africa: Experience and expression*. London: James Currey, 1994.

Bocock, Robert, and Kenneth Thompson (eds), *Religion and Ideology: A reader*. Manchester: Manchester University Press, 1985.

Bongmba, Elias Kifon, 'Toward a hermeneutics of Wimbus *tfu*', *African Studies Review*, vol. 41, nr. 3, pp. 165-91.

——— 'African witchcraft: from ethnography to critique', in George Clement Bond and Diane M. Ciekawy (eds), *Witchcraft Dialogues: Anthropological and philosophical exchanges*, Athens: Ohio University Press, 2001, pp. 39-79.

——— *African Witchcraft and Otherness: A philosophical and theological critique of intersubjective relations*. Albany: SUNY Press, 2001.

Bonhoeffer, Dietrich, *Letters and Papers from Prison*. London: SCM Press, 1971.

Bosch, David J., *Transforming Mission: Paradigm shifts in theology of mission*. Maryknoll: Orbis Books, 1991.

Bostridge, Ian, *Witchcraft and Its Transformations, c.1650-1750*. Oxford: Oxford University Press, 1997.

Bourdillon, M., *Religion and Society: A text for Africa*. Mambo Press, Harare, 1990.

Brandsma, Christine, 'HIV/AIDS and witchcraft: an exploration of a possible relationship on the discourse of HIV/AIDS and witchcraft in South Africa', MA diss., Utrecht University, 2004.

Briggs, Robin, *Witches and Neighbours: The social and cultural context of European witchcraft*. London: Fontana, 1997 [1996].

Chambers, R., *Rural Development: Putting the last first*. London: Longman Group, 1983.

Charles, William, *Witchcraft*. New York: Meridian, 1959.

Ciekawy, Diane and Peter Geschiere, 'Containing witchcraft: conflicting scenarios in post-colonial Africa', *African Studies Review*, vol. 41, no 3, 1998, pp. 1-14 [Special issue].

Clark, Stuart, *Thinking with Demons: The idea of witchcraft in early modern Europe*. Oxford: Clarendon Press, 1997.

Cochrane, James R., *Circles of Dignity: Community wisdom and theological reflection*. Minneapolis: Fortress Press, 1999.

Cohn, Norman, *Europe's Inner Demons: An inquiry inspired by the great witch-hunt*. London: Sussex University Press, 1975.

Comaroff, Jean and John Comaroff (eds), *Modernity and its Malcontents: Ritual and power in postcolonial Africa*. Chicago and London: University of Chicago Press, 1993.

Crawford, J. R., *Witchcraft and Sorcery in Rhodesia*. Oxford: OUP for the International African Institute, 1967.

Crick, Malcolm, *Explorations in Language and Meaning: Towards a semantic anthropology*. London: Malaby Press, 1976.

Crozier, H. David and Roger M. Blench (eds), *An Index of Nigerian Languages*. Dallas: Summer Institute of Linguistics, 1992 [1977].

Cumes, David M., *Africa in My Bones: A surgeon's odyssee into the spirit world of African healing*. Claremont: Spearhead, 2004.

Daly, M., *Pure Lust: Elemental Feminist Philosophy*. London: The Women's Press, 1984.

Daneel, Marthinus L., 'Exorcism as a means of combating wizardry: liberation or enslavement?', *Missionalia*, vol. 18, nr. 1, 1990, pp. 220-47.

——— *African Earthkeepers: Environmental Mission and Liberation in Christian Perspective*. Vol. 2. Pretoria: University of South Africa Press, 1999.

Danfulani, Umar H. D., 'Islam, Christianity and traditional religion in a changing Nigerian society: case study of the Ngas of Plateau State', BA long essay, Department of Religious Studies, University of Jos, 1982.

——— 'A historico-missiological analysis of fifty years of COCIN in Mupunland', MA diss., Department of Religious Studies, University of Jos, 1986.

——— *Pebbles and Deities: Pa divination patterns among the Ngas, Mupun and Mwaghavul in Nigeria*. Peter Lang: Frankfurt am Main, 1995.

Danfulani, Umar, Simon Mwadkwon and Vincent Parlong, 'Children at the centre of witchcraft accusations: the rise of modern witchery, secret societies and anti-witchcraft Christian prayer houses in Nigeria'. Paper presented at the International Workshop on Religion and Human Rights, 4-8 November, 2002, Dodowa, Ghana.

Davies, R. T., *Four Centuries of Witch-beliefs*. New York: New York Times Company, 1980.

De Boeck, Filip and Marie-Françoise Plissart, *Kinshasa: Tales of the Invisible City*. Gent: Ludion, 2004.

De Certeau, Michel, *La possession de Loudun*. Paris: Julliard, 1970.

De Craemer, Willy, Jan Vansina and Renée Fox, 'Religious movements in central Africa: a theoretical study', *Comparative Studies in Society and History*, vol. 18, nr. 4, 1976, pp.458-75.

De Rosny, Eric, *Les yeux de ma chèvre: Sur les pas des maîtres de la nuit en pays douala (Cameroon)*. Paris: Karthala, 1981 [translated into English as *Healers in the Night*, Maryknoll, NY: Orbis Books, 1985].

——— *L' Afrique des guérisons*. Paris: Karthala, 1992.

Debrunner, Hans, *Witchcraft in Ghana: A study on the belief in destructive witches and its effects on the Akan tribes*. Accra: Presbyterian Book Depot, 1961 [Kumasi, 1959].

Detienne, Marcel, 'L'art de construire des comparables: entre historiens et anthropologues', *Critique internationale*, nr. 14, 2002, pp. 68-78.

Dhavamony, Mariasusai, *Phenomenology of Religion*. Rome: Gregorian University Press, 1973.

Dopamu, Ade, 'Magic and Medicine in Yoruba Traditional Religion', Ph.D. thesis, University of Ibadan, 1977.

Douglas, Mary, 'Witchcraft beliefs in central Africa', *Africa*, vol. 37, nr. 1, 1967, pp. 72-80.

——— (ed), Witchcraft, Confessions and Accusations [ASA Monograph nr. 9]. London: Tavistock, 1970.

——— 'Sorcery accusations unleashed: the Lele revisited, 1987', *Africa*, vol. 69, nr. 2, 1999, pp. 177-93.

Downes, Rupert M., *Tiv Religion*. Ibadan: Ibadan University Press, 1971.

Dzurgba, A., 'The ethical dimension of Tiv religion', *Africana Marburgensia*, vol. 25, nr. 1/2, 1992, pp. 29-43.

Eboussi-Boulaga, Fabien, *Christianity Without Fetishes: An African critique and recapture of Christianity* [transl. Robert Barr]. Maryknoll, NY: Orbis Books, 1984.

Ellis, Stephen, *The Mask of Anarchy: The destruction of Liberia and the religious dimension of an African civil war*. London: Hurst and Co., 1999.

——— 'Mystical weapons: some evidence from the Liberian war', *Journal of Religion in Africa*, vol. 31, nr. 2, 2001, pp. 222-36.

———'Witch-hunting in central Madagascar, 1828-1861', *Past and Present*, nr. 175, 2002, pp. 90-123.

Ellis, Stephen and Gerrie ter Haar, 'Religion and politics in sub-Saharan Africa', *Journal of Modern African Studies*, vol. 36, nr. 2, 1998, pp. 175-201.

——— *Worlds of Power: Religious thought and political practice in Africa*. London: Hurst and Co./New York: Oxford University Press, 2004.

Erivwo, Sam U., 'Christian attitude to witchcraft', *AFER*, nr. 17, 1975, pp. 23-31.

Evans-Pritchard, Edward E., *Witchcraft, Oracles and Magic among the Azande*. Oxford: Clarendon Press, 1976 [1937].

——— *Social Anthropology and Other Essays*. New York: Free Press, 1962 [1948].

——— *The Zande Trickster*. Oxford: Clarendon Press, 1967.

Fadiman, Jeffrey A., *When We Began There Were Witchmen: An oral history from Mount Kenya*. Berkeley: University of California Press, 1993.

Falk Moore, Sally, *Anthropology and Africa: Changing perspectives on a changing scene*. Charlottesville and London: University Press of Virginia, 1994.

Feierman, Steven, 'African histories and the dissolution of world history', in R.H. Bates, V.Y. Mudimbe and Jean O'Barr (eds), *Africa and the Disciplines: The contributions of research in Africa to the social sciences and humanities*, Chicago and London: University of Chicago Press,1993, pp. 167-212.

Field, Margaret J., *Search for Security: An ethno-psychiatric study of rural Ghana*. London: Faber and Faber, 1960.

Fields, Karen E., 'Political contingencies of witchcraft in colonial central Africa: culture and the state in Marxist theory', *Canadian Journal of African Studies*, vol. 16, nr. 3, 1982, pp. 567-93.

Fisiy, Cyprian F. and Peter Geschiere, 'Judges and witches, or how is the State to deal with witchcraft: examples from southeast Cameroon', *Cahiers d'études africaines*, vol. 30, cah. 118, 1990, pp. 135-56.

———, 'Sorcery, witchcraft and accumulation: regional variations in south and west Cameroon', *Critique of Anthropology*, vol. 11, nr. 3, 1991, pp. 251-78.

Fortes, M. and G. Dieterlen (eds), *African Systems of Thought*. London: Oxford University Press, 1965.

Fowler, A., *Striking a Balance: A guide to enhancing the effectiveness of non- governmental organisations in international development*. London: Earthscan Publications, 1997.

Frazer, J.G. *The Golden Bough* (abridged edition). London: Macmillan, 1933 [1890].

Gadamer, Hans Georg, *Truth and Method* [transl. Joel Weinsheimer and Donald G. Marshall]. New York: Crossroad, 1989 [2nd. rev. edition].

Geertz, Hildred, 'An anthropology of religion and magic' [part 1], *Journal of Interdisciplinary History*, vol. 6, nr. 1, 1975, pp.71-89.

Geschiere, Peter, *The Modernity of Witchcraft: Politics and the occult in postcolonial Africa*. Charlottesville and London: University Press of Virginia, 1997.

Getty, J. Arch and Oleg V. Naumov, *The Road to Terror: Stalin and the self-destruction of the Bolsheviks, 1932-1939*. New Haven and London: Yale University Press, 1999.

Gibson, W.B., *Witchcraft: A history of the black art*. London: Arthur Barker Ltd., 1973.

Giddens, Anthony, *Sociology*. Cambridge: Polity Press, 1997 [2nd. edition].

Ginzburg, Carlo, *Ecstasies: Deciphering the witches' sabbath*. Harmondsworth: Penguin, 1992 [originally published in Italian, 1989].

Girard, René, *The Scapegoat*. Baltimore: Johns Hopkins University Press, 1982.

Golooba-Mutebi, Frederick, 'Witchcraft, social cohesion and participation in a South African village', *Development and Change*, vol. 36, nr. 5, 2005, pp. 937-58.

Gray, Richard, *Black Christians and White Missionaries*. New Haven and London: Yale University Press, 1990.

Grove, C. P., *Africa South of the Sahara*. London: Lutherwirth, 1970.

Habermas, Jürgen, *The Theory of Communicative Action: Reason and rationalization of society*. Vol. I. Boston: Beacon Press, 1984.

Hallen, Barry and J.O. Sodipo, *Knowledge, Belief and Witchcraft: Analytic experiments in African philosophy*. London: Ethnographica, 1986.

Handa, M., 'The political economy of adult education'. Paper read at UNISA for the International Council for Adult Education, 1984.

Hastings, Adrian, *The Church in Africa, 1450-1950*. Oxford: Clarendon Press, 1994.

Hayes, Stephen, 'Christian responses to witchcraft and sorcery', *Missionalia*, vol. 23, nr. 3, 1995, pp. 339-54.

Healey, Joseph G. and Donald Sybertz, *Towards an African Narrative Theology*. Maryknoll, NY: Orbis Books, 1996.

Hebga, Meinrad P., *Croyance et guérison*. Yaounde: Éditions CLE, 1973.

——— *Émancipation d'églises sous tutelle: Essay sur l'ère post-mission-naire*. Paris: Présence Africaine, 1976.

——— *Sorcellerie: chimère dangereuse?* Abidjan: Inades, 1979.

——— 'Sorcellerie et maladie en Afrique noire: jalons pour un approche catéchétique et pastorale', *Telema*, vol. 8, nr. 32, 1982, pp. 5-48.

——— *Sorcellerie et prière de délivrance: Réflexion sur une expérience*. Paris/Abidjan: Présence Africaine/Inades, 1982.

Hill, Harriet, 'Witchcraft and the gospel: insights from Africa', *Missiology*, vol. 24, nr. 3, 1996, pp. 323-44.

Hiltunen, Maija, *Witchcraft and Sorcery in Ovambo*. Helsinki: Finnish Anthropological Society, 1986.

Himmans-Arday, Daniel, *And the Truth Shall Set You Free*. London: Janus Publishing Company, 1996.

Hoeben, H., 'Who is who in African witchcraft?', *Pro Mundi Vita Dossier*, *Africa Dossier*, 12, 1980, pp. 1-41.

Hoffman, Carl, 'Provisional Check List of Nigerian Languages (by Language Family)' [mimeo], Ibadan: Ibadan University Press, 1976.

Hübsch, Bruno, 'Premiers contacts du christianisme et de Madagascar (XVII et XVIIIe siècles)', in *Madagascar et le christianisme*, Paris: ACCT and Karthala/ Antananarivo: Ambozontany, 1993, pp. 163-84.

Hutton, Ronald, *The Pagan Religions of the Ancient British Isles*. Oxford: Blackwell, 1991.

Idowu, E.Bolaji, 'The challenge of witchcraft', *Orita*, vol 4, nr. 1, 1970, pp. 3-16.

——— *African Traditional Religion: A definition*. London: SCM Press, 1973.

Imo, Cyril Okechukwu, 'Religion and Social Stratification in Jos, Nigeria', Ph.D. thesis, University of Ibadan, 1989.

Interim Report International Workshop on Religion and Human Rights, 4-8 November, Dodowa, Ghana, 2002.

Jackson, Michael, 'Thinking through the body', *Social Analysis*, vol. 14, 1983, pp. 127-49.

Jungraithmayr, Hermann, 'Die Sprache der Sura (Mwaghavul) in Nordnigerien', *Afrika und Übersee*, vol. 47, nr. 1, 1963, pp.8-89.

——— (ed), *The Chad Languages in the Hamito-Semitic-Nigritic Border Area: Proceedings of the Chad Symposion, Marburg, 1-5 October 1979*. Berlin: Reimer, 1982.

Kangethe, Kamuyu wa, *Witchcraft, Magic and Social Structure in Africa*. East Lancing: Michigan State University Press, 1980.

Kapferer, Bruce, *The Feast of the Sorcerer: Practices of consciousness and power*. Chicago and London: University of Chicago Press, 1997.

Kgatla, S. T., 'Beliefs about witchcraft in the Northern region', *Theologia Viatorum*, vol. 22, 1995, pp. 53-79.

——— 'Church and witchcraft'. Paper read at a Seminar of the Northern Province Council of.Churches, 1996.

Kgatla, S.T. and G. ter Haar, 'Crossing witchcraft barriers in South Africa: power, politics, healing, beliefs and social empowerment. Preliminary report' [Utrecht University, 2000].

Kgatla, S.T., G. ter Haar, W.E.A. van Beek and J.J. de Wolf, *Crossing Witchcraft Barriers in South Africa. Exploring witchcraft accusations: causes and solutions*. Utrecht: Utrecht University, 2003 [SANPAD Research Report].

Kiernan, James P., 'The role of the adversary in Zulu Zionist Churches', *Religion in Southern Africa*, vol. 8, nr. 1, 1987, pp. 3-14.

Klaniczay, Gábor, *The Uses of Supernatural Power: The transformation of popular religion in medieval and early-modern Europe* [transl. Susan Singerman]. Cambridge: Polity Press, 1990.

Kors, Alan C. and Edward Peters (eds), *Witchcraft in Europe, 1100-1700: A documentary history*. Pittsburgh, University of Pennsylvania Press, 1972.

Kuit, Stefan, '"Witchcraft is African technology": vertalingen van hekserij in de antropologische literatuur en in Gciriku, Namibia', MA thesis, University of Amsterdam, 2000.

La Fontaine, Jean, *Speak of the Devil: Tales of satanic abuse in contemporary England*. Cambridge: Cambridge University Press, 1998.

Lagerwerf, Leny, *Witchcraft, Sorcery, and Spirit Possession: Pastoral responses in Africa*. Gweru: Mambo Press, 1987. Originally published as special issue of *Exchange*, vol. 14, nr. 41, 1985.

Larner, Christina, *Witchcraft and Religion: The politics of popular belief*. Oxford and New York: Blackwell, 1984.

Levack, Brian P., *The Witch-Hunt in Early Modern Europe*. London: Longman, 1995 [2nd edition].

Levinas, Emmanuel, *Totality and Infinity: An essay on exteriority* [transl. Alphonso Lingis]. Pittsburgh, Penn: Duquesne University Press, 1969.

——— *Time and the Other* [transl. Richard Cohen]. Pittsburgh, Penn: Duquesne University Press, 1987.

Lewis, I.M., *Ecstatic Religion: A study of shamanism and spirit possession*. London: Routledge, 1989 [1971].

——— *Religion in Context: Cults and charisma*. Cambridge: Cambridge University Press, 1986.

Linzey, Andrew, *Animal Theology*. London: SCM Press, 1994.

Loewen, Jacob A., 'Mission churches, independent churches and felt needs in Africa', *Missiology*, vol. 4, nr. 4, 1976, pp. 405-25.

Louw, J. K., 'Witchcraft among the Southern Bantu: Facts, problems, policies', Ph.D thesis, Yale University, 1941.

Lye, William F. and Colin Murray, *Transformations on the Highveld: The Tswana and Southern Sotho*. Cape Town: David Philip, 1980.

Lyons, Diane, 'Witchcraft, gender, power, and intimate relations in Mura compounds in Dela, northern Cameroon', *World Archeology*, vol. 29, nr. 3, 1998, pp. 344-62.

Macfarlane, Alan, *Witchcraft in Tudor and Stuart England*. London: Routledge and Kegan Paul, 1970.

——— 'The root of all evil', in Parkin 1985, pp. 57-76.

Magesa, Laurenti, *African Religion: The moral traditions of abundant life*. Maryknoll, NY: Orbis Books, 1997.

Magesa, Laurenti, and Stephen N. Nyaga, 'Telling their own story: report on history, state and prospects of Christian marriage and family in Bukwaya, Musoma-Rural District, Tanzania', 1999 [unpublished research report].

Maple, E., *Witchcraft: The story of man's search for supernatural power*. London: Octopus Books, 1973.

Marwick, Max (ed), *Witchcraft and Sorcery: Selected readings*. Harmondsworth: Penguin, 1970.

Maxwell, David, 'Witches, prophets and avenging spirits: the second Christian movement in north-east Zimbabwe', *Journal of Religion in Africa*, 1995, vol. 25, nr. 3, pp. 309-39.

Mayer, P., *Witches*. Grahamstown: Rhodes University, 1954.

Mbambo, Samuel Kaveto, 'Magie 'n struikelblok? 'n Ondersoek na die vraag of magie enighe negatiewe uitwerking het op die verkondiging en die uitlewing van die evangelie onder die Vakavango', MA diss., Theological Faculty, University of the North (South Africa), 1990.

——— 'Heal with God': Indigenous healing and religion among the Vagciriku of Kavango region, Namibia. Utrecht: Utrecht University, 2002 [UNITWIN series nr. 14].

Mbiti, John S., African Religions and Philosophy. London: Heinemann, 1969 [2nd rev. and enlarged edition 1990].

——— Bible and Theology in African Christianity. Nairobi: Oxford University Press, 1986.

Mburu, John, 'Witchcraft among the Wimbum', BA thesis, Regional Major Seminary, Bambui, Cameroon, 1979.

McCord, James, My Patients Were Zulus. New York: Rinehart, 1951.

McGuire, Meredith B., Religion: The social context. London: Wadsworth, 1997 [4th edition].

McKeating, H., Living with Guilt. London: SCM Press, 1970.

Meyer, Birgit, '"Delivered from the powers of darkness": confessions of satanic riches in Christian Ghana', Africa, vol. 65, nr. 2, 1995, pp. 236-55.

——— 'Commodities and the power of prayer: pentecostalist attitudes towards consumption in contemporary Ghana', Development and Change, vol. 29, nr. 4, 1998, pp. 751-76.

——— Translating the Devil: Religion and modernity among the Ewe in Ghana. Edinburgh: Edinburgh University Press, 1999.

——— 'Popular Ghanaian cinema and "African heritage"', Africa Today, vol. 46, nr. 2, 1999, pp. 93-114.

——— 'Ghanaian popular cinema and the magic of film', in Birgit Meyer and Peter Pels (eds), Magic and Modernity: Interfaces of revelation and concealment, Stanford: Stanford University Press, 2003, pp. 200-22.

Mijoga, Hilary B.P., 'The Bible in Malawi: a brief survey of its impact on society', in West and Dube 2001, pp. 74-83.

Milingo, E., The World In-Between: Christian healing and the struggle for spiritual survival (edited with introduction, commentary and epilogue by Mona Macmillan). London: Hurst and Co./Maryknoll, NY: Orbis Books, 1984.

Moffat, Robert, Missionary Labours and Scenes in Southern Africa. 1842.

Moore, Henrietta L. and Todd Sanders (eds), Magical Interpretations, Material Realities: Modernity, witchcraft and the occult in post-colonial Africa. London and New York: Routledge, 2001.

Morris, B., *Anthropological Studies of Religion*. Cambridge: Cambridge University Press, 1987.

Mosala, Itumeleng J., *Biblical Hermeneutics and Black Theology in Southern Africa*. Grand Rapids: William B. Eerdmans, 1989.

Mpolo, Jean Masamba ma, 'Psychotherapeutic Dynamics in African Bewitched Patients: Towards a multi-dimensional therapy in social psychiatry', Th.D. diss., The School of Theology at Claremont, 1975.

——— *La libération des envoûtés*. Yaounde: Éditions CLE, 1976.

Mpolo, Jean Masamba ma and Daisy Nwachuku (eds), *Pastoral Care and Counselling in Africa Today*, Frankfurt/M: Peter Lang, 1991.

Mpolo, Jean Masamba ma and Wilhelmina Kalu (eds), *The Risks of Growth: Counselling and pastoral theology in the African context*. Geneva: World Council of Churches, 1985.

Mubengayi, Luakale Mukundi, 'La sorcellerie: problème et fléau', *Telema*, vol. 9, nr. 34, 1983, pp. 19-24.

Myers, B.L., *Walking with the Poor: Principles and practices of transformational development*. Maryknoll: Orbis Books, 1999.

Nabla, Moses, 'Rehabilitation of the witches in Gambaga: The role of the Presbyterian Church of Ghana', BA Hon. diss., Department of Sociology, University of Ghana, 1997.

Nadel, S.F., 'Witchcraft in four African societies: an essay in comparison', *American Anthropologist*, vol. 70, 1968, pp. 18-29.

Narayan, Deepa, with Raj Patel et al., *Can Anyone Hear Us? Voices of the poor*. Oxford University Press for the World Bank, 2000.

Neiers, Marie de Paul, *The Peoples of the Jos Plateau, Nigeria: Their philosophy, manners and customs*. Frankfurt/M: Peter Lang, 1979.

Newman, Paul, 'Chadic classification and reconstructions', *Afroasiatic Linguistics*, vol. 5, nr. 1, 1977, pp. 1-42.

——— 'Nominal and verbal plurality in Chadic', *Publications in African Languages and Linguistics*, vol. 12. Dordrecht and Providence: Foris Publications, 1990.

Niehaus, Isak, 'Witch-hunting and political legitimacy: continuity and change in the Green Valley, Lebowa, 1930-91', *Africa*, vol. 63, nr. 4, 1993, pp. 498-530.

——— '"A witch has no horn": the subjective reality of witchcraft in the South African lowveld', *African Studies*, 1997, vol. 56, nr. 2, pp. 251-78.

——— with Eliazaar Mohlala and Kally Shokane, *Witchcraft, Power and Politics: Exploring the occult in the South African lowveld*. London: Pluto Press, 2001.

Ntiamoah-Mensah, Comfort, 'Gambaga outcast home: The experiences of the Presbyterian Church of Ghana'. Paper presented at the International Workshop on Religion and Human Rights, Dodowa, 4-8 November, 2002.

Ntloedibe-Kuswani, Gomang S., 'Bongaka, women and witchcraft'. Paper presented at the 7th International Conference on Women, Tromsø, Norway, 20-26 June, 1999.

——— 'Ngaka and Jesus as liberators: a comparative reading', in West and Dube 2001, pp. 498-510.

Nukunya, G.K., *Tradition and Change in Ghana: An introduction to sociology*. Accra, Ghana Universities Press, 1992.

Nutini, Hugo G. and John M. Roberts, *Blood-sucking Witchcraft: An epistemological study of anthropomorphic supernaturalism in rural Tlaxcala*. Tucson etc.: University of Arizona Press, 1993.

Oduyoye, Mercy Amba, *Daughters of Anowa: African women and patriarchy*. Maryknoll, NY: Orbis Books, 1995.

Oosthuizen, Gerhardus C., *The Healer-Prophet in Afro-Christian Churches*. Leiden: E.J. Brill, 1992.

Opoku, Kofi Asare, *West African Traditional Religion*. Accra: FEP International Private Limited, 1978.

Parkin, David. (ed), *The Anthropology of Evil*. Oxford: Blackwell, 1985.

Parrinder, Geoffrey, *Witchcraft: European and African*. London: Faber and Faber, 1963 [1958].

Pelgrim, Riekje, *Witchcraft and Policing: South African Police Service attitudes towards witchcraft and witchcraft-related crime in the Northern Province*. Leiden: African Studies Centre, 2003 [African Studies Centre Research Report 72 /2003].

Pels, Peter, 'The magic of Africa: reflections on a Western commonplace', *African Studies Review*, vol. 41, nr. 3, 1998, pp. 193-209.

Radin, Paul, *Primitive Religion: Its nature and origin*. London and New York: Dover Publications, 1957 [1938].

Ralushai, N.V. et al., 'Report of the Commission of Inquiry into Witchcraft Violence and Ritual Murders in the Northern Province of the Republic of South Africa'. Ministry of Safety and Security, Northern Province, RSA, 1996.

Ramsay, J., 'The neo-traditionalist: Sebele II of the Bakwena', in Fred Morton and J. Ramsay (eds), *The Birth of Botswana: A history of the Bechuanaland Protectorate from 1910 to 1966*, Gaborone: Longman, 1987, pp. 30-44.

Raphael, Melissa, *Introducing Thealogy: Discourses on the goddess*. Sheffield: Sheffield Academic Press, 1999.

Razafimbelo-Harisoa, Jacques, 'Les débuts des missions chrétiennes dans l'océan Indien (du XIIIe au XVIIIe siècle)', in *Madagascar et le christianisme*, Paris: ACCT and Karthala/Antananarivo: Ambozontany, 1993, pp. 141-61.

Report on the Round Table Conference on the Treatment of Suspected Witches in Northern Ghana, Picorner Hotel, Tamale, 17th December 1998.

Report on the visit of B.S.R.D. team to Kukuo Witches Village, 7th-12th May 1996, submitted to the Methodist Church, Ghana, in June 1996.

Rosen, B., *Witchcraft*. London: Edward Arnold, 1969.

Rush, J.A., *Witchcraft and Sorcery: An anthropological perspective of the occult*. Springfield: Thomas, 1974.

Rutherford, Blair, 'To find an African witch: anthropology, modernity and witch-finding in north-west Zimbabwe', *Critique of Anthropology*, nr. 19, 1999, pp. 89-109.

Sarpong, Peter, *Ghana in Retrospect: Some aspects of Ghanaian culture*. Accra/Tema: Ghana Publishing Corporation, 1974.

Schmoll, Pamela, 'Black stomachs, beautiful stones: soul-eating among Hausa in Niger', in Comaroff and Comaroff 1993, pp. 193-220.

Schoffeleers, J.M., 'Christ as the medicine-man and the medicine-man as Christ: a tentative history of African christological thought', *Man and Life*, vol. 8, nr. 1/2, 1982, pp. 11-28.

Setiloane, Gabriel M., *The Image of God among the Sotho Tswana*. Rotterdam: Balkema, 1976.

Shorter, Aylward, 'Folk Christianity and functional christology', *AFER*, vol. 24, nr. 3, 1982, pp. 133-7.

——— *Jesus and the Witchdoctor: An approach to healing and wholeness*. Maryknoll, NY: Orbis Books, 1985.

Smith-Bowen, Elenore, *Return to Laughter*. New York: Doubleday, 1954.

Stadler, Jonathan, 'Witches and witch-hunters: witchcraft, generational relations and the life-cycle in a lowveld village', *African Studies*, vol. 55, nr. 1, 1996, pp. 87-110.

Stephens, Walter, *Demon Lovers: Witchcraft, sex, and the crisis of belief.* Chicago: University of Chicago Press, 2002.

Stewart, Charles, *Demons and the Devil.* Princeton, NJ: Princeton University Press, 1991.

Stewart, Pamela J. and Andrew Strathern, *Witchcraft, Sorcery, Rumors and Gossip.* Cambridge: Cambridge University Press, 2004.

Sundkler, B.M.G., *Bantu Prophets in South Africa.* London: Oxford University Press, 1961.

Tempels, Placide, *Bantu Philosophy.* Paris: Présence Africaine, 1959 [originally published in Dutch as *Bantoe-filosofie*, 1946].

Temple, C.L. (ed), *Notes on the Tribes, Provinces, Emirates and States of the Northern Provinces of Northern Nigeria* [compiled from official reports]. London: Frank Cass, 1965 [1919].

Ter Haar, Gerrie, *Spirit of Africa: The healing ministry of Archbishop Milingo of Zambia.* London: Hurst and Co./Trenton, NJ: Africa World Press, 1992.

——— *Halfway to Paradise: African Christians in Europe.* Cardiff: Cardiff Academic Press, 1998.

——— *Rats, Cockroaches and People Like Us: Views of humanity and human rights.* The Hague: Institute of Social Studies, 2000 [Inaugural Address]. Revised and shortened version published in Joseph Runzo, Nancy M. Martin and Arvind Sharma (eds), *Human Rights and Responsibilities in the World Religions*, Oxford: Oneworld, pp. 79-95.

Thiselton, Anthony C., *The Two Horizons: New Testament hermeneutics and philosophical description with special reference to Heidegger, Bultmann, Gadamer and Wittgenstein.* Grand Rapids: William B. Eerdmans, 1980.

——— *New Horizons in Hermeneutics: The theory and practice of transforming biblical reading.* Grand Rapids: Zondervan Publishing House, 1992.

Thomas, Keith, *Religion and the Decline of Magic: Studies in popular beliefs in sixteenth- and seventeenth-century England.* London: Penguin, 1973 [1971].

Thoyandu Declaration on Ending Witchcraft Violence. Johannesburg, Commission on Gender Equality, 1998.

Toulabor, Comi, 'Sacrifices humains et politique: quelques exemples contemporains en Afrique', in G. Hesseling, P. Konings and W. van Binsbergen (eds), *Trajectoires de libération en Afrique*, Paris: Karthala, 2000, pp. 207-21.

Trevor-Roper, H.R. 'Witches and witchcraft', *Encounter*, vol. 28, nr. 5, 1967, pp. 3-25.

Turnbull, Colin M, *The Forest People*. New York: Simon and Schuster, 1961.

Turner, Victor W., *Revelation and Divination in Ndembu Ritual*. Ithaca, NY: Cornell University Press, 1975 [1962].

——— *The Drums of Affliction: A study of religious processes among the Ndembu of Zambia*. Oxford: Clarendon Press, 1968.

——— *The Ritual Process: Structure and anti-stucture*. Chicago: Aldine, 1969.

Ukpong, Justin S., 'Developments in biblical interpretation in Africa: historical and hermeneutical directions', in West and Dube 2001, pp. 11-28.

Van Baal, J. and W.E.A. van Beek, *Symbols for Communication: An introduction to the anthropological study of religion*. Assen: Van Gorcum, 1985 [2nd rev. edition]. Originally published in 1971 by Jan van Baal.

Van Beek, 'The innocent sorcerer: coping with evil in two African societies (Kapsiki and Dogon)', in Blakely et al. 1994, pp. 196-228.

Van Kessel, Ineke, '"From confusion to Lusaka": the youth revolt in Sekhukhuneland', *Journal of Southern African Studies*, vol. 19, no 4, 1993, pp. 593-614.

——— *'Beyond Our Wildest Dreams': The United Democratic Front and the transformation of South Africa*. Charlottesville and London: University Press of Virginia, 2000.

Van Kessel, Ineke and Barbara Oomen, '"One chief, one vote": the revival of traditional authorities in post-apartheid South Africa', *African Affairs*, vol. 96, nr. 385, 1997, pp. 561-85.

Wambutda, Daniel N., *A Study of Conversion among the Angas of Plateau State of Nigeria, with Emphasis on Christianity*. Frankfurt /M: Peter Lang, 1991.

Welbourn, F.B., *Atoms and Ancestors*. London, 1968.

Wessel, W. H., 'Folk healers in South Africa: traditions cannot be ignored', *SALUS*, vol. 15, 1993, pp. 14-5.

West, Gerald O., *Biblical Hermeneutics of Liberation: Modes of reading the Bible in the South African context*. Maryknoll, NY: Orbis Books, 1995 [2nd rev. edition].

West, Gerald O. and Musa W. Dube (eds), *The Bible in Africa: Transactions, trajectories, and trends*. Leiden: Brill, 2001.

Whyte, Susan, 'Uncertain persons in Nyole divination', *Journal of Religion in Africa*, vol. 20, nr.1, 1990, pp. 41-62.

Willis, Roy G., 'Kamcape: an anti-sorcery movement in south-west Tanzania', *Africa*, vol. 38, nr. 1, 1968, pp. 1-15.

——— 'Do the Fipa have a word for it?', in Parkin 1985, pp. 209-23.

Wilson, Monica Hunter, *Communal Rituals of the Nyakyusa*. London: Oxford University Press, 1970.

Wimbush, Vincent L., *African Americans and the Bible: Sacred texts and social textures*. New York: Continuum, 2000.

'Witchcraft violence and the law'. Special issue *African Legal Studies*, vol. 2, 2001.

Yamba, C. Bawa, 'Cosmologies in turmoil: witchfinding and AIDS in Chiawa, Zambia', *Africa*, vol. 67, nr. 2, 1997, pp.183-209.

Zahan, Dominique, *The Religion, Spirituality and Thought of Traditional Africa*. Chicago: University of Chicago Press, 1979 [transl. Kate Ezra Martin and Lawrence M. Martin. Originally published in French as *Religion, spiritualité et pensée africaines*, 1970].

CONTRIBUTORS

ABRAHAM AKRONG is Senior Research Fellow and Head of Religion and Philosophy in the Institute of African Studies at the University of Ghana. He is also Adjunct Professor of African Christianity at Trinity Theological Seminary, Legon. Abraham Akrong holds a Ph.D. from the Lutheran School of Theology in Chicago. He has been a Visiting Professor in various institutions in Chicago, including the University of Chicago, and Adjunct Professor of Theology at MacCormick Theological Seminary in Chicago. He has published various articles on witchcraft and on African traditional religion generally.

ELIAS K. BONGMBA is Associate Professor of Religious Studies at Rice University in Houston, Texas, where he teaches African religions. His 2001 book *African Witchcraft and Otherness* addresses moral aspects of witchcraft from a philosophical and theological perspective. He will shortly publish *On the Dialectics of Transformation in Africa*, a discussion of humanistic perspectives on the transformation of political power. In addition, Elias Bongmba is working on a monograph on HIV/AIDS entitled *Facing a Pandemic: Theological Obligations at a Time of Illness*.

UMAR HABILA DADEM DANFULANI is Professor in the Department of Religious Studies at the University of Jos, Nigeria, where he is also acting Dean of Students. He obtained his Ph.D. at the University of Uppsala, Sweden. He has been a Humboldt Fellow at Bayreuth University, Germany, since 1997, and a STINT Fellow at the University of Uppsala since 2000.

Among his recent publications are *Understanding Nyam: Studies in the History and Culture of the Ngas, Mupun and Mwaghavul in Nigeria* (2003), and *The Sharia Issue and Christian-Muslim Relations in Contemporary Nigeria: Studies on Inter-Religious Relations*.

ELOM DOVLO is Associate Professor in the Department for the Study of Religions, University of Ghana. A former Head of the Department, he is currently the Vice-Dean of the Faculty of Arts. He is also President of the African Association for the Study of Religions (AASR). Elom Dovlo obtained his Ph.D. from the University of Lancaster in the UK. He has held research fellowships at universities in Japan, the USA and the Netherlands. He is currently writing a book on new religious movements in Ghana.

STEPHEN ELLIS is a senior researcher at the African Studies Centre at Leiden, the Netherlands. A historian by training, he has also worked as a journalist and as an official with various non-governmental organisations, most recently as director of the Africa programme at the International Crisis Group. He has published on witch-hunting in nineteenth-century Madagascar. He is the author of *The Mask of Anarchy: The Destruction of Liberia and the Religious Dimension of an African Civil War* (1999).

HUGO F. HINFELAAR is a historian. He received his Ph. D. from the School of Oriental and African Studies, London, for a study about religious change among Zambian women. As a White Father, he has been a Catholic missionary in Zambia for almost 50 years. He has frequently encountered witchcraft-related problems in his pastoral work, and has studied witchcraft beliefs from a theological and anthropological perspective. His most recent book is an extensive study entitled *History of the Catholic Church in Zambia*.

SELAELO THIAS KGATLA is Professor of Theology and Religious Studies in the University of Limpopo, South Africa. He obtained his D.Th. and D.Litt. et Phil. degrees from the

University of South Africa. He is also a minister in the Uniting Reformed Church in Southern Africa. Thias Kgatla was leader of the joint research project *Crossing Witchcraft Barriers in South Africa,* funded by the South Africa-Netherlands Programme on Alternatives in Development, whose final report was released in 2003.

SAMUEL KAVETO MBAMBO was recently appointed Namibian ambassador to the Russian Federation. He holds a Ph.D. from Utrecht University in the Netherlands. He has been a lecturer in African religions at the Theological Faculty of the University of Namibia, and later became Rector of Rundu College of Education in Namibia. Samuel Mbambo is also a minister in the Evangelical Reformed Church of Africa, Namibia, and has been President of the Council of Churches in Namibia.

GOMANG SERATWA NTLOEDIBE-KUSWANI is Senior Lecturer in the Centre for Continuing Education in the University of Botswana, and an instructional designer for humanities study materials in open and distance learning at the same university. She was trained as a teacher of history and religion and holds an M.Th. in non-Western theology from the University of Edinburgh in the UK. Her main research and publications are in the field of African and Asian religions.

STEPHEN NYOKA NYAGA is a lecturer in the Department of Philosophy and Religious Studies in Kenyatta University at Nairobi, Kenya, where he obtained his Ph.D. He also lectures at Tangaza College in Nairobi, a part of the Catholic University of Eastern Africa. He is currently investigating the relation between witchcraft belief and HIV/AIDS, as well as working on a training manual concerning psycho-social healing of victims of conflict in southern Sudan.

GERRIE TER HAAR is Professor of Religion, Human Rights and Social Change in the Institute of Social Studies (ISS) in The Hague, the Netherlands. As a scholar of religion she specialises in the religious traditions of Africa, notably investigating the interface between African traditional religions and Christianity in Africa. She has published extensively on religious trends in Africa and the diaspora. Among her most recent work is *Worlds of Power: Religious Thought and Political Practice in Africa* (with Stephen Ellis).

WALTER E.A. VAN BEEK is a senior researcher at the African Studies Centre in Leiden, the Netherlands. He was formerly Associate Professor of Anthropology at Utrecht University. He has done extensive fieldwork in Africa, especially among the Kapsiki-Higi on the Cameroon-Nigeria border, and among the Dogon in Mali. His main focus is on traditional religion and its relation to local cultures: this includes the dynamics of witch-craft discourses and witchcraft accusations. Walter van Beek has published widely on religion in Africa.

INDEX